HOUGHTON MIFFLIN
Mathematics

Coordinating Author   Ernest R. Duncan

Authors   W.G. Quast
Mary Ann Haubner
William L. Cole
Linda M. Gemmill
Charles E. Allen
Ann Miers Cooper
Lelon R. Capps

Houghton Mifflin Company   BOSTON

Atlanta   Dallas   Geneva, Ill.   Hopewell, N.J.   Palo Alto   Toronto

Authors

Ernest R. Duncan
Rutgers University
New Brunswick, New Jersey

W.G. Quast
Slippery Rock State College
Slippery Rock, Pennsylvania

Mary Ann Haubner
Mount Saint Joseph College
Cincinnati, Ohio

William L. Cole
Michigan State University
Lansing, Michigan

Linda M. Gemmill
Arizona State University
Tempe, Arizona

Charles E. Allen
Los Angeles City Schools
Los Angeles, California

Ann Miers Cooper
Mathematics Consultant
Los Angeles, California

Lelon R. Capps
University of Kansas
Lawrence, Kansas

Editorial Advisor

Andrew Gleason
Harvard University
Cambridge, Massachusetts

Teacher Consultants

Lucille R. Beisner
Educational Consultant
Richmond Community Schools
Richmond, Indiana

Mildred Jerris
Teacher
Nova Middle School
Ft. Lauderdale, Florida

ISBN: 0-395-31309-0

Contents

4 Division

5 Addition, Subtraction of Decimals

6 Multiplication, Division of Decimals

11 Ratio, Probability, Percents

12 Geometry and Measurement

13 Statistics and Integers

Applying Your Skills

Addition, Subtraction, and Numeration

Every year thousands of salmon follow their noses to return to the streams where they were born. Every stream has its own odor which the salmon can recognize. Can you think of 3 places you could recognize by their smell?

1

Properties

You can use the following ideas to make it easier to memorize the addition and subtraction facts.

The Commutative (Order) Property of Addition

Changing the order of the addends does not change the sum.

$$4 + 3 = 7 \qquad 3 + 4 = 7$$
$$\text{so, } 4 + 3 = 3 + 4$$

The Associative (Grouping) Property of Addition

Changing the grouping of the addends does not change the sum.

$$(3 + 5) + 4 = 12 \qquad 3 + (5 + 4) = 12$$
$$\text{so, } (3 + 5) + 4 = 3 + (5 + 4)$$

The Zero Property of Addition

The sum of zero and any number is that number.

$$6 + 0 = 6 \qquad 0 + 6 = 6$$

The Opposites Property of Addition and Subtraction

Addition and subtraction are opposites. One undoes the other.

$$3 + 5 = 8 \qquad 8 - 5 = 3$$

Exercises

Add.

1. $3 + 4$ 7
   $4 + 3$ 7

2. $2 + 5$ 7
   $5 + 2$ 7

3. $4 + 6$ 10
   $6 + 4$ 10

4. $7 + 8$ 15
   $8 + 7$ 15

5. $7 + 3 + 2$ 12
   $2 + 3 + 7$ 12

6. $1 + 5 + 6$ 12
   $6 + 1 + 5$ 12

7. $5 + 8 + 3$ 16
   $8 + 5 + 3$ 16

8. $3 + 8 + 4$ 15
   $4 + 3 + 8$ 15

Complete to show the Commutative Property.

9. $6 + 4 = \boxed{4} + 6$

10. $8 + 5 = 5 + \boxed{8}$

11. $3 + 0 = 0 + \boxed{3}$

12. $4 + 7 = \boxed{7} + 4$

13. $\boxed{3} + 9 = 9 + 3$

14. $2 + \boxed{5} = 5 + 2$

15. $\boxed{7} + 6 = 6 + 7$

16. $\boxed{3} + 8 = 8 + 3$

17. $5 + \boxed{7} = 7 + 5$

Complete to show the Associative Property.

18. $(3 + 7) + 1 = \boxed{3} + (7 + 1)$

19. $(2 + 7) + 5 = \boxed{2} + (7 + 5)$

20. $(2 + 1) + 4 = \boxed{2} + (1 + 4)$

21. $9 + (6 + 8) = (9 + 6) + \boxed{8}$

22. $5 + (3 + 9) = (5 + 3) + \boxed{9}$

23. $2 + (7 + 3) = (2 + \boxed{7}) + 3$

Complete to show the Zero Property.

24. $0 + 8 = \boxed{8}$

25. $7 + 0 = \boxed{7}$

26. $0 + 0 = \boxed{0}$

27. $3 + 0 = \boxed{3}$

Complete to show the Opposites Property.

28. $2 + 4 = \boxed{6}$
$6 - 4 = \boxed{2}$

29. $6 + 7 = \boxed{13}$
$13 - 7 = \boxed{6}$

30. $5 + 2 = \boxed{7}$
$7 - 2 = \boxed{5}$

31. $9 + 3 = \boxed{12}$
$12 - 3 = \boxed{9}$

Just for the Fun of It

32. Find an expression on the decoder ring to match each one below. Write the letters in order to solve the riddle.

What do ducks eat with soup?

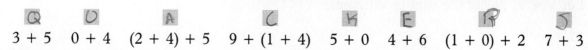

$\boxed{Q}$	$\boxed{U}$	$\boxed{A}$	$\boxed{C}$	$\boxed{K}$	$\boxed{E}$	$\boxed{R}$	$\boxed{S}$
$3 + 5$	$0 + 4$	$(2 + 4) + 5$	$9 + (1 + 4)$	$5 + 0$	$4 + 6$	$(1 + 0) + 2$	$7 + 3$

★ **33.** Are the Commutative and Associative Properties true for subtraction? Give examples to explain your answer.

Using Letters for Numbers

Letters can stand for numbers. For instance you can write
$n + 3$, where n stands for a number.

When you write $n + 3$, suppose you let n stand for 5, 7, or 9.
Then you add 3 to 5, 7, or 9.

Let $n = 5$

$$n + 3 = 5 + 3$$
$$= 8$$

Let $n = 9$

$$n + 3 = 9 + 3$$
$$= 12$$

Let $n = 7$

$$n + 3 = 7 + 3$$
$$= 10$$

You can write a letter and numbers to form an equation.

$3 + n = 11$ $\qquad$ $6 - x = 3$ $\qquad$ $a + 5 = 12$ $\qquad$ $4 - y = 3$

When you find what the letter stands for, you solve the
equation.

$4 + n = 9$

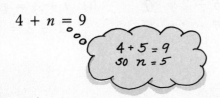
4 + 5 = 9
so n = 5

$t - 4 = 6$

10 - 4 = 6
so t = 10

Exercises

Let $n = 4$. Write the sum or difference.

1. $n + 6$ 10 $\qquad$ **2.** $8 + n$ 12 $\qquad$ **3.** $10 - n$ 14 $\qquad$ **4.** $n + 0$ 4 $\qquad$ **5.** $4 - n$ 0

Let $x = 9$. Write the sum or difference.

6. $x - 6$ 3 $\qquad$ **7.** $8 + x$ 17 $\qquad$ **8.** $15 - x$ 6 $\qquad$ **9.** $x + 5$ 14 $\qquad$ **10.** $x - 7$ 6

Let $a = 7$. Write the sum or difference.

11. $a + 7$ 14 $\qquad$ **12.** $a - 5$ 2 $\qquad$ **13.** $a + 9$ 16 $\qquad$ **14.** $15 - a$ 8 $\qquad$ **15.** $3 + a$ 10

Let $y = 5$. Write the sum or difference.

16. $12 - y$ 7 $\qquad$ **17.** $4 + y$ 9 $\qquad$ **18.** $y - 2$ 3 $\qquad$ **19.** $y + 9$ 14 $\qquad$ **20.** $y - 4$ 1

10

What is the missing number? Solve the equation.

21. 2 + a = 7   **22.** n − 9 = 9   **23.** x − 7 = 5   **24.** 7 + a = 11

25. 4 + y = 9   **26.** 2 + a = 4   **27.** 6 + n = 9   **28.** x + 3 = 12

29. 5 + a = 7   **30.** n − 2 = 7   **31.** x − 4 = 8   **32.** y − 7 = 6

33. y − 3 = 6   **34.** a − 0 = 6   **35.** x − 8 = 2   **36.** x − 5 = 10

37. 3 + n = 3   **38.** 7 + x = 10   **39.** a + 6 = 9   **40.** n + 7 = 7

Math Machine

Imagine a machine that adds 4 to any number that you put into it.

If we let *x* stand for the input number, we can let *x* + 4 stand for the output number. Here's a table to show how the machine works.

Input	Output
x	x + 4
0	4
1	5
5	9
8	12

Copy and complete the table for the machine.

41.

a	a − 7
16	9 ?
14	7 ?
10	3 ?
7	0 ?
11	4 ?

42.

n	n + 3
9	12 ?
0	3 ?
7	10 ?
15	18 ?
19	22 ?

★ **43.**

y	y − 5
11	?
14	?
?	1
?	0
?	5

★ **44.** Write a rule to make the machine work.

X	?
8	15
4	11
3	10
1	8

11

Place Value

In one year 210,715,349,026 phone calls were made in the
United States!

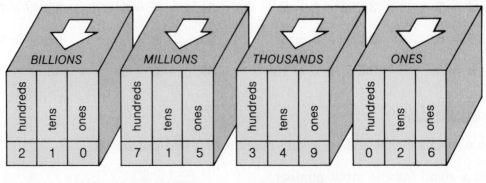

| 210 billion | 715 million | 349 thousand | 26 |

The **standard form** 210,715,349,026 is read, *two hundred ten
billion, seven hundred fifteen million, three hundred forty-nine
thousand, twenty-six.* The **digit 5** is in the millions' place. Its
value is 5,000,000.

Exercises

Write the value of the underlined digit.

1. 19<u>3</u>4

2. 297,<u>6</u>54

3. 4<u>3</u>2,591

4. <u>2</u>7,384,112

5. 40,000,<u>1</u>07,080

6. 4<u>2</u>,773,377,737

7. 3<u>5</u>2,482,796

8. 27,2<u>5</u>3,482

9. 99<u>8</u>,999,999,999

10. 526,<u>4</u>55,301

Write the standard form.

11. 4 thousand 8

12. 2 thousand 83

13. 32 thousand, 438

14. 37 thousand, 15

15. 710 thousand, 208

16. 488 thousand, 622

12

17. 6 million, 250 thousand, 4 hundred

18. 68 billion, 145 thousand, 16

19. 22 million, 973 thousand, 8 hundred

20. sixty-eight

21. two-hundred eleven

22. one hundred twenty-two

23. fifty-seven

24. four hundred eighty-one

25. three hundred thirty-six

26. six thousand twelve

27. two thousand, four hundred fifty-nine

28. eleven billion, five hundred

29. thirty-eight million, five hundred

30. one hundred ninety-five million, three hundred eight thousand

31. nine hundred twenty billion, six hundred fifty-two million, ten

Number Explosion

You can write numbers in expanded notation.

Example.   46,876 = 40,000 + 6000 + 800 + 70 + 6

Write the number in expanded notation.

32. 4332   **33.** 754,882   **34.** 30,091   **35.** 6891   **36.** 111,298

Write the number in standard form.

37. In one year, New York City had 5 million, 945 thousand, 45 telephones in use.

38. A pay phone in Chicago is used to make about ninety-eight thousand, five hundred fifty calls each year.

39. The largest incorrect phone bill ever reported was for 4 billion, 386 million, 800 thousand dollars.

Divide the clock into 6 parts so that the sum of the numbers in each part is the same.

Take a Break

Comparing Numbers

You can compare the prices of the two cars by comparing digits with the same place value starting at the left.

thousands	hundreds	tens	ones
3	8	5	6
3	7	5	7

thousands	hundreds	tens	ones
3	8	5	6
3	7	5	7

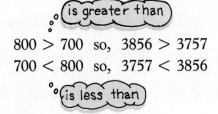

Since the thousands are the same, look at the hundreds.

$800 > 700$ so, $3856 > 3757$

$700 < 800$ so, $3757 < 3856$

A number that has more places than another number is greater than the other number. Since 1,376,212 has a digit in the millions' place, it is greater than 989,227.

Exercises

Write $<$ or $>$ to compare the numbers.

1. 30 ⬛ 20
   300 ⬛ 200

2. 79 ⬛ 81
   179 ⬛ 181

3. 376 ⬛ 476
   476 ⬛ 376

4. 3008 ⬛ 1561
   1561 ⬛ 3008

Write $<$ or $>$ to compare the numbers.

5. 123 ⬛ 127

6. 339 ⬛ 768

7. 654 ⬛ 554

8. 121 ⬛ 122

9. 745 ⬛ 738

10. 486 ⬛ 480

11. 4338 ⬛ 9098

12. 9691 ⬛ 10,020

13. 4910 ▨ 4109

14. 6782 ▨ 4782

15. 3741 ▨ 3746

16. 20,990 ▨ 20,909

17. 2016 ▨ 189

18. 15,486 ▨ 15,493

19. 63,422 ▨ 33,468

20. 59,009 ▨ 50,990

21. 578,376 ▨ 1,578,376

22. 2,367,599 ▨ 1,867,331

23. 1,456,132 ▨ 1,579,943

24. 3,984,303 ▨ 3,909,445

Traffic Jam

The chart shows the number of licensed drivers in some states in a recent year.

State	Number of Drivers
Alaska	225,781
California	14,579,000
Delaware	383,749
Illinois	6,741,192
Ohio	8,505,035
Rhode Island	600,213

25. Which state had the most drivers?

26. Which state had the fewest drivers?

27. Which states had more than 1,000,000 drivers?

★ **28.** The number of licensed drivers in Texas is more than in Illinois but less than in Ohio. What is the greatest number of drivers Texas could have? the least?

Checkpoint A

Complete. (*pages 8-9*)

1. 9 + 6 = ▨ + 9

2. (5 + 2) + 6 = ▨ + (2 + 6)

3. 0 + 7 = ▨

4. 8 + 7 = ▨   15 − 7 = ▨

Solve the equation. (*pages 10-11*)

5. 7 + a = 12

6. y + 3 = 6

7. b − 7 = 14

8. w − 9 = 2

Write the standard form. (*pages 12-13*)

9. 4 million, 12 thousand, 6

10. five hundred three

11. 31 million, 100 thousand

12. 45 billion, 506 million

Write < or > to compare the numbers. (*pages 14-15*)

13. 457 ▨ 452

14. 9836 ▨ 9736

15. 78,345 ▨ 87,406

16. 4,473,326 ▨ 473,326

Extra practice on page 378

Addition

How many walkie-talkies were shipped? Since you want to find a total, you add.

Add the ones.
Regroup.

Add the tens.
Regroup.

Add the hundreds.

```
    1              11              11
  168            168             168
+ 336          + 336           + 336
-----          -----           -----
    4             04             504
```

Answer: 504 walkie-talkies were shipped.

Exercises

Add.

1. 65 +26	**2.** 78 +53	**3.** 29 + 8	**4.** 55 +97	**5.** 31 + 9	**6.** 42 + 5
7. 37 +35	**8.** 57 + 8	**9.** 47 +25	**10.** 47 +23	**11.** 379 +355	**12.** 345 +208
13. 883 + 15	**14.** 545 +689	**15.** 791 + 98	**16.** 246 +373	**17.** 682 + 9	**18.** 341 +859

19. 87	**20.** 69	**21.** 49	**22.** 134	**23.** 487
61	28	0	22	526
+43	+15	+31	+421	+ 65

24. 456	**25.** 78	**26.** $8.14	**27.** $9.29	**28.** $2.75
4	221	+2.79	+3.81	+8.23
424	45			
+ 89	+625			

29. 463 + 35   **30.** 507 + 372   **31.** 348 + 27   **32.** $9.63 + $4.75

33. 659 + 2   **34.** 462 + 393   **35.** 247 + 505   **36.** $6.58 + $7.03

Special Sale

Solve.

37. If you buy 2 jigsaw puzzles, how much do you spend?

38. How much do you need to buy a puzzle and a record?

39. During their special sale, Toys Galore sold 78 tapes on Thursday, 102 on Friday, and 97 on Saturday. How many did they sell in all?

40. If you have $25.00, can you buy a pair of skates and a record?

★ **41.** After the sale, the cost of each item will double. How much will each item cost?

TOYS GALORE
Special Sale!
3 days only
Electronics Kit $14.99 over 100 experiments
Skates $15.98
Chess Sets $5.95
All records and tapes NOW just $4.98
King Size Jigsaw Puzzles $6.98 1,000 pieces
Chemistry Sets $19.89

Calculator Corner

What do you call the workers in a honey factory? Complete the computations, then turn your calculator upside-down to read the answer.

639 + 8765 − 2974 + 999 − 3848 + 739 + 1018

Subtraction

Did you know that Hank Aaron hit a record 755 home runs in his major league career? Frank Robinson hit 169 fewer. You can figure out how many home runs Frank Robinson hit by subtracting.

Regroup. Subtract the ones.	Regroup. Subtract the tens.	Subtract the hundreds.
$\begin{array}{r} {\scriptstyle 4\,15} \\ 7\,5\,5 \\ -1\,6\,9 \\ \hline 6 \end{array}$	$\begin{array}{r} {\scriptstyle 14} \\ {\scriptstyle 6\,4\,15} \\ 7\,5\,5 \\ -1\,6\,9 \\ \hline 8\,6 \end{array}$	$\begin{array}{r} {\scriptstyle 14} \\ {\scriptstyle 6\,4\,15} \\ 7\,5\,5 \\ -1\,6\,9 \\ \hline 5\,8\,6 \end{array}$

Answer: Frank Robinson hit 586 home runs.

You can add to check your work.

$$\begin{array}{r} 169 \\ +586 \\ \hline 755 \end{array}\ \checkmark$$

Exercises

Subtract.

1. $\begin{array}{r} 45 \\ -27 \\ \hline \end{array}$ 22

2. $\begin{array}{r} 61 \\ -17 \\ \hline \end{array}$

3. $\begin{array}{r} 78 \\ -\ 9 \\ \hline \end{array}$

4. $\begin{array}{r} 83 \\ -58 \\ \hline \end{array}$

5. $\begin{array}{r} 95 \\ -\ 6 \\ \hline \end{array}$

6. $\begin{array}{r} 446 \\ -122 \\ \hline \end{array}$ 324

7. $\begin{array}{r} 582 \\ -\ 37 \\ \hline \end{array}$

8. $\begin{array}{r} 446 \\ -359 \\ \hline \end{array}$

9. $\begin{array}{r} 846 \\ -332 \\ \hline \end{array}$

10. $\begin{array}{r} 324 \\ -\ 55 \\ \hline \end{array}$

11. $\begin{array}{r} 716 \\ -482 \\ \hline \end{array}$ 234

12. $\begin{array}{r} 626 \\ -\ 7 \\ \hline \end{array}$

13. $\begin{array}{r} 702 \\ -356 \\ \hline \end{array}$

14. $\begin{array}{r} 815 \\ -587 \\ \hline \end{array}$

15. $\begin{array}{r} 723 \\ -\ 66 \\ \hline \end{array}$

16. 673
    − 54
    ‾‾‾‾
    612

17. 501
    −399
    ‾‾‾‾
    102

18. 841
    − 8
    ‾‾‾‾
    833

19. 583
    −156
    ‾‾‾‾
    427

20. 648
    −189
    ‾‾‾‾

21. 927
    −553

22. 416
    − 43

23. 734
    − 98

24. 782
    −643

25. 312
    − 71

26. $5.30
    −2.18

27. $9.08
    −6.34

28. $7.18
    − .49

29. $9.13
    −7.52

30. $6.52
    − .95

31. 688
    − 59

32. 249
    −182

33. 137
    − 68

34. $4.39
    − .89

35. $3.12
    −1.55

36. 675 − 48

37. 895 − 47

38. 913 − 674

39. 323 − 194

40. 563 − 37

41. 758 − 9

42. 830 − 687

43. 211 − 35

Sports Page

The Clarksville Cubs have lost their team records. Use the players' numbers and the clues below to help the team figure out its statistics.

44. The Cubs' total home runs for the season is the sum of the numbers for the 2nd and 3rd base players.

45. The total hits for the season is the difference between 108 and the left fielder's number.

46. The number of games the team won can be found by subtracting the catcher's number from the shortstop's number.

47. The number of errors the Cubs made is the first baseman's number minus the left fielder's number plus the catcher's number.

Player	Number	Position
Boivin	56	Pitcher
Frankland	19	Catcher
Jigarjian	77	1st base
Keay	8	2nd base
Parant	13	3rd base
Draper	32	Shortstop
Bonnema	53	Left Field
Hense	92	Right Field
Kier	39	Center Field

★ 48. For an end-of-the-season party the Cubs collected an amount of money equal to the sum of all the players' numbers. How much was collected?

19

Zeros in Subtraction

Brendan borrowed $9000 to start his own plumbing business. He spent $6869 for a truck. You can subtract to see how much money he had left for other expenses.

First regroup.

```
   8 9 9 10
  $9 0 0 0
 -  6 8 6 9
```

Then subtract.

```
   8 9 9 10
  $9 0 0 0
 -  6 8 6 9
  $2 1 3 1
```

Brendan had $2131 left for other expenses.

Here are some other examples.

```
   4 9 9 12
   5 0 0 2
 -   1 3 5
   4 8 6 7
```

```
   7 9 9 10
   8 0 0 0
 - 5 8 8 1
   2 1 1 9
```

```
   5 9 9 14
   6 0 0 4
 -   3 3 7
   5 6 6 7
```

Exercises

Complete the subtraction.

1.
```
  7 10
   8 0
 - 2 3
```

2.
```
  3 9 10
   4 0 0
 - 1 8 9
```

3.
```
  4 9 9 10
   5 0 0 0
 - 3 2 8 1
```

4.
```
  7 9 9 13
   8 0 0 3
 - 2 1 7 4
```

5.
```
  1 9 9 15
   2 0 0 5
 -   1 8 9
```

6.
```
  2 9 9 10
   3 0 0 0
 -   4 8 6
```

7.
```
  3 9 10 10
   4 0 1 0
 -   2 3 3
```

8.
```
  7 9 9 12
   8 0 0 2
 - 7 7 3 8
```

9.
```
  5 9 9 10
   6 0 0 0
 - 5 4 2 1
```

10.
```
  8 9 9 10
   9 0 0 0
 -     2 7
```

Subtract.

11. 70 − 11	**12.** 90 − 55	**13.** 30 − 9	**14.** 40 − 3	**15.** 20 − 12
16. 700 − 243	**17.** $6.08 − .35	**18.** $5.00 − 3.82	**19.** 801 − 256	**20.** $9.00 − .87
21. 6040 − 2382	**22.** $90.00 − 7.91	**23.** 8003 − 1106	**24.** 6000 − 209	**25.** $40.06 − 7.21

26. $70.00 − $69.09   **27.** 800 − 597   **28.** 200 − 98   **29.** 701 − 333

30. $6.00 − $4.63   **31.** 800 − 251   **32.** 300 − 291   **33.** 500 − 33

Business Sense

Rosie fixes up and sells old furniture. She uses this
formula or rule to figure out the profit on each item.

Profit = Selling Price − Cost of Materials
$$P = S - C$$

Find out how much profit Rosie made on each item.

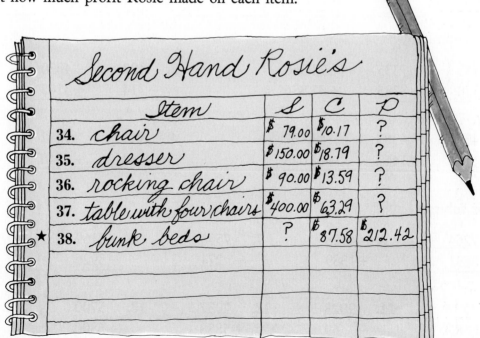

Second Hand Rosie's

	Item	S	C	P
34.	chair	$79.00	$10.17	?
35.	dresser	$150.00	$18.79	?
36.	rocking chair	$90.00	$13.59	?
37.	table with four chairs	$400.00	$63.29	?
★ **38.**	bunk beds	?	$87.58	$212.42

Adding, Subtracting Greater Numbers

How many votes were cast? Add 50,848 and 53,735 to find out.

$$\begin{array}{r} \overset{1\ \ 1}{} \\ 50{,}848 \\ +53{,}735 \\ \hline 104{,}583 \end{array}$$

By how many votes did Jane Godin win? Subtract 50,848 from 53,735 to find out.

$$\begin{array}{r} \overset{16\,12}{} \\ 2\ \overset{}{\cancel{6}}\ \overset{}{\cancel{2}}\ 15 \\ 5\ \cancel{3}{,}\cancel{7}\ \cancel{3}\ \cancel{5} \\ -5\ 0{,}8\ 4\ 8 \\ \hline 2{,}8\ 8\ 7 \end{array}$$

There were 104,583 votes cast and Jane Godin won by 2887 votes.

Exercises

Add or subtract.

1.	733 + 378	7335 + 3785	73,356 + 37,856	**2.**	483 − 314	4830 − 3142	48,302 − 31,426
3.	438 − 146	4383 − 1462	43,837 − 14,628	**4.**	941 + 34	9412 + 348	94,122 + 3,487

Add or subtract.

5.	7264 + 8891	**6.**	4728 + 1389	**7.**	7536 − 274	**8.**	5169 − 3926	**9.**	8989 + 346
10.	3579 + 82	**11.**	9028 − 69	**12.**	2037 + 5888	**13.**	5700 + 6800	**14.**	$36.57 + 2.36

15.	6358 − 1429	16.	$36.50 − 1.80	17.	3197 + 63	18.	$26.50 + 2.09	19.	3786 +6175

20.	7233 − 644	21.	$73.56 − .58	22.	663,582 +227,518	23.	$5373.47 +2548.95	24.	38,865 − 7,593

25.	51,609 + 9,723	26.	$653.58 − 38.21	27.	$4317.71 − 275.85	28.	303,181 − 35,045	29.	9527 +8399

30.	685 4216 387 + 52	31.	75 8168 7 + 892	32.	3004 276 15 +6172	33.	8869 27 348 + 3	34.	68,819 77 850 + 1,136

Election Time

Solve.

35. After the election, Tom Chilbert had 1273 bumper stickers left. How many of the original 10,000 were given away?

36. Beth Roulan spent $87,359 for television advertising and $12,646 for newspaper advertising. How much did she spend on the two types of advertising?

37. When voters were surveyed about whether or not to build a new school, this was the response.

Yes	No	No opinion
2378	1677	303

How many responded to the survey?

Solve the equation.

★ **38.** $5000 + n = 7821$

★ **39.** $10,000 - x = 6500$

23

Roman Numerals

The Romans used a number system without place value. They just combined basic numerals by addition and subtraction rules to form other numerals. No numeral was ever used more than three times.

These are the basic Roman numerals.

You can follow these rules when using Roman numerals.

 Add when a numeral is repeated.

X   X   X
10 + 10 + 10 = 30

C   C   C
100 + 100 + 100 = 300

 Add when a numeral for a lesser number follows a numeral for a greater number.

X   V
10 + 5 = 15

L   XX   VII
50 + 20   + 7   = 77

 Subtract when a numeral for a lesser number comes before a numeral for a greater number.

IV
5 − 1 = 4

XL
50 − 10 = 40

CM
1000 − 100 = 900

Exercises

Write the standard numeral.

1. XII   **2.** VI   **3.** IV   **4.** III   **5.** XVI   **6.** XX

7. XXV   **8.** XL   **9.** XLV   **10.** LXI   **11.** XCVII   **12.** CMXL

13. DCL   **14.** MDC   **15.** CCXX   **16.** CDXCI   **17.** LXVII   **18.** MMDCXXX

Write the Roman numeral.

19. 38	**20.** 36	**21.** 75
22. 13	**23.** 46	**24.** 56
25. 138	**26.** 326	**27.** 545
28. 287	**29.** 985	**30.** 666
31. 1954	**32.** 3026	**33.** 2782
34. 3656	**35.** 2841	**36.** 1368
37. 1475	**38.** 1585	**39.** 1620

Modern Conveniences

Write the standard numeral for the Roman numeral.

40. Sound movies were invented in MCMXXVII.

41. Air conditioning was invented in MCMXL.

42. The toaster was invented in MCMXVIII.

43. The lawn mower was invented in MDCCCLXVIII.

Add. (*pages 16–17*)

1. 675 + 95	**2.** $7.54 +8.09
3. 937 26 207 + 38	**4.** 55 63 +87

Subtract. (*pages 18–19*)

5. 624 − 5	**6.** 839 − 68

Subtract. (*pages 20–21*)

7. 701 − 124	**8.** 9500 − 767
9. 5000 − 623	**10.** $80.00 − 52.36

Add or subtract. (*pages 22–23*)

11. 8536 +2957	**12.** 7114 − 6889
13. 52,754 + 8,968	**14.** $6701.40 − 76.75

Write the standard numeral. (*pages 24–25*)

15. LXII   **16.** MCDI

Write the Roman numeral.

17. 78   **18.** 1168

Problem Solving ·

"Howdy, sports fans," said Biff. "It's half time and the score is 28 to 12. The Longshots lead by ▨ points."

To complete his report, Biff had to solve a problem. The four steps below show how he worked it out.

1	Understand the problem.	What do you know? What do you want to know?	Longshots — 28 points Bisons — 12 points How many more points for the Longshots?
2	Make a plan.	What do you do to solve the problem?	Since you want to know how many more, subtract.
3	Use the plan to do the work.	Show your work.	28 − 12 = 16
4	Write the answer.	Check to see if your answer makes sense.	16 points ✓

For each problem write the last column of a 4-step chart like the one above.

1. The Longshots won the game with a final score of 49 to 19. The Bisons lost by ▨ points.

2. At least ▨ more people can now see a game since seating capacity has been increased from 1782 to 6250.

3. With the price of an adult ticket at $6.75 and a youth ticket at $4.50 it now costs ▮ for a parent and child to attend a game.

4. Even the price of a bag of peanuts has gone up. It now costs 79¢, which gives me only ▮ in change from my dollar.

Add or subtract to solve the problem.

5. During a game a photographer took 53 pictures. Only 5 of the pictures were chosen for the sports section. How many pictures were not used?

6. The reporters in the press box spent $28.50 on sandwiches, $13.75 on milk, and $9.80 on apples. What was the total cost of their lunch?

7. There were 65 woodwinds, 37 brass instruments, 2 drums, and 1 set of cymbals in the band. How many instruments were there in all?

8. The Bisons' star passer completed 19 out of 33 pass attempts. How many passes were incomplete?

For Exercises 9–16 use the Sports Roundup. Write a problem to fit the exercise. Solve the problem.

Here's an example.

SPORTS ROUNDUP

Movers 37, Turtles 38

Quarter	1	2	3	4
Movers	6	7	3	21
Turtles	0	14	18	6

```
      6
    + 7
    ─────
     13
```
The Movers scored 6 points in the first quarter and 7 points in the second quarter. What was their score at halftime?

9.
```
    6
    7
    3
 +21
```

10.
```
   14
   18
 +  6
```

11.
```
   14
 − 13
```

12.
```
   38
 − 37
```

13.
```
   21
 −  6
```

14.
```
   21
 +  3
```

15.
```
   18
 +  6
```

★ 16.
```
   24
 − 14
```

Unit Review

Complete.

1. $4 + 7 = 7 + $ ▨

2. $9 + $ ▨ $ = 3 + 9$

3. $6 + 5 = $ ▨ $ + 6$

4. $0 + 8 = $ ▨ $ + 0$

5. $2 + $ ▨ $ = 0 + 2$

Solve the equation.

6. $a + 9 = 17$

7. $6 + 5 = y$

8. $x - 8 = 4$

9. $n - 7 = 8$

10. $8 + x = 11$

Add or subtract.

11. $367 + 845$

12. $5006 - 897$

13. $15,061 - 3972$

14. $136,782 + 45,896$

15. $23 + 451 + 508$

Match.

16. five thousand, two hundred six

17. three million, eighty-nine

18. five hundred thousand, twenty-six

19. five million, two hundred sixty

20. thirty million, eight hundred ninety

A. 5,000,260

B. 500,026

C. 30,000,890

D. 3,000,089

E. 5206

Write the numbers in order from least to greatest.

21. 11,111   9999   111,111   9111   11,999   1999

22. 347   286   92   1256   338   192

23. 5,076,338   15,668,113   887,345   5,145,998

24. 221,069   231,748   122,231   738,960   1,000,843

25. 3099   4000   3999   3400   400

Solve.

26. Luis earned $7.75 babysitting and $25.25 raking leaves. How much did he earn for the two jobs?

27. Kizzie bought 100 balloons for a school party. She ran out of helium after filling 83 balloons. How many balloons were left without helium?

Complete. (*pages 8–9*)

1. 3 + 8 = ▦ + 3   **2.** 5 + 7 = 7 + ▦   **3.** 6 + (2 + 1) = (▦ + 2) + 1

Solve the equation. (*pages 10–11*)

4. $6 + x = 10$ **5.** $y - 7 = 8$ **6.** $13 + z = 19$ **7.** $m + 7 = 14$

Write the standard form. (*pages 12–13*)

8. 4 thousand 92   **9.** 17 thousand, 48

10. three hundred twenty-two   **11.** nine thousand four

12. ten million, four hundred thousand, sixteen

Write < or > to compare the numbers. (*pages 14–15*)

13. 4765 ▦ 34,765   **14.** 24,363 ▦ 24,361

15. 575,620 ▦ 564,301   **16.** 4,450,362 ▦ 2,045,632

Add or subtract. (*pages 16–21*)

17.	**18.**	**19.**	**20.**	**21.**
368	435	$8.24	4006	$70.00
+297	29	+3.96	−2193	− 9.36
	+366			

Add or subtract. (*pages 22–23*)

22.	**23.**	**24.**	**25.**	**26.**
3008	34,264	$850.47	$500.29	10,819
− 789	+ 8,837	−246.76	− 35.79	78
				+ 264

Write the standard numeral. (*pages 24–25*)

27. XIV   **28.** XXV   **29.** LXXIV   **30.** MCXI   **31.** DCCXLI

Solve. (*pages 26–27*)

32. The attendance at Auburn's home games was 4036, 2784, 982, and 3738. What was the total attendance for the home games?

Time Zones

Do you feel let down when your birthday's over and you have to wait a whole year to have another one? Cheer up! When your birthday is over in your time zone, it's still going on somewhere else in the world.

This happens because the world is divided into 24 time zones that are one hour apart in time. The map shows time zones around the world. As you move east, add one hour for each time zone you pass through. As you move west, subtract one hour for each time zone.

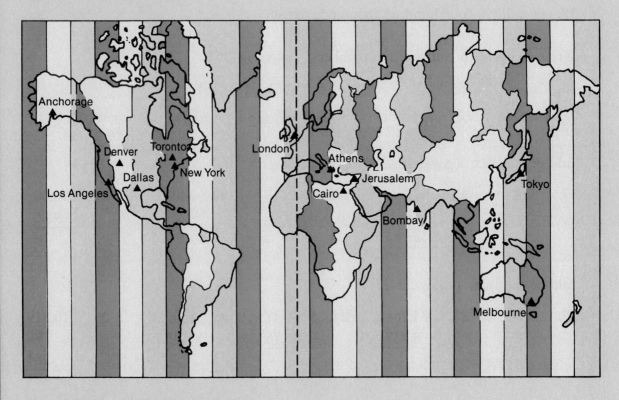

Use the map to answer the questions.

1. What is the time difference between New York and Denver?

2. What is the time difference between Tokyo and Cairo?

3. If it's 2:30 in Dallas, what time is it in Jerusalem?

4. If it's 6:30 in Bombay, what time is it in Melbourne?

The table below shows time differences between some cities. Here's how to find the time in London when it's 2:00 in Toronto. Find the row containing Toronto and follow it over to the column containing London. Add 5 hours to the Toronto time. Since $2 + 5 = 7$, it's 7:00 in London when it's 2:00 in Toronto.

5. Copy and complete the table below. Use the map on page 30 for help.

	Athens	Anchorage	Los Angeles	London	Tokyo	Toronto	New York
Athens	0	−12	−10	−2	+7	−7	−7
Anchorage	+12	0	?	+10	+19	?	+5
Los Angeles	+10	−2	0	?	+17	?	+3
London	+2	?	−8	0	?	?	−5
Tokyo	−7	?	?	−9	0	−14	?
Toronto	+7	−5	−3	+5	?	0	?
New York	+7	?	?	?	+14	?	0

Use the table from Exercise 5 to answer the question.

6. A flight to New York left Los Angeles at 1:00 A.M. The flying time was 6 hours and 25 minutes. At what time did the plane arrive in New York?

7. A flight to Los Angeles left London at 8:00 A.M. The flying time was 11 hours. At what time did the plane arrive in Los Angeles?

8. A flight from Toronto arrived in Athens at 10:40 A.M. The flying time was 9 hours. At what time did the plane leave Toronto?

9. A flight left Anchorage at 6:00 A.M. and arrived in New York at 7:32 P.M. What was the flying time?

Maintaining Skills

Use the position code to find the sum or difference.

2	6	5
7	3	9
8	4	1

Here's how. $\lrcorner + \square \longrightarrow 2 + 3 = 5$

1. $\sqcup + \llcorner$

2. $\urcorner - \llcorner$

3. $\square - \square$

4. $\ulcorner + \square + \lrcorner$

5. $\square + \lrcorner + \ulcorner$

6. $\lrcorner + \llcorner + \sqcup$

7. $\urcorner + \sqcup$

Solve the equation.

8. $4 + a = 12$

9. $b - 4 = 7$

10. $16 - 7 = c$

11. $6 + 9 = d$

Write the standard form.

12. 77 thousand, 7 hundred, 34

13. 3 thousand, 2 hundred, 96

14. 9 million, 428 thousand, 7 hundred

15. fifteen thousand, three

16. Follow the arrows. Compute each sum or difference using the answer to the previous problem. If your final answer isn't 9, go back and check your work!

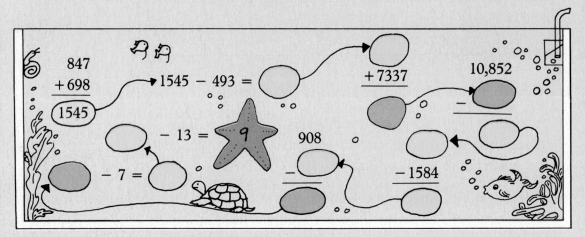

$847 + 698 = 1545$ $1545 - 493 =$ $+ 7337$ $10,852$ $- 13 =$ 9 908 $- 1584$ $- 7 =$

Solve.

17. Sharon bought a bicycle that cost $109.06. She gave the clerk $110.00. How much change did she receive?

18. Erica received $3.00 in change when she bought a fishing lure that cost $2.13. How much money did Erica give the clerk?

32

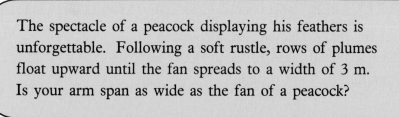

The spectacle of a peacock displaying his feathers is unforgettable. Following a soft rustle, rows of plumes float upward until the fan spreads to a width of 3 m. Is your arm span as wide as the fan of a peacock?

Estimation and Measurement

Rounding Numbers

Rent-a-Ride has 27 bikes for rent. You can use a rounded number and say they have about 30 bikes for rent. Let's look at some examples to see how numbers are rounded.

Round 42 to the nearest ten. Since 42 is nearer to 40 than 50, round down to 40.

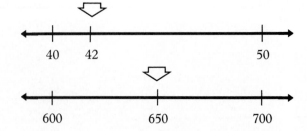

Round 650 to the nearest hundred. Since 650 is exactly halfway between 600 and 700, round up to 700.

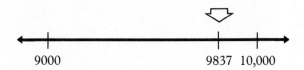

Round 9837 to the nearest thousand. Since 9837 is nearer 10,000 than 9000, round up to 10,000.

When a number is exactly halfway between two numbers, round up.

Exercises

Round to the nearest ten. Use the number line for help.

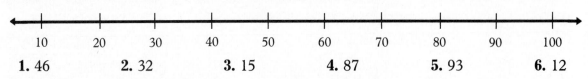

1. 46   **2.** 32   **3.** 15   **4.** 87   **5.** 93   **6.** 12

Round to the nearest hundred. Use the number line for help.

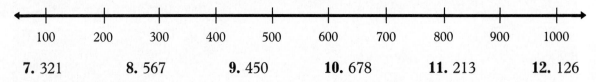

7. 321   **8.** 567   **9.** 450   **10.** 678   **11.** 213   **12.** 126

Round to the nearest thousand. Use the number line for help.

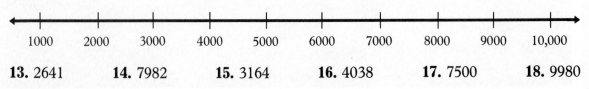

13. 2641   **14.** 7982   **15.** 3164   **16.** 4038   **17.** 7500   **18.** 9980

Round to the nearest ten.

19. 32   **20.** 43   **21.** 58   **22.** 65   **23.** 79   **24.** 68

25. 59   **26.** 31   **27.** 11   **28.** 23   **29.** 13   **30.** 15

Round to the nearest hundred.

31. 421   **32.** 388   **33.** 643   **34.** 770   **35.** 895   **36.** 201

37. 613   **38.** 555   **39.** 439   **40.** 786   **41.** 138   **42.** 517

Round to the nearest thousand.

43. 2813   **44.** 4170   **45.** 8341   **46.** 1259   **47.** 9061   **48.** 5978

49. 3004   **50.** 1304   **51.** 6503   **52.** 9501   **53.** 6769   **54.** 9399

Pedal Around

55. Round each number to the nearest ten. Follow the path of rounded numbers. List the places Ted went on his bike.

1st	2nd	3rd	4th	5th	6th	7th	8th	9th	10th
38	27	6	52	84	57	24	96	88	71

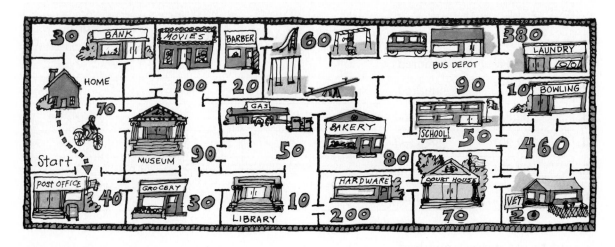

★ **56.** Write ten numbers which are written as 70 when rounded to the nearest ten.

★ **57.** Write ten numbers which are written as 1000 when rounded to the nearest thousand.

Rounding Greater Numbers

Newspapers use rounded numbers every day because they are easier to read.

Look at the table to see how numbers are rounded.

Exact Number	Round to the Nearest	Digit to the Right	Is it 5 or More?	Round
7842	hundred	4	no	down to 7800
15,633	thousand	6	yes	up to 16,000
125,643	ten-thousand	5	yes	up to 130,000

Exercises

Complete the chart.

	Exact Number	Round to the Nearest	Digit to the Right	Is it 5 or More?	Round
1.	8342	hundred	4	No	?
2.	19,672	hundred	7	?	?
3.	32,831	thousand	8	?	?
4.	889,201	thousand	2	?	?
5.	163,071	ten-thousand	3	?	?
6.	4,748,802	ten-thousand	8	?	?

Round to the nearest hundred.

7. 3206 **8.** 8746 **9.** 3385 **10.** 9461 **11.** 7341

12. 41,801 **13.** 88,315 **14.** 60,774 **15.** 74,806 **16.** 50,552

17. 135,781 **18.** 287,003 **19.** 741,819 **20.** 891,197 **21.** 555,402

Round to the nearest thousand.

22. 86,019	**23.** 32,543	**24.** 96,182	**25.** 45,560	**26.** 27,368
27. 170,168	**28.** 247,813	**29.** 554,506	**30.** 428,400	**31.** 367,308
32. 665,708	**33.** 499,516	**34.** 267,813	**35.** 981,875	**36.** 889,568

Round to the nearest ten-thousand.

37. 42,175	**38.** 90,017	**39.** 17,508	**40.** 731,813	**41.** 536,981
42. 339,234	**43.** 813,375	**44.** 209,319	**45.** 922,722	**46.** 826,739
47. 1,598,266	**48.** 6,833,296	**49.** 11,817,567	**50.** 98,275,331	**51.** 35,299,012

Extra! Extra!

Rewrite the sentence as a newspaper headline using a rounded number.

52. There were 55,147 people at an outdoor concert.

53. The governor cut the new state budget by $763,412.

54. A transit strike left 258,694 people without transportation.

55. There were 5894 runners in a recent marathon.

56. An oil tanker spilled 565,014 barrels of oil into the ocean.

57. There were 69,948 cars recalled.

Calculator Corner

Replace each ▦ with a digit from 0 to 9 so that the addition is correct. Use each digit exactly once.

$$
\begin{array}{r}
\blacksquare\ \blacksquare\ \blacksquare \\
+\ \blacksquare\ \blacksquare\ \blacksquare \\
\hline
\blacksquare\ \blacksquare\ \blacksquare
\end{array}
$$

Estimating Sums and Differences

It's easy to make mistakes even when you use a calculator. If
you forget to push the clear button between problems, or if you
enter the wrong number, your answer will be wrong. Estimating
will help you decide if your answer is reasonable.

Let's look at some examples.

Add.

$5\,4\,7\ \boxplus\ 7\,8\,2\ \boxminus\ 1\,3\,2\,9.$

Estimate by adding rounded numbers.

$5\,0\,0\ \boxplus\ 8\,0\,0\ \boxminus\ 1\,3\,0\,0$

The estimate shows that the sum is reasonable.

Subtract.

$8\,7\,3\,6\ \boxminus\ 4\,2\,9\,5\ \boxminus\ 1\,2,\!6\,8\,7$

Estimate by subtracting rounded numbers.

$9\,0\,0\,0\ \boxminus\ 4\,0\,0\,0\ \boxminus\ 5\,0\,0\,0$

The estimate shows that the difference is not reasonable.
Let's clear and subtract again.

$\boxed{C}\ 8\,7\,3\,6\ \boxminus\ 4\,2\,9\,5\ \boxminus\ 4\,4\,4\,1$

Now you have a reasonable answer.

Exercises

Estimate. Write *a*, *b*, or *c* for the most reasonable answer.

1. $3\,3\,9\ \boxplus\ 4\,7\ \boxminus$
  a. 386
  b. 286
  c. 526

2. $1\,8\,7\,5\ \boxminus\ 9\,3\,4\ \boxminus$
  a. 2829
  b. 941
  c. 841

3. $5\,7\,3\,5\ \boxplus\ 4\,3\,3\,1\ \boxminus$
  a. 2404
  b. 11,066
  c. 9386

4. $9\,4\,7\,8\ \boxminus\ 3\,0\,5\,1\ \boxminus$
  a. 12,529
  b. 8527
  c. 6427

5. $3\,5\,2\ \boxplus\ 6\,7\ \boxplus\ 1\,9\,5\ \boxminus$
  a. 6148
  b. 306
  c. 614

6. $7\,1\,3\ \boxminus\ 4\,8\,5\ \boxminus$
  a. 228
  b. 1198
  c. 2287

Round to the nearest hundred. Estimate the sum or difference.

7.	128	8.	422	9.	573	10.	481	11.	142
	354		157		147		374		378
	+328		+124		+283		+285		+691

12.	8147	13.	8043	14.	6947	15.	8432	16.	9573
	−4372		− 681		−3241		− 893		−1747

Round to the nearest thousand. Estimate the sum or difference.

17.	3752	18.	5581	19.	9103	20.	3381	21.	2061
	+2180		+4682		+7615		+7466		+1898

22.	6818	23.	7332	24.	8106	25.	3715	26.	5561
	−3406		−5481		−1725		−3256		−2738

27.	37,841	28.	42,617	29.	78,781	30.	36,716	31.	71,620
	+ 7,650		+57,332		− 2,206		−22,501		−37,232

Educated Guesses

You can estimate to decide if an answer is reasonable. Estimate each sum or difference. Write *yes* or *no* to tell if the answer given is reasonable.

32.	16,782	33.	8441	34.	11,821	35.	63,701	36.	77,382
	+ 3,461		−5316		+73,622		− 8,332		+21,161
	30,243		3125		95,443		15,369		98,543

Solve.

37. The shoe buyer for Save-a-Lot Discount stores ordered 378 pairs of tennis shoes, 182 pairs of clogs, and 593 pairs of sandals. Estimate the total number of pairs ordered.

38. A shipment of 648 cans of tennis balls was received by the sports department. They returned 176 dented cans. Estimate the number of cans they accepted.

Estimating with Money

When you go shopping it's a good idea to estimate the cost of your purchases. You'll want to be sure you have enough money and that you get the correct change.

You can use these rules.

Round prices less than $1.00 to the nearest ten cents.

Round prices greater than $1.00 to the nearest dollar.

$$\begin{array}{r} \$.90 \\ .70 \\ +.50 \\ \hline \$2.10 \end{array}$$

$$\begin{array}{r} \$6.00 \\ 3.00 \\ +4.00 \\ \hline \$13.00 \end{array}$$

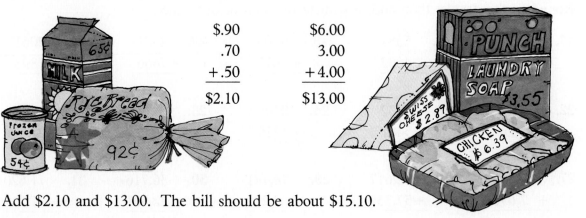

Add $2.10 and $13.00. The bill should be about $15.10.

Exercises

Round to the nearest ten cents.

1. 39¢	**2.** 35¢	**3.** 82¢	**4.** 18¢	**5.** 23¢
6. 41¢	**7.** 98¢	**8.** 13¢	**9.** 11¢	**10.** 93¢

Round to the nearest dollar.

11. $1.45	**12.** $3.86	**13.** $4.57	**14.** $7.33	**15.** $9.84
16. $34.55	**17.** $14.90	**18.** $16.03	**19.** $33.49	**20.** $54.81

Round to the nearest ten cents. Estimate the sum or difference.

21. $.79 +.41	**22.** $.38 −.18	**23.** $.44 +.65	**24.** $.87 −.31	**25.** $.52 +.28
26. $.38 +.72	**27.** $.41 −.18	**28.** $.67 −.25	**29.** $.96 +.81	**30.** $.86 +.22

Round to the nearest dollar.
Estimate the sum or difference.

31.	$3.25	32.	$7.13	33.	$42.89
	+4.25		+3.85		+ 7.50

34.	$6.40	35.	$17.83	36.	$15.78
	−1.09		− 5.71		− 8.68

37.	$3.53	38.	$2.98	39.	$4.95
	4.28		8.08		9.85
	+3.49		+5.17		+4.63

40. $5.83 + $3.47   41. $2.98 + $3.21

42. $12.43 − $4.71   43. $3.09 − $2.47

Shopping Spree

Estimate the total sale. Write *yes* or *no* to tell if $20.00 is enough to pay the bill.

44.
Warm-up Shop	
gloves	$3.49
scarf	2.88
hat	6.79
sweater	6.48
Total	?

45.
Book Nook	
Paperback	$3.95
calendar	6.98
book mark	.65
Total	?

★ **46.** Lena bought 3 cans of corn for $.89, 2 jars of beets for $.65, a bag of dog food for $4.39, and a package of frozen peas for $1.49. She estimated the total bill as $6.60. How close was her estimate to the actual cost?

Checkpoint A

Round to the nearest ten.
(*pages 34–35*)

1. 58   **2.** 72

Round to the nearest hundred.

3. 741   **4.** 389

Round to the nearest thousand.
(*pages 36–37*)

5. 4753   **6.** 18,064

Round to the nearest ten-thousand.

7. 38,719   **8.** 584,531

Estimate the sum or difference.
(*pages 38–39*)

9.	675	10.	987
	+ 28		+236

11.	4836	12.	12,886
	− 1275		− 4,315

Estimate the sum or difference.
(*pages 40–41*)

13.	$.79	14.	$.68
	.28		−.22
	+.14		

15.	$17.85	16.	$89.95
	+ 3.25		−27.50

Using a Centimeter Ruler

Since ancient times people have used the idea of measurement to compare objects. We can use a ruler to measure objects and draw line segments.

$$1 \text{ cm} = 10 \text{ mm}$$

Here's how to draw a segment 7 **centimeters** (cm) or 70 **millimeters** (mm) long.

Use a sharp pencil close to the ruler.

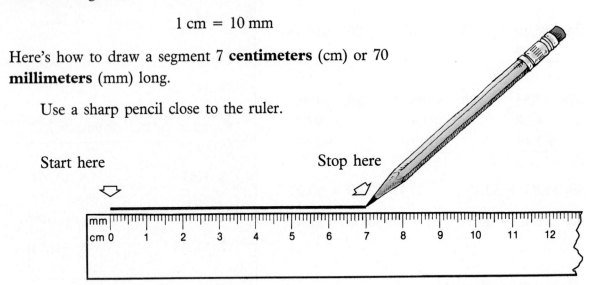

Exercises

Measure the segment to the nearest centimeter.

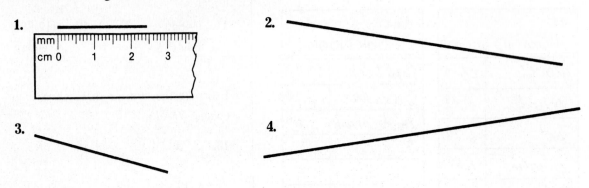

Measure the segment to the nearest millimeter.

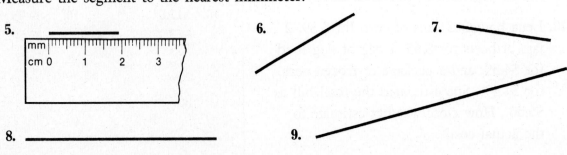

42

Measure to the nearest centimeter.

10.

11.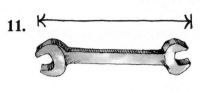

12.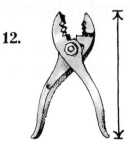

Measure to the nearest millimeter.

13.

14.

15.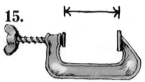

Draw a segment with the given length.

16. 2 cm	**17.** 3 cm	**18.** 18 cm	**19.** 4 cm	**20.** 7 cm
21. 70 mm	**22.** 33 mm	**23.** 85 mm	**24.** 168 mm	**25.** 135 mm

Size Wise

Solve.

26. 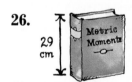 Can the book stand on a shelf that is 25 cm high?

27.  Will the vase fit in a cabinet that is 35 cm deep?

★ **28.** Will the shade cover a window that is 65 cm wide?

★ **29.**  Will the glass fit in a window that is 98 cm tall?

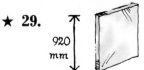

43

Metric Units of Length

You can get an idea of how long metric units are by looking at some familiar objects.

← the width of a thumbtack

← the width of a stripe

About 1 meter (m)   About 1 centimeter (cm)   About 1 millimeter (mm)

Longer distances are measured in **kilometers** (km). You'd have to run around the bases of a softball field about 14 times to cover a distance of 1 km. If you walked a distance of 1 km it would take about ten minutes.

$$10 \text{ mm} = 1 \text{ cm}$$
$$100 \text{ cm} = 1 \text{ m}$$
$$1000 \text{ m} = 1 \text{ km}$$

Exercises

Complete.

1. 10 mm = ▨ cm
   20 mm = ▨ cm
   30 mm = ▨ cm

2. 1 cm = ▨ mm
   3 cm = ▨ mm
   5 cm = ▨ mm

3. 100 cm = ▨ m
   300 cm = ▨ m
   500 cm = ▨ m

Choose the more likely measurement. Write *a* or *b*.

4. the thickness of a dime
   a. 1 mm   **b.** 1 cm

5. the width of a double bed
   a. 135 cm   **b.** 135 m

6. the length of a river
   a. 1080 m   **b.** 1080 km

7. the height of a desk
   a. 73 mm   **b.** 73 cm

8. the length of a pencil
   a. 15 cm   **b.** 150 cm

9. the height of a flagpole
   a. 10 m   **b.** 200 m

10. the height of a room
   a. 240 cm   **b.** 240 km

11. the length of a belt
   a. 65 mm   **b.** 65 cm

Match. Write the letter of the most likely measurement.

12. the length of a carrot

13. the height of a person

14. the height of a tall building

15. the length of a peanut

16. the thickness of a book cover

17. the distance you can hike in an hour

A. 5 km

B. 300 m

C. 170 cm

D. 15 cm

E. 4 cm

F. 2 mm

Write *mm, cm, m* or *km* to tell the best unit for measuring.

18. the length of a crayon

20. the length of a road

22. the width of a book

19. the height of a door

21. the height of a mountain

23. the distance between cities

Solve.

24. An official softball field has a distance of about 1800 cm between the bases. How many meters is this?

25. Home plate is 425 mm wide. Each base is 375 mm wide. How much wider is home plate than a base?

★ **26.** Junior softball fields measure 1350 cm between the bases. How many meters must Joan run to reach second base?

★ **27.** In the third inning, Ryan hit a double. On the next play he scored a run. He didn't get to bat again in that inning. If there are 18 m between bases, how far did he run in that inning?

Metric Units of Volume and Mass

In the metric system, volume is measured in **milliliters** (mL) and **liters** (L).

$$1000 \text{ mL} = 1 \text{ L}$$

Here are some items usually measured in milliliters.

Here are some items usually measured in liters.

Mass is measured in **grams** (g) and **kilograms** (kg).

$$1000 \text{ g} = 1 \text{ kg}$$

These objects are usually measured in grams.

These objects are usually measured in kilograms.

Exercises

Choose the more likely measurement. Write *a* or *b*.

1. the amount of gas in a car
    a. 53 mL   **b.** 53 L

2. the amount of milk in a glass
    a. 240 mL   **b.** 240 L

3. the amount of water in a bathtub
    a. 2 L   **b.** 220 L

4. the amount of glue in a jar
    a. 118 mL   **b.** 118 L

5. the mass of a raisin
    a. 1 g   **b.** 1 kg

6. the mass of a dog
    a. 18 g   **b.** 18 kg

7. the mass of five apples
    a. 50 g   **b.** 500 g

8. the mass of an eraser
    a. 6 g   **b.** 600 g

Match. Write the letter of the most likely measurement.

9. amount of water in an aquarium   **A.** almost 1 mL

10. amount of water in a fish pond   **B.** 1 L

11. amount of water in a raindrop   **C.** 40 L

12. amount of juice in a carton   **D.** 250 mL

13. amount of soup in a bowl   **E.** 70,000 L

Match. Write the letter of the most likely measurement.

14. the mass of a roast beef   **A.** 10 g

15. the mass of a pencil   **B.** 250 g

16. the mass of a piece of cheese   **C.** 10 kg

17. the mass of a heavy suitcase   **D.** 1000 kg

18. the mass of a car   **E.** 3 kg

Fruity Salad

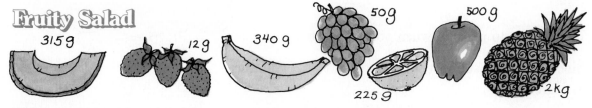

Write the mass of each salad. Remember: 1000 g = 1 kg.

19.    **20.**    **21.**    **22.**

Write the mass of the fruit basket.   Solve.

23.

24. Marilyn added 540 mL of water to 180 mL of orange juice concentrate. How much juice did she make?

★ **25.** Desmond made 2 L of chili for a skating party. After the party he had 125 mL left. How much chili was eaten?

United States Units of Length

In the United States, the most commonly used units of length are the **inch** (in.), **foot** (ft), **yard** (yd), and **mile** (mi).

$$12 \text{ in.} = 1 \text{ ft}$$

$$3 \text{ ft} = 1 \text{ yd}$$

$$5280 \text{ ft} = 1 \text{ mi}$$

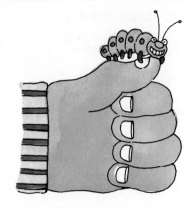

AT ONE TIME AN INCH WAS MEASURED BY PART OF A PERSON'S THUMB.

Here's how to regroup when you add.

First add.

```
   1 ft   4 in.
+         11 in.
   1 ft  15 in.
```

Next regroup the sum.

```
   1 ft   4 in.
+         11 in.
   1 ft  15 in. = 2 ft 3 in.
```

1 ft 15 in. = 1 ft + 1 ft 3 in.

Here's how to regroup when you subtract.

Since you can't subtract 9 from 3, regroup.

1 ft 12 in. + 3 in.

```
   2 ft 3 in.
−  1 ft 9 in.
```

Subtract.

```
    1   15
    2 ft 3 in.
−   1 ft 9 in.
         6 in.
```

Exercises

Complete.

1. 2 ft 16 in. = ▯ ft 4 in.

2. 3 ft 14 in. = 4 ft ▯ in.

3. 3 yd 5 ft = 4 yd ▯ ft

4. 8 yd 4 ft = ▯ yd 1 ft

5. 7 yd 1 ft = 6 yd ▯ ft

6. 4 ft 7 in. = ▯ ft 19 in.

7. 1 yd 1 ft = ▯ ft

8. 3 yd 1 ft = ▯ yd 4 ft

Add or subtract.

9. 2 ft 3 in.
   + 1 ft 7 in.

10. 3 ft 4 in.
   + 3 ft 5 in.

11. 7 ft 8 in.
   + 3 ft 5 in.

12. 3 ft 9 in.
   + 1 ft 2 in.

13. 7 ft 3 in.
   − 3 ft 4 in.

14. 8 ft 6 in.
   − 2 ft 8 in.

15. 4 ft 2 in.
   − 3 ft 8 in.

16. 2 ft 1 in.
   − 1 ft 2 in.

17. 3 yd 2 ft
   + 5 yd 2 ft

18. 7 yd 1 ft
   + 3 yd 1 ft

19. 4 yd 2 ft
   + 3 yd 1 ft

20. 4 yd 1 ft
   + 3 yd 2 ft

21. 8 yd 2 ft
   − 6 yd 1 ft

22. 7 yd 1 ft
   − 2 yd 2 ft

23. 9 yd
   − 2 yd 1 ft

24. 4 yd 1 ft
   − 1 yd 2 ft

Towering Problems

Use the picture to solve the problem.

25. How much taller is the World Trade Center than the Prudential Center?

26. The Empire State Building in New York is 571 ft shorter than the CN Tower in Toronto. How tall is the Empire State Building?

Add.

★ **27.** 3 yd 2 ft 8 in.
   + 7 yd 5 ft 9 in.

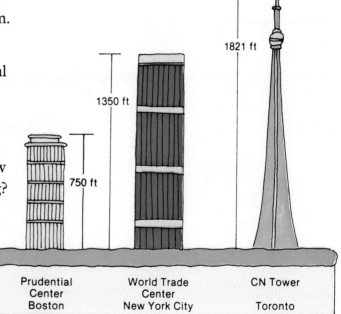

1821 ft

1350 ft

750 ft

Prudential Center Boston

World Trade Center New York City

CN Tower Toronto

Suppose you have red paint, blue paint, and a bunch of cubes. (A cube has 6 faces.) How many different cubes can you paint before two are the same?

Take a Break

49

United States Units of Volume and Weight

In the United States, the most commonly
used units of volume are the **cup** (c), **pint**
(pt), **quart** (qt), and **gallon** (gal).

$$4 \text{ cups} = 1 \text{ qt}$$
$$2 \text{ pt} = 1 \text{ qt}$$
$$4 \text{ qt} = 1 \text{ gal}$$

Weight is measured in **ounces** (oz),
pounds (lb), and **tons** (t).

$$16 \text{ oz} = 1 \text{ lb}$$
$$2000 \text{ lb} = 1 \text{ t}$$

This example shows how to regroup when you add.

First add.

      1 gal 3 qt
   + 2 gal 2 qt
   ─────────────
      3 gal 5 qt

Next regroup the sum.

      1 gal 3 qt
   + 2 gal 2 qt
   ─────────────
      3 gal 5 qt = 4 gal 1 qt

3 gal 5 qt = 3 gal + 1 gal + 1 qt

This example shows how to regroup when you subtract.

Since you can't subtract 7 from
2, regroup.

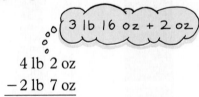

3 lb 16 oz + 2 oz

      4 lb 2 oz
   − 2 lb 7 oz

Subtract.

      3   18
      4̸ lb 2̸ oz
   − 2 lb   7 oz
   ──────────────
      1 lb 11 oz

Exercises

Complete.

1. 5 gal 5 qt = 6 gal ▨ qt

2. 8 gal 6 qt = ▨ gal 2 qt

3. 2 lb 20 oz = 3 lb ▨ oz

4. 8 lb 17 oz = ▨ lb 1 oz

5. 4 lb 2 oz = 3 lb ▨ oz

6. 1 lb 3 oz = ▨ oz

7. 3 lb 12 oz = ▨ lb 28 oz

8. 25 lb 11 oz = 24 lb ▨ oz

Add or subtract.

9. 1 qt 1 pt
      + 2 qt 1 pt

10. 3 qt 1 pt
       + 1 qt

11. 2 gal 2 qt
       + 1 gal 3 qt

12. 5 gal 1 qt
       + 2 gal 3 qt

13. 5 qt
       − 1 qt 1 pt

14. 3 qt 1 pt
       − 1 qt 1 pt

15. 4 gal 2 qt
       − 2 gal 3 qt

16. 6 gal 1 qt
       − 4 gal 3 qt

17. 5 lb 3 oz
       + 2 lb 6 oz

18. 2 lb 7 oz
       + 3 lb 8 oz

19. 1 t 340 lb
       + 2 t 470 lb

20. 2 t 800 lb
       + 5 t 1400 lb

21. 8 lb 7 oz
       + 3 lb 12 oz

22. 15 lb 6 oz
       − 12 lb 7 oz

Solve.

23. Terry made a cheese ball that called for 2 lb of cream cheese, 8 oz of cheddar cheese, and 6 oz of blue cheese. How much more cream cheese is needed than cheddar cheese?

★ **24.** Betty made a gallon of tomato sauce. She used 1 cup of the sauce for meatball sandwiches, 1 pint for a casserole, and 2 pt for lasagna. How much sauce was left?

Checkpoint B

Measure the segment in millimeters and centimeters. (*pages 42–43*)

1. ━━━━━━━━━━━━━

2. ━━━━━━━

Choose the more likely measurement. Write *a* or *b*. (*pages 44–45*)

3. the thickness of a quarter
  a. 2 mm   **b.** 2 cm

4. the length of a football
  a. 30 cm   **b.** 300 cm

5. the distance from Chicago to Miami
  a. 2221 m   **b.** 2221 km

Choose the more likely measurement. Write *a* or *b*. (*pages 46–47*)

6. the amount of tea in a cup
  a. 240 mL   **b.** 240 L

7. the amount of paint in a large can
  a. 4 mL   **b.** 4 L

8. the mass of a carrot
  a. 100 g   **b.** 100 kg

Add or subtract. (*pages 48–49*)

9. 2 ft 8 in.
      +   10 in.

10. 2 ft 3 in.
       − 1 ft 7 in.

Add or subtract. (*pages 50–51*)

11. 1 qt 1 pt
       + 1 qt 1 pt

12. 3 gal 2 qt
       + 1 gal 3 qt

Extra practice on page 380

Problem Solving · FINDING THE FACTS

1	Understand
2	Plan
3	Work
4	Answer

Find the missing clue. Solve the problem.

1. Detective Dooley has to find a certain locker. She knows that the locker number is her height in centimeters plus 29. What is the locker number?

2. Detective Dooley is receiving an Otto Award in April. She knows that the exact date is her house number plus 15. When is the award being given?

3. In 1982, Detective Dooley located a missing uncle who had inherited $45,000. How long was the uncle missing?

4. On Tuesday Detective Dooley flew to Chicago, rented a car, and drove 179 km to meet a client. How much did the trip cost?

Use Detective Dooley's files to solve the problem. Use only the information you need.

5.
Case 382

On 5/30, 186 trading cards were reported missing from 19 Wall Street. I spent 18 hours questioning witnesses and 23 hours following clues. The cards were found in Sis's closet.

How many hours were spent in all?

6.
Case 733

A 35 year old violin was reported missing at 3:30 on 6/12. It took me 45 minutes to find the violin under the sofa. Junior was on time for his music lesson at 4:30.

When was the violin found?

7.
Case 1007

At 6:05 on Monday, Butch Brady was reported late for dinner. It was the fifth time in 7 days. To find Butch I drove 3 km to the playground, then 5 km to the zoo, and 4 km to the library. Butch was found reading mystery books.

How many kilometers were driven?

8.
Case 899

Sally Smart of 35 Bay Road was late for her tuba lesson at 12:08 on Friday. She was last seen wearing a number 15 shirt. I spent $1.85 on phone calls, $5.89 on gas, and $.65 on tolls to find Sally. She was practicing her curve ball in the park.

How much was spent to find Sally?

Solve the problem. Supply a reasonable fact if you do not have enough information.

9. Detective Dooley earns $485.00 each week. How much money does she have left after she buys groceries?

10. Detective Dooley bought a size 10 coat for $179.89, gloves for $15.98, and a hat for $18.98. How much did the coat and hat cost?

11. On Monday, Detective Dooley drove to Gates. The odometer on her car read 63,412 when she started. How far did she travel that day?

12. Detective Dooley wrote 5 reports on Monday, 3 on Tuesday, and 4 on Friday. Each report took about 45 minutes. How many reports did she write in the 3 days?

13. There are 482 students enrolled in Detective Training School. There were 38 absent on Monday and 27 absent on Tuesday. How many were absent on the two days?

★ **14.** Nancy, Chuck, and Amy are sharing a reward. Nancy is getting $500 more than Chuck. Chuck is getting $250 less than Amy. How much is each person getting?

Unit Review

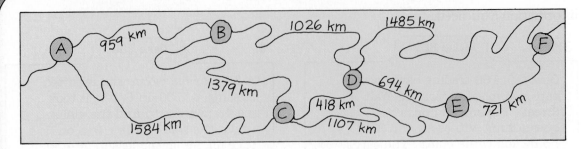

Round the distances to the nearest hundred kilometers.

1. From C to B is about how far?

2. The shortest route from D to F is about how far?

3. The shortest route from E to B is about how far?

4. D is about 2000 km from which city?

Match. Write the letter of the most likely measurement.

5. The thickness of a nickel   **A.** 3 g

6. The amount of juice in a glass   **B.** 12 m

7. The mass of a grape   **C.** 2 mm

8. The height of a kite   **D.** 240 mL

Draw a segment with the given length.

9. 6 cm   **10.** 11 cm   **11.** 17 mm   **12.** 121 mm

True or false? Write *T* or *F*.

13.
$$\begin{array}{r} 6 \text{ ft } 8 \text{ in.} \\ + 11 \text{ ft } 9 \text{ in.} \\ \hline 18 \text{ ft } 7 \text{ in.} \end{array}$$

14.
$$\begin{array}{r} 5 \text{ ft } 5 \text{ in.} \\ + 7 \text{ ft } 7 \text{ in.} \\ \hline 13 \text{ ft} \end{array}$$

15.
$$\begin{array}{r} 3 \text{ qt } 1 \text{ pt} \\ - 2 \text{ qt } 1 \text{ pt} \\ \hline 1 \text{ qt} \end{array}$$

16.
$$\begin{array}{r} 18 \text{ lb } 7 \text{ oz} \\ - 9 \text{ lb } 9 \text{ oz} \\ \hline 8 \text{ lb } 14 \text{ oz} \end{array}$$

Solve.

17. Ingrid drove 113 km before lunch. She spent $3.98 for a fish plate and received $1.02 in change. After lunch she drove 268 km. How far did she drive in all?

Round to the nearest hundred. (*pages 34–37*)

1. 733   **2.** 473   **3.** 1052   **4.** 68,431   **5.** 188,861

Estimate the sum or difference. (*pages 38–41*)

6. 483 + 241   **7.** 638 − 498   **8.** 3712 − 1248   **9.** 5559 + 9143   **10.** 8001 − 4982

11. $.22, .89, + .75   **12.** $1.49, 2.15, + 8.75   **13.** $75.98 − 16.50   **14.** $13.89 − 4.25   **15.** $3.85 + 2.85

Measure the segment to the nearest centimeter. (*pages 42–43*)

16. ———   **17.** ———————   **18.** ——

Measure the segment to the nearest millimeter.

19. ———   **20.** ——   **21.** —   **22.** ———

Choose the better unit for measuring. Write *a* or *b*. (*pages 44–47*)

23. the length of a pen
  a. 15 cm   **b.** 15 m

24. the distance from Boston to Chicago
  a. 1600 m   **b.** 1600 km

25. the amount of gas in a lawn mower
  a. 4 mL   **b.** 4 L

26. the mass of a bag of potatoes
  a. 2 g   **b.** 2 kg

Add or subtract. (*pages 48–51*)

27. 7 ft 9 in. + 3 ft 2 in.   **28.** 2 yd 1 ft + 3 yd 1 ft   **29.** 4 qt − 2 qt 1 pt   **30.** 6 lb 8 oz + 3 lb 12 oz

Solve. (*pages 52–53*)

31. Mario received $10.00 for his birthday. He spent $1.59 for a book and $3.65 for a model. How much did he spend?

Extra practice on page 381

Celsius Temperature

Temperature in the metric system is measured in degrees Celsius (°C). Water was chosen as the temperature standard because it has two temperature points that are easy to see. We call the point at which water freezes 0°C (zero degrees Celsius). We call the point at which water boils 100°C. You can get an idea of some other temperatures by looking at the thermometer.

The normal body temperature is about 38°C.

water boils — 100
— 90
— 80
— 70
— 60
— 50
body temperature — 40
hot summer day — 30
hot shower
room temperature — 20
cold milk — 10
water freezes — 0
cold winter day — -10
— -20

Choose the most likely temperature. Write *a*, *b*, or *c*.

1. Raking leaves
  a. 40°C
  b. 13°C
  c. 2°C

2. Planting a garden
  a. 25°C
  b. 0°C
  c. 5°C

3. Ice skating on a pond
  a. 20°C
  b. 35°C
  c. −1°C

4. Picking strawberries
  a. 3°C
  b. 24°C
  c. −10°C

5. Wearing a winter coat
  a. 75°C
  b. 28°C
  c. −6°C

6. Building a snowperson
  a. 22°C
  b. −5°C
  c. 35°C

7. Washing a car
  a. 25°C
  b. 5°C
  c. −10°C

8. Playing tennis outdoors
  a. 0°C
  b. −20°C
  c. 31°C

The temperature map shows average July temperatures around the world. Places having the same average temperature are joined by a smooth curve called an isotherm.

You can tell, by looking at the key, that most of Australia is warm in July. Temperatures there will vary from about 10°C to 21°C.

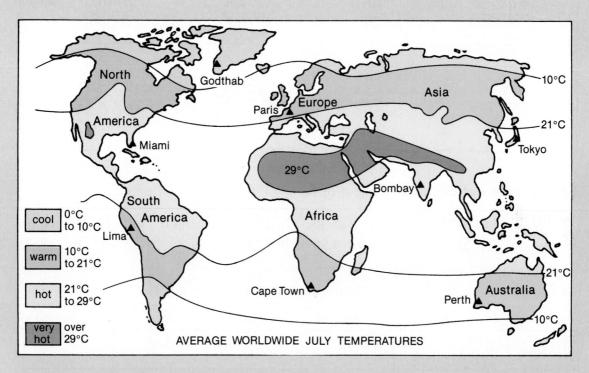

AVERAGE WORLDWIDE JULY TEMPERATURES

Use the temperature map to answer the question.

9. Which continents do not have areas that could be called very hot?

10. Would you expect the temperature in Lima to be 28°C in July?

11. Find three cities on the map where you could expect a temperature of 15°C.

12. By how many degrees does the temperature vary in a hot region?

13. Write reasonable temperatures for Bombay, Godthab, and Cape Town.

Check Tom's homework. Write *C* if the answer is correct. If not, write the correct sum or difference.

Name __Tom R.__

1.
$$\begin{array}{r} 54 \\ +42 \\ \hline 86 \end{array}$$

2.
$$\begin{array}{r} 97 \\ -46 \\ \hline 51 \end{array}$$

3.
$$\begin{array}{r} 72 \\ -29 \\ \hline 42 \end{array}$$

4.
$$\begin{array}{r} 608 \\ +3040 \\ \hline 3748 \end{array}$$

5.
$$\begin{array}{r} 87 \\ 87 \\ +87 \\ \hline 261 \end{array}$$

6.
$$\begin{array}{r} 136 \\ 136 \\ +136 \\ \hline 308 \end{array}$$

7.
$$\begin{array}{r} 4,608 \\ 5,760 \\ +172,800 \\ \hline 183,168 \end{array}$$

8.
$$\begin{array}{r} 3,213 \\ 36,720 \\ +137,700 \\ \hline 166,633 \end{array}$$

Choose the better estimate. Write *a* or *b*.

9.
$$\begin{array}{r} \$1.49 \\ +4.56 \end{array}$$
a. $6.00
b. $5.00

10.
$$\begin{array}{r} \$28.46 \\ -\ 4.98 \end{array}$$
a. $24.00
b. $23.00

11.
$$\begin{array}{r} \$40.32 \\ -23.47 \end{array}$$
a. $60.00
b. $17.00

Bottles for Re-cycling

	Mon	Tues	Wed	Thurs	Fri
Clare	2	3	1	4	1
Ray	2	3	3	3	2

Each ⌷ stands for 15 bottles

Clare and Ray collected bottles for recycling. The table shows how many bottles they collected one week.

12. Who collected more bottles?

13. On Thursday how many more bottles did Clare collect than Ray?

14. Who collected between 160 and 170 bottles?

15. How many bottles were collected altogether for the week?

In the centers of many sunflowers there are 21 spirals in one direction. The next term in the Fibonacci sequence 1,1,2,3,5,8,13,21, ... is the number of spirals in the other direction. How many spirals are in the other direction?

Multiplication

Properties of Multiplication

The **Properties of Multiplication** make it easier to remember
the multiplication facts.

The Commutative (Order) Property

Changing the order of the factors does
not change the product.

$$8 \times 3 = 24 \qquad 3 \times 8 = 24$$
$$\text{so } 8 \times 3 = 3 \times 8$$

The Associative (Grouping) Property

Changing the grouping of the factors
does not change the product.

$$(2 \times 3) \times 4 = 24 \qquad 2 \times (3 \times 4) = 24$$
$$\text{so } (2 \times 3) \times 4 = 2 \times (3 \times 4)$$

The Zero Property

The product of zero and any number is
zero.

$$4 \times 0 = 0 \qquad 0 \times 4 = 0$$

The Property of One

The product of one and any number is
that number.

$$7 \times 1 = 7 \qquad 1 \times 7 = 7$$

Exercises

Multiply. See how fast you can go.

1. 4×3	**2.** 7×2	**3.** 5×6	**4.** 9×8	**5.** 4×5	**6.** 8×0
3×4	2×7	6×5	8×9	5×4	0×8
7. 1×4	**8.** 6×3	**9.** 2×9	**10.** 7×6	**11.** 3×5	**12.** 4×8
4×1	3×6	9×2	6×7	5×3	8×4
13. 5×9	**14.** 8×7	**15.** 8×3	**16.** 2×6	**17.** 7×9	**18.** 9×3
9×5	7×8	3×8	6×2	9×7	3×9
19. 6×8	**20.** 4×7	**21.** 5×8	**22.** 9×6	**23.** 3×7	**24.** 6×4
8×6	7×4	8×5	6×9	7×3	4×6

Complete to show the Commutative Property.

25. $4 \times 6 = 6 \times$ ▨

26. $1 \times 5 =$ ▨ $\times 1$

27. $8 \times$ ▨ $= 9 \times 8$

28. $2 \times 7 =$ ▨ $\times 2$

29. $4 \times 8 = 8 \times$ ▨

30. $5 \times$ ▨ $= 7 \times 5$

31. ▨ $\times 9 = 9 \times 4$

32. ▨ $\times 8 = 8 \times 2$

33. $3 \times 4 =$ ▨ $\times 3$

Complete to show the Associative Property.

34. $2 \times (3 \times 6) = (2 \times 3) \times$

35. $4 \times (1 \times 9) = (4 \times$ $) \times 9$

36. $3 \times (4 \times 7) = ($ $\times 4) \times 7$

37. $2 \times ($ $\times 3) = (2 \times 5) \times 3$

38. $2 \times (6 \times 2) = ($ $\times 6) \times 2$

39. $1 \times ($ $\times 3) = (1 \times 5) \times 3$

Complete to show the Zero Property.

40. $0 \times 5 =$

41. $7 \times 0 =$

42. $3 \times 0 =$

43. $0 \times 8 =$

Complete to show the Property of One.

44. $3 \times 1 =$

45. $1 \times 7 =$

46. $8 \times 1 =$

47. $1 \times 6 =$

Office Equipment

Solve.

48. Renata is a computer programmer. She tested 15 programs on Monday and 8 on Tuesday. How many programs did she test?

49. The Globe Bank has 2 computer terminals at each branch. The bank has 7 branches. How many terminals does the bank have?

50. Sidney operates a word processor. The printer unit can produce about 5 copies of a letter in a minute. About how many copies can the printer produce in 9 minutes?

51. Barry ordered 9 boxes of typewriter ribbons. How many ribbons is this if there are 6 ribbons in each box?

★ **52.** Francine needs 6 copies of a 2-page memo, 8 copies of a 3-page letter, and 10 copies of a 5-page report. How many copies does she need?

Multiplying by One-Digit Numbers

The Baker School reserved 3 buses for a field trip. How many people can go?

Multiply 3 by 68 since you want to combine 3 groups of equal size.

You can rewrite one of the factors to make the multiplication easier. This is an example of the **Distributive Property.**

$$3 \times 68 = 3 \times (60 + 8) = (3 \times 60) + (3 \times 8)$$

Multiply the ones by 3.
Regroup 24 ones as 2 tens 4 ones.

Multiply the tens by 3. Add the 2 tens.

```
    2
   68
  × 3
    4
```

```
    2
   68
  × 3
  204
```

Answer: 204 people can go.

Exercises

Multiply.

1. 2	20	22	**2.** 5	30	35	**3.** 6	70	76
×3	×3	×3	×4	×4	×4	×8	×8	×8

4. 3	60	63	**5.** 6	350	356	**6.** 3	200	203
×4	×4	×4	×7	×7	×7	×5	×5	×5

Multiply.

7. 45	**8.** 63	**9.** 89	**10.** 97	**11.** 24	**12.** 18
×8	×7	×8	×7	×9	×7

13. 47	**14.** 63	**15.** 96	**16.** 82	**17.** 78	**18.** 33
×4	×8	×6	×9	×3	×7

19. 916
×3

20. 159
×5

21. 901
×9

22. 154
×5

23. 253
×7

24. 352
×6

25. 472
×3

26. 583
×8

27. 752
×5

28. 163
×2

29. 1042
×3

30. 3153
×9

31. 5264
×7

32. 8719
×7

33. 2457
×8

34. 55,319
×3

35. 12,086
×5

36. 42,208
×6

37. 31,975
×4

38. 86,319
×9

39. 8 × 486

40. 3 × 374

41. 5 × 8076

42. 2 × 6688

43. 4 × 86,231

44. 7 × 33,422

45. 9 × 721,338

46. 7 × 132,485

Number Pun

47. Use the Decoder to solve the riddle.

Here's how. 157 × 3 = I

Why is twice 15 like twice 16?

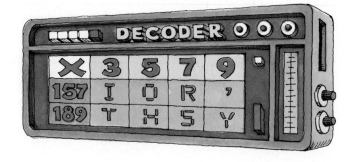

471 567 1413 1323 | 567 945 471 1099 567 1701 | 567 785 785

Solve.

48. At the Outdoor Center there are 13 workshops on Friday and 21 on Saturday. How many more are on Saturday?

49. In a workshop, Dale learned that it takes about 32 L of sap to make 1 L of maple syrup. How many liters of sap are needed to make 8 L of syrup?

★ **50.** The Outdoor Center is sending 5 free tickets, worth $2.75 apiece, to each of 9 schools. What is the value of the tickets?

Multiplying by Tens, Hundreds, Thousands

Looking for patterns makes it easier to multiply by 10, 100, or 1000.

$$
\begin{array}{r} 615 \\ \times 10 \\ \hline 6150 \end{array}
\qquad
\begin{array}{r} 615 \\ \times 100 \\ \hline 61,500 \end{array}
\qquad
\begin{array}{r} 615 \\ \times 1000 \\ \hline 615,000 \end{array}
$$

Look for a similar pattern in these examples.

$$
\begin{array}{r} 318 \\ \times 20 \\ \hline 6360 \end{array}
\qquad
\begin{array}{r} 318 \\ \times 200 \\ \hline 63,600 \end{array}
\qquad
\begin{array}{r} 318 \\ \times 2000 \\ \hline 636,000 \end{array}
$$

Exercises

Multiply. Look for the pattern in the products.

1.
$\begin{array}{r} 25 \\ \times 10 \\ \hline \end{array}$
$\begin{array}{r} 25 \\ \times 100 \\ \hline \end{array}$
$\begin{array}{r} 25 \\ \times 1000 \\ \hline \end{array}$
2.
$\begin{array}{r} 68 \\ \times 10 \\ \hline \end{array}$
$\begin{array}{r} 68 \\ \times 100 \\ \hline \end{array}$
$\begin{array}{r} 68 \\ \times 1000 \\ \hline \end{array}$

3.
$\begin{array}{r} 436 \\ \times 20 \\ \hline \end{array}$
$\begin{array}{r} 436 \\ \times 200 \\ \hline \end{array}$
$\begin{array}{r} 436 \\ \times 2000 \\ \hline \end{array}$
4.
$\begin{array}{r} 733 \\ \times 40 \\ \hline \end{array}$
$\begin{array}{r} 733 \\ \times 400 \\ \hline \end{array}$
$\begin{array}{r} 733 \\ \times 4000 \\ \hline \end{array}$

Multiply.

5. $\begin{array}{r} 57 \\ \times 10 \\ \hline \end{array}$
6. $\begin{array}{r} 87 \\ \times 200 \\ \hline \end{array}$
7. $\begin{array}{r} 482 \\ \times 40 \\ \hline \end{array}$
8. $\begin{array}{r} 679 \\ \times 700 \\ \hline \end{array}$
9. $\begin{array}{r} 346 \\ \times 1000 \\ \hline \end{array}$

10. $\begin{array}{r} 37 \\ \times 20 \\ \hline \end{array}$
11. $\begin{array}{r} 458 \\ \times 300 \\ \hline \end{array}$
12. $\begin{array}{r} 1825 \\ \times 100 \\ \hline \end{array}$
13. $\begin{array}{r} 3795 \\ \times 10 \\ \hline \end{array}$
14. $\begin{array}{r} 18 \\ \times 500 \\ \hline \end{array}$

15. $\begin{array}{r} 100 \\ \times 10 \\ \hline \end{array}$
16. $\begin{array}{r} 217 \\ \times 80 \\ \hline \end{array}$
17. $\begin{array}{r} 300 \\ \times 20 \\ \hline \end{array}$
18. $\begin{array}{r} 468 \\ \times 200 \\ \hline \end{array}$
19. $\begin{array}{r} 34,578 \\ \times 800 \\ \hline \end{array}$

20. $\begin{array}{r} 11 \\ \times 100 \\ \hline \end{array}$
21. $\begin{array}{r} 40 \\ \times 700 \\ \hline \end{array}$
22. $\begin{array}{r} 1000 \\ \times 100 \\ \hline \end{array}$
23. $\begin{array}{r} 13,982 \\ \times 30 \\ \hline \end{array}$
24. $\begin{array}{r} 787 \\ \times 600 \\ \hline \end{array}$

25. 318	**26.** 99,755	**27.** 871	**28.** 27	**29.** 648
×2000	×500	×900	×400	×3000

30. 100 × 875 **31.** 20 × 436 **32.** 10 × 844 **33.** 60 × 409

34. 700 × 39,674 **35.** 50 × 783 **36.** 100 × 1358 **37.** 1000 × 2000

Taxi Please!

Mary Puffins is using her computer to write a new fare schedule for Rocket Ride Taxi. Use the video display to complete the computer printout.

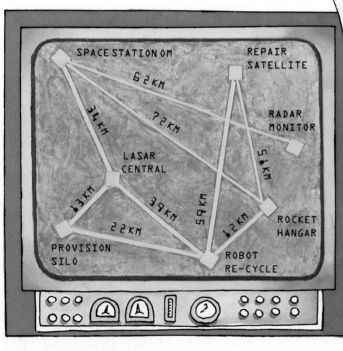

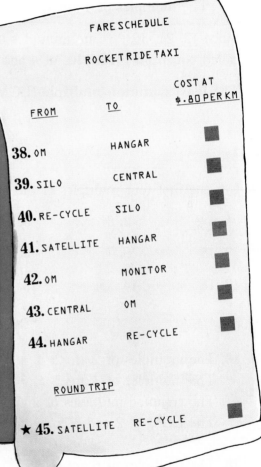

FARE SCHEDULE

ROCKET RIDE TAXI

FROM	TO	COST AT $.80 PER KM
38. OM	HANGAR	
39. SILO	CENTRAL	
40. RE-CYCLE	SILO	
41. SATELLITE	HANGAR	
42. OM	MONITOR	
43. CENTRAL	OM	
44. HANGAR	RE-CYCLE	

ROUND TRIP

★ **45.** SATELLITE RE-CYCLE

12	17	6	31
22	21	19	16
14	19	10	25
8	23	25	18

Find numbers in three squares that touch each other and have a product of 7600.

Take a Break

Multiples, Least Common Multiples

When you multiply a number by 1, 2, 3, 4, . . . , each product is a **multiple** of the number. The three dots mean that the list goes on and on.

Let's look at some examples.

The multiples of 6 are 6, 12, 18, 24, 30, 36, . . .
The multiples of 4 are 4, 8, 12, 16, 20, 24, 28, 32, 36, . . .

Since 12, 24, 36, . . . are multiples of both 4 and 6 they are called **common multiples** of 4 and 6.

The **least common multiple** (LCM) of 4 and 6 is 12.

Exercises

List the first four multiples of the number.

1. 4	**2.** 8	**3.** 5	**4.** 6	**5.** 11	**6.** 20
7. 15	**8.** 7	**9.** 30	**10.** 40	**11.** 100	**12.** 200
13. 18	**14.** 25	**15.** 150	**16.** 12	**17.** 19	**18.** 500

Complete.

19. The multiples of 2 are 2, 4, ▮, ▮, ▮, 12, . . .
The multiples of 3 are 3, 6, ▮, ▮, ▮, 18, . . .
The common multiples of 2 and 3 are ▮, ▮, . . .
The LCM of 2 and 3 is ▮.

20. The multiples of 6 are 6, ▮, ▮, ▮, ▮, 36, . . .
The multiples of 9 are 9, ▮, ▮, ▮, 45, . . .
The common multiples of 6 and 9 are ▮, ▮, . . .
The LCM of 6 and 9 is ▮.

21. The multiples of 20 are 20, ▮, ▮, ▮, ▮, 120, . . .
The multiples of 30 are 30, ▮, ▮, ▮, 150, . . .
The common multiples of 20 and 30 are ▮, ▮, . . .
The LCM of 20 and 30 is ▮.

Write the LCM of the numbers.

22. 3 and 4   **23.** 2 and 6

24. 4 and 6   **25.** 3 and 9

26. 5 and 10   **27.** 6 and 8

28. 6 and 10   **29.** 6 and 12

30. 5 and 9   **31.** 8 and 12

32. 4 and 8   **33.** 6 and 5

34. 2 and 9   **35.** 10 and 15

36. 10 and 25   **37.** 12 and 15

38. 8 and 5   **39.** 5 and 4

40. 4 and 9   **41.** 10 and 12

42. 10 and 20   **43.** 3 and 5

44. 3 and 10   **45.** 16 and 24

46. 18 and 36   **47.** 20 and 25

Hobby Time

Solve.

48. Mia wants to buy 20 stamps that cost 47¢ each. How much change should she get from $10.00?

49. Jay receives Stamp Fan News every 6 weeks and Stamp World every 8 weeks. How often will he receive two magazines in the same week?

★ **50.** The Collector's Showcase has displays of stamps worth 20¢, 30¢, 40¢, and 50¢. If the value of each display is the same, what is the least possible value each display could have?

Checkpoint A

Complete. (*pages 60–61*)

1. 8 × 6 = ▮ × 8

2. 0 × 8 = ▮

3. 3 × (2 × 5) = (3 × 2) × ▮

4. 6 × 1 = ▮

Multiply. (*pages 62–63*)

5. 74
     ×6

6. 803
     ×7

7. 9335
     ×6

8. 84,286
        ×5

Multiply. (*pages 64–65*)

9. 369
      × 10

10. 498
       × 100

11. 732
       × 500

12.   48
        × 700

Write the LCM of the numbers. (*pages 66–67*)

13. 3 and 4

14. 3 and 15

15. 12 and 18

16. 20 and 25

Multiplying by Two-Digit Numbers

Hi!   *April 7*

Today is World Friendship Day. All of the 34 classes in town are sending up helium balloons with messages attached. Every class gets to release 28 balloons.

Sincerely,
T. Barre

To find out how many balloons were released, multiply 34 × 28.

Multiply by 4.

```
   28
 × 34
  112
```

Multiply by 30.

```
   28
 × 34
  112
  840
```

Add.

```
   28
 × 34
  112
  840
  952
```

Wow! Imagine 952 balloons in the sky!

Exercises

Multiply.

1.
```
   42        42        42
  × 2      × 10      × 12
```

2.
```
   31        31        31
  × 4      × 20      × 24
```

3.
```
  357       357       357
  × 5      × 40      × 45
```

4.
```
  963       963       963
  × 7      × 50      × 57
```

5.
```
 1348      1348      1348
  × 6      × 10      × 16
```

6.
```
 2055      2055      2055
  × 3      × 40      × 43
```

Multiply.

7. 52 ×27	**8.** 37 ×81	**9.** 86 ×95	**10.** 91 ×49	**11.** 274 ×68	**12.** 165 ×36
13. 488 ×29	**14.** 9706 ×28	**15.** 1253 ×26	**16.** 585 ×38	**17.** 686 ×92	**18.** 8039 ×17
19. 46 ×52	**20.** 299 ×29	**21.** 6868 ×79	**22.** 107 ×82	**23.** 35 ×47	**24.** 5775 ×70
25. 845 ×68	**26.** 6578 ×83	**27.** 65 ×42	**28.** 78 ×67	**29.** 4351 ×24	**30.** 356 ×84

31. 39 × 15   **32.** 65 × 537   **33.** 87 × 4387   **34.** 76 × 7117

35. 11 × 782   **36.** 26 × 2435   **37.** 88 × 945   **38.** 65 × 5355

It's a Small World

Solve.

39. The carnival committee hoped to raise $350 by selling admission tickets. They sold 428 tickets for $.75 each. Did they reach their goal?

40. Geraldine is slicing each of 25 packages of cheese into 16 pieces. Will she have enough to serve 500 people?

41. Carlos handed out travel folders at the Olé Mexico booth. He had 15 boxes with 25 folders in each box. If all the folders were gone at the end of the day, how many folders did he give away?

★ **42.** A mime group charges $15.75 per hour to perform. They did 1 two hour show on Friday, 2 two hour shows on Saturday, and 3 one hour shows on Sunday. How much did they earn for the 3 days?

Calculator Corner

Multiply. What do you notice about the sum of the first and last digits in the product?

2222 × 9   3333 × 9   4444 × 9
5555 × 9   6666 × 9   7777 × 9

Multiplying by Greater Numbers

To multiply 273×519 we remember that $273 = 2$ hundreds, 7 tens, and 3 ones.

First multiply by 3.   Next multiply by 70.   Finally multiply by 200 and add.

```
      519                 519                    519
    ×273                ×273                   ×273
     1557                1557                   1 557
                        36330                  36 330
                                              103 800
                                              141,687
```

Exercises

Complete the multiplication.

1.
```
      321
    ×524
     1  4
     420
   160500
   1  ,20
```

2.
```
      728
    ×673
     21
    50960
      68
    4 9, 44
```

3.
```
     8142
    ×365
    40710
    48  2
      42  0
     ,  1,83
```

4.
```
    16,276
    ×542
    32
    6  04
    8  8000
     ,82 ,592
```

Multiply.

5.   251
    ×349

6.   617
    ×181

7.   284
    ×686

8.   317
    ×408

9.   215
    ×763

10. 1345
    ×222

11. 3302
    ×687

12. 4345
    ×955

13. 8458
    ×4213

14. 5451
    ×282

15. 18,146
    ×278

16. 33,526
    ×979

17. 42,395
    ×257

18. 26,428
    ×397

19. 63,104
    ×774

20. 4121
    ×5323

21. 122
    ×637

22. 52,521
    ×708

23. 6121
    ×327

24. 122
    ×535

25. 71,465	26. 813	27. 9561	28. 55,792	29. 652
×333	×287	×6357	×621	×193

30. 615 × 580   **31.** 1299 × 9486   **32.** 549 × 22,710   **33.** 3808 × 1348

34. 252 × 34,915   **35.** 345 × 6781   **36.** 769 × 47,862   **37.** 473 × 48,133

Live and Learn

Solve.

38. The Science Museum sent 140 passes to each of 135 schools. How many passes were sent out?

39. A display at the museum says that a bobwhite can eat as many as 5000 weedseeds in a day. At this rate how many weedseeds could a bobwhite eat in a year?

★ **40.** The average twelve-year-old child has a heart rate of about 71 beats per minute. A peregrine falcon has a heart rate of 347 beats per minute. In an hour how many more times will a falcon's heart beat than a twelve-year-old's?

Arrange the numbers to get the answers given.

187   215   637

★ **41.** ▨ × ▨ + ▨ = 137,142

347   6089   591

★ **42.** ▨ × ▨ − ▨ = 198,988

Estimating Products

Henry is buying food for a family reunion. He thinks each person will eat about 225 g of chicken. About how much chicken should he buy to feed 61 people?

Since an exact answer isn't needed, you can round the factors and multiply to get an estimate.

$$
\begin{array}{ccc}
225\text{ g} & \Rightarrow & 200\text{ g} \\
\times 61 & \Rightarrow & \times 60 \\
\hline
& & 12{,}000\text{ g or }12\text{ kg}
\end{array}
$$

Henry estimates that he needs 12 kg of chicken but he's buying 13 kg to make sure everybody has enough.

Exercises

Round to the nearest ten cents.

1. $.75   **2.** $.33   **3.** $.17

4. $.82   **5.** $.96   **6.** $.49

Round to the nearest dollar.

7. $3.45   **8.** $12.98   **9.** $4.72

10. $78.98   **11.** $21.20   **12.** $13.50

Round to the nearest ten.

13. 45 kg   **14.** 38 mL

15. 23 m   **16.** 77 L

17. 14 km   **18.** 13 mm

Round to the nearest hundred.

19. 845 mL   **20.** 363 cm

21. 790 m   **22.** 675 kg

23. 129 km   **24.** 934 L

Estimate the product.

25. $.39
  $\times 2$

26. $.64
  $\times 3$

27. $.78
  $\times 5$

28. 82 mm
  $\times 7$

29. 93 cm
  $\times 8$

30. $.48
  $\times 36$

31. $.51
  $\times 64$

32. 25 mL
  $\times 53$

33. 17 mL
  $\times 89$

34. 66 kg
  $\times 72$

35. $5.18
  $\times 69$

36. $8.47
  $\times 12$

37. $2.85
  $\times 76$

38. 334 cm
  $\times 97$

39. 602 mm
  $\times 45$

40. 715 mm
  $\times 377$

41. 464 g
  $\times 283$

42. 853 mL
  $\times 192$

43. $1.32
  $\times 963$

44. $9.47
  $\times 231$

45. $5.91
  $\times 473$

46. 172 kg
  $\times 874$

47. 365 cm
  $\times 627$

48. $8.03
  $\times 361$

49. 754 mm
  $\times 945$

Making Plans

Estimate.

50. Aunt Minnie is making her special lima bean soup. Each serving should be about 245 mL. Since only 17 people will eat lima bean soup, about how much should Aunt Minnie make?

51. If Uncle Ernie drives the 1168 km to the reunion and back, he thinks the trip will cost about $.08 per kilometer. A round-trip bus ticket will cost $77.45. Estimate to see which method of travel will cost less.

★ **52.** Cousin Jerry is bringing a fruit salad to the reunion.

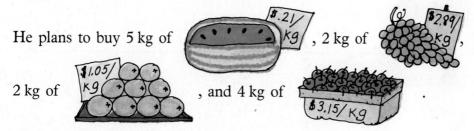

He plans to buy 5 kg of 🍉 $.21/kg, 2 kg of 🍇 $2.99/kg, 2 kg of 🍊 $1.05/kg, and 4 kg of 🍓 $3.15/kg.

Estimate the cost of all the fruit.

Powers and Exponents

In 3^4 the raised 4 is called an **exponent.** It means that 3 is used as a factor four times. We read 3^4 as *three to the fourth power.*

$$3^4 = 3 \times 3 \times 3 \times 3$$
$$= 81$$

The number 3^2 is usually read *three squared* and 3^3 is read *three cubed.*

Any number raised to the first power is that number since the number is used as a factor only once.

$$3^1 = 3 \qquad 17^1 = 17 \qquad 375^1 = 375$$

Exercises

Complete.

1. $3^2 = \boxed{} \times \boxed{}$ **2.** $4^2 = \boxed{} \times \boxed{}$ **3.** $5^2 = \boxed{} \times \boxed{}$

4. $2^3 = \boxed{} \times \boxed{} \times \boxed{}$ **5.** $3^3 = \boxed{} \times \boxed{} \times \boxed{}$ **6.** $4^3 = \boxed{} \times \boxed{} \times \boxed{}$

7. $5 \times 5 \times 5 = 5^{\boxed{}}$ **8.** $6 \times 6 = 6^{\boxed{}}$ **9.** $2 \times 2 \times 2 \times 2 \times 2 = 2^{\boxed{}}$

10. $7 \times 7 \times 7 = \boxed{}^3$ **11.** $4 \times 4 \times 4 = \boxed{}^3$ **12.** $8 \times 8 = \boxed{}^2$

Write the product.

13. 5×5 **14.** $6 \times 6 \times 6$ **15.** $2 \times 2 \times 2 \times 2$

16. $7 \times 7 \times 7$ **17.** $4 \times 4 \times 4$ **18.** $10 \times 10 \times 10$

19. 11×11 **20.** $3 \times 3 \times 3$ **21.** $9 \times 9 \times 9$

Write the product.

22. 3^2 **23.** 5^1 **24.** 8^3 **25.** 4^2 **26.** 6^2 **27.** 2^3

28. 4^3 **29.** 6^1 **30.** 7^2 **31.** 3^3 **32.** 2^1 **33.** 7^3

34. 10^2 **35.** 9^2 **36.** 17^2 **37.** 14^2 **38.** 19^2 **39.** 15^2

40. 12^2 **41.** 40^2 **42.** 50^2

43. 4^4 **44.** 8^2 **45.** 2^5

46. 11^3 **47.** 25^2 **48.** 9^1

49. 11^1 **50.** 20^3 **51.** 3^5

Fair and Square

When you square 3, you get 9.

$$3^2 = 9$$

The **square root** of 9, written $\sqrt{9}$, is 3.

$$\sqrt{9} = 3$$

52. Complete the table of squares. Use the table to find the square root and break the code.

n	12	13	15	16	18	19	23	24	25
n^2									
	L	S	E	Y	O	I	N	H	A

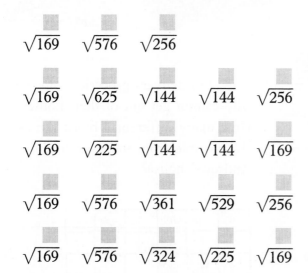

Try saying the tongue twister quickly five times.

Checkpoint B

Multiply. (*pages 68–69*)

1.	42	**2.**	68
	$\times 37$		$\times 54$

3. 3967   **4.** 9786
    $\times 14$ $\times 62$

Multiply. (*pages 70–71*)

5.   687   **6.**   431
    $\times 983$ $\times 556$

7. 6508   **8.** 64,889
    $\times 281$ $\times 672$

Estimate the product. (*pages 72–73*)

9.   46 cm   **10.**   78 mL
    $\times 7$ $\times 36$

11. \$4.16   **12.** \$5.51
    $\times 28$ $\times 326$

Write the product. (*pages 74–75*)

13. 10^1 **14.** 6^3

15. 5^3 **16.** 2^4

Problem Solving · USING A PICTURE

1	Understand
2	Plan
3	Work
4	Answer

The Canal Street After School Club wants to saw a log into 10 pieces to make stools for their clubhouse. If it takes 5 minutes to saw through the log, how long will it take to cut the log into 10 pieces?

Drawing a picture may help you solve the problem.

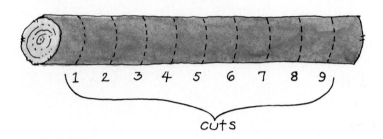

You can see from the picture that there will be 9 cuts.

Since each cut takes 5 minutes it will take $9 \times 5 = 45$ minutes to cut the log into 10 pieces.

Use the picture to help solve the problem.

1. The Club has a tent to use for a clubhouse. If each side of the tent needs 3 stakes, how many stakes are needed for the whole tent?

2. The club delivers groceries for people who cannot get out of their houses. How many different 4-block routes are possible from the store to the Andrews' house?

3. Nan is putting new tiles in Mrs. O'Brien's bathroom. She needs 5 rows with 6 tiles in each row. If she has completed all of 2 rows and half of the other rows, how many more tiles does she need?

4. Every time a club member enters the tent everyone present must shake hands with everyone else. The person entering pays a nickel for each handshake. If you enter the tent and there are already 3 people there, how much must you pay?

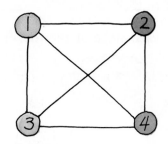

5. The members are choosing a club sweatshirt. Their color choices are red, blue, and green. Their emblem choices are dolphin, leopard, and panda. How many different ways can they choose a club sweatshirt?

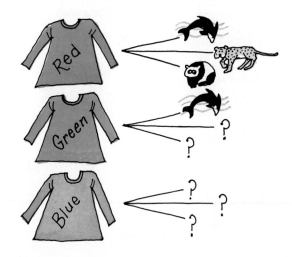

Solve. Drawing a picture may help.

6. Each member volunteers to do one indoor job and one outdoor job each week. The indoor jobs are vacuuming, dusting, and washing floors. The outdoor jobs are mowing and raking. How many weeks can a member go without doing the same two jobs again?

7. Cia is setting up tables for a party. Four people can sit at each square table. How many people can sit at 8 square tables if the tables are placed end-to-end?

8. Harry has a 14 link chain to make a plant hanger. He wants to cut it into 2 pieces so that one piece has 4 more links than the other. How many links will be on each piece?

★ **9.** Sarah and Garret are shoveling a sidewalk that is 30 m long. They start at opposite ends and work towards each other. If Sarah clears 3 m per minute and Garret clears 2 m per minute, how long will it take them to finish the walk?

Multiply each stage of the rocket by the number on the base.

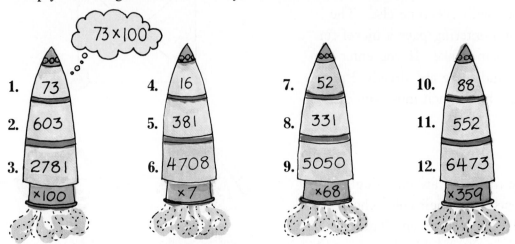

73 × 100

1. 73
2. 603
3. 2781
×100

4. 16
5. 381
6. 4708
×7

7. 52
8. 331
9. 5050
×68

10. 88
11. 552
12. 6473
×359

True or false? Write *T* or *F*.

13. $5^2 = 25$　　　　　**14.** $7^3 = 49$　　　　　**15.** $2^4 = 8$

16. $4^2 = 16$　　　　　**17.** $3^3 = 9$　　　　　**18.** $15^2 = 225$

19. The LCM of 3 and 5 is 15.　　　**20.** The LCM of 8 and 24 is 16.

21. The LCM of 6 and 30 is 30.　　　**22.** The LCM of 2 and 9 is 18.

Estimate the cost.

	Sell to: Tempo Bicycle Equipment	
	Description	**Total**
23.	63 cable locks at $6.46 each	?
24.	37 combination locks at $4.86 each	?
25.	74 chain locks at $9.21 each	?

Solve. Drawing a picture may help.

26. Joseph washes the dishes every third day and sets the table every fifth day. If he washes the dishes on Monday and sets the table on Wednesday when is the next day that he will have to do both jobs?

Multiply. (*pages 60–63*)

1. 7
　×6

2. 21
　×8

3. 419
　×3

4. 2186
　×7

5. 67,739
　×8

Multiply. (*pages 64–65*)

6. 32
　×10

7. 174
　×100

8. 803
　×40

9. 291
　×3000

10. 910
　×500

Write the LCM of the numbers. (*pages 66–67*)

11. 6 and 14

12. 16 and 24

13. 4 and 15

14. 5 and 7

Multiply. (*pages 68–71*)

15. 57
　×43

16. 89
　×64

17. 8206
　×57

18. 759
　×428

19. 9964
　×315

Estimate the product. (*pages 72–73*)

20. 48 mL
　×3

21. 86 g
　×52

22. $2.98
　×21

23. $5.75
　×427

24. $8.09
　×678

Write the product. (*pages 74–75*)

25. 2^4

26. 8^2

27. 5^3

28. 12^2

29. 1^{10}

Solve. Drawing a picture may help. (*pages 76–77*)

30. At a local restaurant you can have a choice of 2 different appetizers, 3 different main courses, and 3 different drinks. How many different dinners are possible if you must choose one item from each group?

31. A total of 36 handshakes were exchanged at a family gathering. Each person shook hands with every one else exactly once. How many people were at the party?

Base Two Numbers

We call ten the **base** of our numeration system because we group in powers of ten. We use the ten digits, 0 through 9, to write numbers. In the base two numeration system we use only two digits, 0 and 1, to write numbers. The symbol 1101_{two} is read *"one one zero one, base two."*

The use of base two numbers makes it possible for computers to complete complicated computations in a very short time.

Compare the place value charts for base ten and base two to see how the number 5_{ten} is written in each system.

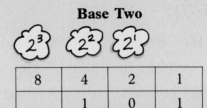

Base Ten			
10^3	10^2	10^1	
1000	100	10	1
			5

Base Two			
2^3	2^2	2^1	
8	4	2	1
	1	0	1

$$5_{ten} = (5 \times 1)$$
$$= 5$$

$$101_{two} = (1 \times 2^2) + (0 \times 2^1) + (1 \times 1)$$
$$= \quad 4 \quad + \quad 0 \quad + \quad 1$$
$$= 5_{ten}$$

1. Copy and complete the table for powers of two.

Powers of 2		
$2^1 = $ ▨	$2^2 = $ ▨	$2^3 = $ ▨
$2^4 = $ ▨	$2^5 = $ ▨	$2^6 = $ ▨
$2^7 = $ ▨	$2^8 = $ ▨	$2^9 = $ ▨

Use the table from Exercise 1. Write the base ten number for the base two number.

2. 1001_{two} **3.** 11_{two} **4.** 1000_{two} **5.** 1010_{two} **6.** 11111_{two}

Now try these. Write the base ten number for the base two number.

7. The average sixth grader is 10010110_{two} cm tall.

8. The school year is usually 10110100_{two} days long.

9. The movie was 101001_{two} minutes long.

10. Jerry spent 101101_{two} minutes on his homework.

A set of lights on a computer can stand for a base two number. A light turned on stands for the digit 1. A light turned off stands for the digit 0.

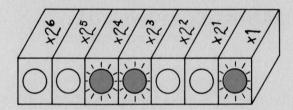

The computer shows the base two number 11001_{two}. In base ten the number becomes 25_{ten}.

$$11001_{two} = (1 \times 2^4) + (1 \times 2^3) + (0 \times 2^2) + (0 \times 2^1) + (1 \times 1)$$
$$= 16 + 8 + 0 + 0 + 1$$
$$= 25_{ten}$$

Write the base two number shown on the computer. Then write the base ten number that stands for the same number.

11.

12.

13.

14.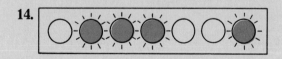

15.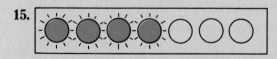

16.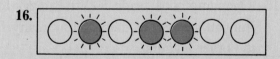

17.

18.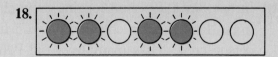

Match.

1. 12^2 **A.** 729

2. 7^3 **B.** 81

3. 3^4 **C.** 144

4. 27^2 **D.** 32

5. 2^5 **E.** 343

True or false? Write *T* or *F*.

6. 200 mm = 2 cm

7. 50 mm = 500 cm

8. 1 cm = 100 mm

9. 8 cm = 800 mm

10. 6000 m = 6 km

Use the clues to complete the squares.

11. Clues: multiply by 4
multiply by 9

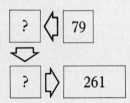

12. Clues: multiply by 33
subtract 26,000

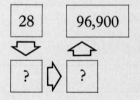

13. Clues: multiply by 182
subtract 14,299
add 182

14. Clues: multiply by 32
add 73
multiply by 100

Solve.

15. The camp cook made 500 fried eggs for breakfast. Paul Bunyan ate 386 of them. How many fried eggs were left for the other loggers?

16. In one day a 7 person logging crew chopped down 279 trees. Paul Bunyan chopped down 5 times as many as the 7 person crew. How many trees did Paul chop down?

It's cogwheels that make the hands on a clock go around. In this clock, the large wheel has 36 teeth. It turns once an hour. The small wheel has 12 teeth. It turns 3 times an hour. How long does it take the small wheel to make a complete turn?

4

Division

Multiplication and Division Equations

Multiplication and division by the same number are opposites.
One undoes the other.

$$4 \times 7 = 28$$
$$28 \div 7 = 4$$

$$\begin{array}{r} 7 \\ \times 4 \\ \hline 28 \end{array}$$

$$\begin{array}{r} 4 \\ 7\overline{)28} \end{array}$$

This idea can help you recall the division facts. It can also help you solve some multiplication and division equations.

You can solve an equation such as $3 \times n = 12$ by thinking of the multiplication facts.

$$3 \times n = 12$$

3×4=12
so n=4

You can solve an equation such as $n \div 4 = 6$ by thinking of the division facts.

$$n \div 4 = 6$$

24÷4=6
so n=24

Exercises

Complete.

1. $32 \div 8 = $ ▨
$4 \times 8 = $ ▨

2. $54 \div 9 = $ ▨
$6 \times 9 = $ ▨

3. $42 \div 7 = $ ▨
$6 \times 7 = $ ▨

4. $72 \div 9 = $ ▨
$8 \times 9 = $ ▨

5. $49 \div 7 = $ ▨
$7 \times 7 = $ ▨

6. $16 \div 8 = $ ▨
$2 \times 8 = $ ▨

Let $n = 5$. Write the product or quotient.

7. $n \times 3$ **8.** $n \times 8$ **9.** $25 \div n$ **10.** $15 \div n$ **11.** $7 \times n$

12. $6 \times n$ **13.** $n \div 1$ **14.** $45 \div n$ **15.** $9 \times n$ **16.** $0 \times n$

Let $y = 9$. Write the product or quotient.

17. $y \div 3$ **18.** $54 \div y$ **19.** $3 \times y$ **20.** $y \div 9$ **21.** $y \times 7$

22. $36 \div y$ **23.** $6 \times y$ **24.** $y \div 1$ **25.** $8 \times y$ **26.** $y \times 9$

Solve.

27. $28 \div 4 = n$ **28.** $a \div 6 = 6$ **29.** $36 \div 9 = y$

30. $n \div 3 = 8$ **31.** $72 \div 9 = a$ **32.** $n \div 9 = 5$

33. $y \div 7 = 7$ **34.** $a \div 8 = 2$ **35.** $9 \times n = 81$

36. $5 \times a = 25$ **37.** $3 \times y = 12$ **38.** $n \times 7 = 56$

39. $18 \div 6 = a$ **40.** $n \div 7 = 6$ **41.** $y \div 4 = 4$

42. $64 \div 8 = a$ **43.** $9 \times y = 18$ **44.** $n \times 4 = 36$

45. $5 \times a = 45$ **46.** $8 \times y = 72$ **47.** $63 \div 7 = n$

48. $y \times 8 = 40$ **49.** $a \div 6 = 5$ **50.** $n \div 9 = 9$

Giant Food

Solve the equation to complete the sentence.

51. The largest pineapple on record had a mass of nearly $3 \times n = 21$ kilograms.

52. A carrot with a mass of almost $y \div 5 = 1$ kilograms was grown in Victoria, Australia.

53. A North Carolina resident reported growing a peanut with a length of more than $6 \times a = 48$ centimeters.

★ **54.** The tallest sunflower on record reached a height of between $9 \times n = 63$ meters and $a \div 4 = 2$ meters.

Calculator Corner

How Big is a Billion?

A million minutes is about ▮ years.

A billion minutes is about ▮ years.

Dividing by Ones

Here's one way to divide 177 by 5.

Think of 5)17.

divisor ⟶ 5) 177 ⟵ dividend

3

−15
2

subtract 3 × 5

Is 2 less than 5? Yes.

Division is elementary if you memorize the basic facts.

Think of 5)27.

quotient ⟶ 35 R2 ⟵ remainder
5) 177
−15↓
27
−25
2

subtract 5 × 5

Check.
```
    35
  × 5
   175
  +  2
   177  √
```

Exercises

Complete.

1. 4) 51
  1▮ R▮
−▮
11
−▮
▮

2. 2) 57
  2▮ R▮
−▮
17
−▮▮
▮

3. 5) 667
  1▮▮ R▮
−▮
16
−▮▮
▮7
−▮▮
▮

4. 7) 1888
  2▮▮ R▮
−14
▮▮
−▮▮
▮8
−▮▮
▮

Divide.

5. 6)325   6)3259   6)32,590   **6.** 5)194   5)1946   5)19,462

7. 8)488   8)4889   8)48,891   **8.** 4)179   4)1796   4)17,966

Divide and check.

9. $8\overline{)89}$ **10.** $7\overline{)84}$ **11.** $2\overline{)59}$ **12.** $9\overline{)100}$ **13.** $5\overline{)133}$

14. $4\overline{)6639}$ **15.** $8\overline{)2034}$ **16.** $6\overline{)9254}$ **17.** $9\overline{)1935}$ **18.** $4\overline{)3168}$

Divide.

19. $3\overline{)23,605}$ **20.** $5\overline{)24,061}$ **21.** $7\overline{)898}$ **22.** $2\overline{)16,675}$ **23.** $3\overline{)2149}$

24. $4\overline{)1769}$ **25.** $6\overline{)37,555}$ **26.** $8\overline{)48,997}$ **27.** $5\overline{)42,687}$ **28.** $9\overline{)1573}$

29. $375 \div 5$ **30.** $188 \div 2$ **31.** $328 \div 8$ **32.** $1134 \div 3$ **33.** $7936 \div 8$

34. $51,534 \div 8$ **35.** $62,946 \div 7$ **36.** $26,841 \div 5$ **37.** $77,833 \div 9$

Using Your Head

You can use short division to find $3\overline{)775}$. At each stage just divide, multiply, and subtract in your head.

Here's how. $3\overline{)7^17\,5}$ (2) $3\overline{)7^17^2\,5}$ (2 5) $3\overline{)7^17^2\,5}$ (2 5 8 R1)

Complete the short division.

38. $4\overline{)6^27^39}$ R▦ **39.** $7\overline{)8^148}$ R▦ **40.** $5\overline{)9^43^36^18}$ R▦ **41.** $6\overline{)38^25^14}$ R▦

Divide using short division.

42. $3\overline{)286}$ **43.** $4\overline{)2751}$ **44.** $9\overline{)87,915}$ **45.** $8\overline{)65,010}$

Solve.

46. Lucy Rodriguez set a school record by making a chain of paper clips 4371 cm long. Each paper clip was 3 cm long. How many paper clips were in Lucy's chain?

★ **47.** Write a word problem to fit the equation. $y \div 6 = 1800$

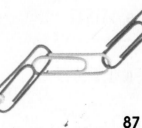

Zeros in the Quotient

In 7 days, the Jandrons drifted 3558 km. About how many kilometers did they drift each day?

We divide 3558 by 7 in three stages.

Think of $7\overline{)35}$.
The quotient is 5.

$$
\begin{array}{r}
5 \\
7\overline{)\ 3558} \\
-35
\end{array}
$$

Think of $7\overline{)5}$.
The quotient is 0.

$$
\begin{array}{r}
50 \\
7\overline{)\ 3558} \\
-35\downarrow \\
\hline
5 \\
-0 \\
\hline
5
\end{array}
$$

Think of $7\overline{)58}$.
The quotient is 8.

$$
\begin{array}{r}
508\ \text{R2} \\
7\overline{)\ 3558} \\
-35 \\
\hline
5 \\
-0\downarrow \\
\hline
58 \\
-56 \\
\hline
2
\end{array}
$$

They drifted about 508 km each day.

Exercises

Complete.

1.
$$
\begin{array}{r}
20\blacksquare\ \text{R}\blacksquare \\
4\overline{)\ 815} \\
-\blacksquare \\
\hline
1 \\
-\blacksquare \\
\hline
15 \\
-12 \\
\hline
3
\end{array}
$$

2.
$$
\begin{array}{r}
\blacksquare\blacksquare\ \text{R}\blacksquare \\
5\overline{)\ 154} \\
-15 \\
\hline
4 \\
-\blacksquare \\
\hline
4
\end{array}
$$

3.
$$
\begin{array}{r}
4\blacksquare 9\ \text{R}\blacksquare \\
6\overline{)\ 8456} \\
-6 \\
\hline
24 \\
-\blacksquare\blacksquare \\
\hline
5 \\
-0 \\
\hline
56 \\
-\blacksquare\blacksquare \\
\hline
\blacksquare
\end{array}
$$

4.
$$
\begin{array}{r}
\blacksquare\blacksquare\blacksquare\ \text{R6} \\
7\overline{)\ 2246} \\
-\blacksquare\blacksquare \\
\hline
14 \\
-14 \\
\hline
\blacksquare \\
-\blacksquare \\
\hline
6
\end{array}
$$

5.
$$
\begin{array}{r}
2\blacksquare 0\ \text{R}\blacksquare \\
7\overline{)1542}
\end{array}
$$

6.
$$
\begin{array}{r}
5\blacksquare 0\blacksquare\ \text{R}\blacksquare \\
8\overline{)40{,}035}
\end{array}
$$

7.
$$
\begin{array}{r}
4\blacksquare\blacksquare\blacksquare\ \text{R}\blacksquare \\
9\overline{)36{,}272}
\end{array}
$$

8.
$$
\begin{array}{r}
5\blacksquare\blacksquare \\
5\overline{)2845}
\end{array}
$$

9.
$$
\begin{array}{r}
9\blacksquare\blacksquare\blacksquare\ \text{R}\blacksquare \\
3\overline{)27{,}077}
\end{array}
$$

10.
$$
\begin{array}{r}
3\blacksquare\blacksquare\blacksquare\ \text{R}\blacksquare \\
5\overline{)17{,}042}
\end{array}
$$

11.
$$
\begin{array}{r}
1\blacksquare\blacksquare\blacksquare\ \text{R}\blacksquare \\
4\overline{)6123}
\end{array}
$$

12.
$$
\begin{array}{r}
8\blacksquare\blacksquare\ \text{R}\blacksquare \\
6\overline{)5223}
\end{array}
$$

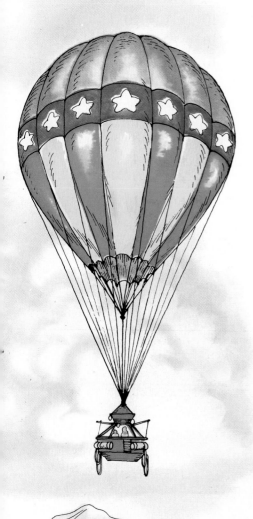

Divide and check.

13. $3\overline{)7042}$ **14.** $2\overline{)16,100}$ **15.** $9\overline{)8172}$

16. $8\overline{)97,631}$ **17.** $6\overline{)44,457}$ **18.** $5\overline{)3000}$

Divide.

19. $8\overline{)23,210}$ **20.** $4\overline{)16,123}$ **21.** $6\overline{)42,457}$

22. $7\overline{)24,503}$ **23.** $7\overline{)63,546}$ **24.** $8\overline{)16,647}$

25. $4\overline{)16,322}$ **26.** $3\overline{)21,025}$ **27.** $6\overline{)63,020}$

28. $2\overline{)13,000}$ **29.** $5\overline{)35,352}$ **30.** $9\overline{)78,030}$

31. $78,025 \div 5$ **32.** $21,068 \div 2$ **33.** $10,542 \div 3$

34. $48,186 \div 6$ **35.** $63,873 \div 9$ **36.** $37,632 \div 4$

Ship Shape

37. Solve the equation. Match the quotient with a letter to solve the riddle.

$14,515 \div 5 = C$ $\qquad$ $20,510 \div 7 = E$

$21,510 \div 9 = I$ $\qquad$ $12,234 \div 6 = P$

$11,545 \div 5 = R$ $\qquad$ $16,744 \div 8 = L$

What kind of ship does a barber sail?

2903 $\quad$ 2093 $\quad$ 2390 $\quad$ 2039 $\quad$ 2039 $\quad$ 2930 $\quad$ 2309

What number can you write on each side of the equation to make the equation true?

★ **38.** $36 + \blacksquare = 405 \div \blacksquare$

★ **39.** $6 \times \blacksquare = 294 \div \blacksquare$

★ **40.** $2106 \div \blacksquare = 357 - \blacksquare$

Factors, Greatest Common Factors

Numbers which divide 10 with no remainder
are called **factors** of 10.

$$10 \div 1 = 10$$
$$10 \div 2 = 5$$
$$10 \div 5 = 2$$
$$10 \div 10 = 1$$

The factors of 10 are 1, 2, 5, and 10.

You can also find the factors of 8 by
dividing.

$$8 \div 1 = 8$$
$$8 \div 2 = 4$$
$$8 \div 4 = 2$$
$$8 \div 8 = 1$$

The factors of 8 are 1, 2, 4, and 8.

Since 1 and 2 are factors of both 10 and 8,
they are called **common factors** of 10 and 8.

The **greatest common factor** (GCF) of 10 and 8 is 2.

Exercises

Complete the chart.

	Numbers	Factors	Common Factors	GCF
1.	18	1, 2, 3, ▦, ▦, ▦	1, ▦, ▦	▦
	27	1, 3, ▦, ▦		
2.	45	1, 3, 5, ▦, ▦, ▦	1, ▦	▦
	21	1, ▦, ▦, ▦		
3.	15	1, 3, ▦, ▦	1, ▦	▦
	20	1, 2, 4, ▦, ▦, ▦		
4.	6	1, 2, ▦, ▦	1, 2, ▦, ▦	▦
	12	1, 2, 3, ▦, ▦, ▦		

Write the factors.

5. 50   **6.** 14   **7.** 11   **8.** 22   **9.** 26   **10.** 23

11. 28   **12.** 29   **13.** 32   **14.** 35   **15.** 36   **16.** 24

Write the common factors of the numbers.

17. 16 and 20   **18.** 36 and 60   **19.** 24 and 48   **20.** 20 and 100

21. 27 and 63   **22.** 55 and 75   **23.** 85 and 51   **24.** 90 and 150

25. 16 and 28   **26.** 45 and 60   **27.** 33 and 55   **28.** 17 and 51

Write the GCF of the numbers.

29. 16 and 24   **30.** 40 and 130   **31.** 16 and 12   **32.** 8 and 48

33. 30 and 200   **34.** 75 and 30   **35.** 41 and 17   **36.** 52 and 33

37. 18 and 36   **38.** 26 and 39   **39.** 14 and 42   **40.** 27 and 36

Prime Time

What's so special about these numbers?

2, 3, 5, 7, 11, 13, 17, 19, 23, 29, 31, 37, . . .

Each is a **prime number.** A prime number is one that has exactly two factors, 1 and itself.

The numbers 4, 6, 8, 9, 10, 12, 14, 15, 16, 18, . . . are **composite numbers** since each has more than 2 factors.

0 AND 1 ARE NEITHER PRIME NOR COMPOSITE SINCE EACH HAS ONLY ONE FACTOR.

Is the number prime or composite? Write *P* or *C*.

41. 90   **42.** 71   **43.** 51   **44.** 43   **45.** 35   **46.** 63

47. 102   **48.** 40   **49.** 91   **50.** 75   **51.** 89   **52.** 18

53. 145   **54.** 39   **55.** 182   **56.** 144   **57.** 511   **58.** 151

★ **59.** The numbers 4 and 9 each have exactly three factors. What are the next two numbers that have exactly three factors?

★ **60.** Two numbers between 40 and 50 have common factors of 1, 2, and 4. What are these numbers?

Divisibility Rules

The Busby Helicopter Company likes to get tire shipments in sets of 3. This allows each helicopter to be completed as it passes through the assembly line. If 29,307 tires are delivered, can they all be used 3 at a time?

You can solve this problem quickly without division if you know a divisibility rule for 3.

A number is divisible by 3 if the sum of its digits is divisible by 3.

29,307 is **divisible** by 3 since 2 + 9 + 3 + 0 + 7 = 21, and 21 is divisible by 3.

The tires can all be used 3 at a time.

ONE NUMBER IS DIVISIBLE BY ANOTHER IF IT CAN BE DIVIDED BY THE NUMBER WITH NO REMAINDER.

Here are some other divisibility rules to remember.

Rule	Example
A number is divisible by 2 if the digit in the ones' place is 0, 2, 4, 6, or 8.	37,858 is divisible by 2.
A number is divisible by 5 if the digit in the ones' place is 0 or 5.	30,015 is divisible by 5.
A number is divisible by 10 if the digit in the ones' place is 0.	68,170 is divisible by 10.

Exercises

Is the first number divisible by the second? Write *Yes* or *No*.

1. 27; 2   **2.** 105; 5   **3.** 30; 3   **4.** 206; 10   **5.** 78; 2

6. 703,490; 10   **7.** 4761; 3   **8.** 71,613; 5   **9.** 6790; 2   **10.** 158,601; 3

11. 64; 10   **12.** 85; 5   **13.** 789; 2

14. 168; 3   **15.** 426; 2   **16.** 3008; 10

17. 790; 5   **18.** 334; 3   **19.** 4283; 2

20. 87; 10   **21.** 888; 3   **22.** 202; 2

23. 49; 3   **24.** 5681; 2   **25.** 8000; 5

26. 368; 2   **27.** 401; 3   **28.** 39,010; 10

29. 279; 5   **30.** 71,589; 3   **31.** 99,734; 2

32. 4890; 10   **33.** 6000; 2   **34.** 81,810; 3

35. 2778; 2   **36.** 7121; 3   **37.** 420; 5

Keep Going

Use the numbers in the chart for the exercises below.

78,450	564	88
910	6684	871,154
4793	831	3025

38. Which numbers are divisible by 2?

39. Which numbers are divisible by 3?

40. Which numbers are divisible by both 5 and 10?

41. Which numbers are divisible by 2, 5, and 10?

★ **42.** Which numbers are divisible by 2, 3, 5, and 10?

★ **43.** Which number is not divisible by any of the factors 2, 3, 5, or 10?

★ **44.** Write a divisibility rule for 6.

Checkpoint A

Solve. (*pages 84–85*)

1. $n \div 4 = 6$ **2.** $w \div 3 = 5$

3. $7 \times a = 21$ **4.** $9 \times y = 54$

Divide. (*pages 86–87*)

5. $8\overline{)67}$ **6.** $5\overline{)163}$

7. $6\overline{)937}$ **8.** $7\overline{)24,615}$

Divide. (*pages 88–89*)

9. $2\overline{)619}$ **10.** $7\overline{)912}$

11. $6\overline{)7825}$ **12.** $8\overline{)18,461}$

Write the GCF of the numbers. (*pages 90–91*)

13. 15 and 25   **14.** 21 and 30

15. 35 and 21   **16.** 18 and 36

Is the first number divisible by the second? Write *Yes* or *No*. (*pages 92–93*)

17. 42; 2   **18.** 700; 5

19. 631; 3   **20.** 655; 10

Dividing by Tens

The Sea View Company packs snorkels in boxes of 20. How many boxes can be filled with 7953 snorkels?

Divide 7953 by 20 since you want to know how many boxes of 20 there are.

Think of $2\overline{)7}$.

$$
\begin{array}{r}
3 \\
20\overline{)7953} \\
-60 \\
\hline
19
\end{array}
$$

Think of $2\overline{)19}$.

$$
\begin{array}{r}
39 \\
20\overline{)7953} \\
-60\downarrow \\
\hline
195 \\
-180 \\
\hline
15
\end{array}
$$

Think of $2\overline{)15}$.

$$
\begin{array}{r}
397 \text{ R13} \\
20\overline{)7953} \\
-60 \\
\hline
195 \\
-180\downarrow \\
\hline
153 \\
-140 \\
\hline
13
\end{array}
$$

There will be 397 boxes of 20 snorkels and 13 snorkels left over.

Exercises

Divide.

1. $30\overline{)120}$ 2. $40\overline{)160}$ 3. $70\overline{)420}$ 4. $50\overline{)500}$

   $30\overline{)90}$ $40\overline{)280}$ $70\overline{)210}$ $50\overline{)300}$

   $30\overline{)270}$ $40\overline{)360}$ $70\overline{)630}$ $50\overline{)150}$

5. $30\overline{)60}$ 6. $40\overline{)80}$ 7. $60\overline{)180}$ 8. $70\overline{)490}$

   $30\overline{)72}$ $40\overline{)95}$ $60\overline{)197}$ $70\overline{)526}$

Complete the division.

9.
$$
\begin{array}{r}
5 \text{ R}\blacksquare\blacksquare \\
40\overline{)228} \\
-\blacksquare\blacksquare\blacksquare \\
\hline
\blacksquare\blacksquare
\end{array}
$$

10.
$$
\begin{array}{r}
6\blacksquare \text{ R}\blacksquare\blacksquare \\
40\overline{)2628} \\
-240 \\
\hline
228 \\
-200 \\
\hline
\blacksquare\blacksquare
\end{array}
$$

11.
$$
\begin{array}{r}
\blacksquare\blacksquare \text{ R}\blacksquare\blacksquare \\
70\overline{)3028}
\end{array}
$$

12.
$$
\begin{array}{r}
\blacksquare\blacksquare \text{ R}\blacksquare\blacksquare \\
90\overline{)3828}
\end{array}
$$

Divide and check.

13. $20\overline{)502}$ **14.** $30\overline{)1038}$ **15.** $50\overline{)1352}$ **16.** $40\overline{)1204}$

17. $80\overline{)8055}$ **18.** $70\overline{)2730}$ **19.** $60\overline{)4212}$ **20.** $90\overline{)7483}$

Divide.

21. $50\overline{)918}$ **22.** $20\overline{)719}$ **23.** $30\overline{)1266}$ **24.** $70\overline{)731}$

25. $60\overline{)4702}$ **26.** $90\overline{)3562}$ **27.** $80\overline{)4286}$ **28.** $40\overline{)825}$

29. $30\overline{)1970}$ **30.** $20\overline{)608}$ **31.** $20\overline{)672}$ **32.** $70\overline{)6674}$

33. $1980 \div 60$ **34.** $3400 \div 40$ **35.** $6660 \div 90$ **36.** $4560 \div 60$

37. $5840 \div 80$ **38.** $6930 \div 70$ **39.** $700 \div 50$ **40.** $420 \div 30$

Sea Scene

Solve.

41. Finn's Scuba ordered 150 face masks. There were 10 cartons of masks delivered. How many masks were in each carton?

42. Flippers are packed in cartons of 30 pairs. How many cartons should be ordered if 1260 pairs are needed?

43. There are 20 wetsuits in a carton. The Diver's Den needs 80 wetsuits. Will 3 cartons be enough?

44. There are 420 people signed up for scuba diving classes. Each class can accept 10 people. How many classes will there be?

Two-Digit Divisors

Here's one way to divide 72 by 26.

Round 26 up to 30.
To estimate the quotient, think of $3\overline{)7}$.

$$\begin{array}{r} 2\text{ R}20 \\ 26\overline{)72} \\ -52 \\ \hline 20 \end{array}$$

(30)

Sometimes your first estimate isn't large enough. Look at 631 divided by 75.

Round 75 up to 80. Think of $8\overline{)63}$.

(80)
$$\begin{array}{r} 7 \\ 75\overline{)631} \\ -525 \\ \hline 106 \end{array}$$

◁ Since 106 is greater than 75, try a larger quotient.

Try 8 as the quotient.

$$\begin{array}{r} 8\text{ R}31 \\ 75\overline{)631} \\ -600 \\ \hline 31 \end{array}$$

Sometimes your first estimate is too large. Look at 121 divided by 44.

Round 44 down to 40. Think of $4\overline{)12}$.

(40)
$$\begin{array}{r} 3 \\ 44\overline{)121} \\ -132 \end{array}$$

◁ Since you can't subtract 132 from 121, try a smaller quotient.

Try 2 as the quotient.

$$\begin{array}{r} 2\text{ R}33 \\ 44\overline{)121} \\ -88 \\ \hline 33 \end{array}$$

Exercises

Divide.

1. $20\overline{)81}$ $19\overline{)81}$ 2. $30\overline{)65}$ $27\overline{)65}$ 3. $40\overline{)243}$ $36\overline{)243}$

4. $60\overline{)186}$ $64\overline{)186}$ 5. $50\overline{)316}$ $54\overline{)316}$ 6. $70\overline{)436}$ $66\overline{)436}$

Divide and check.

7. $28\overline{)60}$ 8. $34\overline{)65}$ 9. $39\overline{)170}$ 10. $25\overline{)163}$ 11. $44\overline{)153}$

12. $53\overline{)193}$ 13. $88\overline{)753}$ 14. $74\overline{)400}$ 15. $34\overline{)259}$ 16. $72\overline{)588}$

Divide.

17. $65\overline{)264}$ **18.** $12\overline{)463}$

19. $53\overline{)174}$ **20.** $44\overline{)364}$

21. $78\overline{)393}$ **22.** $85\overline{)782}$

23. $25\overline{)118}$ **24.** $18\overline{)110}$

25. $50\overline{)462}$ **26.** $62\overline{)289}$

27. $32\overline{)165}$ **28.** $30\overline{)211}$

29. $225 \div 45$ **30.** $164 \div 41$

31. $217 \div 31$ **32.** $280 \div 35$

Limited Editions

Solve.

33. Jeff can print 60 T-shirts from one stencil. How many T-shirts can he print from 15 stencils?

34. Shirley needs 38 leather loops to make one belt. How many belts can she make from 160 loops?

35. Chris has 357 beads. He wants to make 37 necklaces. How many beads will each necklace have?

★ **36.** Melba sold 38 clay pots at a craft show. She collected $119.70 which included $5.70 for tax. How much did she charge for each pot?

Lenny and Lulu each have 12 coins that total 49¢. Lulu has one coin that Lenny doesn't have. What coins does each have?

Take a Break

97

Two-Stage Division

Lucky Larry won 715 pairs of tennis shoes on a quiz show. Larry shared his prize with 27 friends.

Divide 715 by 28 (don't forget Larry) to see how many pairs of shoes each person will get.

Round 28 to 30. Think of $3\overline{)7}$.

Think of $3\overline{)15}$.

Write the remainder.

$$\begin{array}{r} 2 \\ 28\overline{)715} \\ -56 \\ \hline 15 \end{array}$$

$$\begin{array}{r} 25 \\ 28\overline{)715} \\ -56\downarrow \\ \hline 155 \\ -140 \\ \hline 15 \end{array}$$

$$\begin{array}{r} 25\ \text{R15} \\ 28\overline{)715} \\ -56 \\ \hline 155 \\ -140 \\ \hline 15 \end{array}$$

Everyone gets 25 pairs of tennis shoes and Larry gets an extra 15 pairs.

Exercises

Divide.

1. $40\overline{)875}$

2. $30\overline{)1285}$

3. $60\overline{)689}$

4. $80\overline{)895}$

$37\overline{)875}$

$26\overline{)1285}$

$55\overline{)689}$

$78\overline{)895}$

Divide and check.

5. $33\overline{)757}$

6. $18\overline{)537}$

7. $93\overline{)6542}$

8. $44\overline{)1425}$

9. $51\overline{)789}$

10. $64\overline{)4973}$

11. $38\overline{)714}$

12. $77\overline{)873}$

Divide.

13. $29\overline{)2143}$ **14.** $17\overline{)984}$ **15.** $50\overline{)2475}$ **16.** $76\overline{)6238}$

17. $56\overline{)1512}$ **18.** $39\overline{)1238}$ **19.** $85\overline{)7025}$ **20.** $14\overline{)290}$

21. $19\overline{)493}$ **22.** $82\overline{)2986}$ **23.** $13\overline{)285}$ **24.** $10\overline{)826}$

25. $54\overline{)1850}$ **26.** $17\overline{)361}$ **27.** $24\overline{)613}$ **28.** $38\overline{)1304}$

29. $82\overline{)1000}$ **30.** $87\overline{)7118}$ **31.** $35\overline{)1273}$ **32.** $21\overline{)461}$

33. $1320 \div 40$ **34.** $2660 \div 28$ **35.** $4712 \div 76$ **36.** $5950 \div 85$

37. $816 \div 17$ **38.** $2765 \div 79$ **39.** $1408 \div 32$ **40.** $902 \div 41$

Shoe Biz

Use the production report to solve the problem.

41. Cartons hold 36 pairs of shoes. How many cartons are needed to pack each style?

42. The Footprint received a shipment of tennis shoes. The bill was $1296. How many pairs of tennis shoes were in the shipment?

43. Twinkle Toes Shoe Co. employs 56 people to make sandals. About how many pairs of sandals did each employee make that week?

TWINKLE TOES SHOE CO.
Production Report
Week of _March 18_ Dept. _23_

Style Number	Type	Number of Pairs	Price Per Pair
68	tennis shoes	1512	$18.00
59A	sandals	2016	15.00
90C	rainboots	3564	20.00
90B	workboots	2664	25.00

Solve.

★ **44.** Twinkle Toes Shoe Co. has only 5 days to fill an emergency order for 1440 pairs of boots. If 6 people work on the project, how many pairs of boots must each person make each day?

Three-Stage Division

Since wood is needed to make paper, many paper companies
plant their own forests. The Southern Pine Paper Company
wants to plant 15,648 trees. They intend to plant 84 trees in a
row. How many complete rows will there be?

Since you want to know how many groups, divide 15,648 by 84.

$$
\begin{array}{r}
1 \\
84\overline{)\ 15{,}648} \\
-\ 84 \\
\hline
7\ 2
\end{array}
\qquad
\begin{array}{r}
18 \\
84\overline{)\ 15{,}648} \\
-\ 84\downarrow \\
\hline
7\ 24 \\
-6\ 72 \\
\hline
52
\end{array}
\qquad
\begin{array}{r}
186\ \text{R}24 \\
84\overline{)\ 15{,}648} \\
-\ 84 \\
\hline
7\ 24 \\
-6\ 72\downarrow \\
\hline
528 \\
-504 \\
\hline
24
\end{array}
$$

There will be 186 complete rows.

Exercises

Divide.

1. $38\overline{)842}$ $\qquad$ $38\overline{)8429}$ $\qquad$ 2. $27\overline{)1122}$ $\qquad$ $27\overline{)11{,}223}$

3. $81\overline{)983}$ $\qquad$ $81\overline{)9835}$ $\qquad$ 4. $81\overline{)3413}$ $\qquad$ $81\overline{)34{,}135}$

5. $46\overline{)5128}$ $\qquad$ $46\overline{)51{,}287}$ $\qquad$ 6. $63\overline{)2440}$ $\qquad$ $63\overline{)24{,}401}$

Divide and check.

7. $48\overline{)6576}$ **8.** $47\overline{)12{,}376}$ **9.** $66\overline{)7173}$ **10.** $24\overline{)15{,}997}$

11. $92\overline{)48{,}321}$ **12.** $35\overline{)23{,}520}$ **13.** $69\overline{)37{,}536}$ **14.** $73\overline{)20{,}052}$

Divide.

15. $27\overline{)5808}$ **16.** $29\overline{)3430}$ **17.** $78\overline{)60{,}996}$ **18.** $37\overline{)25{,}019}$

19. $70\overline{)28{,}241}$ **20.** $31\overline{)9427}$ **21.** $25\overline{)10{,}070}$ **22.** $72\overline{)54{,}884}$

23. $84\overline{)19{,}020}$ **24.** $85\overline{)15{,}995}$ **25.** $19\overline{)10{,}971}$ **26.** $64\overline{)23{,}296}$

27. $46\overline{)10{,}050}$ **28.** $35\overline{)13{,}354}$ **29.** $89\overline{)82{,}173}$ **30.** $73\overline{)8314}$

31. $65\overline{)62{,}991}$ **32.** $34\overline{)22{,}984}$ **33.** $58\overline{)39{,}004}$ **34.** $29\overline{)12{,}905}$

35. $17{,}577 \div 81$ **36.** $28{,}576 \div 32$ **37.** $13{,}464 \div 66$ **38.** $12{,}384 \div 24$

39. $7587 \div 27$ **40.** $25{,}152 \div 48$ **41.** $15{,}168 \div 16$ **42.** $28{,}476 \div 84$

Planting Time

Solve.

43. One wagon can move 85 pine trees. How many wagons are needed to move 15,648 pine trees?

44. One bag of fertilizer is needed for every 64 trees planted. How many trees can be fertilized with 205 bags?

★ **45.** A forest worker can plant 96 trees in one day. How many workers are needed to plant 15,648 trees in two days?

★ **46.** Divide and study the quotients. Tell why the quotients on the left belong and those on the right don't.

THESE BELONG	THESE DON'T BELONG
$15\overline{)675}$	$69\overline{)4899}$
$75\overline{)6075}$	$36\overline{)16{,}488}$
$47\overline{)3384}$	$82\overline{)3526}$

Three-Digit Divisors

Sodium is a big part of salt. Most people need no more than 250 milligrams (mg) of sodium a day.

This sandwich has about 1592 mg of sodium. Divide to see how many times more this is than our daily need.

Round 250 to 300. Think of $3\overline{)15}$.

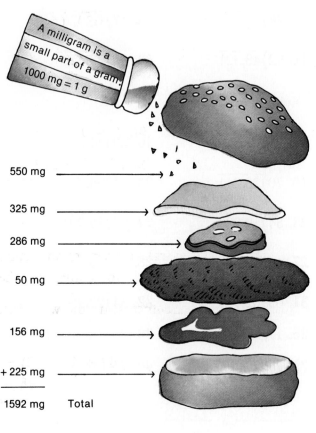

A milligram is a small part of a gram. 1000 mg = 1 g

550 mg

325 mg

286 mg

50 mg

156 mg

+ 225 mg

1592 mg   Total

$$
\begin{array}{r}
5 \\
250\overline{)1592} \\
-1250 \\
\hline
342
\end{array}
$$

(300)

Is 342 less than 250? No.

Try 6 as the quotient.

$$
\begin{array}{r}
6 \text{ R92} \\
250\overline{)1592} \\
-1500 \\
\hline
92
\end{array}
$$

Is 92 less than 250? Yes.

One hamburger with all the fixings has about 6 times as much sodium as a person needs in a day.

Exercises

Divide.

1. $200\overline{)76,875}$ **2.** $500\overline{)93,116}$ **3.** $700\overline{)56,608}$ **4.** $400\overline{)28,773}$

$179\overline{)76,875}$ $492\overline{)93,116}$ $665\overline{)56,608}$ $382\overline{)28,773}$

Divide and check.

5. $375\overline{)15,789}$ **6.** $202\overline{)36,675}$ **7.** $495\overline{)75,461}$ **8.** $917\overline{)75,679}$

9. $422\overline{)26,984}$ **10.** $901\overline{)78,954}$ **11.** $322\overline{)46,721}$ **12.** $608\overline{)85,030}$

Divide.

13. $781 \overline{)15{,}799}$ **14.** $239 \overline{)39{,}766}$ **15.** $358 \overline{)97{,}618}$ **16.** $607 \overline{)85{,}515}$

17. $346 \overline{)91{,}861}$ **18.** $159 \overline{)54{,}616}$ **19.** $708 \overline{)43{,}708}$ **20.** $645 \overline{)37{,}691}$

21. $491 \overline{)28{,}776}$ **22.** $248 \overline{)84{,}307}$ **23.** $831 \overline{)70{,}661}$ **24.** $965 \overline{)77{,}650}$

25. $51{,}761 \div 191$ **26.** $71{,}610 \div 682$ **27.** $28{,}124 \div 316$ **28.** $50{,}368 \div 787$

29. $45{,}875 \div 367$ **30.** $25{,}056 \div 522$ **31.** $95{,}893 \div 133$ **32.** $14{,}014 \div 637$

Just Following Orders

When you have several numbers to add, subtract, multiply, or divide, the order in which you compute makes a difference.

When you have parentheses, do the work inside the parentheses first.

Example.
$$48 + (20 \div 5) - (3 \times 9) = a$$
$$48 + 4 - 27 = a$$
$$52 - 27 = a$$
$$25 = a$$

When you don't have parentheses, do all the multiplications and divisions first, working in order from left to right. Next do all the additions and subtractions, working in order from left to right.

Example.
$$4 \times 8 \div 16 + 3 = n$$
$$32 \div 16 + 3 = n$$
$$2 + 3 = n$$
$$5 = n$$

Solve.

33. $(4 \times 9) + (15 \div 3) - 8 = y$ **34.** $17 - 6 + (9 \times 7) = n$

35. $(100 \div 10) - (2 \times 3) = a$ **36.** $99 \div 11 + 35 \times 3 \div 5 = n$

37. $2955 + 475 - 5 = y$ **38.** $87 + 55 \div 5 + 3 \times 40 - 218 = a$

★ **39.** $16 + 15{,}918 \div 758 + 7 \times 5 + 68 \times 94 - 6430 = n$

★ **40.** $100 \div 5 \times 5 + 99 \div 3 \times 3 - 3 \times 25 \div 5 = a$

Estimating Quotients

Dorothy is earning $325 per week. Could she earn more in the position advertised? We can answer the question by simply estimating the weekly salary.

Round the dividend and divisor, then estimate the quotient.

$$18{,}395 \div 52 \implies \begin{array}{r} \$360 \\ 50\overline{)18{,}000} \\ -150 \\ \hline 300 \\ -300 \\ \hline 00 \end{array}$$

The estimate shows that Dorothy could earn more in the job advertised.

Exercises

Complete.

1. $24\overline{)671}$ $\implies$ $20\overline{)700}$

2. $46\overline{)487}$ $\implies$ $50\overline{)500}$

3. $12\overline{)375}$ $\implies$ $10\overline{)400}$

4. $26\overline{)928}$ $\implies$ $30\overline{)900}$

5. $44\overline{)1571}$ $\implies$ $40\overline{)1600}$

6. $65\overline{)2118}$ $\implies$ $70\overline{)2100}$

Estimate the quotient.

7. $72\overline{)2832}$ **8.** $46\overline{)3147}$ **9.** $17\overline{)5217}$ **10.** $34\overline{)2657}$

11. $85\overline{)7242}$ **12.** $29\overline{)1153}$ **13.** $51\overline{)4832}$ **14.** $68\overline{)5640}$

15. $93\overline{)44,687}$

16. $21\overline{)4723}$

17. $64\overline{)31,477}$

18. $42\overline{)2541}$

19. $76\overline{)6842}$

20. $92\overline{)27,113}$

21. $35\overline{)27,431}$

22. $83\overline{)3642}$

23. $52\overline{)50,432}$

24. $18\overline{)1741}$

25. $39\overline{)7056}$

26. $74\overline{)28,471}$

27. $189\overline{)9932}$

28. $621\overline{)538,009}$

29. $246\overline{)5875}$

30. $773\overline{)478,554}$

31. $427\overline{)3611}$

32. $582\overline{)239,112}$

Job Hunting

```
┌─────────────────────────────────┐
│          BOOKKEEPER             │
│  Full charge, $19,865 plus      │
│  benefits. Send resume to:      │
│       Box L                     │
│       Phoenix, AZ 85008         │
└─────────────────────────────────┘
```

```
┌─────────────────────────────────┐
│          PROGRAMMER             │
│  Excellent opportunity with a   │
│  small computer firm.           │
│  Experience neces-              │
│  sary, $22,480. Send resume to: │
│  Box R Boulder, CO 80301        │
└─────────────────────────────────┘
```

Solve.

33. John earns $300 a week. Could he earn more in the bookkeeping job described?

34. Sally earns $415 a week. Would she earn more or less in the programming job described?

Checkpoint B

Divide. (*pages 94–95*)

1. $60\overline{)420}$

2. $20\overline{)85}$

3. $40\overline{)461}$

4. $30\overline{)2465}$

Divide. (*pages 96–97*)

5. $27\overline{)61}$

6. $38\overline{)125}$

7. $25\overline{)155}$

8. $31\overline{)292}$

Divide. (*pages 98–99*)

9. $44\overline{)545}$

10. $76\overline{)3116}$

11. $24\overline{)853}$

12. $40\overline{)1727}$

Divide. (*pages 100–101*)

13. $27\overline{)5808}$

14. $19\overline{)18,671}$

15. $89\overline{)12,098}$

16. $63\overline{)29,376}$

Divide. (*pages 102–103*)

17. $681\overline{)26,108}$

18. $233\overline{)105,083}$

19. $419\overline{)7968}$

20. $906\overline{)393,038}$

Estimate the quotient.
(*pages 104–105*)

21. $52\overline{)3870}$

22. $81\overline{)48,380}$

23. $376\overline{)163,081}$

24. $514\overline{)746,381}$

Problem Solving · CHOOSING THE OPERATION

1	Understand
2	Plan
3	Work
4	Answer

Choosing the correct operation is often the most difficult part of problem solving. Study the examples to see why the operation was chosen.

Add since you want to find a total.
17 + 9 + 23 + 12 = 61

Multiply since you want to combine groups of equal size.
15 × 9 = 135

CAMP GRANOLA

How many campers signed up for an activity?

Tuesday's Activities

Volleyball (17)   Hiking (9)

Dramatics (12)   Crafts (23)

Each hiker brought back 15 wild flowers. How many wild flowers is that altogether?

There are 3082 beads for crafts. How many beads can each camper have?

How many more chose volleyball than hiking?

Divide since you want to know how many in each group.
3082 ÷ 23 = 134

Subtract since you want to find how much greater one group is than another.
17 − 9 = 8

Write add, subtract, multiply, or divide to tell which operation you'd use to solve the problem.

1. A canoe can carry ▨ campers. How many canoes are needed to carry ▨ campers?

2. Max bought ▨ postcards that cost ▨ each. How much did he spend?

3. Teddy says that his cat Hippo has a mass of ▨ kg. Arnold says his cat Lillian has a mass of ▨ kg. How much heavier is Arnold's cat?

4. Susan got ▨ mosquito bites in the morning and ▨ bites in the afternoon. How many bites did she get in all?

Match each problem with the correct example. Solve the problem.

A. $15 \div 3$ **B.** $15 + 3$ **C.** 15×3 **D.** $15 - 3$

5.

Dear Sam,
Today I found 15 spiders.
I'll give three of them to
you when I get home.
Your friend,
Bruce

How many spiders will Bruce keep?

6.

Dear Emily,
We went hiking today and
3 kids got poison ivy. The
other 15 of us just got blisters.
See you soon,
Laurie

How many campers went on the hike?

7.

Dear Willy,
Today was my turn to cook.
I made Campfire Nuggets
for 15 people. Everyone ate 3.
Yours truly,
Ned

How many Nuggets were eaten?

8.

Dear Carol,
I've collected 15 different
beetles. I'll split them
with you and Ellie when
I get home.
Your sister,
Mimi

How many beetles will each girl get?

Solve. Be sure to check your answer.

9. In a camp softball game, the Donkeys beat the Mules by 9 runs. If the Donkeys' final score was 37, what was the Mules' final score?

10. In her first week at camp, Melina spent $1.89 on insect spray, $.98 on bandages, and $1.57 on snacks. If she has $10.56 left, how much did she have to start with?

11. "I played Magic Maze with the camp computer 41 times today," said Lorna, "and I won 15 times." How many times did the computer win?

12. James took 7 rolls of film to camp. Each roll had 24 pictures. If he used 5 complete rolls, how many pictures did he take?

★ **13.** The camp cook makes granola for cereal. The recipe he uses makes enough for 15 servings. How many times should he increase the recipe to make enough for 140 people?

Unit Review

Divide the numbers on the target by the number in the center.

1.   **2.**   **5.**   **6.**

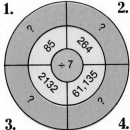

3.   **4.**   **7.**   **8.**

9.   **10.**   **13.**   **14.**

11.   **12.**   **15.**   **16.**

17. Write $\times$ or $\div$ to make the equations true for the same value of n.

$n \,\blacksquare\, 6 = 54$ $n \,\blacksquare\, 9 = 1$ $n \,\blacksquare\, 8 = 72$ $n \,\blacksquare\, 3 = 3$

Write the GCF.

18. 14 and 21   **19.** 8 and 16   **20.** 10 and 18   **21.** 25 and 30

True or false? Write T or F.

22. 942 is divisible by 2 and 3.   **23.** 51 is divisible by 3 and 10.

24. 3570 is divisible by 2, 3, 5 and 10.   **25.** 6111 is divisible by 3.

Choose the better estimate. Write a or b.

26. $63\overline{)35{,}691}$ **27.** $17\overline{)83{,}916}$ **28.** $37\overline{)47{,}561}$
    a. 500   **b.** 600   **a.** 4200   **b.** 420   **a.** 1200   **b.** 1600

Solve.

29. Harrison knitted sweaters for each of his three dogs. He used 387 g of yarn for each sweater. How much yarn did he use for the three sweaters?

Solve. (*pages 84–85*)

1. $36 \div 4 = n$ **2.** $a \div 8 = 3$ **3.** $y \div 6 = 9$ **4.** $7 \times n = 21$

Divide. (*pages 86–87*)

5. $7\overline{)38}$ **6.** $4\overline{)274}$ **7.** $7\overline{)3898}$ **8.** $5\overline{)33,849}$

Divide. (*pages 88–89*)

9. $6\overline{)1239}$ **10.** $5\overline{)4352}$ **11.** $3\overline{)3306}$ **12.** $9\overline{)6215}$

Write the GCF. (*pages 90–91*)

13. 8 and 12   **14.** 24 and 60   **15.** 16 and 32   **16.** 20 and 30

Is the first number divisible by the second number? Write *Yes* or *No*. (*pages 92–93*)

17. 87;3   **18.** 904;5   **19.** 2094;3   **20.** 1390;10

Divide. (*pages 94–101*)

21. $70\overline{)3650}$ **22.** $63\overline{)462}$ **23.** $72\overline{)6341}$ **24.** $62\overline{)32,216}$

Divide. (*pages 102–103*)

25. $486\overline{)53,719}$ **26.** $891\overline{)206,417}$ **27.** $398\overline{)42,320}$ **28.** $540\overline{)837,512}$

Estimate the quotient. (*pages 104–105*)

29. $53\overline{)4000}$ **30.** $38\overline{)8423}$ **31.** $12\overline{)648}$ **32.** $77\overline{)7742}$

Solve. (*pages 106–107*)

33. A recipe for fish chowder calls for 450 g of codfish and 240 g of perch. How much fish is in the chowder?

34. Ramona bought 4 dozen rolls for a picnic. If there are 24 people at the picnic, how many rolls will each person get?

35. Bernie spent $1.29 for a flea collar and $1.45 for cat food. How much did he spend?

Extra practice on page 385

Enrichment

Flow Charts

Flow charts are like treasure maps. They are often used by computer programmers to help plan the steps needed to solve a problem.

A palindrome is a number that reads the same forwards and backwards such as 12321. You can use a flow chart to show the steps needed to turn a number into a palindrome.

Here's how.

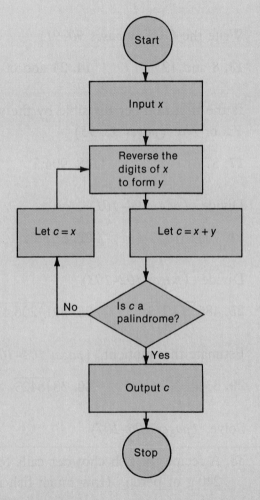

Input *x*.	*x* = 367
Reverse the digits of *x* to get *y*.	*y* = 763
Add *x* + *y* to get *c*.	367 + 763 = 1130
Is *c* a palindrome?	*c* = 1130 No.
Let *c* = *x*.	*x* = 1130
Reverse the digits of *x* to get *y*.	*y* = 311
Add *x* + *y* to get *c*.	1130 + 311 = 1441
Is *c* a palindrome?	*c* = 1441 Yes.
Output *c*.	*c* = 1441

Use the flow chart above. Write the number as a palindrome.

1. 487   **2.** 6218   **3.** 756   **4.** 7681   **5.** 46,071

6. 9816   **7.** 3592   **8.** 2297   **9.** 68   **10.** 827

Suppose you live in Atlanta, Georgia and want to call a friend in Albuquerque, New Mexico.

The table below shows sample rates.

Sample Rates from Atlanta to Albuquerque	8:00–5:00 Weekdays	5:00–11:00 Evenings	11:00–8:00 Nights/ Weekends
First minute	$.55	$.35	$.22
Each additional minute	$.38	$.25	$.16

You can use the flow chart to find the cost of the phone call.

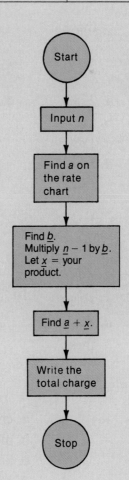

The flow chart uses the following variables.

n = length of phone call in minutes

a = charge for the first minute

b = charge for each additional minute

Find the cost of making a weekday call and talking for the given number of minutes.

11. 10   **12.** 25   **13.** 40

Find the cost of making an evening call and talking for the given number of minutes.

14. 15   **15.** 20   **16.** 37

Find the cost of making a weekend call and talking for the given number of minutes.

17. 32   **18.** 58   **19.** 75

Maintaining Skills

Choose the best answer. Write *a*, *b*, *c*, or *d*.

Add.

1. 113 **a.** 632
  + 529 **b.** 641
  c. 642
  d. None of
  these

2. 1098 **a.** 1785
  + 687 **b.** 1675
  c. 1685
  d. None of
  these

3. 7,256 **a.** 51,349
  +44,093 **b.** 41,349
  c. 41,249
  d. None of
  these

Subtract.

4. 609 **a.** 278
  − 431 **b.** 178
  c. 238
  d. None of
  these

5. 1086 **a.** 1668
  − 582 **b.** 1504
  c. 594
  d. None of
  these

6. 25,091 **a.** 18,653
  − 7,438 **b.** 18,663
  c. 17,653
  d. None of
  these

Multiply.

7. 95 **a.** 2280
  ×24 **b.** 570
  c. 1280
  d. None of
  these

8. 879 **a.** 12,594
  ×86 **b.** 12,306
  c. 75,594
  d. None of
  these

9. 4307 **a.** 232,578
  ×54 **b.** 23,598
  c. 222,578
  d. None of
  these

Divide.

10. 38)408 **a.** 13 R24
  b. 11 R28
  c. 10 R28
  d. None of
  these

11. 45)8826 **a.** 198 R16
  b. 19 R31
  c. 196 R6
  d. None of
  these

12. 97)37,421 **a.** 385 R26
  b. 375 R46
  c. 374 R143
  d. None of
  these

Choose the best answer.

13. Nick is 148 ▨ tall. **a.** cm
  b. m
  c. km
  d. None of
  these

14. Doris drank 240 ▨ of
  milk for lunch. **a.** mm
  b. mL
  c. L
  d. None of
  these

15. The distance from New York to Boston is about 346 ▨.

a. cm
b. m
c. km
d. None of these

16. A stew recipe calls for 454 ▨ of meat.

a. L
b. g
c. kg
d. None of these

17. Elise bought 8 ▨ of paint to paint her room.

a. mL
b. L
c. g
d. None of these

18. Toby used 2 ▨ of fabric to make a backpack.

a. m
b. L
c. g
d. None of these

Estimate the total.

19. $ .79
        4.15
         .29
      + 1.79

a. $6.30
b. $7.10
c. $8.00
d. None of these

20. $ .89
        3.16
         .48
       + .75

a. $5.20
b. $6.00
c. $7.00
d. None of these

21. $2.98
        1.79
        3.78
       + .47

a. $6.50
b. $8.00
c. $9.50
d. None of these

22. $3.39
        1.52
         .69
       + .28

a. $6.00
b. $5.00
c. $7.00
d. None of these

23. $5.29
        3.65
         .75
       + .75

a. $12.00
b. $9.60
c. $10.60
d. None of these

24. $8.85
        2.86
        3.59
       + .42

a. $16.40
b. $17.00
c. $14.00
d. None of these

Solve.

25. A large paper cup holds 335 mL. A small paper cup holds 240 mL. How much more does a large cup hold?

a. 775 mL
b. 95 mL
c. 95 L
d. None of these

Applying Your Skills

Footwork

Sometimes, joggers have to use math.
You'll see how as you do the exercises
on these pages.

Jogger's World
1238 Spring Street

We've taken
$3 off all shoes!

For men and women
NOW $32.50

For men
NOW $24.65

For men and women
NOW $26.89

For children
NOW $23.69

Choosing needed facts is one of the first things you need to do in
solving problems. Use the newspaper ad. Write the shoe prices
you need to solve the problem. Then solve.

1. What is the cost of outfitting 3 children with running shoes?

2. How much would 15 women and 12 men save by buying shoes on sale?

3. Ten women and 8 men in a jogging club bought the cheapest shoes possible. How much did all the shoes cost?

4. Four women all need new running shoes. What is the least it can cost for all their shoes? What is the most it can cost?

5. Three men each bought the same kind of shoes. Their total bill was $80.67. What price shoes did each buy?

6. What is the difference in cost between the least and most expensive shoes for men? for women?

PLAN FOR BEGINNING JOGGERS				
Days	**First Week**	**Second Week**	**Third Week**	**Fourth Week**
1, 3, 5	Walk 15 min	Walk 15 min Jog 1 min Total: 16 min	Walk 15 min Jog 1 min Total: 16 min	Walk 15 min Jog 2 min Total: 17 min
2, 4, 6	Walk 5 min Jog 1 min Repeat for total of 17 min	Walk 5 min Jog 3 min Repeat for total of 21 min	Walk 6 min Jog 4 min Repeat for total of 26 min	Walk 3 min Jog 2 min Repeat for total of 30 min
7	Rest	Rest	Rest	Rest

Use the chart. Is the statement true or false? Write *T* or *F*.

7. If the rest day is on a Wednesday, the plan starts on a Tuesday.

8. If the plan is started on a Monday, the rest day is on a Sunday.

9. During the first week, a jogger walks a total of 90 minutes.

10. During the fourth week, a jogger jogs a total of 42 minutes.

11. During the second week, the plan takes a total of more than 2 hours.

12. The program never takes longer than two and a half hours.

Applying Your Skills

Supermarket Strategy

People are in a problem solving situation when they go grocery shopping these days. It's a real challenge to try to save money.

Suppose you are doing the family shopping.

Compare prices of equal amounts of the item. Use the pictures and what you know about equal measurements. Decide whether it costs less to buy a large size or more than one of a smaller size.

Find the best bargain. How much does it cost? You'll need your answers to Questions 1 through 5 for Question 6.

Shopper's List

1. 1 lb. cottage cheese

2. 4 bars soap

3. 8 tomatoes

4. 1 pkg. napkins

5. 1 roll aluminum foil

1.

$1.26 $.75

2.

$1.74 $1.07

3.

$.15 each

$.98 per pkg

4.

$1.40 $1.29

5.

$1.98   2 for $1.50

6. Suppose you buy all the best bargains. Is the total cost of your groceries more or less than $10?

The chart shows some codes that appear on supermarket cash register tapes.

MT meat GR groceries PR produce (fruits and vegetables)	SUB subtotal for CR credit for coupons TX taxed item or tax	TL total bill CA cash paid CH change returned

Here are two pieces of a cash register tape. In Exercises 7–12, complete the second part of the tape, step by step.

These were the coupons used to get credit (CR) on the tape.

Show amounts that should be on the tape. Answer the questions.

7. What is the first subtotal of the supermarket bill?

8. What subtotal should be entered for the first coupon? the second?

9. What subtotal should be entered for the two coupons?

10. What is the new subtotal after taking off the amount for the coupons?

11. If the tax was $.41, what is the total amount of the bill?

12. How much change would the customer receive from $20?

Solve.

13. Each of 25 families attended a neighborhood block party. Each family gave $15.75 to cover grocery costs. How much money was collected in all?

14. There were 34 people at the family reunion. The grocery bill came to $105.75. About how much per person did the reunion cost?

Looking Into Trucks

Loading trucks can be a mathematical puzzle.

Suppose you are the manager of an oil company in charge of dispatching, or sending out, delivery trucks A, B, C and D that hold the amount of oil listed below. Which of your trucks would you send to fill the order? Write **A, B, C, D,** or a combination of the letters.

A. 5500 gal   **B.** 4500 gal   **C.** 3000 gal   **D.** 6050 gal

1.

SURE DELIVERY OIL

Order 2570   Date 10/16

Deliver: 240 gal. To each
of 22 new homes
Dispatch: Smallest
Possible Truck To
take care of
whole Order

2.

SURE DELIVERY OIL

Order 2568   Date 10/16

Deliver: 135,000 gal

Dispatch: 45 of the
same Kind of
truck to deliver
whole amount

3.

SURE DELIVERY OIL

Order 2567   Date 10/16

Deliver: 14,550 gal

Dispatch: 3 different
trucks for exact
amount

4.

SURE DELIVERY OIL

Order 2569   Date 10/16

Deliver: 1120 gal. In The
afternoon, after a morning
delivery of 2480 gal.
Dispatch: Smallest Truck
To Take Care of
whole Job

Emptying boxes that trucks deliver is a lot of work. Use the chart to find how many items have to be put on a shelf or in a pile one by one.

5. 6 boxes of liquid detergent

6. 8 boxes of beans

7. 14 boxes of paper towels

8. 2 boxes of carrots

9. 35 boxes of tomato juice

AMOUNT OF GROCERIES PER BOX	
Item	Number
carrots	48 bunches
oranges	108 oranges
beans	24 cans
tomato juice	12 cans
liquid detergent	24 bottles
paper towels	24 rolls

Solve.

10. A 31,700-pound truckload of groceries is being delivered to a supermarket. Each carton on the truck weighs about 25 lb. How many cartons are on the truck?

11. With mechanical help, it takes two people one hour to unload a truckload of groceries. The people each work an 8-hour day. How many trucks could they unload during a 5-day work week?

★ 12. A whole truckload of groceries weighed 32,083 pounds. It held 1268 cartons of groceries. First round each amount. Then find how much each carton weighed.

★ 13. A supermarket received 1300 cartons of groceries during February on every day but Sundays and holidays. February started on a Sunday and ended on a Saturday. Washington's Birthday was celebrated on a Monday. How many cartons were delivered in February?

119

Enrichment

A Different Way to Multiply

John Napier, a Scottish mathematician, invented a set of rods with numbers. By putting the rods, or "bones," together in different ways, he found a shortcut for doing multiplication.

A set of Napier's "bones" showed the multiplication tables.

An extra "bone" was used for multipliers.

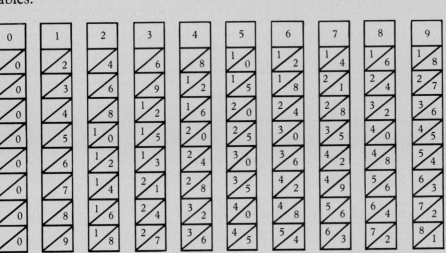

You can use Napier's short cut without a set of "bones." This is how to multiply 56 × 78.

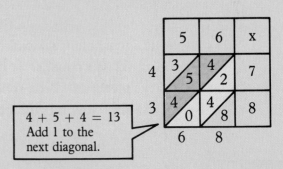

4 + 5 + 4 = 13
Add 1 to the next diagonal.

1. Draw a square 3 squares across and 3 squares down.

2. Draw diagonals as shown.

3. Write 56 and the times sign at the top. Write 78 down the right side.

4. Multiply 56 × 7, then 56 × 8. Do not regroup.

5. Add along the diagonals. Be sure to regroup.

6. Read the answer beginning on the left side. 56 × 78 = 4368

Use Napier's short cut to multiply.

1. 47 × 23   2. 84 × 69   3. 69 × 29   4. 38 × 46   5. 63 × 27

6. 84 × 35   7. 86 × 29   8. 741 × 360   9. 609 × 324   10. 700 × 281

Addition, Subtraction of Decimals

5

On your mark. Get set . . . go! Bicycle racing sometimes takes place on portable tracks called velodromes. They are 333.3 m around and have fine wooden surfaces to allow high speeds. A sprint is 3 laps around the track. How far does a sprinter race?

Numbers with Tenths and Hundredths

When something is divided into ten equal parts or a hundred equal parts, you can write **decimals** to describe the parts.

1 whole

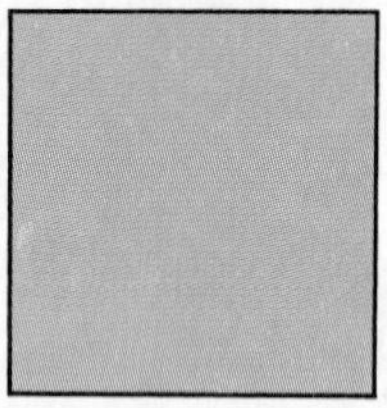

one whole ⇨ 1.00

10 equal parts

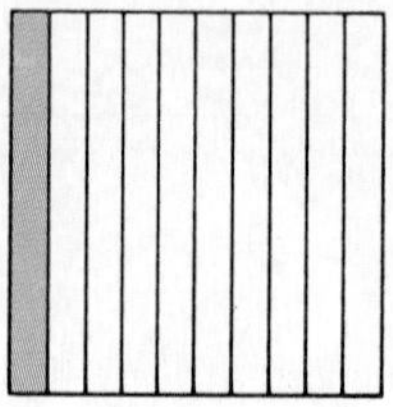

one tenth ⇨ 0.1

100 equal parts

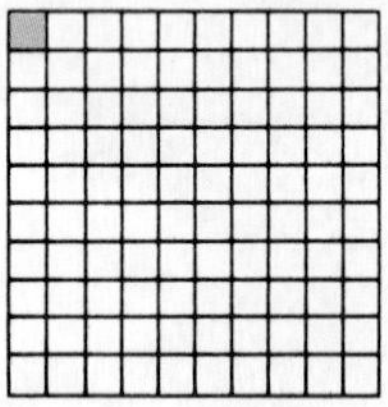

one hundredth ⇨ 0.01

You can see how decimals fit into our place-value system by looking at the place-value chart. A **decimal point** is used to separate whole numbers from tenths and hundredths.

hundreds	tens	ones		tenths	hundredths	
		6	.	8		⇨ 6.8 ⇨ 6 and 8 tenths
		0	.	2	7	⇨ 0.27 ⇨ 27 hundredths
1	5	8	.	0	6	⇨ 158.06 ⇨ 158 and 6 hundredths

Exercises

Complete.

1. 0.7 = ▢ tenths
0.07 = ▢ hundredths

2. 0.9 = ▢ tenths
0.09 = ▢ hundredths

3. 0.4 = ▢ tenths
0.04 = ▢ hundredths

4. 0.37 = ▢ hundredths

5. 0.8 = ▢ tenths

6. 0.66 = ▢ hundredths

7. 0.84 = ▢ hundredths

8. 0.07 = ▢ hundredths

9. 0.01 = ▢ hundredth

10. 6.08 = ▢ and ▢ hundredths

11. 5.33 = ▢ and ▢ hundredths

12. 17.28 = ▢ and ▢ hundredths

13. 3.05 = ▢ and ▢ hundredths

Write the decimal.

14. 8 and 2 tenths

15. 6 tenths

16. 4 and 1 tenth

17. 3 hundredths

18. 27 hundredths

19. 4 tenths

20. 58 and 49 hundredths

21. 73 and 27 hundredths

22. 329 and 7 tenths

23. 495 and 3 hundredths

24. 634 and 2 hundredths

25. 703 and 47 hundredths

26. 241 and 3 tenths

27. 53 and 70 hundredths

28. 71 and 20 hundredths

29. 2 and 8 hundredths

30. 6 hundredths

31. 11 hundredths

32. 177 and 2 tenths

33. 892 and 7 hundredths

34. 568 and 5 hundredths

On the Road

There are 10 vehicles parked at a highway rest area. Write a decimal to show what decimal part of the 10 vehicles is named in the problems below.

35. cars

36. trucks

37. motorcycles

38. vehicles from Missouri

39. vehicles from Idaho

40. cars from Idaho

41. trucks from Missouri

★ **42.** not cars or trucks from Missouri

Decimals to Hundred-Thousandths

tens	ones		tenths	hundredths	thousandths	ten-thousandths	hundred-thousandths
4	2	.	3	5	6		
	4	.	0	0	0	3	
1	6	.	3	4	7	9	2

▷ 42 and 356 thousandths
▷ 4 and 3 ten-thousandths
▷ 16 and 34,792 hundred-thousandths

LEAGUE LEADERS

Player	Batting Average
Alonzo	0.324
Colyer	0.321
Meyer	0.307
Woznik	0.287
Kerouak	0.285

In 42.356, the 6 is in the **thousandths'** place. Its value is 6 thousandths.

In 4.0003, the 3 is in the **ten-thousandths'** place. Its value is 3 ten-thousandths.

In 16.34792, the 2 is in the **hundred-thousandths'** place. Its value is 2 hundred-thousandths.

You can read decimals in another way. The decimal 42.356 can be read *forty-two point three five six.*

Exercises

Complete.

1. 0.3 = ▧ tenths
0.37 = ▧ hundredths
0.374 = ▧ thousandths

2. 0.9 = ▧ tenths
0.91 = ▧ hundredths
0.917 = ▧ thousandths

3. 0.25 = ▧ hundredths
0.256 = ▧ thousandths
0.2568 = ▧ ten-thousandths

4. 0.403 = ▧ thousandths
0.4031 = ▧ ten-thousandths
0.40316 = ▧ hundred-thousandths

Write the value of the underlined digit.

5. 75.$\underline{8}$

6. 78.3$\underline{2}$

7. 36.04$\underline{2}$9

8. 78.923$\underline{1}$

9. 2.169$\underline{4}$

10. 4.$\underline{5}$682

11. 21.6038$\underline{7}$

12. 52.6$\underline{4}$81

Write the decimal.

13. 6 and 123 thousandths

14. 2 and 41 hundredths

15. 3 and 4128 ten-thousandths

16. 427 thousandths

17. 64 hundredths

18. 5 and 5243 ten-thousandths

19. 47 and 241 thousandths

20. 52 and 20 hundredths

21. 59 and 104 ten-thousandths

22. 471 and 47 ten-thousandths

23. 593 and 3 tenths

24. 89 and 28 thousandths

25. 621 hundred-thousandths

26. 932 and 9 ten-thousandths

27. 9 thousandths

28. 472 and 8 tenths

29. 77 and 37 ten-thousandths

30. 89 and 80 thousandths

31. 42 hundred-thousandths

32. 4172 ten-thousandths

Place Value

658.01492

Look at the number above. Write the digit that is in each place.

33. tens' place

34. hundreds' place

35. ten-thousandths' place

36. tenths' place

37. thousandths' place

38. hundred-thousandths' place

Use the numbers on the cards.

★ **39.** Write all the decimals you can make with a 3 in the tenths' place and an 8 in the ones' place.

★ **40.** Write all the decimals you can make with a 7 in the thousandths' place and a 2 in the ten-thousandths' place.

Comparing Decimals

Writing zeros after the last digit in a decimal doesn't change its value.

The models show that 0.3 = 0.30.

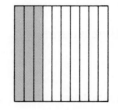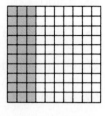

3 tenths	=	30 hundredths
0.3	=	0.30

To compare 0.2 and 0.17, you can rewrite 0.2 as 0.20.

You can see from the shaded squares that 0.20 > 0.17, so 0.2 > 0.17.

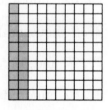

0.2 = 0.20   0.17

0.2 > 0.17

Exercises

True or false? Write *T* or *F*.

1. 4.3 = 4.30   **2.** 0.80 = 0.8   **3.** 0.51 = 0.510

4. 6.08 = 6.80   **5.** 0.9 = 0.09   **6.** 3.80 = 3.800

7. 48.3 = 48.30   **8.** 17.7 = 170.7   **9.** 3.7 > 3.6

10. 0.03 < 0.01   **11.** 0.15 > 0.2   **12.** 1.68 < 1.680

Write <, >, or = to compare the numbers.

13. 0.3 ▒ 0.4   **14.** 0.73 ▒ 0.71   **15.** 0.513 ▒ 0.519

16. 0.8 ▒ 0.80   **17.** 0.6 ▒ 0.93   **18.** 0.9 ▒ 0.76

19. 0.56 ▒ 0.65   **20.** 3.82 ▒ 33.8   **21.** 6.52 ▒ 652

22. 8.45 ▒ 0.967   **23.** 1.009 ▒ 0.831   **24.** 6.63 ▒ 3.21

25. 32.45 ▒ .0234   **26.** 123.5 ▒ 12.35   **27.** 18.09 ▒ 28.09

28. 5.64 ▨ 5.5

29. 8.745 ▨ 8.81

30. 0.8 ▨ 0.743

31. 0.449 ▨ 0.5

32. 12.2 ▨ 1.22

33. 6.871 ▨ 68.7

34. 17.35 ▨ 18.35

35. 0.384 ▨ 0.4

36. 7.5 ▨ 7.024

37. 0.0251 ▨ 0.026

38. 0.1456 ▨ 0.15

39. 7.2 ▨ 7.197

40. 0.8031 ▨ 17.3781

41. 1.23 ▨ 1.023

42. 5.81 ▨ 5.9

43. 17.38 ▨ 17.3791

44. 4.005 ▨ 4.01

45. 6.02 ▨ 6.0189

Track Meet

Arrange the finishers in order from first place to last.

46.

EVENT: LONG JUMP	
Student	Distance in Meters
David	3.78
Costa	4.02
George	3.90
James	4.10

47.

EVENT: 80 METER HURDLES	
Student	Time in Seconds
Sasha	26.806
Marie	28.371
Joanne	25.916
Leslie	26.842

Can you make 4 stacks of coins, with 2 coins in each stack, using only 4 moves? Each move must jump exactly 2 other coins either in a line or in a stack. For example, A could jump over B and C to D. Then C could jump over the stack with A and D to E.

Take a Break

Addition of Decimals

Warren complained that his feet hurt after climbing 3.7 km up Jackson's Ravine. By the time he reached the top, 4.7 km further, he was having such a good time that he forgot about his sore feet.

You can add to see just how far Warren climbed.

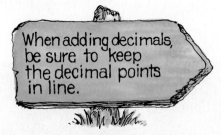

When adding decimals, be sure to keep the decimal points in line.

$$\begin{array}{r} 3.7 \\ +4.7 \\ \hline 8.4 \end{array}$$

Warren climbed 8.4 km. No wonder his feet hurt!

Here are some other examples.

$$\begin{array}{r} 82.43 \\ +65.96 \\ \hline 148.39 \end{array} \qquad \begin{array}{r} 77.5 \\ +36.76 \\ \hline 114.26 \end{array}$$

Exercises

Complete.

1. $\begin{array}{r} 0.3 \\ +0.5 \\ \hline 0.\blacksquare \end{array}$

2. $\begin{array}{r} 0.8 \\ +0.8 \\ \hline 1.\blacksquare \end{array}$

3. $\begin{array}{r} 0.9 \\ +0.41 \\ \hline 1.\blacksquare\blacksquare \end{array}$

4. $\begin{array}{r} 27.3 \\ +48.5 \\ \hline \blacksquare\blacksquare.8 \end{array}$

5. $\begin{array}{r} 7.46 \\ +2.9 \\ \hline 10.\blacksquare\blacksquare \end{array}$

6. $\begin{array}{r} 324.5 \\ +468.9 \\ \hline \blacksquare\blacksquare\blacksquare.4 \end{array}$

7. $\begin{array}{r} 7.8 \\ +1.45 \\ \hline 9.\blacksquare\blacksquare \end{array}$

8. $\begin{array}{r} 17.9 \\ +\ 6.7 \\ \hline \blacksquare4.\blacksquare \end{array}$

9. $\begin{array}{r} 4.68 \\ +7.7 \\ \hline 12.\blacksquare\blacksquare \end{array}$

10. $\begin{array}{r} 11.3 \\ +\ 2.61 \\ \hline 13.\blacksquare\blacksquare \end{array}$

Add.

11. 3.8
+4.7

12. 4.12
+6.38

13. 5.29
+6.4

14. 4.1497
+2.3786

15. 4.129
+47.384

16. 8.057
+59.128

17. 12.3
+324.7

18. 7.098
+6.98

19. 33.981
+ 4.83

20. 4.8
2.0
+4.9

21. 8.23
3.4
+7.01

22. 7.621
3.8
+6.91

23. 27.64
38.2
10.61
+ 5.84

24. 3.4914
7.0057
2.421
+3.2811

25. 28.97
3.2
4.39
+11.68

26. 5.28 + 6.3

27. 7.8 + 9.73

28. 4.8 + 6.28

29. 4.8 + 3.6 + 2.41

Hearty Hikers

Solve.

30. Amos hiked 14.4 km on Monday and 14.8 km on Wednesday. How far did he hike on the two days?

31. Leah hiked 7.5 km in 1.2 hours. She hiked a further 3.7 km in 0.6 hours. How far did she hike?

Add.

★ **32.** 14.07 + 375.611 + 146.0089 + 3.0

★ **33.** 761.33 + 810.01 + 6.16 + 0.0651

Checkpoint A

Write the decimal.
(*pages 122–123*)

1. 7 tenths

2. 4 hundredths

3. 31 and 25 hundredths

4. 19 and 5 tenths

Write the decimal.
(*pages 124–125*)

5. 4 and 52 thousandths

6. 23 and 4735 ten-thousandths

7. 384 thousandths

8. 470 and 59 ten-thousandths

Write $<$, $>$, or $=$ to compare the numbers. (*pages 126–127*)

9. 3.43 ▧ 3.53

10. 12.8 ▧ 12.80

11. 1.093 ▧ 1.092

12. 0.8 ▧ 0.74

Add. (*pages 128–129*)

13. 19.15
+38.29

14. 1.489
+0.123

15. 7.69
25.138
+34.35

16. 5.901
2.31
44.8
+ 7.6

Subtraction of Decimals

You can subtract to find how much can be saved by buying cashews on sale rather than at the regular price.

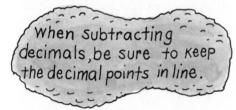
When subtracting decimals, be sure to keep the decimal points in line.

$$\begin{array}{r} \$16.25 \\ -14.98 \\ \hline \$1.27 \end{array}$$

Here are some more examples.

$$\begin{array}{r} 597.3 \\ -326.4 \\ \hline 270.9 \end{array} \qquad \begin{array}{r} 48.26 \\ -5.90 \\ \hline 42.36 \end{array} \qquad \begin{array}{r} 3.70 \\ -0.29 \\ \hline 3.41 \end{array}$$

Exercises

Complete.

1.	2.	3.	4.	5.
0.8	7.8	46.3	92.81	4.81
−0.5	−1.5	−27.8	−24.8	−2.5
0.▪	▪.3	▪▪.5	▪▪.▪1	.3▪

6.	7.	8.	9.	10.
37.5	74.9	8.871	13.02	108.35
−18.8	−30.84	−6.43	−6.33	−76.97
▪▪.7	▪▪.▪6	▪.▪41	▪.▪9	▪▪.▪8

Subtract.

11. 2.3 -1.6	**12.** 17.8 $-\ 9.7$	**13.** 23.2 $-\ 4.6$	**14.** 16.8 $-\ 7.9$	**15.** 67.3 -43.6
16. 3.82 -1.2	**17.** 7.38 -2.9	**18.** 13.3 $-\ 0.6$	**19.** 9.81 -3.9	**20.** 41.07 $-\ 2.68$
21. 4.38 -0.09	**22.** 4.27 -1.836	**23.** 2.483 -1.97	**24.** 16.08 $-\ 3.751$	**25.** 179.4 $-\ 59.6$

26. $3.926 - 1.845$ **27.** $9.831 - 6.725$ **28.** $9.005 - 2.346$ **29.** $163.5 - 76.35$

30. $75.8 - 1.09$ **31.** $7.5 - 1.239$ **32.** $83.5 - 7.2$ **33.** $37.9 - 28.8$

34. $9.483 - 2.68$ **35.** $48.41 - 22.4$ **36.** $266.8 - 13.75$ **37.** $0.308 - 0.02$

Clip and Save

Which product costs less if the coupon is used?

38. Duzn't Detergent $3.15
 Sudzup Detergent $2.89

39. Slurp Apple Juice $1.39
 Chuckles Apple Juice $1.59

40. Fido Dog Chow $1.59
 Yelp Dog Chow $1.69

41. Blunt Cheddar $2.98
 Keen Cheddar $2.69

42. Broccoli Bonanza $3.75
 Broccoli Bonus $3.20

★ **43.** Betts' Clam Chowder $.89
 Ling's Clam Chowder $.75

Checking Accounts

When you have a checking account it's important to record the checks you write and the deposits you make.

DATE	CHECK NUMBER	CHECKS OR DEPOSITS	AMOUNT OF CHECK		✓	AMOUNT OF DEPOSIT		BALANCE	
		BALANCE BROUGHT FORWARD →						289	13
12/1	325	Village Market	18	45				270	68
12/7	326	Hot Shot Electric	62	89				207	79
12/10		Deposit				165	85	373	64
12/13	327	Dr. Tracy (dentist)	32	00				341	64
12/22		Deposit				75	00	416	64
12/27	328	Brighton Lumber	84	12				?	
12/27	329	Alpha Airlines	119	65				?	
1/5		Deposit				165	85	?	

Subtract when you write a check.

$$\begin{array}{ll} \$289.13 & \Diamond \quad \text{balance} \\ -\ 18.45 & \Diamond \quad \text{check number 325} \\ \hline \$270.68 & \Diamond \quad \text{new balance} \end{array}$$

Add when you make a deposit.

$$\begin{array}{ll} \$341.64 & \Diamond \quad \text{balance} \\ +\ 75.00 & \Diamond \quad \text{deposit of 12/22} \\ \hline \$416.64 & \Diamond \quad \text{new balance} \end{array}$$

Exercises

Use the checkbook record above.

1. What was the amount of the check to Hot Shot Electric?

2. What was the amount of the deposit made on December 10th?

3. What was the balance before check number 327 was written?

4. What was the balance after check number 326 was written?

5. To whom was check number 325 made out?

6. What was the amount of the check written to Dr. Tracy?

Complete to show the new balance.

7. $416.64 - \$84.12 = $ ▓ $ - \$119.65 = $ ▓ $ + \$165.85 = $ ▓

Use the checkbook record below. Write the balance after the check or deposit.

	DATE	CHECK NUMBER	CHECKS OR DEPOSITS	AMOUNT OF CHECK		✓	AMOUNT OF DEPOSIT		BALANCE	
				BALANCE BROUGHT FORWARD →					839	02
8.	6/17	541	Last National Bank	315	27				?	
9.	6/20	542	Heat Wave Insulation	75	89				?	
10.	6/23	543	Sea Breeze Health Club	125	00				?	
11.	6/25		Deposit				289	75	?	
12.	6/27	544	A-1 Garage	49	75				?	
13.	6/30		Deposit				150	00	?	
14.	7/3	545	Cash	50	00				?	
15.	7/9	546	Green Leaf Tree Service	89	90				?	
16.	7/18	547	Last National Bank	315	27				?	
17.	7/25		Deposit				289	75	?	

Checks and Charges

The Last National Bank makes the following charges for checking accounts.

LAST NATIONAL BANK SERVICE CHARGES		
Monthly Service Charge	**Monthly Check Charge**	**Check Printing Charge**
$2.50	$.10 per check	$7.50 for 200 checks

Solve.

18. Maud has a balance of $347.58. What will her balance be after she deducts the service charge?

★ **19.** Don wrote 7 checks and ordered 200 new checks last month. What are the total bank charges for the month?

Calculator Corner

In a magic square, the sum of the numbers in each row, column, and diagonal is the same. Copy and complete the magic square.

?	61.4	56.4
?	51.4	?
46.4	?	?

Rounding Decimals

Sometimes you need exact numbers and sometimes rounded ones will do.

The winning diver scored 402.39 points.

The pool is about 9 m deep.

Study the table to see how decimals are rounded.

Exact Number	Round to the Nearest	Digit to the Right	Is it 5 or More?	Round
48.65	whole number	6	Yes	up to 49
31.52	tenth	2	No	down to 31.5
8.204	hundredth	4	No	down to 8.20
73.8425	thousandth	5	Yes	up to 73.843

Exercises

Write the missing word and number.

	Exact Number	Round to the Nearest	Digit to the Right	Is it 5 or More?	Round
1.	3.7	whole number	7	Yes	up to ?
2.	48.26	tenth	6	?	?
3.	0.342	hundredth	2	?	?
4.	0.6878	thousandth	8	?	?
5.	126.08	tenth	8	?	?
6.	37.003	hundredth	3	?	?
7.	19.61	whole number	6	?	?
8.	682.1105	thousandth	5	?	?

Round to the nearest whole number.

9. 1.2   **10.** 2.6   **11.** 1.7   **12.** 5.3   **13.** 8.5

14. 20.6   **15.** 138.1   **16.** 229.5   **17.** 5.86   **18.** 10.011

Round to the nearest tenth.

19. 0.87   **20.** 0.13   **21.** 3.76   **22.** 18.12   **23.** 49.08

24. 6.95   **25.** 156.64   **26.** 350.45   **27.** 24.072   **28.** 9.1882

Round to the nearest hundredth.

29. 0.664   **30.** 0.875   **31.** 5.082   **32.** 10.796   **33.** 59.051

34. 32.1075   **35.** 6.9962   **36.** 8.2038   **37.** 74.934   **38.** 46.135

Round to the nearest thousandth.

39. 0.4832   **40.** 0.5917   **41.** 0.3245   **42.** 0.4174   **43.** 3.4198

44. 4.7331   **45.** 5.2416   **46.** 9.4763   **47.** 7.0428   **48.** 7.3174

Modern Art

49. Round each decimal to the nearest hundredth. Write the letters in order to name the picture.

A — 0.045   L — 0.082
B — 0.1990   M — 0.3901
E — 0.073   N — 0.273
F — 0.4346   O — 0.286
G — 0.181   R — 0.043
H — 0.435   S — 0.085
I — 0.3831   U — 0.1932

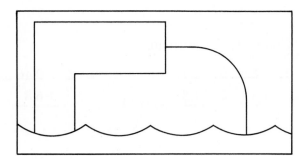

0.09   0.05   0.38   0.08   0.29   0.04

0.43   0.38   0.09   0.44   0.38   0.27   0.18 | 0.43   0.04   0.29   0.39

0.05 | 0.09   0.19   0.20   0.39   0.05   0.04   0.38   0.27   0.07

Estimating Decimal Sums and Differences

Harriet bought 8.3 m of fabric for chair covers and 2.6 m more for pillow covers. She estimated that she had about 11 m of fabric in all. The example shows how she made her estimate.

Round each decimal to the nearest whole number.

Add the rounded numbers.

$$
\begin{array}{ccc}
8.3 & \Rightarrow & 8 \\
+\,2.6 & \Rightarrow & +\,3 \\
\end{array}
\qquad
\begin{array}{c}
8 \\
+\,3 \\
\hline
11
\end{array}
$$

To estimate a decimal sum or difference, round each number to the same place. Then add or subtract as with whole numbers.

Actual Sum		Estimate		Actual Difference		Estimate
17.89	$\Rightarrow$	18		0.38	$\Rightarrow$	0.4
$+\,35.682$	$\Rightarrow$	$+\,36$		$-\,0.165$	$\Rightarrow$	$-\,0.2$
53.572		54		0.215		0.2

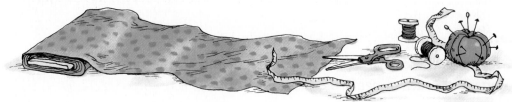

Exercises

Complete the estimate.

1.
$\begin{array}{ccc} 6.5 & \Rightarrow & 7 \\ +\,3.1 & \Rightarrow & +\,3 \\ \hline & & \blacksquare \end{array}$

2.
$\begin{array}{ccc} 9.46 & \Rightarrow & \blacksquare \\ +\,6.8 & \Rightarrow & +\,7 \\ \hline & & \blacksquare \end{array}$

3.
$\begin{array}{ccc} 7.6 & \Rightarrow & \blacksquare \\ -\,4.31 & \Rightarrow & -\,4 \\ \hline & & \blacksquare \end{array}$

4.
$\begin{array}{ccc} 18.31 & \Rightarrow & 18 \\ -\,4.5 & \Rightarrow & -\,\blacksquare \\ \hline & & \blacksquare \end{array}$

5.
$\begin{array}{ccc} 0.73 & \Rightarrow & 0.7 \\ -\,0.37 & \Rightarrow & -\,0.4 \\ \hline & & \blacksquare \end{array}$

6.
$\begin{array}{ccc} 3.71 & \Rightarrow & 4 \\ -\,1.823 & \Rightarrow & -\,\blacksquare \\ \hline & & \blacksquare \end{array}$

7.
$\begin{array}{ccc} 0.99 & \Rightarrow & 1.0 \\ +\,0.156 & \Rightarrow & +\,0.2 \\ \hline & & \blacksquare \end{array}$

8.
$\begin{array}{ccc} 72.34 & \Rightarrow & \blacksquare \\ +\,6.79 & \Rightarrow & +\,7 \\ \hline & & \blacksquare \end{array}$

9.
$\begin{array}{ccc} 4.78 & \Rightarrow & \blacksquare \\ -\,1.34 & \Rightarrow & -\,\blacksquare \\ \hline & & 4 \end{array}$

Round to the nearest whole number.
Estimate.

10.	5.36 +2.75	11.	8.98 −4.79	12.	10.29 + 3.471

13.	13.87 − 5.62	14.	20.01 +11.22	15.	6.83 +13.376

16.	6.05 −4.69	17.	12.95 − 2.49	18.	13.9 − 6.91

Round to the nearest tenth. Estimate.

19.	0.72 +0.86	20.	0.60 −0.21	21.	0.086 +0.71

22.	18.71 + 3.09	23.	0.74 −0.368	24.	0.259 −0.0768

25.	0.85 +1.03	26.	0.42 +0.33	27.	0.861 −0.1694

House Beautiful

Solve.

28. Beatrice needs 7.6 L of paint for the front porch and 6.9 L of paint for the back porch. Estimate the amount of paint needed to paint the two porches.

29. Aaron is buying a refrigerator. He saw one marked down from $595 to $485.99. Estimate the amount he can save by buying on sale.

★ 30. Suppose you spend $2.69 for wallpaper remover, $1.75 for sandpaper, $3.37 for scrapers, and $16.85 for paint. Estimate your change from $30.00.

Subtract. (*pages 130–131*)

1.	21.8 − 16.9	2.	49.00 − 15.43

3.	7.4938 −2.159	4.	6.8 −3.92

Write the new balance.
(*pages 132–133*)

	AMOUNT OF CHECK		BALANCE	
			745	68
5.	13	15	?	
6.	16	49	?	
7.	290	00	?	
8.	78	25	?	

Round. (*pages 134–135*)

9. Round 14.8 to the nearest whole number.

10. Round 81.44 to the nearest tenth.

Round to the nearest whole number. Estimate. (*pages 136–137*)

11.	4.863 +5.75	12.	87.18 − 24.621

Round to the nearest tenth. Estimate.

13.	68.39 + 8.61	14.	141.36 − 65.22

Problem Solving · TRIAL AND ERROR

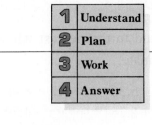

1	Understand
2	Plan
3	Work
4	Answer

Sometimes the best way to solve a problem is to try several answers. Each trial will give you information to help reach the correct answer.

Leon opened his book and said to Connie, "The product of these 2 page numbers is 1190. What are the page numbers?"

Connie used three trials to solve the problem. Here's how she did it.

Trial 1 — First she squared several numbers. This helped her decide where to start choosing factors.

$$10^2 = 100 \qquad 20^2 = 400 \qquad 30^2 = 900 \qquad 40^2 = 1600$$

Trial 2 — Connie saw that 1190 was between 900 and 1600. She knew the page numbers should be between 30 and 40. She decided to start with 36 and 37.

$$36 \times 37 = 1332$$

Trial 3 — Since 1332 is greater than 1190, Connie tried 34 and 35.

$$34 \times 35 = 1190$$

The page numbers are 34 and 35.

Solve. Use the hint for your first trial.

1. Jackie has $4.60 in quarters and dimes. She has 4 more dimes than quarters. How many quarters does she have?

Hint:
$(8 \times \$.25) + (12 \times \$.10) = $ ▨

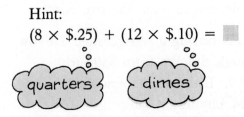
quarters   dimes

2. Karen is 7 years older than Lee. In 5 years she will be twice as old as Lee. How old are Karen and Lee now?

Hint:
If Karen is 10, then Lee is 3. In 5 years Karen will be 15 and Lee will be 8. Is $2 \times 8 = 15$ true?

3. The sum of 3 consecutive numbers is 219. What are the 3 numbers?

Hint:
$75 + 76 + 77 = $

4. Craig bought 72 cm of wood trim to frame a painting. The frame has to be 4 cm longer than it is wide. How wide is the painting?

Hint:
If the length is 16, the width must be 12.
Is $16 + 16 + 12 + 12 = 72$ true?

Solve.

5. The product of 3 consecutive numbers is 1320. What are the numbers?

6. What is the greatest number you can multiply by 78 to get a product between 2000 and 2500?

7. Pedro collected $6.50 in tips. He had twice as many dimes as nickels. He had 8 more quarters than dimes. How many of each coin did he have?

8. In a class election, Wally received twice as many votes as Tammy. Tammy received twice as many votes as Tina. There were 35 votes altogether. How many votes did Tina receive?

★ **9.** Rosco, May, and Lindsey played Rocket Derby. May scored 27 more points than Rosco. Lindsey scored 17 fewer points than May. The sum of all the players scores was 115. What was each player's score?

★ **10.** At a school party there were 8 times as many teachers as bus drivers. There was 1 more teacher aide than bus drivers. There was 1 principal. There were 32 adults at the party. How many teachers were there?

Unit Review

True or false? Write *T* or *F*.

1. 8 tenths = 0.8   **2.** 352 thousandths = 3.52   **3.** 26 and 3 tenths = 26.3

4. 0.37 > 0.35   **5.** 7.3 = 7.03   **6.** 0.59 < 0.61   **7.** 3.9 = 3.90

Add or subtract the number on each stripe and the number on the heel of the sock.

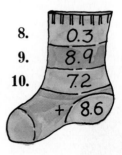

8. 0.3
9. 8.9
10. 7.2
+ 8.6

11. 4.68
12. 12.09
13. 1.60
− 0.37

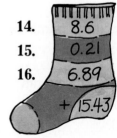

14. 8.6
15. 0.21
16. 6.89
+ 15.43

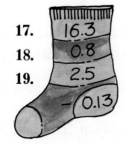

17. 16.3
18. 0.8
19. 2.5
− 0.13

Choose the best estimate. Write *a*, *b*, or *c*.

20. 0.77   **a.** 1.20
    − 0.43   **b.** 0.40
            c. 0.30

21. 5.3   **a.** 11
    + 2.8   **b.** 2
          c. 8

22. $72.88   **a.** $81.00
    + 7.50   **b.** $63.00
           c. $140.00

Write the new balance.

	DATE	CHECK NUMBER	CHECKS OR DEPOSITS	AMOUNT OF CHECK	✓	AMOUNT OF DEPOSIT	BALANCE
			BALANCE BROUGHT FORWARD →				1719 82
23.	3/1	216	Polly's Pet Shop	79 85			?
24.	3/12	217	Acme Barber Shop	6 75			?
25.	3/15		Deposit			351 16	?
26.	3/15	218	Clark's Drug Store	15 89			?
27.	3/20		Deposit			351 16	?

Solve.

28. The sum of 3 consecutive numbers is 342. What are the numbers?

29. At a school picnic there were 52 L of cider. There were 4 times as many 2 L containers as 5 L containers. How many 5 L containers were there?

Write the decimal. (*pages 122-125*)

1. 7 tenths   **2.** 151 thousandths   **3.** 8 hundredths

4. 3051 ten-thousandths   **5.** 18 and 4 tenths   **6.** 3 and 18 hundredths

Write $<$ or $>$ to compare the numbers. (*pages 126-127*)

7. 0.28 ▨ 0.29   **8.** 5.8 ▨ 5.08   **9.** 0.83 ▨ 0.091

Add. (*pages 128-129*)

10. 0.7	**11.** 9.2471	**12.** 0.49	**13.** 12.000
$+0.8$	$+2.3188$	$+0.21$	$+10.135$

Subtract. (*pages 130-131*)

14. 13.79	**15.** 87.981	**16.** 132.4	**17.** 0.837
$-\ 9.81$	-25.492	$-\ 69.52$	-0.45

Find the new balance. (*pages 132-133*)

	DATE	CHECK NUMBER	CHECKS OR DEPOSITS	AMOUNT OF CHECK		✓	AMOUNT OF DEPOSIT		BALANCE	
				BALANCE BROUGHT FORWARD →					361	87
18.	8/1	101	Rocky's Running Center	35	00				?	
19.	8/7	102	Cash	125	00				?	
20.	8/22	103	Belmont Meat Market	27	89				?	
21.	8/30		Deposit				322	18	?	

Estimate the sum or difference. (*pages 134-137*)

22. 0.89	**23.** 347.98	**24.** 19.309	**25.** 0.745
$+0.32$	$-\ 26.321$	$+25.87$	-0.3871

Solve. (*pages 138-139*)

26. Cora has \$2.50 in nickels and dimes. She has 8 more nickels than dimes. How many dimes does she have?

27. The product of 2 consecutive numbers is 60,270. What are the numbers?

Extra practice on page 387

Logic

Each card has a number, either 3, 6, or 7, on the back. Can you use the clues below to find out which number is on which card?

Clue a. The number on ◯ is less than the number on △.

Clue b. The number on ☆ is an odd number.

Clue c. The number on ◯ is not an even number.

To solve the problem, make a chart showing all the possibilities. Make an X in each box as the possibilities are eliminated.

	☆	△	◯
3		X	
6	X		X
7			X

From clue a you know that 7 is not on ◯ and 3 is not on △.

From clue b you know that 6 is not on ☆.

From clue c you know that 6 is not on ◯.

Since ◯ has all possibilities crossed out except one, 3 is on ◯.
You can see that 6 is on △ so 7 must be on ☆.

Make a chart to solve the problem.

1. Each card has a number, 4, 8, or 12 on the back. Use the clues to decide which number is on which card.

   a. The number on ☐ is greater than the number on ⬡.

   b. The number on ☾ is a factor of the number on ⬡.

2. Each card has a number, 12, 15, 18, or 20 on the back. Use the clues to decide which number is on which card.

   a. The number on 🍐 is less than the number on 🥕.

   b. The number on 🍋 is greater than the number on 🍎.

   c. The numbers on 🥕 and 🍎 have 5 as a factor.

Now try these!

3. Sue Brown, Mary Green, and Jane Blue are flying brown, green, and blue kites. What color kite is each girl flying? You have these clues.

  a. No girl's kite color is the same as her name color.
  b. Sue Brown is not flying a green kite.

4. The president, vice-president, and treasurer of a company are Mr. Great, Mrs. Wonder, and Miss Super. Which job does each person hold? You have these clues.

  a. The president has the highest salary.
  b. Mr. Great earns less than Mrs. Wonder.
  c. The treasurer is the brother-in-law of Miss Super.
  d. The president has no brothers or sisters.

★ **5.** Sonya, Richard, Caitlin, and Dylan are artists. Each is a writer, dancer, painter, or singer. Which person is which? You have these clues.

  a. Sonya and Caitlin have seen the singer perform.
  b. Both Richard and the writer have portraits done by the painter.
  c. The writer has written biographies of both Dylan and Sonya.
  d. Sonya has never met Caitlin.

★ **6.** Ms. Ling, Mr. White, Miss Coe, and Mr. Cole work in the same office building. Each is an engineer, architect, accountant, or private detective. Which person has which job? You have these clues.

  a. Miss Coe is younger than Mr. Cole but older than the accountant.
  b. The engineer earns more than either Ms. Ling or Mr. Cole.
  c. The detective is the oldest and Mr. White is the youngest.
  d. The accountant makes the most money and Ms. Ling makes more than the detective.

Maintaining Skills

Write the missing unit.

1. 100 ▦ = 1 m

2. 1000 ▦ = 1 L

3. 1000 ▦ = 1 km

4. Follow the footprints. Your final answer will tell you how much money is in the treasure chest.

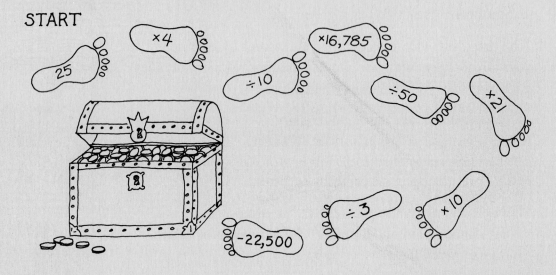

START

Correct or incorrect? Write *C* or *I*.

5.
```
  16,759
+  3,806
  20,565
```

6.
```
   7
  81
+  4
  82
```

7.
```
 178,300
-   5,261
 173,049
```

8.
```
 6421
 × 7
44,947
```

9.
```
      123
78)9633
```

10. 5684 has a 4 in the tens' place.

11. 79,016 has a 6 in the ones' place.

12. 534,098 has a 0 in the hundreds' place.

13. 339,128 has a 3 in the tens' place.

Solve.

14. The Delaware River bridge is 493.2 m long. The Fremont Bridge in Oregon is 376.5 m long. Which bridge is longer? How much longer?

15. The price of a chair increased from $329.86 to $360.59. What was the amount of the increase?

The colors in this photo show the relative temperatures on the surface of this house. Adding storm windows could save up to $250 per year and lower the window temperature to that of the walls. What color would you then expect the windows to be?

Multiplication, Division of Decimals

Multiplying Decimals and Whole Numbers

When you multiply a decimal by a whole number, the product will have the same number of decimal places as the decimal. Look at the examples below to see why this happens.

$$
\begin{array}{r}
3.8 \\
3.8 \\
3.8 \\
+\,3.8 \\
\hline
15.2
\end{array}
\qquad
\begin{array}{r}
3.8 \\
\times\,4 \\
\hline
15.2
\end{array}
$$

3.8 ◁ 1 decimal place
×4
15.2 ◁ 1 decimal place

$$
\begin{array}{r}
47.039 \\
47.039 \\
+\,47.039 \\
\hline
141.117
\end{array}
$$

47.039 ◁ 3 decimal places
×3
141.117 ◁ 3 decimal places

Exercises

Multiply.

1. 24	2.4	0.24	**2.** 32	3.2	0.32
×6	×6	×6	×7	×7	×7

3. 5431	543.1	54.31	**4.** 45	4.5	0.45
×2	×2	×2	×36	×36	×36

5. 702	70.2	7.02	**6.** 28	0.28	0.028
×15	×15	×15	×94	×94	×94

Multiply.

7. 8.7	**8.** 17.8	**9.** 37.6	**10.** 27.84	**11.** 72.69
×4	×9	×8	×3	×5

12. 7.9	**13.** 41.6	**14.** 0.87	**15.** 55.45	**16.** 278.1
×4	×7	×6	×2	×3

17. 45.9
×36

18. 32.8
×92

19. 3.212
×41

20. 45.09
×83

21. 33.65
×59

22. 12.5
×38

23. 3.784
×47

24. 6.892
×56

25. 1.785
×69

26. 2.432
×78

27. 78.3
×823

28. 68.4
×946

29. 39.44
×125

30. 6.472
×232

31. 8.119
×349

32. 24.71
×5334

33. 4.123
×6247

34. 19.8
×5641

35. 5.981
×9056

36. 7.247
×6617

37. 7 × 3.58

38. 85 × 4.8

39. 53 × 38.43

40. 76 × 4.382

41. 62 × 93.6

42. 44 × 7.102

Check Please

Food Glorious Food

SANDWICHES

Titan Tuna .... $ 3.65
Colossal Club ...... $ 4.35
Burly Burger...... $ 3.95
Chunky Chicken..... $ 5.60
Hippo Ham
and Cheese .... $ 4.60

SIDE ORDERS

Super Soup......$ 1.25
Spinach Salad ..... $ 2.75
Veggies and Dip.... $ 3.85
Cheese Choice....$ 2.75

DRINKS

Milk ....$ .85
Juice ....$ .95

Find the cost of the order.

43. 6 Colossal Clubs

44. 15 Burly Burgers

45. 5 orders of the Cheese Choice

46. 7 Titan Tunas

★ 47. The Magicians' Club is meeting at Food Glorious Food.
Each of the 12 members orders Chunky Chicken, Spinach
Salad, and milk. Is $100.00 enough to pay the bill?

Multiplying Decimals

The models show what happens when you multiply decimals.

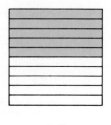

0.5

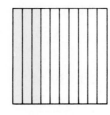

0.3

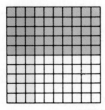

0.3 of 0.5 is 0.15

0.3 × 0.5 = 0.15

You can see that when you multiply tenths times tenths the product is hundredths.

$$0.3 \times 0.5 = 0.15$$

When you multiply tenths times hundredths the product is thousandths.

$$1.2 \times 0.16 = 0.192$$

The number of decimal places in a product is the sum of the number of decimal places in the factors.

Look at these examples.

0.2	◊	1 decimal place		4.116	◊	3 decimal places
×0.8	◊	+1 decimal place		×3	◊	+0 decimal places
0.16	◊	2 decimal places		12.348	◊	3 decimal places

Exercises

Choose the correct product. Write *a* or *b*.

1. 0.4 × 6.1
  a. 2.44
  b. 24.4

2. 1.7 × 0.33
  a. 56.1
  b. 0.561

3. 10.2 × 1.11
  a. 11.322
  b. 113.22

4. 1.5 × 5.5
  a. 8.25
  b. 0.825

5. 1.36 × 0.02
  a. 0.0272
  b. 27.2

6. 25.1 × 0.3
  a. 75.3
  b. 7.53

7. 5.5 × 0.05
  a. 0.275
  b. 27.5

8. 0.98 × 0.02
  a. 1.96
  b. 0.0196

Multiply.

9. 0.8×0.9 **10.** 5.1×0.3 **11.** 7.2×0.24 **12.** 0.8×0.35

13. 0.2×15.3 **14.** 0.05×4.6 **15.** 213.1×0.01 **16.** 1.2×0.11

17. 1.2
     $\times 2.3$

18. 3.2
     $\times 0.8$

19. 0.207
     $\times 1.2$

20. 36.5
     $\times 0.3$

21. 10.4
     $\times 2.5$

22. 28.1
     $\times 6.9$

23. 2.071
     $\times 21.3$

24. 61.2
     $\times 0.8$

25. 25.4
     $\times 35.6$

26. 32.84
     $\times 0.15$

27. 14.317
     $\times 2.1$

28. 15.6
     $\times 267.9$

29. 1.148
     $\times 10.16$

30. 0.4
     $\times 167.5$

31. 2.53
     $\times 175.9$

Underwater World

Solve.

32. Sound is used to measure ocean depth. In one second a sound will travel 1.5 km through water. If it takes 2.6 seconds for a sound to reach the bottom of the ocean, how deep is the water?

33. With scuba gear, a beginning diver can dive to a depth of about 30.5 m. A professional diver can reach a depth 48.8 m deeper. To what depth can a professional diver go?

★ **34.** Underwater, a fish appears to be 1.25 times larger than it actually is. To a diver underwater, how many meters long would a 33.8 cm fish appear to be?

Calculator Corner

A stack of 100 one-dollar bills is about 9.485 mm high.

How high is $575? $2582? $13,685? $1,480,650?

Zeros in the Product

Polly wants to buy 1.25 m of Smiles. How much will it cost if Smiles are $.07 per meter?

Multiply to find out.

$$\begin{array}{r} \$.07 \\ \times 1.25 \\ \hline \$.0875 \end{array} \Rightarrow \$.09$$

Since stores always round up, it will cost $.09 for 1.25 m of Smiles.

Notice that we had to write an extra zero in the product to make the correct number of decimal places.

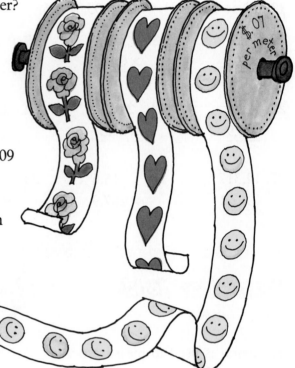

Here are more examples.

4.08	◁	2 decimal places
×0.002	◁	+3 decimal places
0.00816	◁	5 decimal places

0.06	◁	2 decimal places
×0.03	◁	+2 decimal places
0.0018	◁	4 decimal places

Exercises

Copy and correct the product. Write the decimal point in the correct place.

1.	2.	3.	4.	5.
0.19	0.25	0.149	0.38	2.48
×0.06	×0.07	×0.4	×0.003	×0.06
114	175	596	114	1488

6.	7.	8.	9.	10.
0.49	0.29	5.1	0.31	2.5
×0.13	×0.68	×0.24	×0.2	×0.03
637	1972	1224	62	75

150

Multiply.

11. 0.05
×0.1

12. 0.04
×0.3

13. 0.08
×0.6

14. 0.4
×0.08

15. 0.05
×0.4

16. 0.22
×0.4

17. 0.19
×0.3

18. 0.35
×0.4

19. 0.56
×0.2

20. 0.047
×0.6

21. 1.45
×0.05

22. 4.79
×0.2

23. 0.388
×0.09

24. 7.42
×0.3

25. 0.98
×0.08

26. 1.89
×0.03

27. 0.21
×0.08

28. 0.39
×0.102

29. 0.09
×0.06

30. 0.07
×0.005

31. 1.6 × 0.63

32. 0.025 × 0.98

33. 1.2 × 0.027

34. 0.38 × 0.12

35. 0.73 × 0.06

36. 0.018 × 0.05

37. 2.9 × 0.004

38. 0.09 × 0.34

Miniatures

Each item in the Sunshine Store is actually 8.5 times larger than the model. Use the picture of the model below to find the height of the item.

39. Barrel of Laughs

40. Stack of Puns

41. Pile of Smiles

42. Baskets of Scents

43. Canister of Curiosities

44. Crate of Wishes

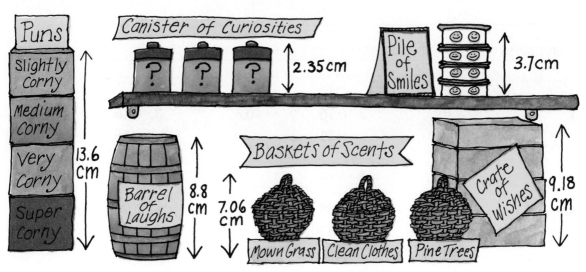

Estimating Decimal Products

It's a good idea to estimate decimal products to make sure the decimal point is in the correct place. The rules below show a good way to round decimals when you estimate products.

Rule 1 Round numbers only when they have more than one digit.

Rule 2 Round whole numbers and decimals greater than 1 to the nearest one, ten, or hundred.

$$63 \Rightarrow 60 \qquad 721 \Rightarrow 700 \qquad 86.7 \Rightarrow 90 \qquad 334.81 \Rightarrow 300$$

Rule 3 Round decimals less than 1 to the nearest tenth or hundredth.

$$0.15 \Rightarrow 0.2 \qquad 0.82 \Rightarrow 0.8 \qquad 0.065 \Rightarrow 0.07 \qquad 0.346 \Rightarrow 0.3$$

Now look at some examples.

Estimate		Actual Product		Estimate		Actual Product
1.8 $\Rightarrow$	2	1.8		48.72 $\Rightarrow$	50	48.72
$\times 6.3$ $\Rightarrow$	$\times 6$	$\times 6.3$		$\times 0.03$ $\Rightarrow$	$\times 0.03$	$\times 0.03$
	12	11.34			1.50	1.4616

Since the estimate is close to the product, the decimal point is in the correct place.

Exercises

Complete the estimate.

1.
$$\begin{array}{r} 12 \\ \times 0.8 \\ \hline \end{array} \Rightarrow \begin{array}{r} 10 \\ \times 0.8 \\ \hline \blacksquare \end{array}$$

2.
$$\begin{array}{r} 0.76 \\ \times 24 \\ \hline \end{array} \Rightarrow \begin{array}{r} 0.8 \\ \times 20 \\ \hline \blacksquare \end{array}$$

3.
$$\begin{array}{r} 0.46 \\ \times 55 \\ \hline \end{array} \Rightarrow \begin{array}{r} 0.5 \\ \times 60 \\ \hline \blacksquare \end{array}$$

4.
$$\begin{array}{r} 3.9 \\ \times 2.1 \\ \hline \end{array} \Rightarrow \begin{array}{r} 4 \\ \times \blacksquare \\ \hline \blacksquare \end{array}$$

5.
$$\begin{array}{r} 0.65 \\ \times 33 \\ \hline \end{array} \Rightarrow \begin{array}{r} \blacksquare \\ \times 30 \\ \hline \blacksquare \end{array}$$

6.
$$\begin{array}{r} 0.709 \\ \times 184 \\ \hline \end{array} \Rightarrow \begin{array}{r} \blacksquare \\ \times 200 \\ \hline \blacksquare \end{array}$$

Estimate the product.

7. 235	**8.** 3.42	**9.** 11.6
×0.7	×18	×8.5

10. 0.759	**11.** 2.31	**12.** 86.5
×38	×5.5	×0.47

13. 53.9	**14.** 9.22	**15.** 13.95
×27.3	×3.6	×66.1

Estimate, then multiply. Use the estimate to make sure the decimal point is in the right place.

16. 0.54	**17.** 178	**18.** 0.473
×2.9	×3.06	×42

19. 85.2	**20.** 21.53	**21.** 8.75
×21.8	×10.5	×6.7

Foreign Exchange

Country	Money Used	Recent Value in U.S. dollars
England	pound	$2.398
France	franc	0.2041
Saudi Arabia	riyal	0.3011
West Germany	mark	0.5236

Estimate the number of U.S. dollars equal to the amount of foreign currency.

22. 98 pounds

23. 310 marks

24. 800 riyals

25. 2000 francs

★ **26.** Estimate the number of U.S. dollars equal to 425 marks if the value of a mark increases by $0.038.

Checkpoint A

Multiply. (*pages 146–147*)

1. 33.2	**2.** 8.84
×44	×136

3. 0.729	**4.** 0.216
×9140	×15

Multiply. (*pages 148–149*)

5. 6.8	**6.** 21.3
×0.3	×0.02

7. 32.3	**8.** 7.08
×1.2	×2.8

Multiply. (*pages 150–151*)

9. 0.636	**10.** 0.57
×0.1	×0.048

11. 0.14	**12.** 0.17
×0.2	×0.23

Estimate the product. (*pages 152–153*)

13. 158	**14.** 17.2
×0.21	×0.35

15. 0.86	**16.** 9.03
×5.7	×8.2

Dividing Decimals and Whole Numbers

Look at the example below to see how to divide a decimal by a whole number.

First divide as you would whole numbers.

Then write the decimal point in the quotient above the decimal point in the dividend.

```
      1 9
8) 15.2
    - 8
    ─────
      7 2
    - 7 2
    ─────
        0
```

```
      1.9
8) 15.2
    - 8
    ─────
      7 2
    - 7 2
    ─────
        0
```

Watch out for problems like these.

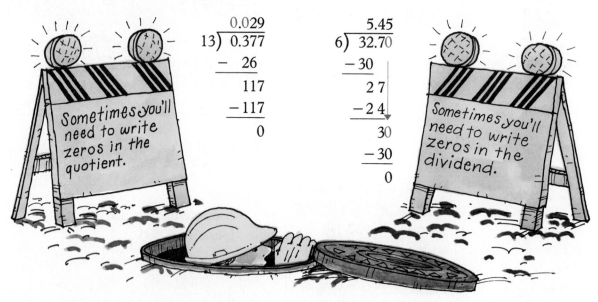

```
    0.029
13) 0.377
    - 26
    ─────
      117
    - 117
    ─────
        0
```

```
     5.45
6) 32.70
   - 30
   ─────
      2 7
    - 2 4
    ─────
       30
     - 30
     ─────
        0
```

Sometimes you'll need to write zeros in the quotient.

Sometimes you'll need to write zeros in the dividend.

Exercises

Divide.

1. 5)365   5)36.5   **2.** 4)506   4)50.6

3. 12)516   12)51.6   **4.** 35)7070   35)70.70

5. 78)117   78)1.17   **6.** 54)6858   54)6.858

Divide.

7. $3\overline{)38.4}$ **8.** $6\overline{)11.7}$ **9.** $4\overline{)5.2}$ **10.** $8\overline{)249.6}$

11. $9\overline{)97.2}$ **12.** $4\overline{)34.16}$ **13.** $7\overline{)448.7}$ **14.** $3\overline{)128.04}$

15. $8\overline{)0.72}$ **16.** $7\overline{)101.64}$ **17.** $6\overline{)0.084}$ **18.** $5\overline{)15.52}$

19. $7\overline{)1.141}$ **20.** $8\overline{)2.462}$ **21.** $9\overline{)0.72}$ **22.** $6\overline{)3.453}$

23. $38\overline{)5.51}$ **24.** $15\overline{)16.2}$ **25.** $29\overline{)83.52}$ **26.** $41\overline{)2.1156}$

27. $59\overline{)1.1977}$ **28.** $24\overline{)152.4}$ **29.** $18\overline{)2.43}$ **30.** $32\overline{)280.32}$

Short Cut Division

You can use short division to find $5\overline{)68.5}$. At each stage just divide, multiply, and subtract in your head.

Here's how.
$$5\overline{)6\,^1 8.5} \qquad \begin{array}{c} 1\ 3 \\ 5\overline{)6\,^1 8.^3 5} \end{array} \qquad \begin{array}{c} 1\ 3.\ 7 \\ 5\overline{)6\,^1 8.^3 5} \end{array}$$

Divide using short division. Be sure to write the decimal point in the quotient.

31. $7\overline{)37.1}$ **32.** $8\overline{)65.04}$ **33.** $4\overline{)3.396}$ **34.** $6\overline{)46.014}$

Solve.

35. Batik Designs Unlimited received a shipment of wax weighing 6.5 kg. There were 5 boxes of wax in the shipment. How much did each box weigh?

36. Suppose your bill for 12 m of fabric is $35.76. What would be the cost of one meter of that fabric?

★ **37.** You have 10 m of cloth. An elephant requires 0.9 m of cloth. A bear requires 1.3 m. If you make 5 elephants, how many bears can you make?

Multiplying or Dividing by 10, 100, or 1000

Multiplying or dividing a decimal by 10 moves the decimal point 1 place.

$$74.5 \times 10 = 745.$$

$$74.5 \div 10 = 7.45$$

Multiplying or dividing a decimal by 100 moves the decimal point 2 places.

$$6.831 \times 100 = 683.1$$

$$6.831 \div 100 = 0.06831$$

Multiplying or dividing a decimal by 1000 moves the decimal point 3 places.

$$4.25 \times 1000 = 4250.$$

$$4.25 \div 1000 = 0.00425$$

MULTIPLYING BY 10, 100, OR 1000 MAKES A NUMBER GREATER, SO MOVE TO THE RIGHT.

DIVIDING BY 10, 100, OR 1000 GIVES A LESSER NUMBER, SO MOVE TO THE LEFT.

Exercises

Copy and correct the product. Write the decimal point in the correct place.

1. $10 \times 3.15 = 315$
$100 \times 3.15 = 315$
$1000 \times 3.15 = 315$

2. $10 \times 0.78 = 78$
$100 \times 0.78 = 78$
$1000 \times 0.78 = 78$

3. $10 \times 22.9 = 229$
$100 \times 22.9 = 229$
$1000 \times 22.9 = 229$

Copy and correct the quotient. Write the decimal point in the correct place.

4. $64.3 \div 10 = 643$
$64.3 \div 100 = 643$
$64.3 \div 1000 = 643$

5. $8.61 \div 10 = 861$
$8.61 \div 100 = 861$
$8.61 \div 1000 = 861$

6. $0.21 \div 10 = 21$
$0.21 \div 100 = 21$
$0.21 \div 1000 = 21$

Multiply or divide.

7. 100×82.11 **8.** $0.473 \div 1000$ **9.** 1000×210.5 **10.** $0.762 \div 100$

11. $93.84 \div 10$ **12.** 1000×7.48 **13.** $12.3 \div 100$ **14.** 10×10.78

15. 1000×24.7 **16.** $36.43 \div 100$ **17.** 10×83.01 **18.** $2.755 \div 1000$

19. $0.371 \div 10$ **20.** 100×0.146 **21.** $0.8615 \div 1000$ **22.** 100×0.315

23. 100×5.84 **24.** $31.6 \div 1000$ **25.** 100×43.615 **26.** $11.15 \div 10$

27. $83.65 \div 1000$ **28.** 1000×7.61 **29.** $92.71 \div 10$ **30.** 100×84.45

31. 10×16.3 **32.** $178.6 \div 100$ **33.** 1000×0.37 **34.** $14.6 \div 100$

35. $397.6 \div 100$ **36.** 1000×0.919 **37.** $9.81 \div 1000$ **38.** 1000×37.16

Table Talk

Complete the table.

39.

×	0.315	6.217	8.75	17.6
10	3.15	?	?	?
100	?	?	?	?
1000	?	?	?	?

40.

÷	16.5	4.08	9.65	27.31
10	1.65	?	?	?
100	?	?	?	?
1000	?	?	?	?

41.

×	0.59	0.18	13.67	9.21
30	?	?	?	?
300	?	?	?	?
3000	?	?	?	?

42.

÷	3.7	14.9	22.6	0.351
50	?	?	?	?
500	?	?	?	?
5000	?	?	?	?

Solve.

★ **43.** Theater tickets are 4.5 cm long. How long is a roll of 2000 tickets?

★ **44.** Theater seats are 40 cm wide. How many seats can fit in a row that is 10 m wide?

Dividing by Tenths

These examples show that multiplying the dividend and the divisor by the same number doesn't change the quotient.

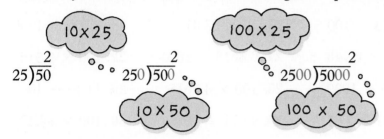
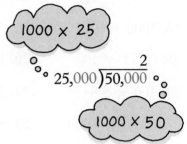

$$
25\overline{)50} \qquad 250\overline{)500} \qquad 2500\overline{)5000} \qquad 25{,}000\overline{)50{,}000}
$$

You can use this fact to divide 25.75 by 0.5.

First multiply the dividend and the divisor by the multiple of 10 that will make the divisor a whole number.

$$
0.5\overline{)25.75} \qquad \Rightarrow \qquad 5.\overline{)257.5}
$$

Next, divide as with whole numbers and write the decimal point in the quotient.

$$
\begin{array}{r} 51.5 \\ 5.\overline{)257.5} \end{array}
$$

Exercises

Complete.

1. $10 \times 0.6 = $ ▨

2. $10 \times 4.7 = $ ▨

3. $10 \times 16.1 = $ ▨

4. $100 \times 18.51 = $ ▨

5. $100 \times 7.63 = $ ▨

6. $100 \times 8.69 = $ ▨

7. $100 \times 42.91 = $ ▨

8. $1000 \times 0.681 = $ ▨

9. $1000 \times 5.02 = $ ▨

10. $0.7\overline{)4.2}$ ⟹ $7.\overline{)42.}$

11. $0.9\overline{)6.48}$ ⟹ $9.\overline{)64.8}$

12. $1.6\overline{)3.36}$ ⟹ $16.\overline{)33.6}$

13. $2.8\overline{)4.48}$ ⟹ $28.\overline{)44.8}$

Divide.

14. $0.6 \overline{)7.8}$ **15.** $0.4 \overline{)4.8}$ **16.** $0.3 \overline{)1.56}$ **17.** $0.5 \overline{)0.395}$

18. $0.8 \overline{)2.512}$ **19.** $0.6 \overline{)13.92}$ **20.** $0.9 \overline{)0.774}$ **21.** $0.7 \overline{)2.464}$

22. $1.3 \overline{)27.82}$ **23.** $2.7 \overline{)8.424}$ **24.** $4.2 \overline{)35.49}$ **25.** $1.8 \overline{)0.234}$

26. $2.4 \overline{)2.244}$ **27.** $3.3 \overline{)0.891}$ **28.** $1.6 \overline{)9.088}$ **29.** $4.5 \overline{)30.78}$

30. $23.9 \overline{)320.26}$ **31.** $22.1 \overline{)18.785}$ **32.** $55.8 \overline{)887.22}$ **33.** $23.6 \overline{)42.48}$

Fill'er Up

Samantha's notebook shows how much she spent on gas on some recent business trips. Complete Samantha's notes to show the price of a liter of gas in each city. Round answers to the nearest thousandth. The first one is done for you.

	City	Amount Spent	Liters	Price per Liter
	Eureka	$38.49	59.3	64.9¢
34.	Fargo	$19.84	30.2	?
35.	Tallahassee	$15.41	25.3	?
36.	Terre Haute	$10.00	16.7	?
37.	Hannibal	$33.55	48.6	?
★ **38.**	Gettysburg	?	38.4	73.8¢
★ **39.**	Oshkosh	$71.13	?	76.9¢

Claude found two dollars and added it to the money he already had. He then had five times as much money as he would have had if he'd lost two dollars. Claude started with less than $10.00. How much did he have after his lucky find?

Take a Break

Dividing by Hundredths and Thousandths

 ← This is Marty holding his fish. It weighed 2.88 kg!

 ←This is Marty cooking his fish. Everyone got 0.24 kg of fish.

You can divide 2.88 by 0.24 to find how many people got to eat some of Marty's fish.

First multiply the dividend and divisor by 100. This will make the divisor a whole number.

100×0.24

$0.24 \overline{)2.88}$ ⟹ $0\,24. \overline{)2\,88.}$

100×2.88

Next divide as with whole numbers and write the decimal point in the quotient.

$$0\,24. \overline{)2\,88.}^{\;12}$$

Marty fed 12 people with his fish.

To divide by thousandths multiply the dividend and divisor by 1000.

1000×0.842

$0.842 \overline{)993.560}$

1000×993.56

Divide. Write the decimal point in the quotient.

$$0\,842. \overline{)993\,560.}^{\;1\,180.}$$

Exercises

Divide.

1. $8 \overline{)192}$ $0.08 \overline{)1.92}$ **2.** $742 \overline{)24{,}486}$ $0.742 \overline{)244.86}$

3. $13 \overline{)364}$ $0.13 \overline{)3.64}$ **4.** $53 \overline{)3392}$ $0.053 \overline{)3.392}$

5. $142 \overline{)3976}$ $1.42 \overline{)3.976}$ **6.** $6.2 \overline{)318.06}$ $0.062 \overline{)0.31806}$

Divide.

7. $0.03\overline{)0.837}$ **8.** $0.005\overline{)1.425}$ **9.** $0.009\overline{)7.56}$ **10.** $0.03\overline{)7.194}$

11. $0.04\overline{)0.956}$ **12.** $0.007\overline{)1.512}$ **13.** $0.59\overline{)9.44}$ **14.** $0.11\overline{)2.783}$

15. $0.08\overline{)3.936}$ **16.** $0.005\overline{)13.15}$ **17.** $2.34\overline{)13.572}$ **18.** $0.315\overline{)7.56}$

19. $0.047\overline{)94}$ **20.** $0.028\overline{)6.916}$ **21.** $5.04\overline{)957.6}$ **22.** $0.816\overline{)3.9984}$

23. $0.17\overline{)68}$ **24.** $0.12\overline{)5.532}$ **25.** $7.01\overline{)24.535}$ **26.** $8.83\overline{)35.32}$

27. $0.602\overline{)28.294}$ **28.** $0.023\overline{)22.08}$ **29.** $0.035\overline{)12.88}$ **30.** $0.985\overline{)0.788}$

Fish Story

Fishing lures cost $1.39 each. How many lures can you buy
with the given amount of money?

31. $4.17 **32.** $8.34 **33.** $15.29 **34.** $23.63 **35.** $41.70

Deluxe fishing hooks cost $.75 each. How many hooks can you
buy with the given amount of money?

36. $3.75 **37.** $7.50 **38.** $11.25 **39.** $21.00 **40.** $27.00

Swordfish costs $9.59 per kilogram. How much will it cost to
buy the given amount of swordfish?

41. 3 kg **42.** 7 kg **43.** 5.5 kg **44.** 0.8 kg **45.** 10.75 kg

★ **46.** Work backwards to find the starting number.

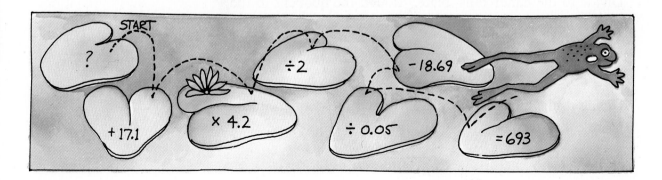

Rounding the Quotient

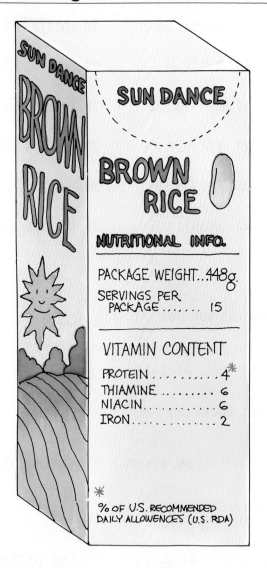

To the nearest gram, how large is one serving?

Divide 448 by 15 to find out. Divide to the tenths' place since you want to round to the nearest whole number.

$$
\begin{array}{r}
29.8 \\
15{\overline{\smash{\big)}\,448.0}} \\
-30 \\
\hline
148 \\
-135 \\
\hline
130 \\
-120 \\
\hline
10
\end{array}
$$

To the nearest gram, each serving is about 30 g.

Always divide to one place further than the place to which you're rounding. When rounding to the nearest tenth, divide to the hundredths' place. When rounding to the nearest hundredth, divide to the thousandths' place.

Exercises

Divide to the hundredths' place. Round the quotient to the nearest tenth.

1. $6{\overline{\smash{\big)}\,2.23}}$ **2.** $8{\overline{\smash{\big)}\,7.15}}$ **3.** $0.3{\overline{\smash{\big)}\,0.52}}$ **4.** $1.2{\overline{\smash{\big)}\,3.46}}$

Divide to the thousandths' place. Round the quotient to the nearest hundredth.

5. $16{\overline{\smash{\big)}\,37.8}}$ **6.** $82{\overline{\smash{\big)}\,0.991}}$ **7.** $3.7{\overline{\smash{\big)}\,6.812}}$ **8.** $15.2{\overline{\smash{\big)}\,9.681}}$

Divide. Round the quotient to the nearest tenth.

9. $7\overline{)125}$ **10.** $9\overline{)22.4}$ **11.** $4\overline{)31.7}$ **12.** $3\overline{)74}$

13. $0.6\overline{)3.85}$ **14.** $0.04\overline{)1.431}$ **15.** $0.7\overline{)92.5}$ **16.** $0.9\overline{)16.18}$

17. $1.32\overline{)0.756}$ **18.** $0.231\overline{)0.7441}$ **19.** $8.71\overline{)2.235}$ **20.** $6.07\overline{)13}$

Divide. Round the quotient to the nearest hundredth.

21. $8\overline{)45.3}$ **22.** $4\overline{)11.5}$ **23.** $6\overline{)52.19}$ **24.** $7\overline{)61.03}$

25. $0.3\overline{)22.9}$ **26.** $0.08\overline{)0.795}$ **27.** $0.6\overline{)45.2}$ **28.** $0.7\overline{)3.893}$

29. $4.44\overline{)73.6}$ **30.** $0.361\overline{)4.793}$ **31.** $1.75\overline{)31.47}$ **32.** $2.09\overline{)58.8}$

Divide to the tenths' place. Round to the nearest whole number.

33. $28\overline{)813}$ **34.** $7\overline{)423}$ **35.** $47\overline{)1002}$ **36.** $86\overline{)942}$

Using Your Skill

Solve.

37. There are 64 dinner rolls in a package. Each roll weighs 28.5 g. How much does the package weigh?

★ **38.** A 356 page book is 14.5 mm thick. To the nearest hundredth of a millimeter, find the thickness of one page.

Calculator Corner

Diamonds are measured in units called carats. Suppose a diamond in a ring has a mass of 0.35 carats. How many rings of this size could be made from these famous diamonds?

Hope   44 carats   Cullinan   3106 carats

Kohinoor   108.33 carats   Great Mogul   287.5 carats

Estimating Decimal Quotients

When you divide decimals you can estimate to check the placement of the decimal point in the quotient.

To estimate a decimal quotient, round the dividend and divisor to the nearest one, ten, hundred, or thousand. Divide.

Estimate $\qquad\qquad$ Actual quotient to the nearest tenth.

$$7.36\overline{)42.8} \quad \Rightarrow \quad 10\overline{)40}^{\;4} \qquad\qquad 7.36\overline{)42.80} \quad \Rightarrow \quad 7.36.\overline{)42\;80.0}^{\;5.8}$$

Since 4 is close to 5.8, the decimal point is in the right place.

Exercises

Estimate the quotient.

1. $3.2\overline{)12.7} \quad \Rightarrow \quad 3\overline{)10}$ $\qquad$ **2.** $5.9\overline{)311.3} \quad \Rightarrow \quad 6\overline{)300}$

3. $28.9\overline{)598.4} \quad \Rightarrow \quad 30\overline{)600}$ $\qquad$ **4.** $8.14\overline{)5298.5} \quad \Rightarrow \quad 10\overline{)5000}$

5. $4.89\overline{)91.8} \quad \Rightarrow \quad 5\overline{)90}$ $\qquad$ **6.** $1.84\overline{)15.732} \quad \Rightarrow \quad 2\overline{)20}$

Estimate the quotient.

7. $4.7\overline{)29.47}$ $\qquad$ **8.** $7.9\overline{)68.43}$ $\qquad$ **9.** $2.1\overline{)718.8}$ $\qquad$ **10.** $9.1\overline{)425.7}$

11. $2.93\overline{)89.431}$ $\qquad$ **12.** $6.74\overline{)215.7}$ $\qquad$ **13.** $4.21\overline{)19.472}$ $\qquad$ **14.** $5.28\overline{)29.531}$

15. $0.93\overline{)16.489}$ $\qquad$ **16.** $0.81\overline{)4.813}$ $\qquad$ **17.** $12.9\overline{)49.73}$ $\qquad$ **18.** $47.3\overline{)928.34}$

19. $61.5\overline{)453.2}$ $\qquad$ **20.** $78.4\overline{)76.9}$ $\qquad$ **21.** $22.5\overline{)245.73}$ $\qquad$ **22.** $53.9\overline{)543.12}$

23. $29.7\overline{)7849.2}$ $\qquad$ **24.** $8.91\overline{)514.3}$ $\qquad$ **25.** $37.8\overline{)41.98}$ $\qquad$ **26.** $92.8\overline{)764.3}$

27. $13.6\overline{)46.19}$ $\qquad$ **28.** $28.2\overline{)910}$ $\qquad$ **29.** $15.3\overline{)670.2}$ $\qquad$ **30.** $4.91\overline{)14.80}$

Estimate to correctly place the decimal point in the quotient.

$$\begin{array}{r} 30 \\ 31.\ 78.4\overline{)235.81} \end{array} \qquad \begin{array}{r} 1\ 5 \\ 32.\ 37.6\overline{)578.9} \end{array} \qquad \begin{array}{r} 88 \\ 33.\ 83.2\overline{)732.55} \end{array} \qquad \begin{array}{r} 19 \\ 34.\ 2.89\overline{)56.89} \end{array}$$

$$\begin{array}{r} 52 \\ 35.\ 55.7\overline{)289.76} \end{array} \qquad \begin{array}{r} 34 \\ 36.\ 12.7\overline{)43.81} \end{array} \qquad \begin{array}{r} 19 \\ 37.\ 37.9\overline{)7.338} \end{array} \qquad \begin{array}{r} 28 \\ 38.\ 9.46\overline{)270.80} \end{array}$$

$$\begin{array}{r} 2\ 6 \\ 39.\ 1.3\overline{)33.8} \end{array} \qquad \begin{array}{r} 45 \\ 40.\ 54.7\overline{)246.15} \end{array} \qquad \begin{array}{r} 171 \\ 41.\ 3.8\overline{)6.498} \end{array} \qquad \begin{array}{r} 1\ 32 \\ 42.\ 2.89\overline{)381.48} \end{array}$$

$$\begin{array}{r} 8\ 2 \\ 43.\ 41.3\overline{)3386.6} \end{array} \qquad \begin{array}{r} 289 \\ 44.\ 4.87\overline{)14.0743} \end{array} \qquad \begin{array}{r} 203 \\ 45.\ 2.5\overline{)5075} \end{array} \qquad \begin{array}{r} 25 \\ 46.\ 69.7\overline{)174.25} \end{array}$$

Up, Up and Away

Estimate.

47. An airplane flew 1449 km in 2.8 hours. About how far did it fly in 1 hour?

★ **48.** An airplane uses 1.9 L of gasoline per minute. About how many hours can it fly on 705 L of gasoline?

★ **49.** The Apollo 10 command module reached a speed of 39,896.16 km/h. How many kilometers per minute is this?

Changing Metric Units

Dr. Brodie bought new file cabinets that are 70 cm tall. Will they fit under a shelf that is 1.2 m tall?

When you compare measurements, you should be certain they are written in the same units.

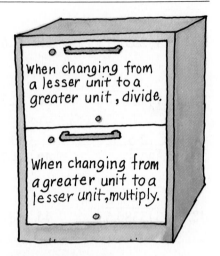

When changing from a lesser unit to a greater unit, divide.

When changing from a greater unit to a lesser unit, multiply.

You can write 1.2 m as 120 cm.
$$1 \text{ m} = 100 \text{ cm}$$
$$1.2 \text{ m} \times 100 = 120 \text{ cm}$$

Since 70 cm is less than 120 cm, the cabinets will fit under the shelf.

You can change any unit in the metric system by multiplying or dividing by 10, 100, or 1000.

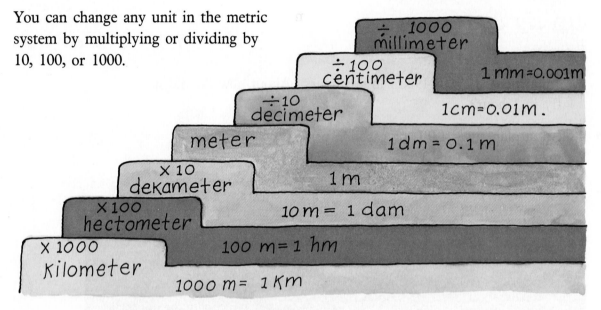

Exercises

Multiply by 100 to write the measure in centimeters.

1. 3.8 m	**2.** 14.9 m	**3.** 7.2 m	**4.** 3.67 m	**5.** 75.71 m
6. 0.9 m	**7.** 0.54 m	**8.** 17 m	**9.** 32.98 m	**10.** 0.315 m

Multiply by 1000 to write the measure in meters.

11. 4.8 km	**12.** 63.9 km	**13.** 115.7 km	**14.** 9.08 km	**15.** 0.7 km
16. 3.71 km	**17.** 22.4 km	**18.** 16.9 km	**19.** 0.31 km	**20.** 11.006 km

Divide by 10 to write the measure in centimeters.

21. 0.51 mm　**22.** 63.4 mm　**23.** 115.6 mm

24. 0.01 mm　**25.** 482.6 mm　**26.** 7.21 mm

Write the missing number.

27. 48.9 m = ▨ cm　**28.** 0.86 km = ▨ m

29. 598 cm = ▨ m　**30.** 9.51 km = ▨ m

31. 751 m = ▨ km　**32.** 0.25 cm = ▨ mm

33. 27 mm = ▨ cm　**34.** 0.08 m = ▨ mm

35. 0.6 m = ▨ cm　**36.** 117.2 m = ▨ km

37. 168 cm = ▨ m　**38.** 90.7 cm = ▨ m

39. 0.85 km = ▨ m　**40.** 82.6 cm = ▨ mm

Office Space

True or false? Write *T* or *F*.

41. An extension cord that is 58 m long will be long enough to connect a typewriter to an outlet that is 485 cm away.

42. A wastebasket that is 36.5 cm tall will fit under a desk that is 0.66 m high.

★ **43.** A photograph that is 88 mm wide and 128 mm long will fit in a frame that is 9.1 cm wide and 11 cm long.

Divide. (*pages 154–155*)

1. $6\overline{)5.4}$　　　　　**2.** $48\overline{)1564.8}$

3. $72\overline{)417.6}$　　　　**4.** $29\overline{)194.59}$

Multiply or divide. (*pages 156–157*)

5. 100×0.17　　　**6.** $4.7 \div 100$

7. 1000×9.08　　**8.** $75.6 \div 1000$

Divide. (*pages 158–159*)

9. $0.8\overline{)9.92}$　　　　**10.** $2.7\overline{)1.161}$

11. $13.9\overline{)75.06}$　　　**12.** $61.2\overline{)201.96}$

Divide. (*pages 160–161*)

13. $1.72\overline{)8.772}$　　　**14.** $3.61\overline{)27.797}$

15. $0.123\overline{)0.4674}$　　**16.** $0.505\overline{)0.303}$

Divide. Round the quotient to the nearest tenth. (*pages 162–163*)

17. $0.5\overline{)68.37}$　　　**18.** $3.91\overline{)48.6}$

19. $4.8\overline{)31.08}$　　　**20.** $2.7\overline{)152.5}$

Estimate the quotient. (*pages 164–165*)

21. $6.1\overline{)54.2}$　　　**22.** $2.5\overline{)58.2}$

23. $0.8\overline{)39.7}$　　　**24.** $71.6\overline{)628.9}$

Write the missing number. (*pages 166–167*)

25. 3.2 m = ▨ cm

26. 67.5 km = ▨ m

27. 47.8 cm = ▨ mm

Problem Solving · MULTI-STEP PROBLEMS

1	Understand
2	Plan
3	Work
4	Answer

The East Egg Athletic Club is buying new soccer equipment. They are ordering everything from the Gold Medal Sports' catalog.

Order Form

GOLD MEDAL SPORTS

Ship to: *East Egg Athletic Club*

Item	How many?	What is it?	Price	Cost
22B	15	soccer uniform	$12.50	$187.50
25R	5	soccer ball	$26.99	$134.95
		Total Cost		$322.45
		Postage and Handling		10.00
		Total Order		$332.45

To find the total cost of the order, you need to solve four small problems.

◁ $15 \times \$12.50 = \$187.50$

◁ $5 \times \$26.99 = \$134.95$

◁ $\$187.50 + \$134.95 = \$322.45$

◁ $\$322.45 + \$10.00 = \$332.45$

Complete the order form.

1.

Order Form

GOLD MEDAL SPORTS

Ship to: *Buckeye Senior Citizen Center*

Item	How many?	What is it?	Price	Cost
173	5	billiard cue	$21.99	?
267	4	inflatable raft	$57.85	?
		Total Cost		?
		Postage and Handling		$12.50
		Total Order		?

2.

Order Form

GOLD MEDAL SPORTS

Ship to: *Great Neck Cycle Club*

Item	How many?	What is it?	Price	Cost
122X	25	bikes	$179.99	?
317X	25	helmets	$14.50	?
482C	1	whistle	$3.98	?
		Total Cost		?
		Postage and Handling		$37.50
		Total Order		?

Solve.

3. Gerald wants to buy the following items:

- speedometer for $9.99
- tire pump for $18.99
- mirror for $3.99

How much change should he receive if he pays with 2 twenty dollar bills?

4. Gloria is using Gold Medal's Layaway Plan. She is buying the following:

- a table tennis table for $48.97
- a set of paddles for $15.88
- three table tennis balls for $1.98

Gloria made a deposit of $12.50. How much more does she owe?

5. Heinrich bought a basketball for $21.99. He returned it and bought a football for $13.99 and a jersey for $10.99. How much more does he owe the store?

6. Paulette wants to buy a bike that costs $88.99. She has saved $35.00. How long will it take to save the rest of the money if she saves $5.00 each week?

7.

Gold Medal Sports
334 Marathon Way
Olympia, WA 98507

Dear Sir/Madam,

We recently ordered 50 life jackets at a price of $18.95 each. We received a bill for $1037.50, which is incorrect.

Please send a corrected bill as soon as possible.

Sincerely,

Sandra Pinney
Cheboygan Boat Club

a. What should the corrected amount be?

b. How much was the club overcharged?

★ **8.** Gold Medal Sports gives G & M stamps on all purchases. Customers receive 1 stamp for every 25¢ spent up to $50.00. Amounts over $50.00 receive 1 stamp for every 10¢ spent. How many stamps would you receive if you bought hiking boots for $39.95 and a first-aid kit for $12.75?

Unit Review

1. Begin with the number at start. Follow the directions at each step on the race track. Your answer is the number of meters from start to finish.

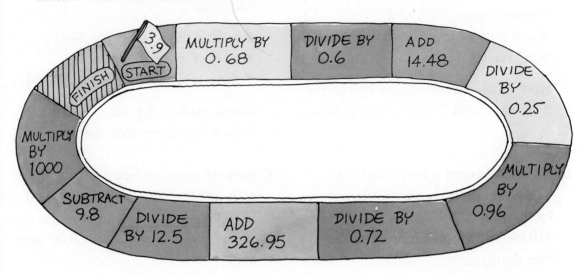

Multiply.

2. 0.439
×100

3. 0.036
×1000

4. 74.8
×3.26

5. 509
×0.87

Divide. Round the quotient to the nearest hundredth.

6. 0.03)‾0.727‾

7. 0.74)‾4647.3‾

8. 0.68)‾7.8609‾

9. 14.8)‾108.72‾

Estimate the product or quotient. Match.

10. 11.12 × 47.3   **A.** 5

11. 951.3 × 5.1   **B.** 50

12. 3.9)‾23.246‾   **C.** 500

13. 14.6)‾451.03‾   **D.** 5000

Solve.

14. Barry ran 3.2 km on Monday, 4.3 on Tuesday, 1.9 on Wednesday, and 3.7 on Thursday. If his goal for the week is 15 km, how many more kilometers must he run?

Multiply. (*pages 146–151*)

1. 5.9	**2.** 4.27	**3.** 6.8	**4.** 31.9	**5.** 0.23
$\times 13$	$\times 5.6$	$\times 4.32$	$\times 0.003$	$\times 0.08$

Divide. (*pages 154–155*)

6. $3\overline{)8.7}$　　　　**7.** $8\overline{)3.68}$　　　　**8.** $29\overline{)19.72}$　　　　**9.** $34\overline{)0.918}$

Multiply or divide. (*pages 156–157*)

10. 1000×56.8　　**11.** $49.83 \div 100$　　**12.** 100×0.71　　**13.** $13.09 \div 10$

Divide. (*pages 158–161*)

14. $0.6\overline{)1.494}$　　　**15.** $0.63\overline{)8.82}$　　　**16.** $0.018\overline{)9.567}$　　　**17.** $0.302\overline{)157.04}$

Divide. Round the quotient to the nearest hundredth. (*pages 162–163*)

18. $9\overline{)16}$　　　　　**19.** $7\overline{)3.2}$　　　　**20.** $5.5\overline{)22}$　　　　**21.** $0.38\overline{)1.61}$

Estimate. (*pages 152–153; 164–165*)

22. $6.2\overline{)43.81}$　　　**23.** $0.9\overline{)72.85}$　　　**24.** 0.19　　　**25.** 419.8
　　　　　　　　　　　　　　　　　　　　$\times 7.6$　　　　　$\times 2.23$

Write the missing number. (*pages 166–167*)

26. 4.2 cm = ▦ m

27. 0.5 km = ▦ m

28. 15.9 m = ▦ cm

29. 68.2 cm = ▦ mm

Solve. (*pages 168–169*)

30. Nancy bought a thermometer for $37.50 and two bird feeders that cost $29.95 each. How much change should she receive from $100?

31. Isaac needs a sweatshirt and shorts. Sweatshirts cost $4.98 and $6.98. Shorts cost $10.98 and $13.49. What is the most he can spend? the least?

Extra practice on page 389

Enrichment

Arrangements

Benjamin Raymond Arthur Turner
wants to use his initials for a
4-letter code for his savings account.
How many different combinations
are possible if each letter is used
only once?

You can list all the possible ways of writing the initials.

BRAT	BRTA	BTRA	BTAR	BATR	BART
TBRA	TBAR	TABR	TARB	TRAB	TRBA
ATBR	ATRB	ABTR	ABRT	ARBT	ARTB
RATB	RABT	RTAB	RTBA	RBTA	RBAT

Since this is a lot of work, let's look at the problem in another way.

With 1 initial there is only 1 possible code.	$1 \times 1 = 1$
With 2 initials there are 2 possible codes.	$2 \times 1 = 2$
With 3 initials there are 6 possible codes.	$3 \times 2 \times 1 = 6$
With 4 initials there are 24 possible codes.	$4 \times 3 \times 2 \times 1 = 24$

Use a pattern like the one above to solve the problem.

1. How many different radio stations can be identified using the
call letters K, L, and M. Assume the letters can't be
repeated.

2. In how many ways can Hugh, Shelly, Elliot, and Norma line
up at the lunch counter?

3. A witness to a robbery told the police that the getaway car
had these numbers on the license plate: 4, 7, 3, 2, 8, and 9.
How many license plates will the police have to check if they
don't know the order?

4. How many different batting orders are possible for a baseball
team with 9 players?

Here's another way to look at the pattern you just used. Suppose there are *a* ways of doing one thing, *b* ways of doing a second thing, and *c* ways of doing a third thing. Then there are $a \times b \times c$ ways of doing the three things.

There are 15 people in a spelling contest. In how many different ways can 3 prizes be won if no one can win more than one prize?

Here's how to use the rule.

There are 15 people who can win 1st prize.

After the 1st prize is won, there are 14 people who can win 2nd prize.

Then there are 13 people left to win 3rd prize.

Altogether, there are $15 \times 14 \times 13 = 2730$ ways to win the three prizes.

Solve.

5. Suppose you have 7 books on a shelf. How many ways can you choose 4 of the books?

6. Your new house needs a number. You can choose any 4-digit number using the digits from 1 through 9. How many choices do you have if no number can be repeated? if numbers can be repeated?

7. Suppose you want to fly from Philadelphia to Kansas City and then take a bus to Pasadena. There are 3 different airlines and 4 different bus companies you can use. How many different ways can you make the round trip without using any plane or bus twice?

Maintaining Skills

Measure to the nearest centimeter and millimeter.

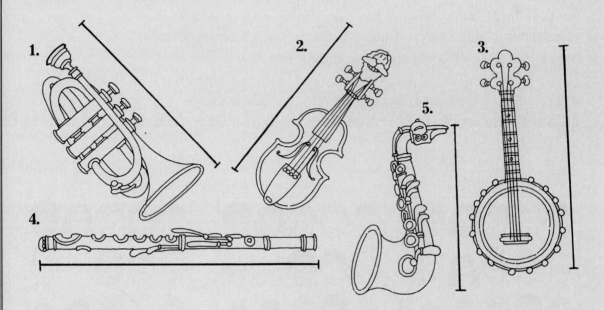

1.

2.

3.

4.

5.

Add or subtract.

6. 3.407
    +0.596

7. 29.05
    − 6.3

8. 13.038
    −12.929

9. 65.48
    + 7.543

10. 5.02 + 62.831 + 0.94   11. 20.048 − 0.8134   12. 65.4 − 7.368

Correct or incorrect? Write C or I.

13. 6 lb 8 oz
    +1 lb 9 oz
    _____
     8 lb 9 oz

14. 6 ft 3 in.
    −4 ft 6 in.
    _____
     2 ft 3 in.

15. 4 gal 1 qt
    −3 gal 3 qt
    _____
         2 qt

16. 2 yd 1 ft
    +1 yd 2 ft
    _____
         4 yd

Write the product.

17. 6^2 18. 3^3 19. 2^4 20. 8^2 21. 4^1 22. 5^2

Solve.

23. The orchestra played four pieces last night. The first was
    15.23 minutes long, the second was 9.03 minutes, the third
    was 21.94 minutes, and the fourth was 11.6 minutes. How
    long did the orchestra play?

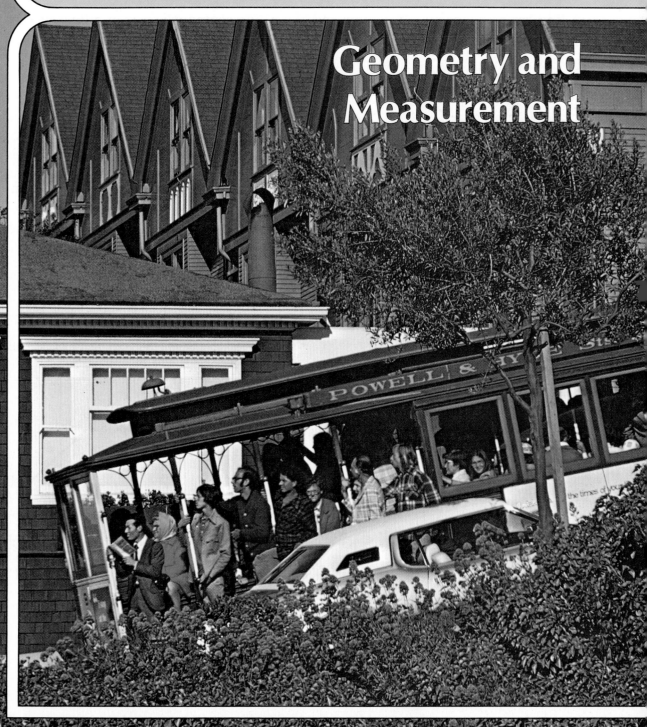

Cable cars were invented to navigate the hilly streets of San Francisco. You can see the steep angle at which this cable car is descending one street. Can you find other geometric figures hidden in the photo?

7

Geometry and Measurement

Lines, Segments, Rays, and Angles

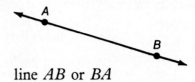

line *AB* or *BA*

A **line** has no endpoints. It goes on and on in two directions.

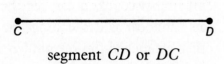

segment *CD* or *DC*

A line **segment** is part of a line. It has two endpoints.

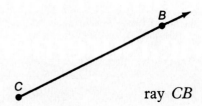

ray *CB*

A **ray** is a part of a line. It has only one endpoint. To name a ray state the endpoint first.

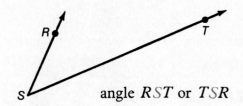

angle *RST* or *TSR*

Two rays with a common endpoint form an **angle**. Point *S* is called the **vertex** of angle *RST*. To name an angle always read the vertex letter in the middle.

Exercises

Name the figure.

Example:  line *XY*

1.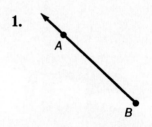

2.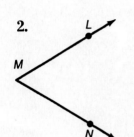

3.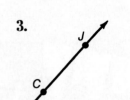

4.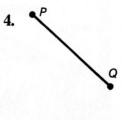

5.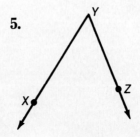

6.

7.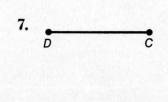

8.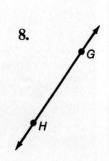

176

9. Name two rays.

10. Name three angles.

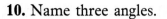
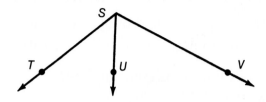

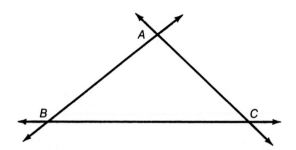

Use the figure at the left.

11. Name three lines.

12. Name six rays.

13. Name three angles.

Use the figure at the right.

14. Name four lines.

15. Name six segments.

16. Name ten rays.

17. Name seven angles.

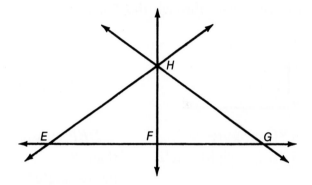

Figures Around Us

Use the picture below.

18. List three examples each of segments, rays, and angles.

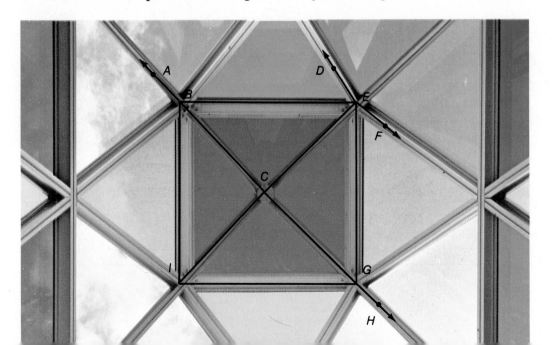

Acute, Obtuse, and Right Angles

Angles are measured using a small unit angle called a **degree.**
The instrument used is called a **protractor.**

Here's how to measure angle ABC
(written $\angle ABC$).

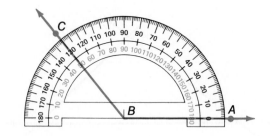

- Place the center of the protractor on
  the vertex, B.

- Place the base of the protractor on
  the ray BA.

- Read the measure of the angle where
  ray BC passes through the scale.

Angle ABC measures 130 degrees (130°).
$$\angle ABC = 130°$$

$\angle ABC$ measures 90°.
$\angle ABC$ is a **right angle.**

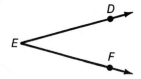

$\angle DEF$ measures less
than 90°. $\angle DEF$ is an
acute angle.

$\angle GHI$ measures more than
90°, but less than 180°.
$\angle GHI$ is an **obtuse angle.**

Exercises

Write A, O, or R to show whether the angle is acute, obtuse,
or right.

1.

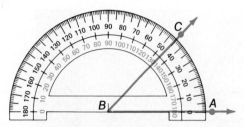

2.

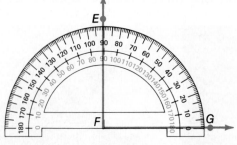

3.

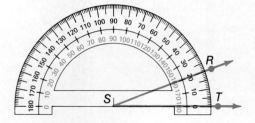

4.

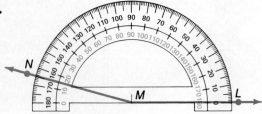

Write *A*, *O*, or *R* to show whether the angle is acute, obtuse, or right.

5. 27° **6.** 98° **7.** 46° **8.** 120° **9.** 90° **10.** 75°

11. 106° **12.** 88° **13.** 31° **14.** 90° **15.** 91° **16.** 168°

Measure the angle. Write *A*, *O*, or *R* to show whether it is acute, obtuse, or right.

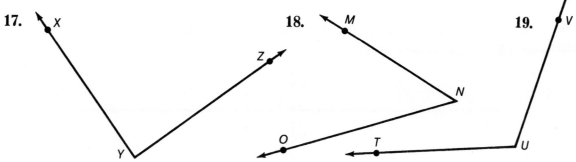

17. **18.** **19.**

Drawing Angles

You can use a protractor to draw angles. Here's how.

a. To draw ∠*DCE* with a measure of 45°, first draw ray *CD*.

b. Place the protractor on ray *CD*. Make sure the center is on *C* and the zero mark is on the ray.

c. Using the scale with the zero mark, mark point *E* at 45°.

d. Draw ray *CE*.

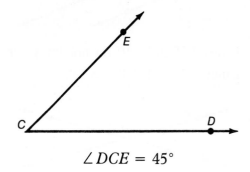

∠*DCE* = 45°

Draw an angle of the given size.

20. 20° **21.** 80° **22.** 90° **23.** 125° **24.** 38° **25.** 145°

Parallel, Perpendicular, and Intersecting Lines

Lines AB and CD meet or **intersect** in point E.

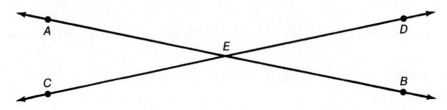

Line UW and XY intersect to form right angles (90°). Lines UW and XY are **perpendicular.**

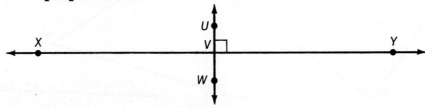

Lines LM and OP do not intersect. They are **parallel.**

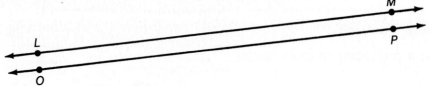

Exercises

Complete.

1.

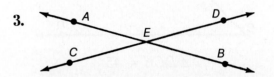

Lines XY and ZW do not intersect.
Lines XY and ZW are ▨.

2.

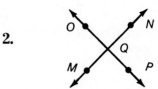

Lines MN and OP form right
angles. Lines MN and OP are ▨.

3.

Lines AB and CD intersect but don't
form right angles. Lines AB and
CD are not ▨.

4.

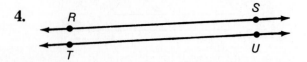

Lines RS and TU are parallel.
Lines RS and TU do not ▨.

Write *parallel*, *perpendicular*, or *intersecting* to describe the way
the lines look to you.

5. lines *AB* and *CD*

6. lines *EF* and *AI*

7. lines *IJ* and *BJ*

8. lines *EF* and *GH*

9. lines *DC* and *BJ*

10. lines *GH* and *AI*

11. lines *AI* and *IJ*

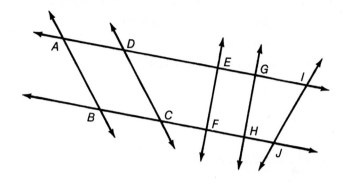

Tell if the statement is true or false.
Write *T* or *F*.

12. Perpendicular lines must intersect.

13. Intersecting lines must form right
angles.

14. Parallel lines must intersect.

15. Intersecting lines are sometimes
perpendicular.

16. Lines can be both intersecting and
perpendicular.

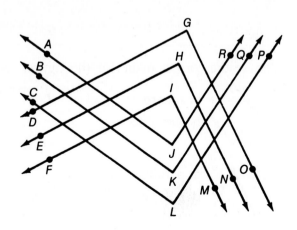

Math Around Us

Use the figure at the right.

17. Find three examples of parallel
lines.

18. Find three examples of
perpendicular lines.

19. Find three examples of
intersecting lines that are not
perpendicular.

Polygons and Quadrilaterals

A figure formed by joining three or more segments is called a **polygon.** The segments that form a polygon are called **sides.** The points where the sides intersect are called **vertexes.**

A four-sided polygon is called a **quadrilateral.**

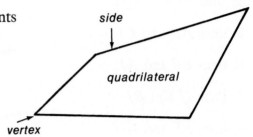

Some quadrilaterals have special properties.

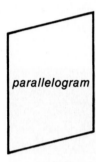

A **parallelogram** is a quadrilateral with opposite sides parallel.

A **rhombus** is a parallelogram with four equal sides.

A **trapezoid** is a quadrilateral with exactly one pair of opposite sides parallel.

A **rectangle** is a parallelogram with four right angles.

A **square** is a rhombus with four right angles.

Exercises

Choose the correct name for the figure. Write *a* or *b*.

1.   **a.** square   **b.** rhombus

2. **a.** rhombus   **b.** rectangle

3. **a.** trapezoid   **b.** square

4. **a.** parallelogram   **b.** polygon

5. 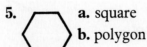 **a.** square   **b.** polygon

6. **a.** trapezoid   **b.** rhombus

Complete.

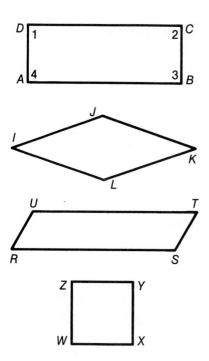

7. Quadrilateral *ABCD* is a rectangle. Angles 1, 2, 3, and 4 are ▓ angles.

8. Parallelogram *IJKL* is a rhombus. Sides *IJ*, *JK*, *KL*, and *LI* are ▓.

9. Quadrilateral *RSTU* is a parallelogram. The opposite sides are ▓.

10. Quadrilateral *WXYZ* is a square. It has four equal ▓ and four ▓ angles.

Shapes Have Names

All polygons have special names determined by the number of sides. A segment that joins two vertexes but is not a side is called a **diagonal.**

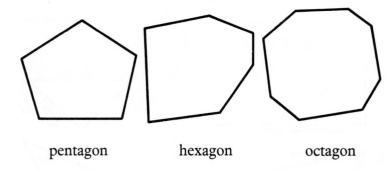

pentagon   hexagon   octagon

11. Complete the table.

Polygon	Number of		
	sides	vertexes	diagonals
Quadrilateral	?	?	?
Pentagon	?	?	?
Hexagon	?	?	?
Octagon	?	?	?

I live on a street in Dundee
And my house number's last digit's three.

The square of the first is the two digits reversed.

So what must my house number be?

Take a Break

Triangles

A three sided polygon is called a **triangle.**
Here are some triangles with special properties.

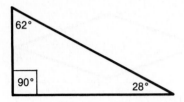

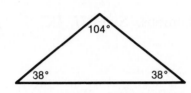

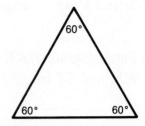

A **right** triangle has one
right angle.

An **isosceles** triangle has
two equal sides and two
equal angles.

An **equilateral** triangle
has three equal sides and
three equal angles.

The sum of the angles of any triangle is 180°. You can use this
fact to find $\angle BCA$ in the triangle below.

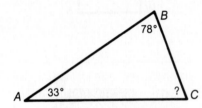

$\angle BAC + \angle ABC = 33° + 78° = 111°$
$\angle BCA = 180° - 111°$
$= 69°$

Exercises

Is the triangle right, equilateral, or isosceles? Write *R*, *E*, or *I*.

1.

2.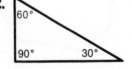

3.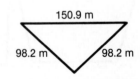

4.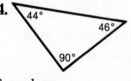

5.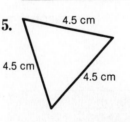

6.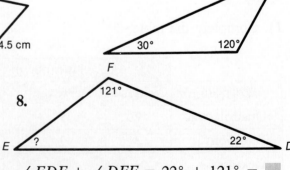

Complete.

7.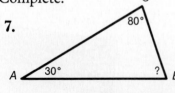

8.

$\angle CAB + \angle BCA = 30° + 80° = \blacksquare$
$\angle ABC = 180° - \blacksquare = \blacksquare$

$\angle EDF + \angle DFE = 22° + 121° = \blacksquare$
$\angle DEF = 180° - \blacksquare = \blacksquare$

184

Is the triangle right, equilateral, or isosceles? Write *R*, *E*, or *I*.

9. sides: 3 cm, 7 cm, and 7 cm

10. sides: 4.5 m, 4.5 m, and 4.5 m

11. angles: 35°, 55°, and 90°

12. angles: 37°, 90°, and 53°

13. angles: 60°, 60°, and 60°

14. angles: 55°, 55°, and 70°

15. sides: 6.2 cm, 4 cm, and 6.2 cm

16. sides: 7 m, 7 m, and 7 m

How big is the third angle of the triangle?

17. 20°, 30°	**18.** 45°, 20°
19. 10°, 90°	**20.** 35°, 35°
21. 70°, 70°	**22.** 65°, 10°
23. 80°, 33°	**24.** 45°, 95°
25. 29°, 29°	**26.** 37°, 82°

Angle Tangle

★ **27.** Compute the measure of the angle.

a. ∠*DBC*	**b.** ∠*ABD*
c. ∠*BAC*	**d.** ∠*ADB*

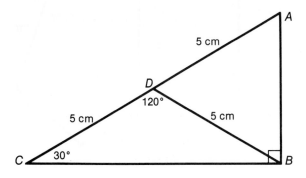

Use the figure below.
(*pages 176–177*)

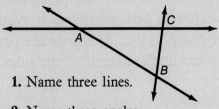

1. Name three lines.

2. Name three angles.

Write *A*, *O*, or *R* to show whether the angle is acute, obtuse, or right.
(*pages 178–179*)

3. 37°	**4.** 68°
5. 90°	**6.** 105°

Write *parallel*, *perpendicular*, or *intersecting* to describe the lines.
(*pages 180–181*)

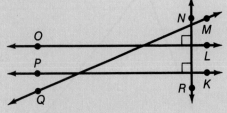

7. lines *KP* and *RN*

8. lines *OL* and *PK*

9. lines *MQ* and *RN*

Choose the correct name for the figure. Write *a* or *b*. (*pages 182–183*)

10.
    a. square
    b. rectangle

How big is the third angle of the triangle? (*pages 184–185*)

11. 30°, 55°	**12.** 98°, 10°

Perimeter

The **perimeter** of a figure is the distance around the figure.

Rita needs to know the perimeter of the window to decide how much weather stripping to use. She finds the perimeter by adding the lengths of the sides.

$$\begin{array}{r} 90 \text{ cm} \\ 120 \text{ cm} \\ 90 \text{ cm} \\ +120 \text{ cm} \\ \hline \end{array}$$
perimeter = 420 cm

Rita needs 420 cm of weather stripping.

Exercises

What is the perimeter of the figure?

1.
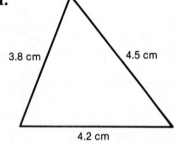
3.8 cm, 4.5 cm, 4.2 cm

2.
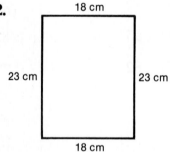
18 cm, 23 cm, 23 cm, 18 cm

3.
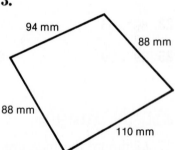
94 mm, 88 mm, 88 mm, 110 mm

4.
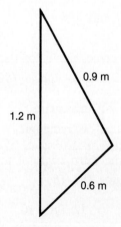
0.9 m, 1.2 m, 0.6 m

5.
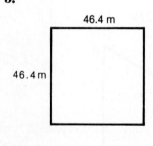
46.4 m, 46.4 m

6.
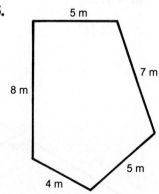
5 m, 8 m, 7 m, 4 m, 5 m

186

What is the perimeter of the triangle with sides of the given lengths?

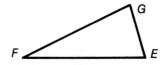

7. EF = 5.5 cm
FG = 4.9 cm
GE = 2.8 cm

8. EF = 8.8 m
FG = 3.7 m
GE = 6.4 m

9. EF = 50.34 cm
FG = 38.76 cm
GE = 21.09 cm

10. EF = 11.16 m
FG = 9.07 m
GE = 5.88 m

11. EF = 21 km
FG = 17.09 km
GE = 7 km

What is the perimeter of a figure with sides of the given lengths?

12. 4 cm, 5 cm, 2 cm, 1 cm

13. 7.5 cm, 8.2 cm, 3.2 cm, 5.9 cm

14. 2.1 m, 3.7 m, 8.4 m, 4.5 m

15. 9.5 km, 8.0 km, 7.5 km, 3.2 km

16. 27 mm, 38 mm, 41 mm, 29 mm

17. 56 mm, 38 mm, 92 mm, 31 mm

18. 4 sides, each 176 m

19. 3 sides, each 98.7 cm

Energy Saving

Solve.

20. How much weather stripping is needed for all three windows?

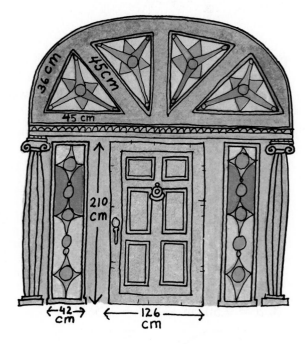

★ **21.** A roll of weather stripping is 27 m long. How many rolls are needed to weather-strip all the windows and the door?

Circles

In a circle the **diameter** (d) is twice as long as the **radius** (r).

$$d = 2 \times r$$

The **circumference** (C) is the distance around a circle. The quotient $C \div d$ is the same number for all circles. We use the symbol π, the Greek letter Pi, to stand for this number.

Although π has been calculated to thousands of decimal places, we usually use the rounded decimal 3.14 for π. We use the symbol $\approx$ to mean *is approximately equal to.*

$$\pi \approx 3.14$$

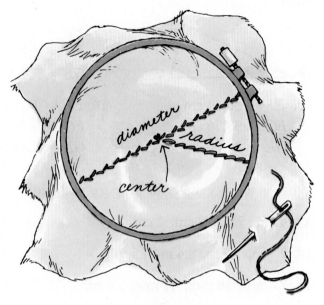

$$C \div d = \pi$$
$$C = \pi \times d$$
$$C \approx 3.14 \times d$$

Exercises

What is the circumference? Round answers to the nearest hundredth.

1. $d = 20$ mm $\qquad C = \pi \times d$
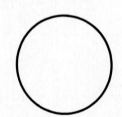 $\qquad \approx 3.14 \times$
$\qquad \approx$ ▨ mm

2. $d = 70$ cm $\qquad C = \pi \times d$
$\qquad \approx 3.14 \times$ ▨
$\qquad \approx$ ▨ cm

3. $d = 7.50$ cm $\qquad C = \pi \times d$
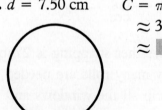 $\qquad \approx 3.14 \times$
$\qquad \approx$ ▨ cm

4. $d = 31.4$ m $\qquad C = \pi \times d$
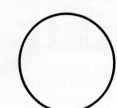 $\qquad \approx 3.14 \times$
$\qquad \approx$ ▨ m

What is the diameter of the circle with the given radius?

5. 30 cm   **6.** 40 cm   **7.** 16 m   **8.** 25 m   **9.** 35 m

10. 12 mm   **11.** 45 mm   **12.** 38 m   **13.** 167 cm   **14.** 22.9 mm

15. 83.6 m   **16.** 45.91 cm   **17.** 33.9 cm   **18.** 145.91 m   **19.** 32.6 mm

What is the circumference of the circle with the given diameter?
Round answers to the nearest hundredth.

20. 5 cm   **21.** 10 m   **22.** 100 mm   **23.** 30 cm   **24.** 45 mm

25. 15 m   **26.** 75 cm   **27.** 150 m   **28.** 20 mm   **29.** 0.36 cm

30. 69.71 m   **31.** 736 cm   **32.** 16.81 cm   **33.** 0.456 mm   **34.** 73.34 km

Moving in Circles

Solve.

35. A ferris wheel has a diameter of 15 m. How far will you travel if a ride makes 12 complete turns?

36. The diameter of Tim's bicycle wheel is 68 cm. How many centimeters will the wheel travel in 8 complete turns?

Use the figure at the right.

★ **37.** What is the distance around the track?

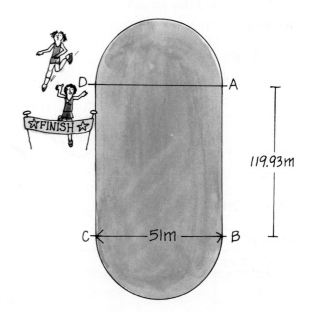

Calculator Corner

A rectangle in which the length divided by the width is about 1.6 is called a Golden Rectangle. Which of the following are Golden Rectangles?

$l = 0.8$ m $l = 0.71$ m $l = 57.6$ m $l = 119$ m
$w = 0.5$ m $w = 0.33$ m $w = 36.0$ m $w = 74.4$ m

Area of Rectangles and Right Triangles

The **area** of a figure is the amount of surface inside it.

You can count the square units to find the area of the rectangle.

In a right triangle the sides next to the right angle are called the base (*b*) and the height (*h*).

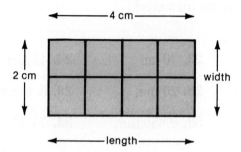

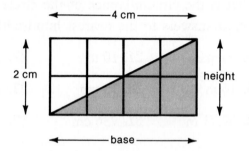

You can also find the area of a rectangle by multiplying the length (*l*) times the width (*w*).

$$A = l \times w$$
$$= 4 \times 2$$
$$= 8 \text{ cm}^2$$

8 square centimeters

The area of each right triangle shown above is half the area of the rectangle. You can find the area by multiplying the base times the height and dividing by 2.

$$A = (b \times h) \div 2$$
$$= (4 \times 2) \div 2$$
$$= 8 \div 2$$
$$= 4 \text{ cm}^2$$

4 square centimeters

Exercises

Complete.

1. 3 cm 5 cm

$$A = l \times w$$
$$= \blacksquare \times \blacksquare$$
$$= \blacksquare \text{ cm}^2$$

2. 7.3 m 2.1 m

$$A = l \times w$$
$$= \blacksquare \times \blacksquare$$
$$= \blacksquare \text{ m}^2$$

3. 7 cm 4 cm

$$A = (b \times h) \div 2$$
$$= (\blacksquare \times \blacksquare) \div 2$$
$$= \blacksquare \div 2$$
$$= \blacksquare \text{ cm}^2$$

4. 17 cm 24 cm

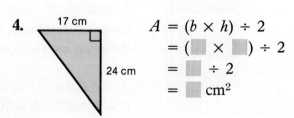

$$A = (b \times h) \div 2$$
$$= (\blacksquare \times \blacksquare) \div 2$$
$$= \blacksquare \div 2$$
$$= \blacksquare \text{ cm}^2$$

What is the area of the rectangle with the given length (*l*) and width (*w*)?

5. *l* = 8.1 cm
   w = 4.0 cm

6. *l* = 0.9 cm
   w = 0.9 cm

7. *l* = 2.3 cm
   w = 4.6 cm

8. *l* = 5.5 cm
   w = 3.0 cm

9. *l* = 170 m
   w = 50 m

10. *l* = 350 m
   w = 170 m

11. *l* = 17 km
   w = 17 km

12. *l* = 3.4 mm
   w = 1.2 mm

What is the area of the right triangle with the given base (*b*) and height (*h*)?

13. *b* = 14 cm
   h = 12 cm

14. *b* = 18 mm
   h = 14 mm

15. *b* = 30 cm
   h = 6 cm

16. *b* = 100 km
   h = 49 km

17. *b* = 22 cm
   h = 21 cm

18. *b* = 50 mm
   h = 30 mm

19. *b* = 9 m
   h = 4 m

20. *b* = 200 km
   h = 200 km

House and Garden

Solve.

21. A garden shaped like a rectangle is 32 m long and 28 m wide. How much fence is needed to enclose the garden?

22. There are two bare spots in the Gridley's back yard. Each is rectangular in shape and measures 20 m by 30 m. Is a bag of grass seed that covers 500 m² enough to cover both spots?

★ **23.** The Mascari's front porch measures 9 m by 5 m and their back porch measures 7 m by 5 m. Both floors are rectangular in shape. One can of paint will cover 45 m². How much paint do they need to paint both porch floors?

Area of a Circle

You can estimate the area (A) of the circle by counting the number of square centimeters that are shaded.

16 ☐ completely shaded

8 ☐ almost completely shaded

<u>+ 4</u> ◩ from other shaded areas

28 cm²

You can use the formula below to calculate the area more accurately.

$$A = \pi \times r^2$$

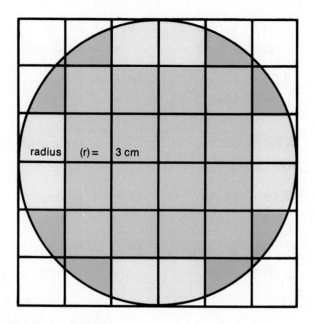
radius (r) = 3 cm

For the circle in the picture you use the formula like this.

$$A = \pi \times r^2$$
$$A \approx 3.14 \times 3^2$$
$$\approx 3.14 \times 9$$
$$\approx 28.26 \text{ cm}^2$$

Exercises

Complete to show the area of the circle. Round to the nearest hundredth.

1.

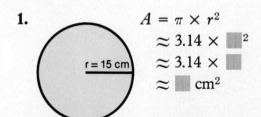
r = 15 cm

$A = \pi \times r^2$
$\approx 3.14 \times \blacksquare^2$
$\approx 3.14 \times \blacksquare$
$\approx \blacksquare$ cm²

2.

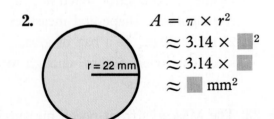
r = 22 mm

$A = \pi \times r^2$
$\approx 3.14 \times \blacksquare^2$
$\approx 3.14 \times \blacksquare$
$\approx \blacksquare$ mm²

3.

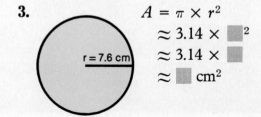
r = 7.6 cm

$A = \pi \times r^2$
$\approx 3.14 \times \blacksquare^2$
$\approx 3.14 \times \blacksquare$
$\approx \blacksquare$ cm²

4.

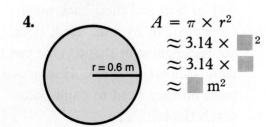
r = 0.6 m

$A = \pi \times r^2$
$\approx 3.14 \times \blacksquare^2$
$\approx 3.14 \times \blacksquare$
$\approx \blacksquare$ m²

What is the area of the circle with the given radius? Round to the nearest hundredth.

5. 2 cm	**6.** 10 m	**7.** 15 m
8. 8 mm	**9.** 20 cm	**10.** 11 cm
11. 7 m	**12.** 12 mm	**13.** 13 cm
14. 30 mm	**15.** 1.6 cm	**16.** 0.9 cm
17. 1.7 m	**18.** 14.8 m	**19.** 22.6 cm
20. 93 m	**21.** 117 cm	**22.** 27.5 m
23. 47.2 m	**24.** 91.5 cm	**25.** 38.2 mm

Work it Out

What is the area of the circle with the given diameter?

26. 6 cm   **27.** 200 cm   **28.** 43.6 cm

Solve.

★ **29.** How much outdoor carpeting is needed to cover the sidewalk between the pool and the fence?

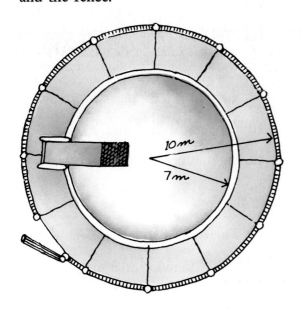

What is the perimeter of the figure with sides of the given lengths? (*pages 186–187*)

1. 7 cm, 12 cm, 6 cm

2. 3.8 cm, 2.6 cm, 4.5 cm

3. 4 m, 28 m, 17 m, 22 m

4. 9.3 m, 2.7 m, 5.4 m, 8.8 m

What is the circumference of the circle with the given diameter? Round to the nearest hundredth. (*pages 188–189*)

5. 12 cm	**6.** 38 cm
7. 7.5 cm	**8.** 16.2 cm

What is the area of the rectangle with the given length (l) and width (w)? (*pages 190–191*)

9. $l = 25$ m	**10.** $l = 38.6$ cm
$w = 5$ m	$w = 10.0$ cm

What is the area of the right triangle with the given base (b) and height (h)?

11. $b = 7$ m	**12.** $b = 42$ cm
$h = 9$ m	$h = 6$ cm

What is the area of the circle with the given radius? Round to the nearest hundredth. (*pages 192–193*)

13. 7 cm	**14.** 6.1 cm
15. 0.8 mm	**16.** 3.5 m

Problem Solving · WRITING EQUATIONS

When you solve word problems it's helpful to be able to write number phrases and equations for word phrases and sentences.

The Hongs bought several tickets to the amusement park for $2.50 each.

Let c be the total cost of the tickets.

Let n be the number of tickets bought.

You can write an equation that shows the total cost of the tickets.

The total cost is the number of tickets times $2.50.

$$c = n \times \$2.50$$

Write the word phrase as a number phrase.

Example.   word phrase ⟹ number phrase
            a minus 12 $a - 12$

1. 6.4 times n **2.** 0.8 less than x **3.** 9.14 more than a

4. the product of 15 and n **5.** 0.26 minus a **6.** 1.2 plus y

7. the quotient of r divided by 3   **8.** the number of hours in n days

9. the number of pennies in t dollars   **10.** the sum of 16.8 and y

11. the difference of 0.47 minus x **12.** the number of days in x weeks

Write an equation for the word sentence. Solve the equation.

13. The product of 6 and w is 4.2.   **14.** The sum of n and 7.25 is 93.6.

15. The quotient of 7.2 divided by 9 is y.   **16.** The difference of b minus 4.87 is 2.9.

Write a number phrase to complete the sentence.

Example.   Ron is 5 cm taller than Joe.
Let j = Joe's height.
Then $j + 5$ = Ron's height.

17. Lynn spent $6.00 more than Pam.
Let p = the amount Pam spent.
Then ▨ = the amount Lynn spent.

18. Norman's books cost $7.50 each.
Let b = the number of books.
Then ▨ = the cost of the books.

19. Liz weighs 8.3 kg less than Donna.
Let w = Donna's weight. Then
▨ = Liz's weight.

20. The price of gas is increased by
$.12. Let p = the original price of
gas. Then ▨ = the new price of gas.

21. Henry, Bo, Mia, and Phil shared the
cost of their dinner equally. Let
c = the cost of the dinner. Then
▨ = the amount paid by each
person.

22. Dave rented a typewriter for $3.50
an hour. Let h = the number of
hours Dave had the typewriter.
Then ▨ = the total cost of the
rental.

Match each problem with an equation. Solve the equation.

23. Each ride at the park costs $.75.
What is the cost of 25 rides?

24. Curt scored 25 points on the ring
toss. He needs 75 points to win.
How many more points does he need?

25. The Glee Club won $75 worth of
free tickets to the park. There are
25 members in the club. How much
is each member's free ticket worth?

A. $75 \div 25 = b$

B. $75 \times 25 = a$

C. $75 + 25 = y$

D. $75 - 25 = n$

Write an equation for the problem. Use
it to complete the table.

★ **26.** You need a total of 75 points to win
a kaleidoscope.
Let n = the number of points
you've scored already.
Let p = the number of points
you need to win.

n	7	13	38	46	59
p	?	?	?	?	?

Use the figure at the right.

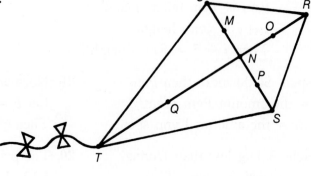

1. Name four segments.

2. Name four angles.

3. Name two lines.

4. Name four rays.

5. Measure ∠RST.

6. Measure ∠QTS.

Use the figure at the right. Tell whether the statement is true or false. Write *T* or *F*.

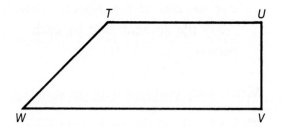

7. Sides *UT* and *WV* are parallel.

8. Angle *TUV* is an acute angle.

9. Angle *WTU* is an obtuse angle.

10. Figure *TUVW* is a quadrilateral.

How big is the third angle of the triangle? Choose the correct answer. Write *a* or *b*.

11. 50°, 20°
   a. 110° **b.** 35°

12. 25°, 40°
   a. 115° **b.** 25°

13. 72°, 16°
   a. 104° **b.** 92°

14. 130°, 8°
   a. 42° **b.** 50°

Use the figure at the right.

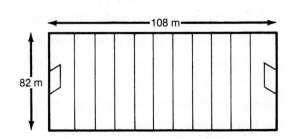

15. How much artificial grass is needed to cover the field?

16. How much tape is needed to make a border around the field?

Use the figure at the right.

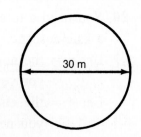

17. How much canvas is needed to cover the fish pond?

18. How much fence is needed to enclose the pond?

Use the figure at the right. (*pages 176–177*)

1. Name three segments.

2. Name four rays.

3. Name three lines.

4. Name three angles.

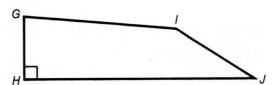

Measure the angle. (*pages 178–179*)

5.

Is the statement true or false? Write *T* or *F*. (*pages 180–183*)

6. Sides *GH* and *GI* are perpendicular.

7. Angle *GHJ* is a right angle.

8. Angle *IJH* is an acute angle.

How big is the third angle of the triangle? (*pages 184–185*)

9. 45°, 45°   10. 50°, 60°   11. 88°, 35°   12. 120°, 50°

What is the perimeter of the figure with sides of the given lengths?
(*pages 186–187*)

13. 20 cm, 35 cm, 45 cm

14. 0.8 m, 1.5 m 2.7 m, 4.2 m

15. 4 sides: 1.8 cm each

16. 63 m, 63 m, 25 m, 25 m

What is the circumference of the circle with the given diameter?
(*pages 188–189*)

17. 45 cm   18. 39 m   19. 8.2 m   20. 7.5 m

Solve. (*pages 190–193*)

21. A rug is 6 m long and 4.5 m wide. Will it cover an area of 25 m²?

22. A round window has a radius of 2.5 m. What is its area?

Extra practice on page 391

Venn Diagrams

A mathematician named Venn
used pictures when he had a yen
to show logical thought
when others had sought
to say it was too hard for them.

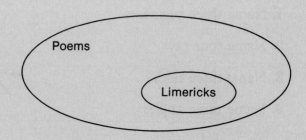

The diagram shows that
  a. *All* limericks are poems.
  b. *Some* poems are limericks.
  c. *If* a verse is a limerick *then* it
  is a poem.

The diagram shows that some but not
all poems are limericks. You cannot be
sure that if a verse is a poem, it is a
limerick. It may be some other kind of
poem.

Use the diagrams to help you. Write *T* or *F* to tell whether each
statement is true or false.

1.

a. All plums are prunes.
b. Some plums are prunes.
c. If a fruit is a prune then it is a
plum.

2.

a. All triangles are polygons.
b. If it is a quadrilateral then it is a
polygon.
c. All polygons are quadrilaterals or
triangles.

Use the diagram to tell which statement is true. Write *a* or *b*.

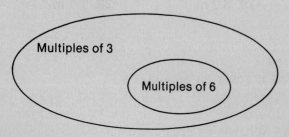

3. a. If a number is a multiple of 6
then it is a multiple of 3.
  b. If a number is a multiple of 3
then it is a multiple of 6.

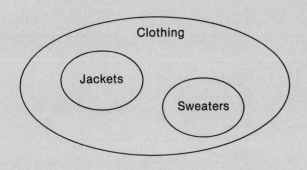

4. a. All pieces of clothing are jackets.
   b. If a garment is a sweater, then it is a piece of clothing.

Draw a Venn diagram for the statements.

5. a. All triangles are polygons.
   b. Some polygons are quadrilaterals.

6. a. All bears are mammals.
   b. Some mammals are whales.

7. a. All diamonds are things that shine.
   b. If a stone is a diamond then it is a thing that shines.

8. a. All tennis games are racket games.
   b. If a game is badminton it is a racket game.

Use the Venn diagrams to write a correct if-then statement.

9.

Spots

Blots

10.

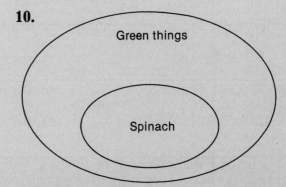

11.

Animals with 4 legs

Rhinoceros

12.

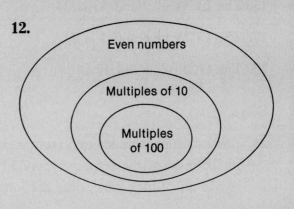

Maintaining Skills

Match the word name with the decimal.

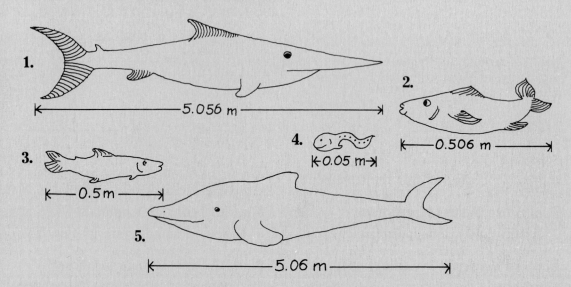

1. 5.056 m
2. 0.506 m
3. 0.5 m
4. 0.05 m
5. 5.06 m

A. 506 thousandths meters

B. 5 and 5 tenths meters

C. 5 and 56 thousandths meters

D. 5 tenths meters

E. 5 and 6 hundredths meters

F. 5 hundredths meters

Write <, >, or = to compare the numbers.

6. 0.9 ▓ 0.82

7. 0.73 ▓ 0.730

8. 0.407 ▓ 0.207

9. 0.380 ▓ 0.308

10. 0.1031 ▓ 0.103

11. 0.965 ▓ 0.9065

12. 0.6201 ▓ 0.6210

13. 0.893 ▓ 0.8930

14. 0.578 ▓ 0.587

True or False? Write *T* or *F.*

15. The LCM of 2 and 12 is 24.

16. The GCF of 19 and 33 is 1.

17. The LCM of 8 and 3 is 24.

18. The GCF of 24 and 32 is 8.

19. The GCF of 8 and 12 is 8.

20. The LCM of 12 and 20 is 2.

Solve.

21. Three whales were spotted from a ship. The first was 18.305 m long, the second was 17.307 m, the third measured 18.315 m. Which whale was the longest?

Fractions

Offshore drilling rigs are used for searching for oil under the ocean. They may perch on floating stands or stand on long legs anchored to the ocean floor. In the near future, $\frac{2}{5}$ of our oil may come from offshore wells.

8

Meaning of Fractions

The garden is divided into 3 equal parts. Peas are planted in 1 of the parts. You write the **fraction** $\frac{1}{3}$, read *one-third*, to tell what part of the garden is planted with peas.

numerator ▷ $\dfrac{1}{3}$
denominator ▷

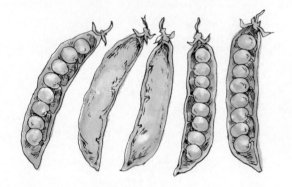

You can write several fractions to describe the pea pods. There are peas in $\frac{3}{5}$ of the pods. There are onions in $\frac{0}{5}$ of the pods. All $\frac{5}{5}$ of the pods are green.

Exercises

Complete. Write a fraction for the shaded part.

1.

numerator ▷ ▨
denominator ▷ ▨

fraction ▷ $\dfrac{▨}{▨}$

2.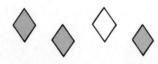

numerator ▷ ▨
denominator ▷ ▨

fraction ▷ $\dfrac{▨}{▨}$

3.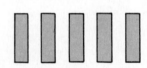

numerator ▷ ▨
denominator ▷ ▨

fraction ▷ $\dfrac{▨}{▨}$

4.

numerator ▷ ▨
denominator ▷ ▨

fraction ▷ $\dfrac{▨}{▨}$

5.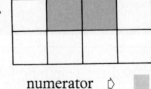

numerator ▷ ▨
denominator ▷ ▨

fraction ▷ $\dfrac{▨}{▨}$

6.

numerator ▷ ▨
denominator ▷ ▨

fraction ▷ $\dfrac{▨}{▨}$

Write the fraction for the shaded part.

7.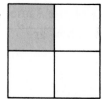

8.

9.

10.

11.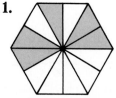

12.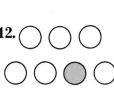

13.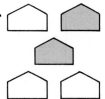

14.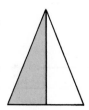

15.

16.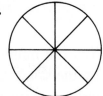

17.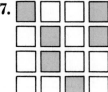

18.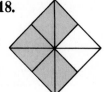

Fraction Action

Write the number.

19. What's a half of 6?

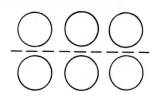

20. What's a third of 12?

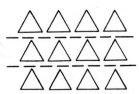

21. What's a fourth of 20?

22. What's $\frac{1}{3}$ of 9?

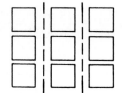

23. What's $\frac{1}{5}$ of 20?

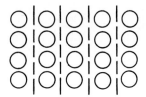

24. What's $\frac{1}{6}$ of 12?

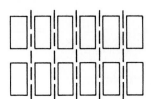

Complete.

★ **25.** $\frac{3}{4}$ of 16 is ▓ .

★ **26.** $\frac{2}{3}$ of 6 is ▓ .

★ **27.** $\frac{4}{10}$ of 30 is ▓ .

Equivalent Fractions

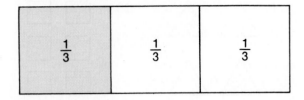

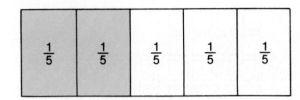

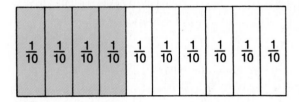

You can see that $\frac{1}{3}$ and $\frac{2}{6}$ of the same shape are the same size. They are **equivalent** fractions.

$$\frac{1}{3} = \frac{2}{6}$$

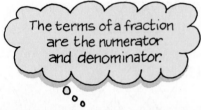

The terms of a fraction are the numerator and denominator.

You can multiply the terms of a fraction by the same number, other than zero, to write an equivalent fraction.

$$\frac{2}{5} = \frac{2 \times 2}{5 \times 2} = \frac{4}{10}$$

Exercises

Complete.

1. $\frac{1}{5} = \frac{1 \times 2}{5 \times 2} = \frac{\blacksquare}{\blacksquare}$

2. $\frac{8}{16} = \frac{8 \times 2}{16 \times 2} = \frac{\blacksquare}{\blacksquare}$

3. $\frac{2}{3} = \frac{2 \times 3}{3 \times 3} = \frac{\blacksquare}{\blacksquare}$

4. $\frac{10}{15} = \frac{10 \times 5}{15 \times 5} = \frac{\blacksquare}{\blacksquare}$

5. $\frac{3}{10} = \frac{3 \times 4}{10 \times 4} = \frac{\blacksquare}{\blacksquare}$

6. $\frac{18}{24} = \frac{18 \times 3}{24 \times 3} = \frac{\blacksquare}{\blacksquare}$

Complete.

7. $\frac{1}{8} = \frac{\blacksquare}{32}$

8. $\frac{1}{2} = \frac{\blacksquare}{10}$

9. $\frac{1}{5} = \frac{\blacksquare}{20}$

10. $\frac{4}{7} = \frac{\blacksquare}{28}$

11. $\frac{8}{12} = \frac{\blacksquare}{36}$

12. $\frac{5}{6} = \frac{\blacksquare}{24}$

13. $\frac{2}{11} = \frac{\blacksquare}{22}$

14. $\frac{8}{32} = \frac{\blacksquare}{64}$

15. $\frac{9}{27} = \frac{\blacksquare}{81}$

16. $\frac{1}{9} = \frac{\blacksquare}{18}$

17. $\frac{3}{7} = \frac{\blacksquare}{14}$ **18.** $\frac{7}{21} = \frac{\blacksquare}{105}$ **19.** $\frac{5}{9} = \frac{\blacksquare}{36}$ **20.** $\frac{2}{3} = \frac{\blacksquare}{27}$ **21.** $\frac{28}{40} = \frac{\blacksquare}{400}$

22. $\frac{20}{25} = \frac{\blacksquare}{125}$ **23.** $\frac{1}{6} = \frac{\blacksquare}{48}$ **24.** $\frac{15}{30} = \frac{\blacksquare}{90}$ **25.** $\frac{4}{24} = \frac{\blacksquare}{72}$ **26.** $\frac{9}{20} = \frac{\blacksquare}{60}$

27. $\frac{4}{7} = \frac{\blacksquare}{56}$ **28.** $\frac{3}{5} = \frac{\blacksquare}{20}$ **29.** $\frac{6}{9} = \frac{\blacksquare}{36}$ **30.** $\frac{5}{9} = \frac{\blacksquare}{18}$ **31.** $\frac{4}{12} = \frac{\blacksquare}{48}$

Secret Mission

32. Your mission is to reach the thief before he steals the rocket design plans. Write the letters of the doors with fractions that can be written with a denominator of 24. Hurry! If you find all five fractions you can catch the thief before the plans are stolen.

Tillie has an old fashioned toaster. It toasts 2 slices of bread at once, but only one side of the bread at a time. Each slice must be toasted for one minute and then turned over. How can Tillie toast 3 slices in 3 minutes?

Take a Break

Fractions in Lowest Terms

You can see that $\frac{4}{8}$ of the lockers are open.

To **simplify** $\frac{4}{8}$, you can divide the numerator and denominator by the same nonzero number.

$$\frac{4}{8} = \frac{4 \div 2}{8 \div 2} = \frac{2}{4}$$

To write $\frac{4}{8}$ in **lowest terms** you can divide the numerator and denominator by 4, their Greatest Common Factor (GCF).

$$\frac{4}{8} = \frac{4 \div 4}{8 \div 4} = \frac{1}{2}$$

Exercises

Complete.

1. $\dfrac{4}{6} = \dfrac{4 \div 2}{6 \div 2} = \dfrac{\blacksquare}{\blacksquare}$

2. $\dfrac{6}{9} = \dfrac{6 \div 3}{9 \div 3} = \dfrac{\blacksquare}{\blacksquare}$

3. $\dfrac{24}{32} = \dfrac{24 \div 8}{32 \div 8} = \dfrac{\blacksquare}{\blacksquare}$

4. $\dfrac{8}{10} = \dfrac{8 \div 2}{10 \div 2} = \dfrac{\blacksquare}{\blacksquare}$

5. $\dfrac{3}{15} = \dfrac{3 \div 3}{15 \div 3} = \dfrac{\blacksquare}{\blacksquare}$

6. $\dfrac{12}{16} = \dfrac{12 \div 4}{16 \div 4} = \dfrac{\blacksquare}{\blacksquare}$

7. $\dfrac{6}{24} = \dfrac{6 \div 6}{24 \div 6} = \dfrac{\blacksquare}{\blacksquare}$

8. $\dfrac{12}{18} = \dfrac{12 \div 6}{18 \div 6} = \dfrac{\blacksquare}{\blacksquare}$

9. $\dfrac{20}{36} = \dfrac{20 \div 4}{36 \div 4} = \dfrac{\blacksquare}{\blacksquare}$

10. $\dfrac{3}{9} = \dfrac{3 \div 3}{9 \div 3} = \dfrac{\blacksquare}{\blacksquare}$

11. $\dfrac{28}{36} = \dfrac{28 \div 4}{36 \div 4} = \dfrac{\blacksquare}{\blacksquare}$

12. $\dfrac{9}{15} = \dfrac{9 \div 3}{15 \div 3} = \dfrac{\blacksquare}{\blacksquare}$

Write in lowest terms.

13. $\dfrac{3}{6}$ 14. $\dfrac{2}{4}$ 15. $\dfrac{14}{21}$ 16. $\dfrac{9}{18}$ 17. $\dfrac{15}{24}$ 18. $\dfrac{7}{35}$

19. $\dfrac{8}{40}$ 20. $\dfrac{6}{15}$ 21. $\dfrac{8}{24}$ 22. $\dfrac{6}{10}$ 23. $\dfrac{5}{36}$ 24. $\dfrac{9}{24}$

25. $\dfrac{7}{28}$ 26. $\dfrac{3}{9}$ 27. $\dfrac{8}{28}$ 28. $\dfrac{7}{21}$ 29. $\dfrac{5}{25}$ 30. $\dfrac{10}{25}$

31. $\dfrac{9}{36}$ 32. $\dfrac{18}{24}$ 33. $\dfrac{12}{36}$ 34. $\dfrac{3}{33}$ 35. $\dfrac{16}{40}$ 36. $\dfrac{20}{25}$

37. $\dfrac{14}{28}$ 38. $\dfrac{18}{48}$ 39. $\dfrac{35}{50}$ 40. $\dfrac{4}{32}$ 41. $\dfrac{16}{20}$ 42. $\dfrac{18}{45}$

A Fraction of the Time

Franklin D. Roosevelt was president of the United States for 12 years. Here's how to write a fraction in lowest terms that tells for what part of a century Roosevelt was president.

$$\frac{12}{100} = \frac{12 \div 4}{100 \div 4} = \frac{3}{25}$$

Write the number of years as a fraction of a century. Be sure your answer is written in lowest terms.

43. 20 years   44. 90 years   45. 50 years

46. 75 years   47. 5 years   48. 22 years

49. 84 years   50. 35 years   51. 38 years

Write the number of years as a fraction of a millennium. Be sure your answer is written in lowest terms.

52. 300 years   53. 250 years   54. 60 years

55. 700 years   56. 800 years   57. 500 years

58. 650 years   59. 125 years   60. 435 years

★ 61. What fraction of a millennium is a century?

Comparing Fractions

It's easy to compare $\frac{2}{5}$ and $\frac{3}{5}$ because they have the same denominator.

$$2 < 3, \text{ so } \frac{2}{5} < \frac{3}{5}$$

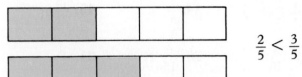

$$\frac{2}{5} < \frac{3}{5}$$

It's not as easy to compare $\frac{2}{3}$ and $\frac{3}{4}$ because they have different denominators.

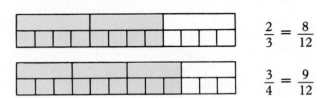

$$\frac{2}{3} = \frac{8}{12}$$

$$\frac{3}{4} = \frac{9}{12}$$

Here's how to compare $\frac{2}{3}$ and $\frac{3}{4}$ when you don't have a model.

Find the LCM of the denominators. Since 12 is the LCM of 3 and 4, it's the **least common denominator** (LCD) of $\frac{2}{3}$ and $\frac{3}{4}$.

Write equivalent fractions with a denominator of 12.

$$\frac{2}{3} = \frac{8}{12} \qquad \frac{3}{4} = \frac{9}{12}$$

Compare the fractions.

$$\frac{8}{12} < \frac{9}{12}, \text{ so } \frac{2}{3} < \frac{3}{4}$$

Exercises

Write $<$ or $>$ to compare the fractions.

1. $\frac{1}{7} \; \blacksquare \; \frac{4}{7}$

$\frac{2}{7} \; \blacksquare \; \frac{4}{7}$

$\frac{3}{7} \; \blacksquare \; \frac{4}{7}$

2. $\frac{2}{5} \; \blacksquare \; \frac{3}{5}$

$\frac{2}{5} \; \blacksquare \; \frac{4}{5}$

$\frac{2}{5} \; \blacksquare \; \frac{5}{5}$

3. $\frac{3}{8} \; \blacksquare \; \frac{3}{4}$

$\frac{5}{8} \; \blacksquare \; \frac{3}{4}$

$\frac{7}{8} \; \blacksquare \; \frac{3}{4}$

4. $\frac{2}{9} \; \blacksquare \; \frac{3}{9}$

$\frac{4}{9} \; \blacksquare \; \frac{3}{9}$

$\frac{6}{9} \; \blacksquare \; \frac{3}{9}$

5. $\frac{1}{3} \; \blacksquare \; \frac{1}{12}$

$\frac{1}{3} \; \blacksquare \; \frac{5}{12}$

$\frac{1}{3} \; \blacksquare \; \frac{7}{12}$

6. $\frac{1}{2} \; \blacksquare \; \frac{1}{8}$

$\frac{1}{2} \; \blacksquare \; \frac{3}{8}$

$\frac{1}{2} \; \blacksquare \; \frac{5}{8}$

7. $\frac{1}{5} \; \blacksquare \; \frac{1}{4}$

$\frac{1}{5} \; \blacksquare \; \frac{2}{4}$

$\frac{1}{5} \; \blacksquare \; \frac{3}{4}$

8. $\frac{3}{6} \; \blacksquare \; \frac{3}{5}$

$\frac{4}{6} \; \blacksquare \; \frac{3}{5}$

$\frac{5}{6} \; \blacksquare \; \frac{3}{5}$

Write < or > to compare the fractions.

9. $\frac{5}{9}$ ▦ $\frac{2}{9}$ **10.** $\frac{5}{16}$ ▦ $\frac{3}{4}$ **11.** $\frac{7}{9}$ ▦ $\frac{2}{3}$

12. $\frac{2}{3}$ ▦ $\frac{1}{3}$ **13.** $\frac{5}{48}$ ▦ $\frac{1}{12}$ **14.** $\frac{5}{9}$ ▦ $\frac{7}{18}$

15. $\frac{3}{7}$ ▦ $\frac{3}{35}$ **16.** $\frac{3}{7}$ ▦ $\frac{5}{21}$ **17.** $\frac{1}{2}$ ▦ $\frac{2}{3}$

18. $\frac{4}{5}$ ▦ $\frac{3}{4}$ **19.** $\frac{5}{6}$ ▦ $\frac{3}{4}$ **20.** $\frac{1}{3}$ ▦ $\frac{3}{4}$

21. $\frac{5}{6}$ ▦ $\frac{7}{8}$ **22.** $\frac{2}{3}$ ▦ $\frac{3}{5}$ **23.** $\frac{4}{7}$ ▦ $\frac{5}{8}$

24. $\frac{2}{9}$ ▦ $\frac{1}{6}$ **25.** $\frac{3}{4}$ ▦ $\frac{7}{10}$ **26.** $\frac{11}{12}$ ▦ $\frac{7}{9}$

Making Comparisons

Solve.

27. Ellen spent $\frac{2}{3}$ of an hour baking and $\frac{7}{8}$ of an hour watching television. On which activity did she spend more time?

28. Alex and Charlie shared a bucket of clams. Alex ate $\frac{1}{2}$ of the clams and Charlie ate $\frac{3}{8}$. Who ate more?

29. Mal cooked $\frac{1}{4}$ of a box of spaghetti on Monday and $\frac{1}{3}$ of a box on Saturday. On which day did he cook more spaghetti?

Write the fractions in order from least to greatest.

★ **30.** $\frac{7}{8}, \frac{2}{5}, \frac{1}{3}, \frac{5}{8}, \frac{3}{5}, \frac{1}{2}$

★ **31.** $\frac{2}{3}, \frac{4}{7}, \frac{3}{8}, \frac{7}{11}, \frac{2}{5}, \frac{4}{5}, \frac{3}{7}, \frac{7}{8}$

Checkpoint A

Write the fraction for the shaded part. (*pages 202–203*)

1. 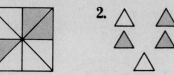   **2.**

3.   **4.**

Complete. (*pages 204–205*)

5. $\frac{1}{2} = \frac{▦}{6}$ **6.** $\frac{1}{3} = \frac{▦}{21}$

7. $\frac{3}{6} = \frac{▦}{12}$ **8.** $\frac{8}{24} = \frac{▦}{72}$

Write in lowest terms. (*pages 206–207*)

9. $\frac{6}{15}$ **10.** $\frac{4}{12}$

11. $\frac{18}{48}$ **12.** $\frac{14}{21}$

Write < or > to compare the fractions. (*pages 208–209*)

13. $\frac{5}{9}$ ▦ $\frac{2}{9}$ **14.** $\frac{3}{7}$ ▦ $\frac{6}{7}$

15. $\frac{2}{3}$ ▦ $\frac{7}{12}$ **16.** $\frac{5}{8}$ ▦ $\frac{7}{10}$

Extra practice on page 392   **209**

Mixed Numbers as Fractions

At the end of the day, Herbie's Deli had two and three-fourths spinach pies left. You can write the number of pies as the mixed number $2\frac{3}{4}$ or as the fraction $\frac{11}{4}$.

$\frac{4}{4}$ and $\frac{4}{4}$ and $\frac{3}{4}$ ⇨ $\frac{11}{4}$

1 and 1 and $\frac{3}{4}$ ⇨ $2\frac{3}{4}$

Here's how to write $2\frac{3}{4}$ as a fraction.

Step 1 Multiply the denominator by the whole number. $2\frac{3}{4}$ $(4 \times 2) = 8$

Step 2 Add the numerator to the product. $8 + 3 = 11$

Step 3 Write the sum over the denominator. $\frac{11}{4}$

Exercises

Complete.

1. $2\frac{1}{3} = \frac{}{3}$

2. $2\frac{1}{2} = \frac{}{2}$

3. $5\frac{1}{6} = \frac{}{6}$

4. $4\frac{1}{2} = \frac{}{2}$

5. $3\frac{2}{3} = \frac{}{}$

6. $6\frac{1}{8} = \frac{}{}$

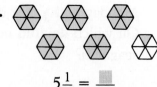

Write as a fraction.

7. $2\frac{1}{2}$ 8. $3\frac{1}{5}$ 9. $2\frac{2}{3}$ 10. $6\frac{1}{7}$ 11. $8\frac{1}{2}$ 12. $8\frac{3}{4}$

13. $4\frac{4}{5}$ 14. $4\frac{1}{8}$ 15. $6\frac{1}{3}$ 16. $7\frac{1}{2}$ 17. $1\frac{3}{7}$ 18. $7\frac{1}{10}$

19. $2\frac{3}{8}$ 20. $5\frac{1}{8}$ 21. $6\frac{7}{9}$ 22. $4\frac{5}{8}$ 23. $1\frac{1}{3}$ 24. $3\frac{2}{3}$

25. $4\frac{1}{5}$ 26. $2\frac{3}{4}$ 27. $7\frac{5}{8}$ 28. $4\frac{5}{12}$ 29. $1\frac{5}{8}$ 30. $6\frac{1}{15}$

31. $3\frac{2}{5}$ 32. $8\frac{3}{8}$ 33. $7\frac{2}{3}$ 34. $4\frac{1}{3}$ 35. $2\frac{5}{7}$ 36. $5\frac{4}{5}$

Puzzling Patterns

Write each mixed number as a fraction.
Look for a pattern. What do you discover?

37. $14\frac{2}{7}$, $28\frac{4}{7}$, $42\frac{6}{7}$

38. $11\frac{1}{9}$, $33\frac{3}{9}$, $55\frac{5}{9}$, $77\frac{7}{9}$, $99\frac{9}{9}$

Write the fraction.

★ 39. I am a mixed number equivalent to $3\frac{5}{8}$. My denominator is 24. Who am I?

★ 40. I am a mixed number equivalent to $10\frac{2}{3}$. My numerator is 6. Who am I?

Calculator Corner

Complete. Look for a pattern. What do you discover?

$\frac{11 \times 11}{1} = $ ▦ $\frac{22 \times 22}{1 + 2 + 1} = $ ▦

$\frac{33 \times 33}{1 + 2 + 3 + 2 + 1} = $ ▦ $\frac{44 \times 44}{1 + 2 + 3 + 4 + 3 + 2 + 1} = $ ▦

Fractions as Mixed Numbers

The Fraction Magician uses division to change fractions to whole numbers or mixed numbers. Here's how she does it.

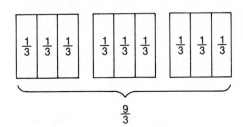 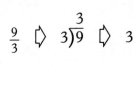 

$$\frac{9}{3} \Rightarrow 3\overline{)9}^{\;3} \Rightarrow 3$$

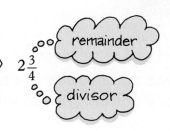

$$\frac{11}{4} \Rightarrow 4\overline{)11}^{\;2} \Rightarrow 2\frac{3}{4}$$
$$\underline{-\;8}$$
$$3$$

remainder

divisor

Exercises

Use the division to write the fraction as a mixed number or whole number.

1. $\frac{9}{4}$, $4\overline{)9}^{\;2}$
   $\underline{-8}$
   1

2. $\frac{13}{4}$, $4\overline{)13}^{\;3}$
   $\underline{-12}$
   1

3. $\frac{15}{4}$, $4\overline{)15}^{\;3}$
   $\underline{-12}$
   3

4. $\frac{9}{8}$, $8\overline{)9}^{\;1}$
   $\underline{-8}$
   1

5. $\frac{11}{8}$, $8\overline{)11}^{\;1}$
   $\underline{-8}$
   3

6. $\frac{15}{8}$, $8\overline{)15}^{\;1}$
   $\underline{-8}$
   7

7. $\frac{12}{7}$, $7\overline{)12}$

8. $\frac{14}{1}$, $1\overline{)14}$

9. $\frac{16}{7}$, $7\overline{)16}$

10. $\frac{11}{10}$, $10\overline{)11}$

11. $\frac{13}{10}$, $10\overline{)13}$

12. $\frac{17}{10}$, $10\overline{)17}$

Write as a mixed number or whole number.

13. $\frac{11}{6}$ **14.** $\frac{8}{8}$ **15.** $\frac{26}{5}$ **16.** $\frac{35}{1}$ **17.** $\frac{32}{4}$ **18.** $\frac{23}{8}$

19. $\frac{17}{11}$ **20.** $\frac{22}{7}$ **21.** $\frac{40}{8}$ **22.** $\frac{51}{8}$ **23.** $\frac{41}{7}$ **24.** $\frac{37}{3}$

25. $\frac{15}{7}$ **26.** $\frac{28}{1}$ **27.** $\frac{25}{3}$ **28.** $\frac{44}{5}$ **29.** $\frac{31}{2}$ **30.** $\frac{53}{6}$

31. $\frac{33}{8}$ **32.** $\frac{35}{6}$ **33.** $\frac{80}{9}$ **34.** $\frac{7}{7}$ **35.** $\frac{88}{9}$ **36.** $\frac{101}{8}$

Fractions and Division

Write the quotient as a mixed number. Write the fraction in lowest terms.

37. $4\overline{)63}$ **38.** $6\overline{)33}$ **39.** $15\overline{)36}$ **40.** $8\overline{)46}$ **41.** $9\overline{)39}$ **42.** $6\overline{)56}$

43. $6\overline{)26}$ **44.** $8\overline{)38}$ **45.** $9\overline{)84}$ **46.** $12\overline{)78}$ **47.** $15\overline{)50}$ **48.** $15\overline{)56}$

Write $<$, $>$, or $=$ to compare the numbers.

49. $\frac{11}{3}$ ▨ 3   **50.** $\frac{5}{2}$ ▨ 2   **51.** $\frac{7}{5}$ ▨ 6   **52.** $\frac{12}{3}$ ▨ 4   **53.** $\frac{30}{4}$ ▨ 9

Solve.

54. One container of berries will fill half a freezer bag. How many bags are needed to hold 6 containers of berries?

55. A recipe for applesauce calls for 4 apples. How many recipes can be made using 48 apples?

56. Art made 30 sandwiches. They were divided equally among 16 people. How many sandwiches did each get?

★ **57.** The average serving of vegetables is 6 oz. How many people can be served with 2 lb of carrots?

Fractions and Decimals

Barbara spent three-tenths of an hour washing the car. You can write three-tenths as a fraction or as a decimal.

Number	Fraction	Decimal
3 tenths	$\frac{3}{10}$	0.3
5 hundredths	$\frac{5}{100}$	0.05
135 thousandths	$\frac{135}{1000}$	0.135
6 and 2 tenths	$6\frac{2}{10}$	6.2

Exercises

Complete.

1. $\frac{3}{10} = 0.\blacksquare$

2. $\frac{31}{100} = 0.\blacksquare\blacksquare$

3. $\frac{315}{1000} = 0.\blacksquare\blacksquare\blacksquare$

4. $\frac{35}{100} = 0.\blacksquare\blacksquare$

5. $\frac{9}{10} = 0.\blacksquare$

6. $\frac{97}{100} = 0.\blacksquare\blacksquare$

7. $8\frac{17}{1000} = 8.\blacksquare\blacksquare\blacksquare$

8. $4\frac{5}{1000} = 4.\blacksquare\blacksquare\blacksquare$

Complete.

9. $0.7 = \frac{\blacksquare}{10}$

$0.17 = \frac{\blacksquare}{100}$

$1.7 = \blacksquare\frac{\blacksquare}{10}$

10. $0.4 = \frac{\blacksquare}{10}$

$0.41 = \frac{\blacksquare}{100}$

$4.1 = \blacksquare\frac{\blacksquare}{10}$

11. $0.38 = \frac{\blacksquare}{100}$

$0.308 = \frac{\blacksquare}{1000}$

$3.08 = \blacksquare\frac{\blacksquare}{100}$

12. $0.75 = \frac{\blacksquare}{100}$

$0.075 = \frac{\blacksquare}{1000}$

$7.5 = \blacksquare\frac{\blacksquare}{10}$

Write as a decimal.

13. $\frac{5}{10}$ 14. $\frac{32}{100}$ 15. $\frac{58}{100}$ 16. $\frac{3}{100}$ 17. $\frac{14}{100}$ 18. $\frac{2}{10}$

19. $\frac{568}{1000}$ 20. $\frac{124}{1000}$ 21. $\frac{24}{1000}$ 22. $\frac{7}{1000}$ 23. $\frac{41}{100}$ 24. $\frac{39}{100}$

25. $5\frac{3}{10}$ 26. $3\frac{7}{10}$ 27. $4\frac{37}{100}$ 28. $2\frac{41}{100}$ 29. $7\frac{87}{100}$ 30. $9\frac{371}{1000}$

31. $4\frac{7}{100}$ 32. $8\frac{307}{1000}$ 33. $8\frac{67}{100}$ 34. $4\frac{17}{100}$ 35. $7\frac{201}{1000}$ 36. $5\frac{92}{1000}$

Write as a fraction or mixed number.

37. 0.1 38. 0.09 39. 0.803 40. 0.01 41. 0.66 42. 0.107

43. 3.15 44. 5.73 45. 7.5 46. 4.003 47. 2.017 48. 9.783

Money Sense

Write the amount of money as a fraction and as a decimal part
of a dollar.

Example.   = 20¢   fraction ⇨ $\frac{20}{100}$ decimal ⇨ $.20

49.    50.

51.    52.

★ 53.

★ 54.

215

Writing Fractions as Decimals

Melanie ordered $\frac{3}{4}$ lb of fish for her cat Bonzo. The reading on the scale was 0.75 lb. Did Melanie get what she ordered? To find out, use division to write the fraction as a decimal.

$$\frac{3}{4} \quad \Rrightarrow \quad 4)\overline{\begin{array}{r} 0.75 \\ 3.00 \\ -2\,8 \\ \hline 20 \\ -20 \\ \hline 0 \end{array}}$$

Since $\frac{3}{4} = 0.75$, Melanie got exactly the amount she ordered.

You can divide to write mixed numbers as decimals too. Here's how to write $2\frac{4}{5}$ as a decimal.

Divide the fractional part of the mixed number.

$$\frac{4}{5} \quad \Rrightarrow \quad 5)\overline{\begin{array}{r} 0.8 \\ 4.0 \end{array}}$$

Add the whole number and the decimal.

$$2 + 0.8 = 2.8$$

Exercises

Write the fraction or mixed number as a decimal.

1. $\frac{1}{5}$, $\quad 5)\overline{1.0}$

2. $\frac{4}{5}$, $\quad 5)\overline{4.0}$

3. $\frac{1}{4}$, $\quad 4)\overline{1.00}$

4. $\frac{3}{8}$, $\quad 8)\overline{3.000}$

5. $2\frac{3}{4}$, $\quad 2 + 4)\overline{3.00}$, $\quad 2.\blacksquare\blacksquare$

6. $2\frac{9}{20}$, $\quad 2 + 20)\overline{9.00}$, $\quad 2.\blacksquare\blacksquare$

Write as a decimal.

7. $\frac{1}{2}$ 8. $\frac{3}{5}$ 9. $\frac{2}{5}$ 10. $\frac{1}{8}$ 11. $\frac{9}{20}$ 12. $\frac{7}{8}$

13. $\frac{16}{25}$ 14. $\frac{11}{20}$ 15. $\frac{5}{8}$ 16. $\frac{8}{25}$ 17. $\frac{13}{20}$ 18. $\frac{9}{40}$

19. $\frac{21}{25}$ 20. $\frac{12}{16}$ 21. $\frac{18}{20}$ 22. $\frac{23}{40}$ 23. $\frac{18}{24}$ 24. $\frac{3}{6}$

25. $2\frac{3}{4}$ 26. $7\frac{1}{2}$ 27. $2\frac{3}{8}$ 28. $3\frac{1}{5}$ 29. $4\frac{7}{20}$ 30. $5\frac{11}{25}$

31. $9\frac{1}{8}$ 32. $3\frac{1}{4}$ 33. $7\frac{2}{5}$ 34. $7\frac{3}{4}$ 35. $4\frac{5}{8}$ 36. $9\frac{3}{5}$

37. $1\frac{3}{8}$ 38. $4\frac{9}{12}$ 39. $8\frac{4}{5}$ 40. $2\frac{15}{20}$ 41. $5\frac{17}{25}$ 42. $3\frac{10}{16}$

Side Trip

Write the fraction or mixed number as a decimal.

43. It took Louis $\frac{3}{5}$ of an hour to shampoo his dog.

44. Pearl spent $2\frac{5}{8}$ hours shopping for bargains.

45. Raymond ate $\frac{7}{8}$ of a pound of grapes before his mother put them away.

46. Della read $\frac{7}{25}$ of a mystery book before figuring out the ending.

47. Terry walked $\frac{3}{8}$ of the way to school before he remembered his homework.

48. Etta ran $6\frac{4}{5}$ mi last week.

Write the whole numbers from 1 to 40 using only the digits 2, 4, 6, and 8.

For example, 27 may be written $(4 \times 6) + \frac{6}{2}$.

Take a Break

Repeating Decimals

When you write a fraction as a decimal and have no remainder, the quotient is a **terminating decimal.**

$$\frac{1}{5} \quad \Rightarrow \quad 5\overline{)1.0} \quad \begin{matrix}0.2\end{matrix}$$

Sometimes, no matter how many zeros you write in the dividend, the division just keeps on going. When the same numbers repeat in the quotient, you have a **repeating decimal.**

THE BAR IN 0.$\overline{36}$ MEANS THE DIGITS 3 AND 6 KEEP REPEATING.

$$\frac{4}{11} \quad \Rightarrow \quad 11\overline{)4.0000} \quad \begin{matrix}0.3636\ldots\end{matrix} \quad \Rightarrow \quad 0.\overline{36}$$

$$
\begin{array}{r}
0.3636\ldots \\
11\overline{)4.0000} \\
-33 \quad\;\; \\
\hline
70 \quad\; \\
-66 \quad\; \\
\hline
40 \; \\
-33 \; \\
\hline
70 \;
\end{array}
$$

Exercises

Complete. Is the quotient a terminating or repeating decimal? Write *T* or *R*.

1. $20\overline{)9.00}$ $\;0.4$

2. $3\overline{)1.00}$ $\;0.3$

3. $11\overline{)8.000}$ $\;0.72$

4. $25\overline{)17.00}$ $\;0.6$

5. $5\overline{)1.00}$ $\;0.2$

6. $12\overline{)5.000}$ $\;0.41$

7. $11\overline{)9.00}$ $\;0.8$

8. $25\overline{)16.00}$ $\;0.6$

Write the repeating decimal using a bar.

9. 0.232323...

10. 0.451451451...

11. 0.444...

12. 0.01010101...

13. 0.003333...

14. 0.5888...

15. 0.04212121...

16. 0.68666...

17. 0.14723723723...

Write as a repeating decimal. Show your answer with a bar.

18. $\frac{5}{6}$ **19.** $\frac{5}{11}$ **20.** $\frac{5}{9}$

21. $\frac{8}{9}$ **22.** $\frac{11}{12}$ **23.** $\frac{6}{9}$

24. $\frac{13}{15}$ **25.** $\frac{7}{12}$ **26.** $\frac{7}{18}$

27. $\frac{4}{30}$ **28.** $\frac{4}{3}$ **29.** $\frac{11}{6}$

Going Ahead

When you have a calculator it's easier to compare fractions if you first write them as decimals.

Example.   Compare $\frac{13}{18}$ and $\frac{21}{27}$

$$\frac{13}{18} = 0.7\overline{2} \qquad \frac{21}{27} = 0.\overline{77}$$

$$0.7\overline{2} < 0.\overline{77} \text{ so } \frac{13}{18} < \frac{21}{27}$$

Write $<$ or $>$ to compare the numbers.

30. $\frac{4}{11}$ ▨ $\frac{6}{9}$ **31.** $\frac{18}{33}$ ▨ $\frac{7}{18}$

32. $\frac{38}{48}$ ▨ $\frac{35}{45}$ **33.** $\frac{51}{81}$ ▨ $\frac{21}{41}$

34. $\frac{12}{17}$ ▨ $\frac{9}{13}$ **35.** $\frac{27}{35}$ ▨ $\frac{33}{59}$

36. $\frac{115}{168}$ ▨ $\frac{246}{275}$ **37.** $\frac{278}{301}$ ▨ $\frac{197}{228}$

Write the fractions in order from least to greatest.

★ **38.** $\frac{23}{24}, \frac{13}{27}, \frac{35}{37}$ ★ **39.** $\frac{16}{9}, \frac{33}{18}, \frac{51}{37}$

Checkpoint B

Write as a fraction.
(*pages 210–211*)

1. $3\frac{1}{3}$ **2.** $4\frac{4}{5}$

3. $6\frac{1}{7}$ **4.** $12\frac{3}{5}$

Write as a mixed number or whole number. (*pages 212–213*)

5. $\frac{12}{5}$ **6.** $\frac{15}{3}$

7. $\frac{25}{3}$ **8.** $\frac{6}{2}$

Write as a decimal.
(*pages 214–215*)

9. $\frac{3}{10}$ **10.** $\frac{15}{100}$

11. $2\frac{9}{10}$ **12.** $9\frac{38}{1000}$

Write as a decimal.
(*pages 216–217*)

13. $\frac{1}{5}$ **14.** $\frac{3}{8}$

15. $8\frac{2}{5}$ **16.** $2\frac{3}{4}$

Write as a repeating decimal using a bar. (*pages 218–219*)

17. $\frac{1}{6}$ **18.** $\frac{5}{12}$

19. $\frac{1}{9}$ **20.** $\frac{5}{3}$

Extra practice on page 392   **219**

Problem Solving · REASONABLE ANSWERS

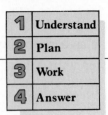

1 Understand
2 Plan
3 Work
4 Answer

Compare the four problems below. Notice how
common sense tells you how to write the quotient
in each case.

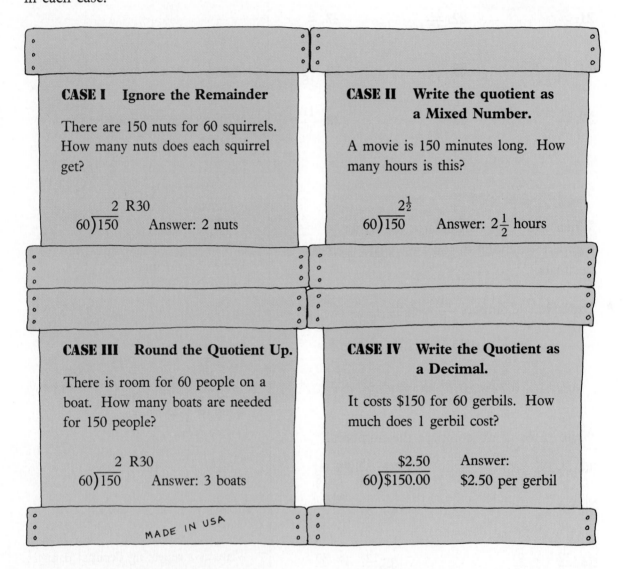

CASE I   Ignore the Remainder

There are 150 nuts for 60 squirrels.
How many nuts does each squirrel
get?

$$2\text{ R}30$$
$$60\overline{)150}$$ Answer: 2 nuts

**CASE II   Write the quotient as
a Mixed Number.**

A movie is 150 minutes long. How
many hours is this?

$$2\tfrac{1}{2}$$
$$60\overline{)150}$$ Answer: $2\tfrac{1}{2}$ hours

CASE III   Round the Quotient Up.

There is room for 60 people on a
boat. How many boats are needed
for 150 people?

$$2\text{ R}30$$
$$60\overline{)150}$$ Answer: 3 boats

MADE IN USA

**CASE IV   Write the Quotient as
a Decimal.**

It costs $150 for 60 gerbils. How
much does 1 gerbil cost?

$$\$2.50$$
$$60\overline{)\$150.00}$$ Answer:
                      $2.50 per gerbil

Solve. Which case describes the quotient? Write *I, II, III* or *IV*.

1. A seal gets 4 fish for every trick
performed. How many tricks must
be done for 25 fish?

2. An acrobat did 12 flips in 30
seconds. What was the time for one
flip?

3. How many hours will it take to
travel 100 km at 30 km per hour?

4. How many days are there in 150
hours?

Solve.

5. A health club ordered 298 sweat shirts. The bill was $1639. How much did each shirt cost?

6. Robin swam 15 km in 6 days. She swam the same distance each day. How far did she swim each day?

7. The principal has 950 book covers to give to 308 students. If each student gets the same number of covers, how many does each get?

8. The Dayton Hat Company ships hats in boxes of 25. How many boxes are needed to fill an order for 480 hats?

9. The Whole Grain Bakery ordered 45 kg of rye flour. They used the same amount for each of 7 days. How many kilograms did they use each day?

10. The cook at the Soup Café made 74 L of vegetable soup. How many 0.24 L servings can be made from this amount?

Write a reasonable problem for the division.

★ 11. $8\overline{)98}$ = $12\frac{1}{4}$

Answer: $12\frac{1}{4}$ mi

★ 12. $28\overline{)4225}$ = 150 R25

Answer: 151 cartons

Use the picture above. Write a fraction in lowest terms.

1. striped hats

2. hats with pom-poms

3. children without hats

4. hats with snowflakes

5. children wearing hats

6. hats with names

Which mitten holds the larger fraction? Write *a* or *b*.

7. a. $\frac{3}{4}$ **b.** $\frac{11}{16}$

8. a. $\frac{2}{3}$ **b.** $\frac{3}{4}$

9. a. $\frac{4}{5}$ **b.** $\frac{5}{6}$

True or false? Write *T* or *F*.

10. $4\frac{3}{5} = \frac{21}{5}$

11. $\frac{3}{10} = 0.3$

12. $6\frac{5}{9} = \frac{59}{9}$

13. $13\frac{345}{1000} = 13.345$

14. $\frac{17}{8} = 2\frac{1}{8}$

15. $\frac{3}{8} = 0.375$

16. $8\frac{6}{10} = 10.6$

17. $\frac{1}{5} = 0.20$

Write as a repeating decimal using a bar.

18. $0.9434343\ldots$

19. $\frac{5}{9}$

20. $\frac{11}{6}$

21. $\frac{7}{12}$

Solve.

22. Mr. Lawson bought 3 jackets for $87.73. About how much did each jacket cost?

23. Earmuffs cost $7.50 per pair. How many pairs can you buy with $35?

Write the fraction for the shaded part. (*pages 202–203*)

1.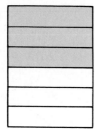

2.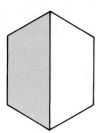

3.

4.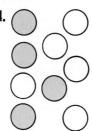

Complete. (*pages 204–205*)

5. $\frac{1}{3} = \frac{\blacksquare}{15}$

6. $\frac{3}{5} = \frac{\blacksquare}{25}$

7. $\frac{5}{9} = \frac{\blacksquare}{27}$

8. $\frac{4}{8} = \frac{\blacksquare}{16}$

Write in lowest terms. (*pages 206–207*)

9. $\frac{6}{10}$

10. $\frac{14}{16}$

11. $\frac{3}{9}$

12. $\frac{2}{12}$

13. $\frac{15}{35}$

14. $\frac{7}{21}$

Write < or > to compare the fractions. (*pages 208–209*)

15. $\frac{3}{5} \; \blacksquare \; \frac{2}{5}$

16. $\frac{2}{3} \; \blacksquare \; \frac{3}{4}$

17. $\frac{6}{7} \; \blacksquare \; \frac{20}{21}$

18. $\frac{4}{6} \; \blacksquare \; \frac{3}{8}$

Write as a fraction. (*pages 210–211*)

19. $2\frac{2}{3}$

20. $3\frac{1}{2}$

21. $7\frac{2}{5}$

22. $6\frac{4}{5}$

23. $3\frac{1}{7}$

24. $11\frac{6}{8}$

Write as a mixed number or whole number. (*pages 212–213*)

25. $\frac{9}{5}$

26. $\frac{10}{3}$

27. $\frac{6}{5}$

28. $\frac{25}{5}$

29. $\frac{18}{7}$

30. $\frac{36}{9}$

Write as a terminating or repeating decimal. (*pages 214–219*)

31. $\frac{8}{10}$

32. $16\frac{87}{100}$

33. $\frac{1}{8}$

34. $1\frac{3}{5}$

35. $\frac{7}{3}$

36. $\frac{3}{11}$

Solve. (*pages 220–221*)

37. There are 155 books to share among 25 students. How many books does each student get?

38. One box holds 30 books. How many boxes are needed for 170 books?

Extra practice on page 393

Networks

Networks are made up of paths and vertexes. A vertex is odd if the number of paths that meet there is odd. A vertex is even if the number of paths that meet there is even.

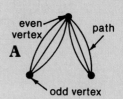 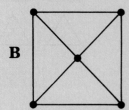 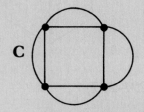 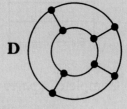

A network is **traversable** if you can draw it without lifting your pencil or retracing any path. You can look for a rule to decide, without drawing, whether or not a network is traversable.

Network	Number of Odd Vertexes	Number of Even Vertexes	Traversable?
A	2	1	yes
B	4	1	no
C	0	4	yes
D	8	0	no

If a network is traversable it cannot have more than 2 odd vertexes.

Complete the table for the networks below.

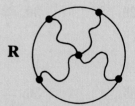 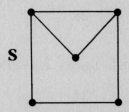 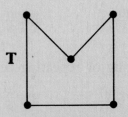 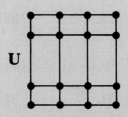

	Network	Number of Odd Vertexes	Number of Even Vertexes	Traversable?
1.	R	?	?	?
2.	S	?	?	?
3.	T	?	?	?
4.	U	?	?	?

The spaces in a network are called regions. Including the region outside the paths, this network has 3 regions.

Copy and complete the table for the networks below.

M 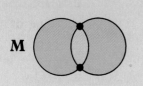   N 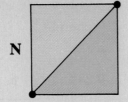   O 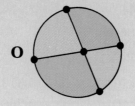   P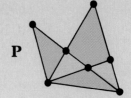

	Network	Vertexes	Regions	Paths
5.	M	?	?	?
6.	N	?	?	?
7.	O	?	?	?
8.	P	?	?	?

9. Add the number of vertexes and the number of regions for each network above. Compare this number with the number of paths. Complete the equation.

$$\text{Vertexes} + \text{Regions} - \text{Paths} = \boxed{}$$

Use the equation from Exercise 9. Solve.

10. A network has 5 vertexes and 4 regions. How many paths does it have?

11. A network has 8 paths and 4 vertexes. How many regions does it have?

12. A network has 3 paths and 2 vertexes. How many regions does it have?

13. A network has 12 paths and 6 regions. How many vertexes does it have?

Copy each network. Try to color the network using 4 or fewer colors. No two touching regions can be the same color.

14.

15.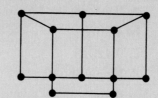

225

Maintaining Skills

Choose the best answer. Write *a*, *b*, *c*, or *d*.
Add.

1. 23.43
    + 9.98
  a. 32.41
  b. 33.41
  c. 23.41
  d. None of these

2. 5.027
    +0.592
  a. 5.619
  b. 5.519
  c. 6.519
  d. None of these

3. 0.53
    +0.918
  a. 1.548
  b. 0.448
  c. 1.458
  d. None of these

4. 47.092
    +88.009
  a. 136.101
  b. 135.101
  c. 135.091
  d. None of these

5. 0.513
    +9.768
  a. 9.281
  b. 10.381
  c. 10.271
  d. None of these

6. 70.506
    + 8.69
  a. 79.206
  b. 78.196
  c. 79.196
  d. None of these

Subtract.

7. 256.08
    − 41.35
  a. 214.23
  b. 214.73
  c. 214.33
  d. None of these

8. 1.036
    −0.827
  a. 0.209
  b. 0.109
  c. 1.209
  d. None of these

9. 13.006
    − 4.513
  a. 8.483
  b. 9.493
  c. 8.493
  d. None of these

10. 29.34
    − 14.128
  a. 15.212
  b. 15.228
  c. 14.222
  d. None of these

11. 50.301
    − 0.643
  a. 50.768
  b. 50.658
  c. 49.758
  d. None of these

12. 32.05
    − 9.361
  a. 22.691
  b. 22.789
  c. 22.689
  d. None of these

Multiply.

13. 6.38
    ×9
  a. 574.2
  b. 57.42
  c. 5.742
  d. None of these

14. 3.47
    ×0.5
  a. 1.735
  b. 1.725
  c. 17.35
  d. None of these

15. 0.38
    ×1.6
  a. 0.608
  b. 6.08
  c. 0.228
  d. None of these

16. 3.002
    ×0.14
  a. 0.40228
  b. 4.2028
  c. 0.42028
  d. None of these

17. 0.07
    ×6.4
  a. 4.48
  b. 4.048
  c. 0.0448
  d. None of these

18. 1.05
    ×0.09
  a. 0.0945
  b. 0.945
  c. 1.945
  d. None of these

Divide. Round the quotient to the nearest hundredth.

19. 8)43.671
a. 5.45
b. 5.36
c. 5.46
d. None of these

20. 5)3.269
a. 6.54
b. 0.65
c. 0.66
d. None of these

21. 21)45.38
a. 2.17
b. 2.07
c. 2.16
d. None of these

22. 0.7)32.461
a. 46.38
b. 4.64
c. 4.63
d. None of these

23. 4.9)0.823
a. 0.16
b. 0.17
c. 1.68
d. None of these

24. 3.1)0.15
a. 0.05
b. 0.48
c. 0.04
d. None of these

Round to the nearest whole number. Estimate the sum or difference.

25. 309.72
  + 53.29
a. 362
b. 364
c. 363
d. None of these

26. 749.51
  − 56.48
a. 694
b. 692
c. 693
d. None of these

27. 2430.45
  − 1928.61
a. 502
b. 501
c. 503
d. None of these

28. 73,429.6
  − 69,834.49
a. 3597
b. 3695
c. 3694
d. None of these

29. 13.508
  + 78.93
a. 91
b. 93
c. 92
d. None of these

30. 4609.47
  + 399.5
a. 5010
b. 5008
c. 5009
d. None of these

Solve.

31. How many slices of bread, 0.75 cm thick, are in a loaf of bread that is 26.25 cm long?

a. 35
b. 37
c. 34
d. None of these

32. A football weighs about 0.4 kg. How many footballs would be in a sack that weighs 16 kg?

a. 6
b. 40
c. 4
d. None of these

Applying Your Skills

Installment Buying

People often pay for expensive items in **installments,** a little at a time. They make a **down payment** at the time of purchase. The rest is paid in monthly installments.

Installment buying costs customers more than paying in full because stores add a **finance charge** for the service. This is how to find the amount of the finance charge on this $800 TV.

TELEVISION SPECIAL!

Pay **$800**
Full cash price or
$85 down payment
and **$67.58**
per month
for 12 months

Multiply the monthly installment amount by the number of months.	Then add the down payment.	Find the difference between the total cost of the plan and the full cash price of $800.
$67.58 $\times 12$ $810.96	$810.96 $+\ \ 85.00$ 895.96 total cost of plan	$895.96 $-\ 800.00$ 95.96 finance charge

Match the installment plan to the finance charge.

1. $ 323.38 full cash price
$ 45.50 down
$ 36.41 per month for 9 months

2. $5258.96 full cash price
$ 930.86 down
$ 136.42 per month for 36 months

3. $ 992.70 full cash price
$ 115.65 down
$ 84.35 per month for 12 months

4. $1564.44 full cash price
$ 221.00 down
$ 75.28 per month for 24 months

A. $135.15

B. $463.28

C. $583.02

D. $ 44.81

These signs were all sent back to the printer for correction. Signs 5, 6, and 7 had mistakes in the number of monthly payments. Signs 8, 9, and 10 had mistakes in the amount of the monthly payment. Correct the mistake in each sign. Remember that the total cost of each plan includes the finance charge.

5.

4 TIRES
$216 total cost
Pay $36 each month
Take 12 months

6.

CAMERA
Only $552
total cost
Pay $46 per month
for 24 months

7.

VIDEO RECORDER
Pay a total of
$1,320
Only
$44 per month
Take **36** months

8.

COMPUTER
$4,085.04
total cost
YOU PAY
$180.20 per month
for 24 months

9.

MOTOR HOME
$15,624 total cost
PAY ONLY
$421.10
per month for
36 months

10.

NEW CAR!
$5,574.30
total cost
JUST **$154.95**
per month
for **30 months**

You'll need to apply your skill in doing multi-step problems to do these. Solve. Then write the number of steps you used.

11. Suppose you buy a winter coat that costs $150. You make a down payment of $35.00 and agree to pay 6 monthly installments of $22.92. What is the total cost of the coat on the installment plan?

12. Maureen bought a new carpet for her living room. She made a down payment of $95.85. She plans to pay the remaining $888 in 12 monthly installments. How much are her monthly installments?

Applying Your Skills

Unit Pricing

Stores use unit pricing to help customers compare prices of different brands or different-sized items. By applying your decimal skills, you can use unit pricing to help you save money.

A **unit price** is the cost of one unit of the amount of a product in a package. In most stores, a unit price tag like this is posted near each product.

You find the unit price by dividing the selling price by the number of units in a package. You round the price to the nearest thousandth.

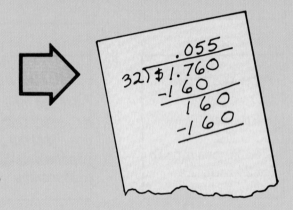

Here are a few unit price tags that need to be completed. Find the missing numbers. Round missing retail prices to the nearest cent. Round missing unit prices to the nearest thousandth.

1.
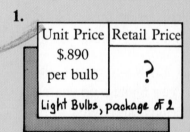

Unit Price	Retail Price
$.890 per bulb	?

Light Bulbs, package of 2

2.
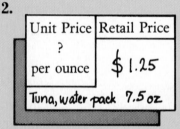

Unit Price	Retail Price
? per ounce	$1.25

Tuna, water pack 7.5 oz

3.
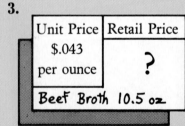

Unit Price	Retail Price
$.043 per ounce	?

Beef Broth 10.5 oz

4.

Unit Price	Retail Price
? per ounce	$.69

Pineapple, own juice 20 oz

5.
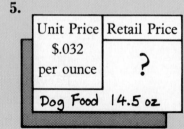

Unit Price	Retail Price
$.032 per ounce	?

Dog Food 14.5 oz

6.

Unit Price	Retail Price
per pound	$1.19

Whole Wheat Bread 1.5 lb

Find the unit price for each size. By comparison, is the larger size or the smaller size the better bargain? Write *larger* or *smaller*.

	Item	Larger Size	Smaller Size
7.	potting soil	10 lb for $1.99	4 lb for $.99
8.	liquid floor cleaner	32 oz for $2.47	16 oz for $1.29
9.	soap pads, box	18 for $2.99	6 for $1.29
10.	window cleaner	32 oz for $3.48	12 oz for $1.59
11.	all-purpose cleaner	64 oz for $2.38	28 oz for $1.64

Sometimes, you have to make quick estimates of food costs when you're shopping. Round prices to the nearest ten cents. Give your quick estimate of the cost.

12. 2 bags of carrots

13. 15 oranges

14. 4 lb squash

15. 3 lb of grapes

16. 2 lb of squash and 10 oranges

17. 5 oranges and 1 lb of grapes

18. 5 bags of carrots and 5 oranges

★**19.** 8 oz grapes and 24 oz of squash

Applying Your Skills

Sizing Up a Skyscraper

Suppose you're in charge of moving your company to new offices. Sky Tower looks like a good place, but you have questions to ask the Building Manager.

Use the facts about Sky Tower. Find the answer that the manager should give to each of your questions.

SKY TOWER
425 Madison Street

Materials: steel and glass
Use: commercial office space

Dimensions:
Height: 40 stories (540 feet)
Outside base: 215 feet by 145 feet
Inside area per floor: 24,375 square feet

Special features
Ocean view and air conditioning
Space still vacant: floors 17, 21, and 31

---

1. The width of each floor inside the building is 125 ft. What is the length?

2. How many times must a person walk around the building to walk at least a mile (5,280 ft)?

3. How many passenger elevators are there?

4. How many different elevators must be taken to visit all vacant floors?

PASSENGER ELEVATOR SERVICE

Number of elevators vs. Floors serviced (2-8, 9-15, 16-25, 26-40)

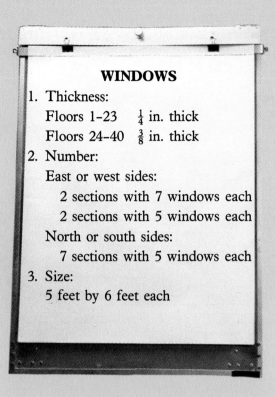

WINDOWS

1. Thickness:
   Floors 1–23 $\frac{1}{4}$ in. thick
   Floors 24–40 $\frac{3}{8}$ in. thick
2. Number:
   East or west sides:
        2 sections with 7 windows each
        2 sections with 5 windows each
   North or south sides:
        7 sections with 5 windows each
3. Size:
        5 feet by 6 feet each

A guide used this chart on a tour of the 27th floor of Sky Tower.

These are some of the questions that the sightseers asked. Use the chart to answer each question.

5. "How many other floors have windows with $\frac{3}{8}$ in. thick glass like these?"

6. "How many windows are there on the east or west side of the floor?" "on the north or south side?" "on the whole floor?"

7. "How much glass surface is there in a window?"

The guide explained that each section of windows lies directly above a section of the same size below it. Window washers call each column of window sections running from the roof to the ground a *drop*. Washers can wash two entire drops in one day.

Use the chart or what the guide said to answer these questions from sightseers.

8. How many drops are there on the north side of the building?

9. How many drops are on the east side of the building?

10. How many drops are there on the entire building?

11. How long would it take to wash all of the windows in the building?

Enrichment

A Special Pattern

A **gear** is a wheel with teeth on its outside edge that interact with teeth on other wheels. When one gear moves, a gear connected to it moves in the opposite direction. A large gear turns more slowly than a smaller gear connected to it.

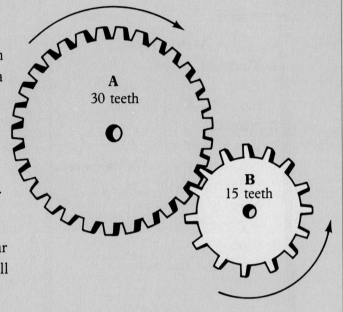

When gear A is turned clockwise, gear B turns counterclockwise.

Gear A has twice as many teeth as gear B. For each complete turn of A, B will turn twice.

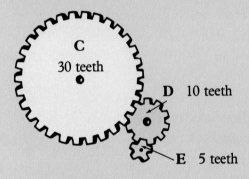

1. Gear C is turned clockwise. How will gear D turn? How will gear E turn?

2. How many times more teeth does gear D have than gear E?

3. How many times more teeth does gear C have than gear D? than gear E?

4. Gear D is turned once. How many times will gear E turn?

5. Gear C is turned once. How many times will gear D turn? How many times will gear E turn?

6. Gear E is turned counterclockwise. How will gear D turn? How will gear C turn?

★ 7. Gear D is turned twice. How many times will gear C turn?

★ 8. Gear E is turned twice. How many times will gear C turn?

Devil's Tower in Wyoming is a volcanic throat that is $865\frac{3}{4}$ ft high and can be seen from $28\frac{1}{4}$ mi away. Suppose Devil's Tower was a skyscraper. About how many floors would it have if each floor was 8 ft high?

Addition, Subtraction of Fractions

Using an Inch Ruler

You can use an inch ruler to measure and draw line segments.
Each inch unit is divided into smaller units to make measuring
more precise.

To the nearest $\frac{1}{4}$ in., the line segment
is $2\frac{1}{4}$ in. long.

The red marks show $\frac{1}{4}$ in. divisions.

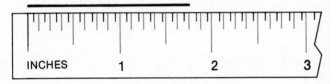

To the nearest $\frac{1}{8}$ in., the line segment
is $1\frac{6}{8}$ in. long.

The red marks show $\frac{1}{8}$ in. divisions.

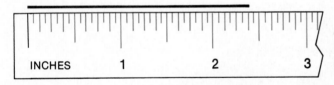

To the nearest $\frac{1}{16}$ in., the line segment
is $2\frac{6}{16}$ in. long.

The red marks show $\frac{1}{16}$ in. divisions.

Exercises

Measure the segment to the nearest $\frac{1}{4}$ in.

1.   **2.**   **3.**   **4.**

Measure the segment to the nearest $\frac{1}{8}$ in.

5.   **6.**   **7.**   **8.**

Measure the segment to the nearest $\frac{1}{16}$ in.

9.   10.   11.   12.

Draw a segment with the given length.

13. $2\frac{5}{8}$ in.   **14.** 6 in.   **15.** $2\frac{3}{4}$ in.   **16.** $3\frac{7}{8}$ in.   **17.** $5\frac{1}{4}$ in.

18. $1\frac{1}{16}$ in.   **19.** $4\frac{7}{16}$ in.   **20.** $3\frac{1}{4}$ in.   **21.** $7\frac{7}{8}$ in.   **22.** $4\frac{11}{16}$ in.

23. $2\frac{4}{16}$ in.   **24.** $\frac{7}{8}$ in.   **25.** $6\frac{1}{2}$ in.   **26.** $10\frac{3}{16}$ in.   **27.** $8\frac{5}{8}$ in.

Game Plan

Measure the path from start to finish to the nearest $\frac{1}{8}$ in.

28.

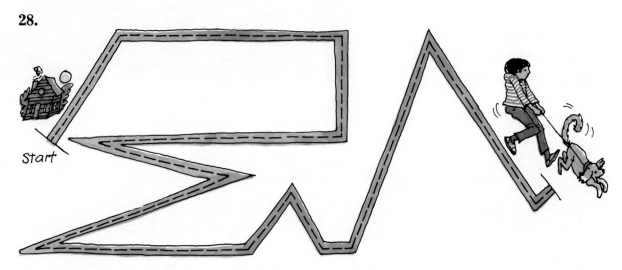

Start

Tim, Tom, Jane and Joan went fishing. Joan caught twice as many fish as Tom. Tim caught 4 more fish than Joan but 3 less than Jane. Jane caught 15 fish. How many fish did Tom catch?

Take a Break

Adding and Subtracting Fractions

William ate $\frac{3}{8}$ of a sandwich and Ann ate $\frac{1}{8}$ of it. Add to see how much of the sandwich was eaten.

Since the denominators are the same, just add the numerators and simplify the sum.

$$\frac{1}{8} + \frac{3}{8} = \frac{4}{8} = \frac{1}{2}$$

Subtract to see how much more William ate than Ann.

$$\frac{3}{8} - \frac{1}{8} = \frac{2}{8} = \frac{1}{4}$$

Together, Ann and William ate $\frac{1}{2}$ of the sandwich. William ate $\frac{1}{4}$ more than Ann.

Exercises

Complete.

1. $\frac{5}{9} + \frac{2}{9} = \frac{\blacksquare}{9}$

2. $\frac{2}{3} - \frac{1}{3} = \frac{\blacksquare}{3}$

3. $\frac{2}{5} + \frac{1}{5} = \frac{\blacksquare}{5}$

4. $\frac{5}{16} + \frac{11}{16} = \frac{\blacksquare}{16} = \blacksquare$

5. $\frac{3}{6} - \frac{1}{6} = \frac{\blacksquare}{6} = \frac{\blacksquare}{3}$

6. $\frac{3}{12} + \frac{6}{12} = \frac{\blacksquare}{12} = \frac{\blacksquare}{4}$

Add or subtract. Write the sum or difference in lowest terms.

7. $\frac{1}{4} + \frac{2}{4}$

8. $\frac{2}{10} + \frac{3}{10}$

9. $\frac{5}{8} - \frac{2}{8}$

10. $\frac{9}{12} - \frac{7}{12}$

11. $\frac{4}{6} - \frac{1}{6}$

12. $\frac{5}{7} + \frac{2}{7}$

13. $\frac{3}{4} - \frac{1}{4}$

14. $\frac{4}{5} - \frac{2}{5}$

15. $\frac{5}{8} + \frac{7}{8}$

16. $\frac{3}{6} + \frac{5}{6}$

17. $\frac{13}{16}$ $-\frac{7}{16}$

18. $\frac{3}{8}$ $+\frac{3}{8}$

19. $\frac{4}{5}$ $+\frac{3}{5}$

20. $\frac{17}{24}$ $-\frac{9}{24}$

21. $\frac{1}{6}$ $+\frac{3}{6}$

22. $\frac{19}{20}$ $-\frac{5}{20}$

23. $\frac{7}{12}$ $+\frac{3}{12}$

24. $\frac{13}{18}$ $-\frac{5}{18}$

25. $\frac{7}{12}$ $-\frac{5}{12}$

26. $\frac{3}{20}$ $+\frac{8}{20}$

27. $\frac{7}{15}$ $+\frac{2}{15}$

28. $\frac{3}{10}$ $+\frac{1}{10}$

29. $\frac{9}{15}$ $-\frac{4}{15}$

30. $\frac{7}{10}$ $-\frac{1}{10}$

31. $\frac{4}{5}$ $+\frac{1}{5}$

32. $\frac{16}{25}$ $+\frac{5}{25}$

33. $\frac{7}{11}$ $+\frac{2}{11}$

34. $\frac{25}{50}$ $-\frac{17}{50}$

Rewriting History

35. Where was the Declaration of Independence signed? To find out, add or subtract. Write the answer in lowest terms. Unscramble the letters with the same numerator.

At the ▨ ▨ ▨ ▨ ▨ ▨ ▨

$\frac{11}{16} - \frac{5}{16}$

$\frac{5}{6} - \frac{2}{6}$

$\frac{17}{25} + \frac{3}{25}$

$\frac{1}{15} + \frac{9}{15}$

$\frac{9}{12} - \frac{5}{12}$

$\frac{2}{8} + \frac{2}{8}$

$\frac{10}{27} - \frac{4}{27}$

$\frac{1}{15} + \frac{2}{15}$

$\frac{33}{48} - \frac{27}{48}$

$\frac{7}{100} + \frac{3}{100}$

$\frac{37}{40} - \frac{9}{40}$

$\frac{29}{42} + \frac{7}{42}$

Unlike Denominators

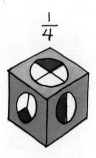

FRACTION TOSS

RULES:
1. Toss the fraction cubes.
2. Write a fraction for each shaded part.
3. Add the two fractions.
4. The player with the higher score wins.

Charlie threw these two cubes.
Let's figure out his score.

First write equivalent fractions with a common denominator.

$$\frac{2}{5} = \frac{8}{20}$$
$$+\frac{1}{4} = \frac{5}{20}$$

20 is the least common denominator of $\frac{2}{5}$ and $\frac{1}{4}$.

Now just add the numerators.

$$\frac{2}{5} = \frac{8}{20}$$
$$+\frac{1}{4} = +\frac{5}{20}$$
$$\frac{13}{20}$$

Charlie's score is $\frac{13}{20}$.

Exercises

Write the least common denominator for the pair of fractions.

1. $\frac{1}{2}, \frac{1}{5}$

2. $\frac{1}{6}, \frac{1}{9}$

3. $\frac{1}{4}, \frac{1}{10}$

4. $\frac{1}{4}, \frac{1}{8}$

5. $\frac{1}{8}, \frac{1}{12}$

6. $\frac{3}{8}, \frac{5}{16}$

7. $\frac{1}{2}, \frac{2}{7}$

8. $\frac{2}{9}, \frac{5}{12}$

9. $\frac{2}{3}, \frac{4}{15}$

10. $\frac{1}{3}, \frac{3}{4}$

Add. Write the sum in lowest terms.

11. $\frac{1}{6}$ $+\frac{1}{2}$

12. $\frac{1}{3}$ $+\frac{1}{4}$

13. $\frac{1}{4}$ $+\frac{1}{5}$

14. $\frac{1}{6}$ $+\frac{1}{4}$

15. $\frac{1}{8}$ $+\frac{1}{2}$

16. $\frac{5}{7}$ $+\frac{1}{3}$

17. $\dfrac{2}{3}$ $+\dfrac{1}{5}$

18. $\dfrac{5}{6}$ $+\dfrac{3}{8}$

19. $\dfrac{3}{7}$ $+\dfrac{1}{2}$

20. $\dfrac{5}{6}$ $+\dfrac{2}{5}$

21. $\dfrac{3}{4}$ $+\dfrac{3}{10}$

22. $\dfrac{1}{8}$ $+\dfrac{5}{12}$

23. $\dfrac{1}{2}$ $+\dfrac{4}{5}$

24. $\dfrac{1}{3}$ $+\dfrac{2}{9}$

25. $\dfrac{2}{3}$ $+\dfrac{3}{8}$

26. $\dfrac{3}{5}$ $+\dfrac{1}{2}$

27. $\dfrac{9}{10}$ $+\dfrac{1}{5}$

28. $\dfrac{5}{8}$ $+\dfrac{5}{6}$

29. $\dfrac{3}{4} + \dfrac{1}{10}$

30. $\dfrac{4}{9} + \dfrac{2}{5}$

31. $\dfrac{5}{12} + \dfrac{5}{9}$

32. $\dfrac{5}{9} + \dfrac{3}{8}$

33. $\dfrac{7}{10} + \dfrac{1}{8}$

34. $\dfrac{3}{8} + \dfrac{1}{4}$

35. $\dfrac{7}{10} + \dfrac{1}{6}$

36. $\dfrac{17}{30} + \dfrac{9}{20}$

High Roller

Use the scoring rules for Fraction Toss to compute the scores for each game below. Compare the sums to decide the winner.

37. Amy

Brad

38. Elena

Erik

39. Kara

Ryan

40. Alex

Alison

★ **41.** Jennifer

Shawn

★ **42.** Phillip

Kathryn

241

Adding Mixed Numbers

Jesse used $4\frac{3}{4}$ yd of fabric to make a bean bag chair. He used $3\frac{2}{3}$ yd for curtains. Add to find the total amount of fabric he used.

Write equivalent fractions with a common denominator.

$$4\frac{3}{4} = 4\frac{9}{12}$$
$$+\,3\frac{2}{3} = 3\frac{8}{12}$$

Add.

$$4\frac{3}{4} = 4\frac{9}{12}$$
$$+\,3\frac{2}{3} = +3\frac{8}{12}$$
$$\rule{0pt}{1pt}$$
$$7\frac{17}{12}$$

Write in lowest terms.

$$7\frac{17}{12} = 7 + 1\frac{5}{12} = 8\frac{5}{12}$$

Jesse used $8\frac{5}{12}$ yd of fabric.

Exercises

Complete.

1. $2\frac{1}{4} = 2\frac{\blacksquare}{8}$

2. $3\frac{1}{5} = 3\frac{\blacksquare}{15}$

3. $6\frac{2}{7} = 6\frac{\blacksquare}{35}$

4. $7\frac{1}{3} = 7\frac{\blacksquare}{6}$

5. $1\frac{1}{8} = 1\frac{\blacksquare}{16}$

6. $2\frac{1}{9} = 2\frac{\blacksquare}{18}$

7. $5\frac{1}{6} = 5\frac{\blacksquare}{18}$

8. $4\frac{3}{4} = 4\frac{\blacksquare}{20}$

Complete.

9. $6\frac{5}{4} = 7\frac{\blacksquare}{4}$

10. $3\frac{7}{6} = 4\frac{\blacksquare}{6}$

11. $8\frac{5}{3} = 9\frac{\blacksquare}{3}$

12. $7\frac{9}{5} = 8\frac{\blacksquare}{5}$

13. $3\frac{3}{2} = 4\frac{\blacksquare}{2}$

14. $5\frac{5}{3} = 6\frac{\blacksquare}{3}$

15. $2\frac{7}{6} = 3\frac{\blacksquare}{6}$

16. $4\frac{10}{7} = 5\frac{\blacksquare}{7}$

Add. Write the sum in lowest terms.

17. $4\frac{1}{4}$
$+3\frac{1}{6}$

18. $3\frac{1}{5}$
$+2\frac{3}{5}$

19. $4\frac{5}{7}$
$+1\frac{4}{7}$

20. $1\frac{1}{4}$
$+1\frac{5}{8}$

21. $6\frac{2}{3}$
$+4\frac{1}{4}$

22. $8\frac{5}{6}$
$+3\frac{5}{8}$

23. $3\frac{1}{5} + 2\frac{7}{10}$

24. $7\frac{4}{9} + 3\frac{1}{6}$

25. $4\frac{1}{3} + 1\frac{1}{8}$

26. $3\frac{1}{3} + 3\frac{4}{5}$

27. $3\frac{1}{2} + 5\frac{3}{8}$

28. $5\frac{3}{4} + 8\frac{1}{6}$

Sew and Save

PROJECT	FABRIC NEEDED
Wall Hanging	$1\frac{1}{4}$ yd
Floor Pillow	$2\frac{1}{3}$ yd
Throw Pillow	$1\frac{1}{8}$ yd
Window Shades	$1\frac{2}{3}$ yd
Sofa Cover	$18\frac{3}{8}$ yd

Solve.

29. How much fabric is needed for a throw pillow and a wall hanging?

30. How much fabric is needed for a sofa cover and a floor pillow?

★ **31.** How much fabric is needed for two window shades, a sofa cover, and a wall hanging?

Checkpoint A

Measure the segment to the nearest $\frac{1}{8}$ in. (*pages 236–237*)

1. _____

2. _____

Add or subtract. Write the answer in lowest terms. (*pages 238–239*)

3. $\frac{3}{5}$
$+\frac{1}{5}$

4. $\frac{5}{8}$
$-\frac{1}{8}$

5. $\frac{1}{8}$
$+\frac{3}{4}$

6. $\frac{2}{10}$
$+\frac{3}{5}$

Add. Write the sum in lowest terms. (*pages 240–241*)

7. $\frac{2}{4}$
$+\frac{5}{6}$

8. $\frac{3}{8}$
$+\frac{2}{5}$

Add. Write the sum in lowest terms. (*pages 242–243*)

9. $2\frac{1}{2}$
$+3\frac{3}{10}$

10. $4\frac{1}{2}$
$+6\frac{3}{5}$

11. $7\frac{2}{3}$
$+3\frac{1}{10}$

12. $5\frac{1}{6}$
$+\frac{3}{5}$

Subtracting Fractions

You can find how much longer Mary's walk was by subtracting.

Write equivalent fractions with a common denominator.

$$\frac{4}{5} = \frac{8}{10}$$

$$-\frac{1}{2} = \frac{5}{10}$$

Now subtract the numerators.

$$\frac{4}{5} = \frac{8}{10}$$

$$-\frac{1}{2} = -\frac{5}{10}$$

$$\frac{3}{10}$$

Mary's walk was $\frac{3}{10}$ mi longer than Kelly's.

Exercises

Complete.

1. $\frac{1}{3} = \frac{\blacksquare}{12}$

$-\frac{1}{4} = -\frac{\blacksquare}{12}$

$\frac{\blacksquare}{12}$

2. $\frac{2}{3} = \frac{\blacksquare}{12}$

$-\frac{1}{4} = -\frac{\blacksquare}{12}$

$\frac{\blacksquare}{12}$

3. $\frac{3}{4} = \frac{\blacksquare}{20}$

$-\frac{1}{5} = -\frac{\blacksquare}{20}$

$\frac{\blacksquare}{20}$

4. $\frac{7}{8} = \frac{\blacksquare}{24}$

$-\frac{1}{6} = -\frac{\blacksquare}{24}$

$\frac{\blacksquare}{24}$

5. $\frac{5}{7} = \frac{\blacksquare}{21}$

$-\frac{1}{3} = -\frac{\blacksquare}{21}$

$\frac{\blacksquare}{21}$

6. $\frac{2}{3} = \frac{\blacksquare}{12}$

$-\frac{1}{4} = -\frac{\blacksquare}{12}$

$\frac{\blacksquare}{12}$

7. $\frac{1}{5} = \frac{\blacksquare}{30}$

$-\frac{1}{6} = -\frac{\blacksquare}{30}$

$\frac{\blacksquare}{30}$

8. $\frac{7}{9} = \frac{\blacksquare}{9}$

$-\frac{2}{3} = -\frac{\blacksquare}{9}$

$\frac{\blacksquare}{9}$

Subtract. Write the difference in lowest terms.

9. $\dfrac{1}{2}$
$-\dfrac{1}{5}$

10. $\dfrac{7}{10}$
$-\dfrac{1}{8}$

11. $\dfrac{1}{3}$
$-\dfrac{1}{5}$

12. $\dfrac{1}{6}$
$-\dfrac{1}{9}$

13. $\dfrac{2}{3}$
$-\dfrac{1}{2}$

14. $\dfrac{1}{2}$
$-\dfrac{1}{4}$

15. $\dfrac{1}{2}$
$-\dfrac{3}{7}$

16. $\dfrac{7}{8}$
$-\dfrac{5}{6}$

17. $\dfrac{2}{3}$
$-\dfrac{1}{9}$

18. $\dfrac{5}{12}$
$-\dfrac{1}{8}$

19. $\dfrac{1}{2}$
$-\dfrac{1}{3}$

20. $\dfrac{3}{10}$
$-\dfrac{1}{4}$

21. $\dfrac{5}{9}$
$-\dfrac{1}{2}$

22. $\dfrac{8}{9}$
$-\dfrac{5}{6}$

23. $\dfrac{2}{5}$
$-\dfrac{1}{4}$

24. $\dfrac{3}{4}$
$-\dfrac{1}{8}$

25. $\dfrac{5}{6}$
$-\dfrac{3}{4}$

26. $\dfrac{4}{5}$
$-\dfrac{3}{4}$

27. $\dfrac{5}{6} - \dfrac{3}{10}$

28. $\dfrac{3}{4} - \dfrac{5}{12}$

29. $\dfrac{1}{4} - \dfrac{1}{12}$

30. $\dfrac{7}{9} - \dfrac{7}{12}$

31. $\dfrac{4}{5} - \dfrac{1}{2}$

32. $\dfrac{9}{10} - \dfrac{3}{4}$

33. $\dfrac{3}{5} - \dfrac{2}{15}$

34. $\dfrac{1}{2} - \dfrac{2}{9}$

Using Fractions

Solve.

35. Tasha's house is $\frac{1}{8}$ mi from school. Mica's house is $\frac{1}{2}$ mi from school. Who lives farther from school? How much farther?

36. Herman lives $\frac{7}{8}$ mi from the library. If he walks for $\frac{1}{5}$ mi and meets a friend, how much farther do they have to walk to the library?

★ 37. A survey showed that $\frac{2}{5}$ of the students at the Brace School ride the bus to school and $\frac{1}{2}$ of the students walk. What fraction of the students use other forms of transportation?

Subtracting Mixed Numbers

To subtract mixed numbers subtract the fractions first, then the whole numbers. Write the difference in lowest terms.

Subtract the fractions.

$$3\frac{7}{9}$$
$$-1\frac{4}{9}$$
$$\overline{\frac{3}{9}}$$

Subtract the whole numbers.

$$3\frac{7}{9}$$
$$-1\frac{4}{9}$$
$$\overline{2\frac{3}{9}}$$

Write the difference in lowest terms.

$$2\frac{3}{9} = 2\frac{1}{3}$$

Subtract $1\frac{1}{8}$ from $4\frac{5}{6}$.

Write equivalent fractions with a common denominator.

$$4\frac{5}{6} = 4\frac{20}{24}$$
$$-1\frac{1}{8} = 1\frac{3}{24}$$

Subtract the fractions.

$$4\frac{5}{6} = \quad 4\frac{20}{24}$$
$$-1\frac{1}{8} = -1\frac{3}{24}$$
$$\overline{\frac{17}{24}}$$

Subtract the whole numbers.

$$4\frac{5}{6} = \quad 4\frac{20}{24}$$
$$-1\frac{1}{8} = -1\frac{3}{24}$$
$$\overline{3\frac{17}{24}}$$

Exercises

Complete.

1. $$2\frac{3}{8}$$
    $$-1\frac{1}{8}$$
    $$\overline{1\frac{\blacksquare}{8}} = 1\frac{\blacksquare}{4}$$

2. $$7\frac{5}{9}$$
    $$-2\frac{2}{9}$$
    $$\overline{5\frac{\blacksquare}{9}} = 5\frac{\blacksquare}{3}$$

3. $$8\frac{2}{3} = \quad 8\frac{\blacksquare}{6}$$
    $$-2\frac{1}{6} = -2\frac{\blacksquare}{6}$$
    $$\overline{\blacksquare\frac{\blacksquare}{6}} = \blacksquare\frac{\blacksquare}{2}$$

4. $$4\frac{7}{10} = \quad 4\frac{\blacksquare}{10}$$
    $$-3\frac{1}{5} = -3\frac{\blacksquare}{10}$$
    $$\overline{\blacksquare\frac{\blacksquare}{10}} = \blacksquare\frac{\blacksquare}{2}$$

5. $$5\frac{3}{5} = \quad 5\frac{\blacksquare}{10}$$
    $$-2\frac{1}{10} = -2\frac{\blacksquare}{10}$$
    $$\overline{\blacksquare\frac{\blacksquare}{10}} = \blacksquare\frac{\blacksquare}{2}$$

6. $$12\frac{5}{6} = \quad 12\frac{\blacksquare}{18}$$
    $$-3\frac{2}{9} = -3\frac{\blacksquare}{18}$$
    $$\overline{\blacksquare\frac{\blacksquare}{18}}$$

Subtract. Write the difference in lowest terms.

7. $6\frac{5}{7}$
    $-4\frac{3}{7}$

8. $5\frac{1}{2}$
    $-2\frac{2}{5}$

9. $8\frac{3}{4}$
    $-2\frac{3}{8}$

10. $4\frac{13}{16}$
    $-1\frac{9}{16}$

11. $5\frac{5}{6}$
    $-4\frac{2}{3}$

12. $3\frac{4}{5}$
    $-2\frac{2}{3}$

13. $6\frac{9}{10}$
    $-1\frac{3}{5}$

14. $4\frac{5}{6}$
    $-2\frac{7}{9}$

15. $5\frac{11}{12}$
    $-3\frac{7}{12}$

16. $7\frac{5}{6}$
    $-5\frac{4}{5}$

17. $16\frac{7}{10}$
    $-\ 5\frac{4}{15}$

18. $11\frac{5}{6}$
    $-\ 3\frac{1}{6}$

19. $15\frac{3}{4}$
    $-\ 8\frac{3}{5}$

20. $9\frac{9}{10}$
    $-7\frac{3}{4}$

21. $8\frac{2}{3}$
    $-4\frac{5}{8}$

22. $4\frac{7}{10} - 3\frac{3}{10}$

23. $2\frac{1}{2} - 1\frac{1}{3}$

24. $3\frac{1}{4} - 2\frac{1}{6}$

25. $4\frac{5}{7} - 1\frac{2}{7}$

26. $5\frac{3}{4} - 1\frac{1}{2}$

27. $7\frac{2}{3} - 2\frac{2}{5}$

28. $8\frac{5}{6} - 2\frac{5}{6}$

29. $3\frac{5}{6} - 1\frac{1}{4}$

Food for Thought

Barney is making roast chicken, baked potatoes, and green beans for supper. He wants everything to be ready at the same time. Here are the cooking times:

roast chicken	$1\frac{1}{2}$ hours
baked potatoes	$1\frac{1}{4}$ hours
green beans	$\frac{1}{6}$ hour

30. How long after the chicken is started should the potatoes go in the oven?

31. How long after the chicken is started should the green beans start cooking?

★ 32. Barney wants to allow $\frac{1}{3}$ hour for the chicken to cool before serving supper. What time should he start cooking in order to serve supper at 7:15?

Subtracting Mixed Numbers

It's often necessary to rewrite a mixed number before you can subtract. Look at these examples.

To subtract $2\frac{1}{4}$ from 6, you first take a 1 from the 6. Then write 6 as $5\frac{4}{4}$.

$$6 = 5 + 1 = 5\frac{4}{4}$$

Now you can subtract.

$$
\begin{array}{rcl}
6 &=& 5\frac{4}{4} \\
-2\frac{1}{4} &=& -2\frac{1}{4} \\
\hline
& & 3\frac{3}{4}
\end{array}
$$

To subtract $2\frac{3}{4}$ from $5\frac{1}{4}$, you first take a 1 from the 5. Then write 5 as $4\frac{4}{4}$ and add $\frac{1}{4}$.

$$5\frac{1}{4} = 4\frac{4}{4} + \frac{1}{4} = 4\frac{5}{4}$$

Now you can subtract.

$$
\begin{array}{rcl}
5\frac{1}{4} &=& 4\frac{5}{4} \\
-2\frac{3}{4} &=& -2\frac{3}{4} \\
\hline
& & 2\frac{2}{4} = 2\frac{1}{2}
\end{array}
$$

Exercises

Complete.

1. $4 = 3\dfrac{\blacksquare}{5}$

2. $6 = 5\dfrac{\blacksquare}{4}$

3. $2 = 1\dfrac{\blacksquare}{6}$

4. $5 = 4\dfrac{\blacksquare}{3}$

5. $2\frac{1}{5} = 1\dfrac{\blacksquare}{5}$

6. $8\frac{2}{5} = 7\dfrac{\blacksquare}{5}$

7. $19\frac{1}{8} = 18\dfrac{\blacksquare}{8}$

8. $6\frac{3}{7} = 5\dfrac{\blacksquare}{7}$

9. $4\frac{1}{6} = 3\dfrac{\blacksquare}{6}$

10. $3\frac{5}{11} = 2\dfrac{\blacksquare}{11}$

11. $13\frac{1}{9} = 12\dfrac{\blacksquare}{9}$

12. $4\frac{3}{8} = 3\dfrac{\blacksquare}{8}$

Subtract. Write the difference in lowest terms.

13. $\begin{array}{r} 4 \\ -2\frac{2}{3} \\ \hline \end{array}$

14. $\begin{array}{r} 8\frac{1}{4} \\ -3\frac{3}{4} \\ \hline \end{array}$

15. $\begin{array}{r} 7\frac{2}{5} \\ -3\frac{4}{5} \\ \hline \end{array}$

16. $\begin{array}{r} 6 \\ -\frac{3}{8} \\ \hline \end{array}$

17. $\begin{array}{r} 9\frac{2}{9} \\ -6\frac{5}{9} \\ \hline \end{array}$

18. $\begin{array}{r} 17 \\ -1\frac{1}{3} \\ \hline \end{array}$

19. $\begin{array}{r} 9\frac{2}{5} \\ -3\frac{4}{5} \\ \hline \end{array}$

20. $\begin{array}{r} 22\frac{1}{8} \\ -19\frac{7}{8} \\ \hline \end{array}$

21. $\begin{array}{r} 63\frac{4}{9} \\ -20\frac{7}{9} \\ \hline \end{array}$

22. $\begin{array}{r} 4\frac{10}{21} \\ -2\frac{15}{21} \\ \hline \end{array}$

23. 5

$\quad -2\dfrac{3}{10}$

24. $9\dfrac{5}{8}$

$\quad -1\dfrac{7}{8}$

25. $10\dfrac{1}{12}$

$\quad -3\dfrac{5}{12}$

26. 9

$\quad -4\dfrac{5}{7}$

27. $12\dfrac{7}{10}$

$\quad -4\dfrac{9}{10}$

28. $15\dfrac{1}{3}$

$\quad -10\dfrac{2}{3}$

29. $10\dfrac{4}{9}$

$\quad -7\dfrac{7}{9}$

30. $8\dfrac{2}{5}$

$\quad -6\dfrac{4}{5}$

31. $6\dfrac{3}{8}$

$\quad -3\dfrac{5}{8}$

32. 8

$\quad -\dfrac{6}{7}$

33. $7 - 4\dfrac{1}{2}$

34. $5\dfrac{1}{6} - 3\dfrac{5}{6}$

35. $10\dfrac{1}{8} - 3\dfrac{5}{8}$

36. $15\dfrac{9}{15} - 8\dfrac{14}{15}$

37. $12\dfrac{2}{7} - 8\dfrac{5}{7}$

38. $1 - \dfrac{1}{3}$

39. $11\dfrac{2}{9} - 4\dfrac{5}{9}$

40. $14\dfrac{3}{8} - 3\dfrac{7}{8}$

Let's Have a Party

Solve.

41. Dan made 16 turkey sandwiches for a party. The dog ate $3\dfrac{1}{2}$ sandwiches before the guests arrived. How many sandwiches were left?

42. Rennie made 3 dishes of Spinach Surprise. The surprise was that only $1\dfrac{1}{8}$ dishes of the casserole were eaten. How many dishes did Rennie have left?

43. Rob bought $3\dfrac{1}{2}$ lb of cream cheese. He used $2\dfrac{3}{4}$ lb for stuffed meatloaf. He used the rest for stuffed celery. How much was used for celery?

Calculator Corner

Write the missing numerator or denominator.

$\dfrac{5}{19} = \dfrac{\blacksquare}{1558}$ $\qquad$ $\dfrac{13}{17} = \dfrac{728}{\blacksquare}$ $\qquad$ $\dfrac{19}{37} = \dfrac{\blacksquare}{999}$ $\qquad$ $\dfrac{29}{53} = \dfrac{3741}{\blacksquare}$

Subtracting Mixed Numbers

Susie tries to practice the piano for $2\frac{1}{2}$ hours a day. Yesterday she only practiced for $1\frac{3}{5}$ hours.

Subtract to see how much longer she should have practiced.

First write equivalent fractions with a common denominator. Notice that you can't subtract the fractions.

$$2\frac{1}{2} = 2\frac{5}{10}$$
$$-1\frac{3}{5} = 1\frac{6}{10}$$

Think of $2\frac{5}{10}$ as $1 + \frac{10}{10} + \frac{5}{10}$.

Rewrite the fraction.

Now subtract as usual.

$$2\frac{5}{10} = 1\frac{15}{10}$$

$$\begin{array}{r} 2\frac{1}{2} = \quad 2\frac{5}{10} = \quad 1\frac{15}{10} \\ -1\frac{3}{5} = -1\frac{3}{5} = -1\frac{6}{10} \\ \hline \frac{9}{10} \end{array}$$

Susie should have practiced for $\frac{9}{10}$ hours longer.

Exercises

Complete to write equivalent fractions.

1. $4\frac{1}{6} = 4\frac{\blacksquare}{12}$ **2.** $5\frac{1}{5} = 5\frac{\blacksquare}{15}$ **3.** $6\frac{1}{6} = 6\frac{\blacksquare}{18}$ **4.** $5\frac{1}{3} = 5\frac{\blacksquare}{9}$

5. $7\frac{2}{5} = 7\frac{\blacksquare}{10}$ **6.** $9\frac{3}{4} = 9\frac{\blacksquare}{12}$ **7.** $2\frac{1}{3} = 2\frac{\blacksquare}{6}$ **8.** $2\frac{4}{7} = 2\frac{\blacksquare}{21}$

9. $3\frac{7}{8} = 3\frac{\blacksquare}{24}$ **10.** $8\frac{4}{5} = 8\frac{\blacksquare}{20}$ **11.** $3\frac{2}{5} = 3\frac{\blacksquare}{25}$ **12.** $6\frac{4}{5} = 6\frac{\blacksquare}{35}$

Subtract. Write the difference in lowest terms.

13. $\begin{array}{r} 8\frac{1}{4} \\ -6\frac{1}{2} \\ \hline \end{array}$ **14.** $\begin{array}{r} 4\frac{3}{8} \\ -2\frac{5}{6} \\ \hline \end{array}$ **15.** $\begin{array}{r} 5\frac{1}{2} \\ -1\frac{2}{3} \\ \hline \end{array}$ **16.** $\begin{array}{r} 8\frac{5}{9} \\ -4\frac{2}{3} \\ \hline \end{array}$ **17.** $\begin{array}{r} 7\frac{3}{10} \\ -3\frac{3}{5} \\ \hline \end{array}$

18. $6\frac{2}{3}$
$-2\frac{3}{4}$

19. $9\frac{1}{6}$
$-5\frac{4}{9}$

20. $5\frac{5}{8}$
$-1\frac{3}{4}$

21. $10\frac{5}{12}$
$-3\frac{2}{3}$

22. $2\frac{1}{4}$
$-\frac{3}{5}$

23. $7\frac{2}{5}$
$-2\frac{1}{2}$

24. $9\frac{2}{7} - 4\frac{2}{3}$

25. $8\frac{2}{5} - 3\frac{3}{4}$

26. $11\frac{2}{5} - 4\frac{7}{10}$

27. $16\frac{1}{6} - 8\frac{3}{8}$

Time Will Tell

Mrs. Nolan's piano students keep a record of how long they practice each week. Last week the record looked like this.

STUDENT	PRACTICE TIME
Tony	$5\frac{3}{4}$ hours
Sarah	$6\frac{1}{2}$ hours
Maria	7 hours
Valdez	$4\frac{2}{3}$ hours

28. How much longer did Maria practice than Valdez?

29. What is the difference in practice times for Sarah and Tony?

30. How much longer did Tony practice than Valdez?

★ **31.** Valdez should practice for $5\frac{1}{2}$ hours a week. If he had practiced for another 45 min would he have reached his goal?

Checkpoint B

Subtract. Write the difference in lowest terms. (*pages 244–245*)

1. $\frac{3}{5}$
$-\frac{1}{4}$

2. $\frac{4}{9}$
$-\frac{1}{6}$

Subtract. Write the difference in lowest terms. (*pages 246–247*)

3. $3\frac{3}{4}$
$-1\frac{1}{4}$

4. $4\frac{7}{10}$
$-3\frac{1}{5}$

5. $2\frac{1}{2}$
$-1\frac{1}{5}$

6. $6\frac{7}{8}$
$-4\frac{3}{4}$

Subtract. Write the difference in lowest terms. (*pages 248–249*)

7. 2
$-\frac{3}{5}$

8. $5\frac{1}{3}$
$-2\frac{2}{3}$

9. 4
$-1\frac{7}{8}$

10. $7\frac{1}{6}$
$-5\frac{5}{6}$

Subtract. Write the difference in lowest terms. (*pages 250–251*)

11. $3\frac{1}{2}$
$-1\frac{3}{4}$

12. $6\frac{1}{3}$
$-2\frac{4}{5}$

Problem Solving · SIMPLIFY THE PROBLEM

1	Understand
2	Plan
3	Work
4	Answer

Sometimes math problems look more difficult than they are. If you rewrite the problem with only the important information and substitute simpler numbers, the solution may become clear.

Problem:
Mount St. Helens was 2948.7 m high before it erupted in May, 1980. After the eruption it was 2559.8 m high. How much of the mountain was blown away by the eruption?

Simpler Problem:
If Mount St. Helens was 5 m high before it erupted and 3 m high after, then how much was blown away?

Plan: Subtract 3 from 5.

Now you can see that subtraction is the method needed to solve the original problem.

$$\begin{array}{r} 2948.7 \text{ m} \\ -2559.8 \text{ m} \\ \hline 388.9 \text{ m} \end{array}$$

There were 388.9 m of the mountain blown away.

USE ANY NUMBERS THAT WILL MAKE THE PROBLEM EASIER.

Use the simpler problem to solve the original problem.

Original Problem	Simpler Problem
1. The eruption of Mount St. Helens leveled a forest that was about 18.6 km wide and 32.15 km long. Estimate the area of the destroyed forests.	The forest was 10 m wide and 20 m long. What was the area?
2. About 2,000,000 new trees were planted on 5000 sections to replace those destroyed by the volcano. About how many trees per section is this?	About 20 new trees were planted on 2 m². How many trees are on 1 m²?

3. The Forest Service estimates that 4986 black-tailed deer, 1487 elk, 215 black bears, 15 mountain goats, and 27,000 grouse were lost on Mount St. Helens. Estimate the total number of animals lost.

There were 10 deer, 7 elks, 5 bears, 2 goats and 20 grouse lost. Estimate the total.

For each problem below, write a simpler problem. Use it to solve the original problem.

4. The eruption of Mount St. Helens created many new lakes and ponds. A channel 885.7 m long was dug in just 14 weeks to prevent one new lake from overflowing. About how much was dug each week?

5. Scientists estimate that the rocks and mud that filled Spirit Lake will raise the water level about 114.82 m. The water level of the lake was 959.40 m before the eruption. What will the new level be?

6. Scientists continue to take measurements in order to predict future earthquakes. A circular warning zone with a radius of 49.5 km surrounds Mount St. Helens. What is the area of the warning zone?

★ **7.** The loggers helping to save the lumber around Mount St. Helens earned $11.80 per hour plus $6.00 a day for hazardous duty. How much would have been earned by a logger who worked 8.5 hours a day for 14 days?

Unit Review

Measure the segment to the nearest $\frac{1}{8}$ in. Match.

1. 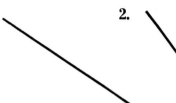 **2.** **3.**  **4.**

A. $1\frac{7}{8}$ in.   **B.** $\frac{6}{8}$ in.   **C.** $1\frac{5}{8}$ in.   **D.** $1\frac{1}{8}$ in.

Add or subtract. Write the sum or difference in lowest terms.

5. $\dfrac{1}{10} + \dfrac{7}{10}$ **6.** $\dfrac{4}{9} + \dfrac{3}{9}$ **7.** $\dfrac{7}{12} - \dfrac{3}{12}$ **8.** $\dfrac{6}{8} - \dfrac{5}{8}$ **9.** $\dfrac{2}{3} + \dfrac{2}{3}$ **10.** $\dfrac{3}{4} - \dfrac{1}{4}$

Add across. Add down. Write the sum in lowest terms.

11.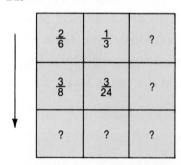

12.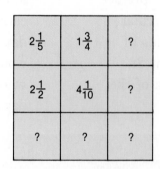

13.

$9\frac{1}{3}$	$6\frac{5}{9}$	?
$4\frac{5}{18}$	$7\frac{1}{6}$	?
?	?	?

Correct or incorrect? Write C or I.

14. $\dfrac{5}{6} - \dfrac{3}{4} = \dfrac{1}{12}$ **15.** $\dfrac{9}{10} - \dfrac{2}{3} = \dfrac{4}{15}$ **16.** $12\frac{4}{5} - 6\frac{1}{2} = 6\frac{3}{10}$ **17.** $6 - 1\frac{1}{5} = 4\frac{4}{5}$ **18.** $3\frac{1}{8} - 2\frac{3}{8} = 1\frac{5}{8}$ **19.** $7\frac{3}{8} - 5\frac{5}{6} = 1\frac{11}{24}$

Solve.

20. In one day 0.38 cm of rain fell from 1:00 to 2:00, 0.25 cm from 2:00 to 3:00, and 0.43 cm from 3:00 to 4:00. How much rain fell from 1:00 to 4:00?

Measure the segment to the nearest $\frac{1}{8}$ in. (*pages 236–237*)

1.    **2.**   **3.**   **4.**

Add or subtract. Write the sum or difference in lowest terms.
(*pages 238–239*)

5. $\frac{1}{5}$ **6.** $\frac{3}{8}$ **7.** $\frac{7}{8}$ **8.** $\frac{5}{9}$ **9.** $\frac{3}{14}$ **10.** $\frac{5}{12}$

$+\frac{2}{5}$ $+\frac{7}{8}$ $-\frac{5}{8}$ $-\frac{2}{9}$ $+\frac{11}{14}$ $-\frac{1}{12}$

Add. Write the sum in lowest terms. (*pages 240–243*)

11. $\frac{3}{4}$ **12.** $\frac{2}{3}$ **13.** $\frac{1}{5}$ **14.** $\frac{3}{8}$ **15.** $4\frac{1}{5}$ **16.** $5\frac{2}{3}$

$+\frac{1}{8}$ $+\frac{5}{9}$ $+\frac{1}{3}$ $+\frac{2}{7}$ $+7\frac{1}{5}$ $+1\frac{1}{7}$

Subtract. Write the difference in lowest terms. (*pages 244–247*)

17. $\frac{4}{9}$ **18.** $\frac{3}{5}$ **19.** $\frac{5}{6}$ **20.** $\frac{3}{4}$ **21.** $7\frac{8}{9}$ **22.** $4\frac{7}{8}$

$-\frac{1}{3}$ $-\frac{3}{10}$ $-\frac{3}{8}$ $-\frac{1}{5}$ $-6\frac{5}{9}$ $-1\frac{5}{6}$

Subtract. Write the difference in lowest terms. (*pages 248–251*)

23. 5 **24.** 8 **25.** $7\frac{5}{12}$ **26.** $6\frac{1}{4}$ **27.** $4\frac{2}{7}$

$-2\frac{2}{3}$ $-6\frac{4}{9}$ $-4\frac{11}{12}$ $-1\frac{2}{3}$ $-2\frac{1}{3}$

Solve. (*pages 252–253*)

28. Cheryl worked $3\frac{1}{2}$ hours on Monday, $5\frac{3}{4}$ on Tuesday, $4\frac{2}{3}$ on
Wednesday, and $6\frac{1}{4}$ on Thursday. How many hours did she
work on the 4 days?

29. Harry wants to see a movie at 7:30. If it's now 5:45 how
long does he have to wait?

Extra practice on page 395

Scientific Notation

You can write standard numbers in expanded notation. Here's an example.

$$4{,}372{,}895 = (4 \times 1{,}000{,}000) + (3 \times 100{,}000) + (7 \times 10{,}000) + (2 \times 1000) +$$
$$(8 \times 100) + (9 \times 10) + (5 \times 1)$$

This form takes a lot of space, and a lot of time writing zeros! Expanded notation can be shortened by using powers of ten.

$$1{,}000{,}000 = 10^6 \text{, so } 4{,}000{,}000 \text{ can be written as } 4 \times 10^6$$
$$4{,}372{,}895 = (4 \times 10^6) + (3 \times 10^5) + (7 \times 10^4) + (2 \times 10^3) + (8 \times 10^2) +$$
$$(9 \times 10^1) + (5 \times 1)$$

Write these numbers in expanded notation using powers of ten. Use the chart to help.

10^9	1,000,000,000
10^8	100,000,000
10^7	10,000,000
10^6	1,000,000
10^5	100,000
10^4	10,000
10^3	1000
10^2	100
10^1	10

1. 243

2. 3879

3. 4821

4. 63,985

5. 486,093

6. 9,429,876

7. 8,302,481

8. 68,937,498

9. 102,365,299

10. 268,539,740

11. 7,368,366,928

12. 5,854,901,407

The nearest Pluto ever comes to Earth is 4,260,800,000 km. Scientists must often make calculations with this type of large number. To make their work easier they use **scientific notation.**

A number in scientific notation is shown as the product of a number between 1 and 10 and a power of 10. Here's how to write 4,260,800,000 in scientific notation.

Standard Number		Scientific Notation
4,260,800,000	⇨	4.2608×10^9

Write the distance in scientific notation.

13. The moon is about 382,000 km away from Earth.

14. The diameter of the sun is 1,384,000 km.

15. When Saturn is closest to Earth, it is 1,630,000,000 km away.

16. At its farthest point, Saturn is 1,228,952,000 km away from Earth.

Write the number in standard form.

17. Venus is 1.069×10^8 km away from the sun.

18. The star Sirius is 8.352×10^{13} km away.

19. The diameter of Jupiter is 1.385×10^5 km.

20. Neptune is 4.48×10^9 km from the sun.

21. Uranus is 2.848×10^9 km from the sun.

22. The star Canopus is 9.6×10^{14} km away from the sun.

23. The orbit of the earth has a diameter of 2.9728×10^8 km.

Write the circumference and area of the circle.

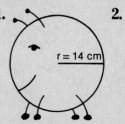 **1.** r = 14 cm

2. r = 9 cm

3. r = 6 cm

4. r = 19 mm

5. r = 16 mm

Write the area of the rectangle or right triangle.

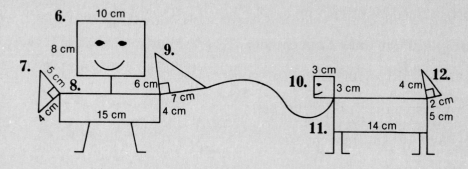

6. 10 cm, 8 cm

7. 5 cm, 4 cm

8. 15 cm

9. 6 cm, 7 cm, 4 cm

10. 3 cm, 3 cm

11. 14 cm

12. 4 cm, 2 cm, 5 cm

What is the perimeter of the polygon?

13. 5 cm, 4 cm, 6 cm, 6 cm, 9 cm

14. 5.2 m, 2.1 m, 3.5 m, 4.9 m, 4.6 m, 2.2 m

15. 13 mm, 12.2 mm, 15.7 mm, 16 mm

Estimate the product or quotient. Match.

16. 29.4 × 8.93   **A.** 100

17. 3.6$\overline{)385.6}$ **B.** 3

18. 206.3 × 49.61   **C.** 270

19. 77.4 × 98.53   **D.** 7700

20. 98.6$\overline{)316.5}$ **E.** 10,000

Solve.

21. The cover for a rectangular swimming pool is 18.7 m long and 11.63 m wide. Estimate the area of the pool cover.

One drop per second from a leaking faucet can amount to a loss of 200 gal of water per month. A quart fills four 8-oz drinking glasses. How many people could have a full glass from the lost water?

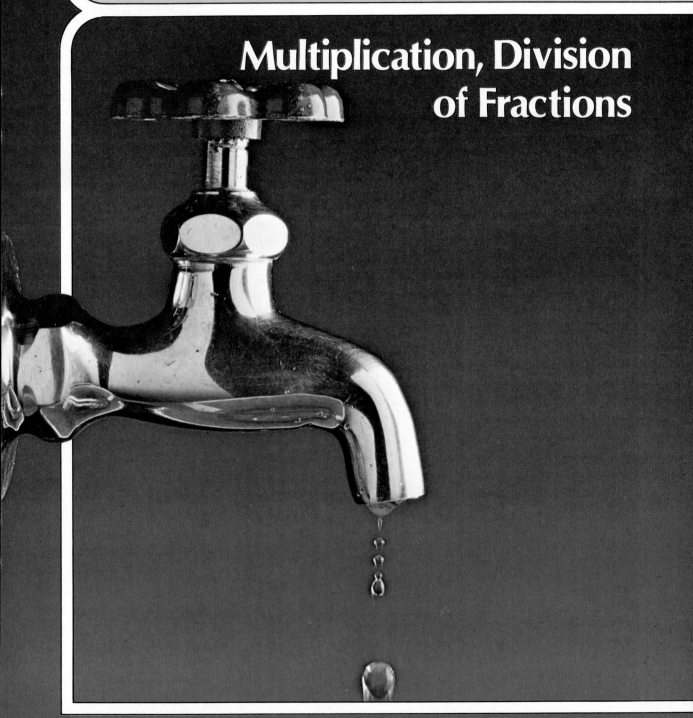

Multiplication, Division of Fractions

Multiplying Fractions and Whole Numbers

Vern had a flat tire after driving $\frac{2}{3}$ the distance to the shore. If the total distance is 6 mi, how far did Vern drive before he got the flat tire?

Since you want to find $\frac{2}{3}$ of 6, multiply.

$$\frac{2}{3} \times 6 = \frac{2 \times 6}{3} = \frac{12}{3} = 4$$

Vern drove 4 mi before getting a flat tire.

Exercises

Complete.

1. $\frac{1}{5} \times 10 = \frac{\blacksquare \times 10}{5} = \frac{\blacksquare}{5} = \blacksquare$

   $10 \times \frac{1}{5} = \frac{\blacksquare \times 1}{5} = \frac{\blacksquare}{5} = \blacksquare$

2. $\frac{1}{8} \times 9 = \frac{1 \times \blacksquare}{8} = \frac{\blacksquare}{8} = 1\frac{\blacksquare}{8}$

   $9 \times \frac{1}{8} = \frac{\blacksquare \times 1}{8} = \frac{\blacksquare}{8} = 1\frac{\blacksquare}{8}$

3. $6 \times \frac{1}{4} = \frac{\blacksquare}{4} = 1\frac{\blacksquare}{4} = 1\frac{\blacksquare}{2}$

   $\frac{1}{4} \times 6 = \frac{\blacksquare}{4} = 1\frac{\blacksquare}{4} = 1\frac{\blacksquare}{2}$

4. $5 \times \frac{1}{7} = \frac{\blacksquare}{7}$

   $\frac{1}{7} \times 5 = \frac{\blacksquare}{7}$

5. $\frac{2}{3} \times 12 = \frac{\blacksquare \times 12}{3} = \frac{\blacksquare}{3} = \blacksquare$

   $12 \times \frac{2}{3} = \frac{\blacksquare \times 2}{3} = \frac{\blacksquare}{3} = \blacksquare$

6. $15 \times \frac{3}{5} = \frac{\blacksquare \times 3}{5} = \frac{\blacksquare}{5} = \blacksquare$

   $\frac{3}{5} \times 15 = \frac{3 \times \blacksquare}{5} = \frac{\blacksquare}{5} = \blacksquare$

Multiply. Write the product in lowest terms.

7. $3 \times \frac{2}{3}$

8. $8 \times \frac{3}{4}$

9. $\frac{1}{6} \times 10$

10. $\frac{1}{5} \times 2$

11. $\frac{1}{9} \times 3$

12. $\frac{1}{8} \times 11$

13. $4 \times \frac{6}{7}$

14. $\frac{2}{9} \times 3$

15. $\frac{3}{10} \times 5$

16. $\frac{1}{2} \times 11$

17. $8 \times \frac{1}{11}$ **18.** $4 \times \frac{5}{6}$ **19.** $4 \times \frac{4}{7}$ **20.** $\frac{5}{8} \times 7$ **21.** $\frac{5}{12} \times 3$

22. $15 \times \frac{4}{5}$ **23.** $\frac{6}{7} \times 8$ **24.** $9 \times \frac{1}{4}$ **25.** $5 \times \frac{2}{3}$ **26.** $\frac{1}{6} \times 12$

27. $\frac{1}{3} \times 7$ **28.** $\frac{3}{4} \times 10$ **29.** $6 \times \frac{2}{3}$ **30.** $6 \times \frac{3}{10}$ **31.** $\frac{5}{9} \times 6$

32. $6 \times \frac{4}{5}$ **33.** $\frac{2}{3} \times 7$ **34.** $\frac{7}{8} \times 11$ **35.** $\frac{3}{4} \times 16$ **36.** $\frac{9}{10} \times 15$

37. $12 \times \frac{1}{8}$ **38.** $\frac{4}{5} \times 30$ **39.** $\frac{7}{12} \times 54$ **40.** $33 \times \frac{2}{9}$ **41.** $65 \times \frac{3}{10}$

At the Pumps

Solve.

42. Monica's station wagon has a 24 gal gas tank. How many gallons are in the tank when the gauge is on $\frac{1}{2}$?

43. Ramon owns a Courser II that has an 18 gal gas tank. He now has $2\frac{1}{2}$ gal of gas in his car. How much gas is needed to fill the tank?

★ **44.** Mrs. Chin owns a Sphinx RX7 with a 20 gal gas tank. How much gas is needed to fill the tank if the gauge is on $\frac{1}{8}$?

Multiplying Fractions

The Arch Street parking lot is divided into 3 equal sections. Spaces for the handicapped occupy $\frac{1}{2}$ of Section A. What part of the lot is this? Multiply to find out.

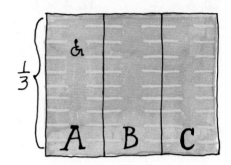 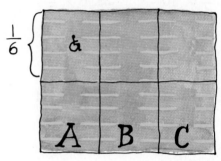

You can see from the diagram that $\frac{1}{2}$ of $\frac{1}{3}$ is $\frac{1}{6}$.

To multiply fractions you multiply the numerators and multiply the denominators.

$$\frac{\text{numerator} \times \text{numerator}}{\text{denominator} \times \text{denominator}} \quad \Rightarrow \quad \frac{1}{2} \times \frac{1}{3} = \frac{1 \times 1}{2 \times 3} = \frac{1}{6}$$

Exercises

Multiply. Write the product in lowest terms.

1.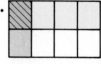
$\frac{1}{2} \times \frac{1}{4}$

2.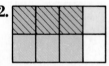
$\frac{1}{2} \times \frac{3}{4}$

3.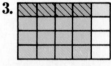
$\frac{1}{4} \times \frac{4}{5}$

4.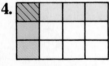
$\frac{1}{3} \times \frac{1}{4}$

5.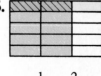
$\frac{1}{5} \times \frac{2}{3}$

6.
$\frac{2}{4} \times \frac{3}{5}$

7.
$\frac{3}{5} \times \frac{1}{3}$

8.
$\frac{5}{6} \times \frac{3}{4}$

Multiply. Write the product in lowest terms.

9. $\frac{1}{3} \times \frac{1}{5}$

10. $\frac{1}{2} \times \frac{1}{8}$

11. $\frac{1}{5} \times \frac{1}{4}$

12. $\frac{1}{3} \times \frac{1}{7}$

13. $\frac{1}{6} \times \frac{1}{3}$

14. $\frac{1}{5} \times \frac{2}{3}$ **15.** $\frac{1}{4} \times \frac{5}{6}$ **16.** $\frac{2}{5} \times \frac{1}{4}$ **17.** $\frac{5}{8} \times \frac{2}{3}$ **18.** $\frac{2}{5} \times \frac{3}{5}$

19. $\frac{4}{7} \times \frac{1}{2}$ **20.** $\frac{2}{3} \times \frac{5}{6}$ **21.** $\frac{3}{4} \times \frac{3}{5}$ **22.** $\frac{1}{2} \times \frac{9}{10}$ **23.** $\frac{3}{5} \times \frac{2}{3}$

24. $\frac{7}{8} \times \frac{3}{4}$ **25.** $\frac{5}{8} \times \frac{1}{6}$ **26.** $\frac{2}{9} \times \frac{2}{3}$ **27.** $\frac{1}{7} \times \frac{7}{8}$ **28.** $\frac{5}{6} \times \frac{7}{10}$

29. $\frac{4}{5} \times \frac{2}{3}$ **30.** $\frac{3}{4} \times \frac{5}{8}$ **31.** $\frac{7}{12} \times \frac{2}{5}$ **32.** $\frac{1}{2} \times \frac{5}{16}$ **33.** $\frac{3}{10} \times \frac{5}{8}$

34. $\frac{2}{8} \times \frac{4}{9}$ **35.** $\frac{7}{12} \times \frac{4}{5}$ **36.** $\frac{8}{10} \times \frac{7}{11}$ **37.** $\frac{10}{15} \times \frac{3}{7}$ **38.** $\frac{8}{19} \times \frac{2}{3}$

39. $\frac{3}{5} \times \frac{9}{11}$ **40.** $\frac{8}{15} \times \frac{3}{4}$ **41.** $\frac{7}{9} \times \frac{6}{13}$ **42.** $\frac{4}{11} \times \frac{3}{4}$ **43.** $\frac{15}{38} \times \frac{2}{3}$

 Half Strength

Kara finds a recipe she wants to try. She decides to make only half the recipe in case she doesn't like it.

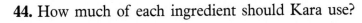

Yogurt Dip for Vegetables

$\frac{1}{2}$ c. cottage cheese
$\frac{1}{3}$ c. yogurt
4 Tablespoons mayonnaise
$\frac{1}{2}$ clove garlic
$\frac{1}{4}$ c. chopped walnuts
$\frac{1}{2}$ teaspoon lemon juice
1 tablespoon chopped parsley
Mix well and chill for 2 hours
Makes about 1 c.

Solve.

44. How much of each ingredient should Kara use?

45. How much dip will half of a recipe make?

When you buy stamps, they are usually connected. How many ways can you buy 3 connected stamps? 4 connected stamps? 5 connected stamps?

Take a Break

Multiplying Fractions

You can multiply fractions, then write the product in lowest terms.

$$\frac{4}{9} \times \frac{3}{5} = \frac{4 \times 3}{9 \times 5} = \frac{12}{45} = \frac{4}{15}$$

It's sometimes easier to divide the numerator and denominator by a common factor before you multiply. Then the product will already be in lowest terms.

$$3 \div 3 = 1$$

$$\frac{4}{9} \times \frac{3}{5} = \frac{4 \times \overset{1}{\cancel{3}}}{\underset{3}{\cancel{9}} \times 5} = \frac{4 \times 1}{3 \times 5} = \frac{4}{15}$$

$$9 \div 3 = 3$$

Exercises

Complete.

1. $\dfrac{2}{3} \times \dfrac{5}{6} = \dfrac{\overset{1}{\cancel{2}} \times 5}{3 \times \underset{3}{\cancel{6}}} = $ ▨

2. $\dfrac{3}{4} \times \dfrac{2}{5} = \dfrac{3 \times \overset{1}{\cancel{2}}}{\underset{2}{\cancel{4}} \times 5} = $ ▨

3. $\dfrac{6}{7} \times \dfrac{1}{3} = \dfrac{\overset{2}{\cancel{6}} \times 1}{7 \times \underset{1}{\cancel{3}}} = $ ▨

4. $\dfrac{3}{4} \times \dfrac{5}{6} = \dfrac{\overset{1}{\cancel{3}} \times 5}{4 \times \underset{2}{\cancel{6}}} = $ ▨

5. $\dfrac{2}{3} \times \dfrac{3}{7} = \dfrac{2 \times \overset{1}{\cancel{3}}}{\underset{1}{\cancel{3}} \times 7} = $ ▨

6. $\dfrac{9}{10} \times \dfrac{5}{6} = \dfrac{\overset{3}{\cancel{9}} \times \overset{1}{\cancel{5}}}{\underset{2}{\cancel{10}} \times \underset{2}{\cancel{6}}} = $ ▨

7. $\dfrac{5}{8} \times \dfrac{6}{7} = \dfrac{5 \times 6}{8 \times 7} = $ ▨

8. $\dfrac{9}{10} \times \dfrac{4}{5} = \dfrac{9 \times 4}{10 \times 5} = $ ▨

9. $\dfrac{2}{9} \times \dfrac{6}{7} = \dfrac{2 \times 6}{9 \times 7} = $ ▨

Multiply. Write the product in lowest terms.

10. $\dfrac{4}{9} \times \dfrac{1}{2}$

11. $\dfrac{5}{8} \times \dfrac{2}{7}$

12. $\dfrac{4}{9} \times \dfrac{5}{6}$

13. $\dfrac{3}{10} \times \dfrac{4}{7}$

14. $\dfrac{5}{6} \times \dfrac{2}{3}$

15. $\dfrac{3}{5} \times \dfrac{7}{9}$

16. $\dfrac{7}{10} \times \dfrac{5}{8}$

17. $\dfrac{4}{5} \times \dfrac{5}{8}$

18. $\dfrac{7}{8} \times \dfrac{3}{4}$

19. $\dfrac{2}{9} \times \dfrac{3}{4}$

20. $\frac{1}{3} \times \frac{6}{7}$ **21.** $\frac{9}{20} \times \frac{5}{6}$ **22.** $\frac{8}{9} \times \frac{3}{4}$ **23.** $\frac{5}{6} \times \frac{8}{15}$ **24.** $\frac{9}{16} \times \frac{8}{9}$

25. $\frac{2}{3} \times \frac{5}{12}$ **26.** $\frac{3}{8} \times \frac{4}{7}$ **27.** $\frac{1}{2} \times \frac{3}{10}$ **28.** $\frac{7}{12} \times \frac{3}{8}$ **29.** $\frac{3}{7} \times \frac{4}{15}$

30. $\frac{5}{16} \times \frac{8}{15}$ **31.** $\frac{3}{14} \times \frac{7}{18}$ **32.** $\frac{9}{10} \times \frac{5}{24}$ **33.** $\frac{8}{15} \times \frac{5}{12}$ **34.** $\frac{9}{25} \times \frac{20}{27}$

35. $\frac{1}{2} \times \frac{8}{9}$ **36.** $\frac{7}{10} \times \frac{4}{5}$ **37.** $\frac{2}{7} \times \frac{3}{8}$ **38.** $\frac{4}{5} \times \frac{16}{20}$ **39.** $\frac{3}{10} \times \frac{17}{21}$

Summer Sounds

When you want to know the temperature but don't have a thermometer, try listening to the crickets. The number of times they chirp in a minute and the following formula can give you a good idea of the temperature.

Let t = degrees Celsius

n = number of chirps in one minute

Then $t = \left(\frac{n}{4} + 8\right) \times \frac{5}{9}$

The example below shows how to use the formula.

Suppose $n = 100$

$t = \left(\frac{100}{4} + 8\right) \times \frac{5}{9}$

$= 33 \times \frac{5}{9}$

$= \frac{165}{9} = 18.3 \approx 18°C$

Find t, to the nearest degree, for the value of n.

40. 120   **41.** 160   **42.** 200

43. 220   ★ **44.** 227   ★ **45.** 155

Multiplying Mixed Numbers

Manson grew a squash that weighed $5\frac{1}{4}$ lb. Kim grew one that weighed $2\frac{2}{3}$ times as much. How many pounds did Kim's squash weigh?

To multiply $5\frac{1}{4}$ by $2\frac{2}{3}$, first write the mixed numbers as fractions.

$$5\frac{1}{4} = \frac{21}{4} \qquad 2\frac{2}{3} = \frac{8}{3}$$

Then simplify, if possible, before multiplying the fractions.

$$5\frac{1}{4} \times 2\frac{2}{3} = \frac{21}{4} \times \frac{8}{3} = \frac{\overset{7}{21} \times \overset{2}{8}}{\underset{1}{4} \times \underset{1}{3}} = \frac{14}{1} = 14$$

Kim's squash weighed 14 lb.

Exercises

Complete.

1. $1\frac{1}{2} = \frac{\blacksquare}{2}$ 2. $3\frac{1}{4} = \frac{\blacksquare}{4}$ 3. $6\frac{2}{5} = \frac{\blacksquare}{5}$ 4. $7\frac{3}{8} = \frac{\blacksquare}{8}$ 5. $2\frac{1}{6} = \frac{\blacksquare}{6}$

6. $4\frac{3}{8} = \frac{\blacksquare}{8}$ 7. $5\frac{2}{7} = \frac{\blacksquare}{7}$ 8. $3\frac{2}{5} = \frac{\blacksquare}{5}$ 9. $4\frac{1}{8} = \frac{\blacksquare}{8}$ 10. $1\frac{2}{3} = \frac{\blacksquare}{3}$

11. $1\frac{3}{5} = \frac{\blacksquare}{5}$ 12. $3\frac{1}{2} = \frac{\blacksquare}{2}$ 13. $2\frac{1}{4} = \frac{\blacksquare}{4}$ 14. $3\frac{1}{3} = \frac{\blacksquare}{3}$ 15. $7\frac{1}{2} = \frac{\blacksquare}{2}$

Multiply. Write the product in lowest terms.

16. $1\frac{1}{4} \times \frac{2}{3}$ 17. $1\frac{1}{9} \times \frac{3}{5}$ 18. $\frac{3}{7} \times 2\frac{1}{3}$ 19. $\frac{2}{3} \times 1\frac{1}{2}$ 20. $1\frac{3}{10} \times 2\frac{1}{2}$

21. $1\frac{5}{6} \times 1\frac{1}{2}$ 22. $1\frac{1}{3} \times 2\frac{1}{4}$ 23. $1\frac{1}{5} \times 3\frac{1}{3}$ 24. $1\frac{1}{2} \times 8$ 25. $1\frac{1}{6} \times 4$

26. $4\frac{1}{6} \times 2\frac{2}{5}$

27. $2\frac{4}{7} \times 10\frac{1}{2}$

28. $1\frac{3}{4} \times 2\frac{1}{2}$

29. $2\frac{1}{3} \times 1\frac{1}{4}$

30. $1\frac{3}{8} \times 2\frac{2}{5}$

31. $2\frac{1}{7} \times 1\frac{5}{9}$

32. $3\frac{3}{4} \times 1\frac{7}{10}$

33. $5\frac{1}{3} \times 1\frac{5}{8}$

34. $3\frac{3}{4} \times 1\frac{2}{9}$

35. $1\frac{1}{6} \times 1\frac{4}{5}$

36. $5\frac{1}{2} \times 4\frac{2}{3}$

37. $7\frac{7}{8} \times 10\frac{1}{5}$

38. $12\frac{2}{3} \times 6\frac{1}{9}$

39. $25\frac{1}{8} \times 10\frac{3}{4}$

Spring Fever

Solve.

40. Jim can weed $3\frac{1}{2}$ rows in his garden in one hour. At this rate, how many rows can he weed in $2\frac{1}{4}$ hours?

41. Steve planted $2\frac{1}{4}$ dozen tomato plants. Only $1\frac{2}{3}$ dozen plants survived. How many dozen plants did not survive?

42. Mabel worked in her garden for $1\frac{1}{2}$ hours a day for 2 weeks. How many hours did she work in her garden?

★ **43.** May grew 37 pumpkins. She used 8 for bread and 12 for gifts. She entered 5 in a perfect pumpkin contest. She sold the rest for $2.50 each. How much did she earn?

Multiply.

★ **44.** $1\frac{1}{2} \times 2\frac{1}{3} \times 3\frac{1}{4}$

★ **45.** $5\frac{1}{8} \times 4\frac{3}{5} \times 3\frac{4}{9}$

Checkpoint A

Multiply. Write the product in lowest terms. (*pages 260–261*)

1. $3 \times \frac{1}{6}$

2. $12 \times \frac{2}{3}$

3. $\frac{1}{5} \times 26$

4. $\frac{7}{8} \times 3$

Multiply. Write the product in lowest terms. (*pages 262–263*)

5. $\frac{1}{8} \times \frac{1}{3}$

6. $\frac{1}{5} \times \frac{2}{3}$

7. $\frac{4}{7} \times \frac{3}{4}$

8. $\frac{5}{8} \times \frac{9}{10}$

Multiply. Write the product in lowest terms. (*pages 264–265*)

9. $\frac{6}{9} \times \frac{1}{3}$

10. $\frac{3}{15} \times \frac{5}{9}$

11. $\frac{4}{7} \times \frac{21}{28}$

12. $\frac{2}{3} \times \frac{9}{10}$

Multiply. Write the product in lowest terms. (*pages 266–267*)

13. $1\frac{3}{8} \times \frac{2}{3}$

14. $2\frac{1}{4} \times \frac{3}{5}$

15. $3\frac{1}{8} \times 2\frac{3}{5}$

16. $4\frac{1}{2} \times 2\frac{1}{3}$

17. $3\frac{1}{2} \times 7\frac{2}{3}$

18. $5\frac{4}{9} \times 2\frac{3}{8}$

Dividing a Whole Number by a Fraction

Fred is serving $\frac{1}{2}$ grapefruit to each of his guests. How many guests can he serve with 3 grapefruit?

There are 6 halves in 3.

$$3 \div \frac{1}{2} = 6$$

Instead of dividing by $\frac{1}{2}$, you can multiply by 2.

$$3 \div \frac{1}{2} = 6 \qquad 3 \times 2 = 6$$

Fred can serve 6 guests with 3 grapefruit.

Two numbers whose product is 1 are called **reciprocals.**
Dividing by a number gives the same result as multiplying by its reciprocal.

$$10 \div 5 = 10 \times \frac{1}{5} = 2 \qquad 7 \div \frac{1}{3} = 7 \times 3 = 21$$

Exercises

Write the reciprocal of the number.

1. $\frac{1}{3}$ **2.** $\frac{1}{4}$ **3.** $\frac{1}{5}$ **4.** $\frac{1}{6}$ **5.** $\frac{1}{8}$ **6.** $\frac{1}{9}$

Complete.

7.

$$2 \div \frac{1}{4} = 2 \times \blacksquare = \blacksquare$$

8.

$$3 \div \frac{1}{6} = 3 \times \blacksquare = \blacksquare$$

9. $3 \div \frac{1}{8} = 3 \times \blacksquare = \blacksquare$

10. $4 \div \frac{1}{5} = 4 \times \blacksquare = \blacksquare$

11. $5 \div \frac{1}{3} = 5 \times \blacksquare = \blacksquare$

12. $6 \div \frac{1}{6} = 6 \times \blacksquare = \blacksquare$

268

Divide.

13. $2 \div \frac{1}{3}$ **14.** $8 \div \frac{1}{5}$ **15.** $4 \div \frac{1}{7}$ **16.** $5 \div \frac{1}{4}$ **17.** $7 \div \frac{1}{7}$

18. $5 \div \frac{1}{5}$ **19.** $1 \div \frac{1}{8}$ **20.** $7 \div \frac{1}{2}$ **21.** $11 \div \frac{1}{4}$ **22.** $8 \div \frac{1}{7}$

23. $3 \div \frac{1}{9}$ **24.** $2 \div \frac{1}{7}$ **25.** $9 \div \frac{1}{5}$ **26.** $1 \div \frac{1}{10}$ **27.** $12 \div \frac{1}{2}$

28. $15 \div \frac{1}{3}$ **29.** $17 \div \frac{1}{4}$ **30.** $6 \div \frac{1}{12}$ **31.** $14 \div \frac{1}{10}$ **32.** $20 \div \frac{1}{13}$

33. $10 \div \frac{1}{3}$ **34.** $18 \div \frac{1}{9}$ **35.** $1 \div \frac{1}{12}$ **36.** $75 \div \frac{1}{2}$ **37.** $157 \div \frac{1}{4}$

38. $110 \div \frac{1}{2}$ **39.** $300 \div \frac{1}{5}$ **40.** $250 \div \frac{1}{25}$ **41.** $138 \div \frac{1}{9}$ **42.** $223 \div \frac{1}{50}$

Figure It Out

Solve.

43. There are 8 c of detergent in a jumbo bottle of Brisk detergent. Each load of wash requires $\frac{1}{4}$ c. How many loads can you do with one bottle?

44. Tina bought $3\frac{1}{2}$ ft of flypaper. She hung $\frac{1}{3}$ of it on her porch. How much did she have left?

45. Lee filled 27 bags with leaves. Each bag can hold 76 L. How many liters of leaves did he rake?

Solve.

★ **46.** $\left(16 \div \frac{1}{4}\right) + \left(13 \div \frac{1}{5}\right)$

★ **47.** $\left(9 \div \frac{1}{3}\right) - \left(5 \div \frac{1}{2}\right)$

★ **48.** $\left(28 \div \frac{1}{2}\right) \times \left(6 \div \frac{1}{4}\right)$

Dividing a Fraction by a Whole Number

In a turtle race, Mick's turtle traveled $\frac{3}{4}$ yd in 2 minutes. At this rate, how far can the turtle travel in 1 minute? Divide $\frac{3}{4}$ by 2.

To divide a fraction by a whole number, first write the reciprocal of the whole number. Then multiply.

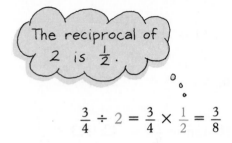

The reciprocal of 2 is $\frac{1}{2}$.

$$\frac{3}{4} \div 2 = \frac{3}{4} \times \frac{1}{2} = \frac{3}{8}$$

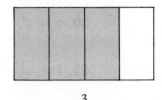

$\frac{3}{4}$

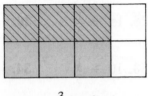

$\frac{3}{4} \div 2$

Mick's turtle can travel $\frac{3}{8}$ yd in 1 minute.

Exercises

Write the reciprocal of the number.

1. 6   **2.** 8   **3.** 11   **4.** 5   **5.** 2   **6.** 26

Complete. Write the answer in lowest terms.

7.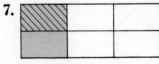

$$\frac{1}{3} \div 2 = \frac{1}{3} \times \frac{1}{2} = \frac{\blacksquare}{\blacksquare}$$

8.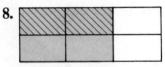

$$\frac{2}{3} \div 2 = \frac{2}{3} \times \frac{1}{2} = \frac{\blacksquare}{\blacksquare}$$

9.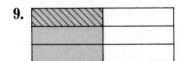

$$\frac{1}{2} \div 3 = \frac{1}{2} \times \frac{1}{3} = \frac{\blacksquare}{\blacksquare}$$

10. $\frac{1}{5} \div 4 = \frac{1}{5} \times \frac{1}{4} = \frac{\blacksquare}{\blacksquare}$ **11.** $\frac{4}{5} \div 4 = \frac{4}{5} \times \frac{1}{4} = \frac{\blacksquare}{\blacksquare}$ **12.** $\frac{1}{2} \div 5 = \frac{1}{2} \times \frac{1}{5} = \frac{\blacksquare}{\blacksquare}$

Divide. Write the quotient in lowest terms.

13. $\frac{1}{2} \div 2$ **14.** $\frac{3}{5} \div 3$ **15.** $\frac{5}{6} \div 2$ **16.** $\frac{1}{3} \div 4$ **17.** $\frac{5}{8} \div 5$

18. $\frac{1}{2} \div 4$ **19.** $\frac{1}{3} \div 3$ **20.** $\frac{2}{5} \div 4$ **21.** $\frac{3}{4} \div 6$ **22.** $\frac{1}{8} \div 2$

23. $\frac{3}{4} \div 4$ **24.** $\frac{4}{9} \div 4$ **26.** $\frac{9}{10} \div 3$ **26.** $\frac{2}{3} \div 4$ **27.** $\frac{6}{7} \div 2$

28. $\frac{1}{6} \div 2$ **29.** $\frac{4}{5} \div 8$ **30.** $\frac{1}{3} \div 5$ **31.** $\frac{5}{8} \div 2$ **32.** $\frac{3}{3} \div 6$

33. $\frac{1}{8} \div 6$ **34.** $\frac{3}{7} \div 4$ **35.** $\frac{2}{9} \div 5$ **36.** $\frac{4}{5} \div 12$ **37.** $\frac{6}{11} \div 10$

38. $\frac{3}{8} \div 9$ **39.** $\frac{4}{7} \div 15$ **40.** $\frac{6}{10} \div 20$ **41.** $\frac{7}{8} \div 21$ **42.** $\frac{10}{12} \div 15$

Race Around

Divide each fraction on the wheel by the number on the center.
Write the quotient in lowest terms.

Solve.

53. Ben spent $58.50 for a new radio. After it fell out of the window, he spent $14.63 to have it fixed. What fraction of the cost were the repairs?

★ **54.** Regina gave $\frac{1}{2}$ the money she won in a race to charity. She shared the rest equally with her friend. What fraction of the money did Regina keep?

Dividing a Fraction by a Fraction

The Sleep Tight Pillow Company received a shipment of $\frac{9}{10}$ t of feathers. The bales of feathers were stacked in piles that weighed $\frac{1}{6}$ t each. Into how many piles were the feathers stacked?

Divide $\frac{9}{10}$ by $\frac{1}{6}$.

To divide a fraction by a fraction, multiply the dividend by the reciprocal of the divisor.

$$\frac{9}{10} \div \frac{1}{6} = \frac{9}{10} \times \frac{6}{1} = \frac{54}{10} = 5\frac{4}{10} = 5\frac{2}{5}$$

There were $5\frac{2}{5}$ piles of feathers.

Exercises

Write the reciprocal of the number.

1. $\frac{2}{3}$ **2.** $\frac{3}{5}$ **3.** $\frac{7}{8}$ **4.** $\frac{1}{5}$ **5.** $\frac{3}{7}$ **6.** $\frac{11}{12}$

Complete. Write the quotient in lowest terms.

7. $\frac{1}{2} \div \frac{4}{5} = \frac{1}{2} \times \frac{\blacksquare}{\blacksquare} = \frac{\blacksquare}{\blacksquare}$ **8.** $\frac{3}{5} \div \frac{2}{3} = \frac{3}{5} \times \frac{\blacksquare}{\blacksquare} = \frac{\blacksquare}{\blacksquare}$

9. $\frac{5}{8} \div \frac{3}{4} = \frac{5}{8} \times \frac{\blacksquare}{\blacksquare} = \frac{\blacksquare}{\blacksquare}$ **10.** $\frac{1}{6} \div \frac{2}{5} = \frac{1}{6} \times \frac{\blacksquare}{\blacksquare} = \frac{\blacksquare}{\blacksquare}$

11. $\frac{2}{7} \div \frac{2}{5} = \frac{2}{7} \times \frac{\blacksquare}{\blacksquare} = \frac{\blacksquare}{\blacksquare}$ **12.** $\frac{3}{8} \div \frac{6}{7} = \frac{3}{8} \times \frac{\blacksquare}{\blacksquare} = \frac{\blacksquare}{\blacksquare}$

Divide. Write the quotient in lowest terms.

13. $\frac{3}{4} \div \frac{1}{2}$ **14.** $\frac{1}{6} \div \frac{5}{9}$ **15.** $\frac{2}{3} \div \frac{1}{5}$ **16.** $\frac{1}{5} \div \frac{4}{5}$ **17.** $\frac{3}{4} \div \frac{2}{3}$

18. $\frac{2}{9} \div \frac{3}{4}$ 19. $\frac{5}{6} \div \frac{7}{12}$ 20. $\frac{1}{2} \div \frac{1}{3}$ 21. $\frac{1}{8} \div \frac{5}{6}$ 22. $\frac{2}{5} \div \frac{5}{9}$

23. $\frac{3}{10} \div \frac{2}{5}$ 24. $\frac{5}{12} \div \frac{1}{4}$ 25. $\frac{7}{8} \div \frac{5}{6}$ 26. $\frac{9}{10} \div \frac{5}{6}$ 27. $\frac{8}{15} \div \frac{2}{3}$

28. $\frac{9}{16} \div \frac{3}{4}$ 29. $\frac{1}{3} \div \frac{4}{9}$ 30. $\frac{3}{7} \div \frac{2}{3}$ 31. $\frac{4}{11} \div \frac{6}{7}$ 32. $\frac{1}{25} \div \frac{7}{5}$

33. $\frac{2}{5} \div \frac{1}{3}$ 34. $\frac{2}{9} \div \frac{3}{4}$ 35. $\frac{5}{8} \div \frac{2}{3}$ 36. $\frac{3}{5} \div \frac{2}{9}$ 37. $\frac{4}{11} \div \frac{12}{22}$

Practice Makes Perfect

Divide to find the missing quotients.

38.

dividend ＼ divisor	$\div$	$\frac{3}{5}$	$\frac{2}{3}$	$\frac{3}{4}$
	$\frac{1}{6}$	$\frac{5}{18}$	?	?
	$\frac{2}{9}$	?	?	?
	$\frac{1}{7}$	?	?	?

39.

dividend ＼ divisor	$\div$	$\frac{7}{8}$	$\frac{4}{9}$	$\frac{12}{13}$
	$\frac{1}{5}$	$\frac{8}{35}$	?	?
	$\frac{2}{9}$	?	?	?
	$\frac{8}{10}$	?	?	?

Solve.

40. A robot can stitch 25 pillow covers in 1 hour. How many covers can it stitch in $7\frac{1}{2}$ hours?

★ 41. A pillow stuffer worked for $8\frac{1}{2}$ hours on Monday, Wednesday, and Friday. He worked for 4 hours on Tuesday and Thursday. How many hours did he work on the 5 days?

Calculator Corner

Most people sleep an average of 8 hours per day. At this rate, how many hours of your life have you spent sleeping? How many weeks?

Dividing with Mixed Numbers

Jacob can complete a model in about $6\frac{1}{2}$ hours. He works on his model for about $1\frac{1}{4}$ hours each day. At this rate, how many days should it take him to complete the model?

Divide $6\frac{1}{2}$ by $1\frac{1}{4}$.

Write the mixed numbers as fractions.

$$6\frac{1}{2} = \frac{13}{2} \qquad 1\frac{1}{4} = \frac{5}{4}$$

Multiply the dividend by the reciprocal of the divisor.

$$\frac{13}{2} \div \frac{5}{4} = \frac{13}{2} \times \frac{4}{5} = \frac{52}{10} = 5\frac{2}{10} = 5\frac{1}{5}$$

The model will be complete in about $5\frac{1}{5}$ days.

Exercises

Write the reciprocal of the number.

1. $\frac{12}{5}$
2. $\frac{9}{4}$
3. $\frac{4}{3}$
4. $\frac{8}{5}$
5. $\frac{15}{10}$
6. $\frac{13}{3}$

Divide. Write the quotient in lowest terms.

7. $\frac{1}{8} \div 3\frac{1}{5}$
8. $\frac{2}{3} \div 3\frac{2}{3}$
9. $7 \div 1\frac{1}{8}$
10. $4\frac{1}{2} \div 6$

11. $3\frac{1}{5} \div \frac{2}{3}$
12. $9\frac{2}{5} \div \frac{1}{2}$
13. $5\frac{1}{2} \div \frac{1}{2}$
14. $8\frac{1}{6} \div 7$

15. $11\frac{1}{3} \div 2\frac{1}{2}$

16. $9\frac{2}{3} \div 4\frac{1}{5}$

17. $8\frac{1}{2} \div 3$

18. $2\frac{1}{5} \div 6$

19. $6 \div 9\frac{1}{2}$

20. $\frac{3}{4} \div 2\frac{3}{4}$

21. $5 \div 4\frac{7}{12}$

22. $2\frac{1}{3} \div 3\frac{1}{9}$

23. $8\frac{2}{3} \div 6\frac{1}{4}$

24. $11 \div 6\frac{7}{8}$

25. $7\frac{1}{5} \div 3$

26. $9\frac{2}{3} \div 8$

27. $4\frac{7}{8} \div 5\frac{2}{3}$

28. $6\frac{2}{5} \div 4\frac{1}{8}$

29. $17\frac{1}{8} \div 16\frac{1}{3}$

30. $25\frac{2}{3} \div 30\frac{3}{4}$

Try These

Write $<$, $>$, or $=$ to compare the numbers.

31. $4\frac{1}{8} \div 2\frac{1}{3}$ ▧ $6\frac{1}{5} \div 1\frac{1}{2}$

32. $6 \div 1\frac{7}{8}$ ▧ $\frac{1}{10} \div \frac{1}{32}$

33. $3\frac{1}{2} + 2\frac{1}{8}$ ▧ $4\frac{2}{3} - 1\frac{7}{8}$

34. $5\frac{1}{4} \times 2\frac{3}{8}$ ▧ $7\frac{1}{3} + 2\frac{1}{4}$

35. $15\frac{1}{2} \div 2\frac{3}{7}$ ▧ $14\frac{2}{3} \times 3\frac{1}{2}$

★ **36.** $\left(4\frac{1}{3} \div 3\frac{1}{3}\right) + 1\frac{7}{8}$ ▧ $\left(8\frac{1}{5} \times 2\frac{1}{2}\right) + 37\frac{2}{3}$

★ **37.** $\left(8\frac{1}{2} \times 5\right) - 2\frac{1}{3}$ ▧ $\left(4\frac{7}{8} \div 3\right) + 1\frac{1}{8}$

Divide. (*pages 268–269*)

1. $4 \div \frac{1}{5}$

2. $6 \div \frac{1}{8}$

3. $5 \div \frac{1}{3}$

4. $12 \div \frac{1}{7}$

Divide. Write the quotient in lowest terms. (*pages 270–271*)

5. $\frac{1}{5} \div 7$

6. $\frac{3}{4} \div 6$

7. $\frac{2}{3} \div 8$

8. $\frac{4}{5} \div 16$

Divide. Write the quotient in lowest terms. (*pages 272–273*)

9. $\frac{1}{8} \div \frac{4}{5}$

10. $\frac{2}{3} \div \frac{8}{9}$

11. $\frac{3}{5} \div \frac{9}{10}$

12. $\frac{7}{8} \div \frac{1}{16}$

Divide. Write the quotient in lowest terms. (*pages 274–275*)

13. $6\frac{1}{8} \div 5$

14. $2\frac{1}{3} \div 1\frac{1}{8}$

15. $4\frac{2}{3} \div 1\frac{1}{2}$

16. $12 \div 1\frac{3}{4}$

17. $2\frac{1}{8} \div 7$

18. $5\frac{7}{8} \div 6\frac{3}{10}$

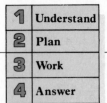

Customers don't always buy 25 envelopes at a time. Brian made a chart to help him keep track of other prices. Here's how he did it.

First he divided to find the cost of 1 envelope.

$$\begin{array}{r} \$\ .17 \\ 25\overline{)\$4.25} \end{array}$$

Then he made a chart.

Envelope Prices

Number	1	2	3	4	5	6	7	8	9	10
Price	$.17	$.34	$.51	$.68	$.85	$1.02	$1.19	$1.36	$1.53	$1.70

When Brian needed the price for 18 envelopes, he found the price for 9 and multiplied by 2.

$$\$1.53 \times 2 = \$3.06$$

He could have chosen to add the prices for 8 and 10.

$$\$1.36 + \$1.70 = \$3.06$$

Use the chart above to solve the problem.

1. What is the cost of 11 envelopes?

2. What is the cost of 100 envelopes?

3. What is the cost of 38 envelopes?

4. What is the cost of 125 envelopes?

The Writer's Block sells 4 stickers for $1.00.

5. Make a chart to show the prices of from 1–10 stickers. Use it for Exercises 6–9.

6. What is the cost of 15 stickers?

7. What is the cost of 25 stickers?

8. What is the cost of 62 stickers?

9. What is the cost of 99 stickers?

Making out a work schedule is part of a manager's job. Imagine you're the manager of The Writer's Block.

10. Use the information below to make a work schedule for a week. The Writer's Block is open from 8:00 A.M. to 6 P.M.

Week of Oct. 15	Mon.	Tues.	Wed
Susan	9 to 5		
Millie			

Susan   Monday 9 to 5, Tuesday 8 to 3, Wednesday 8 to 12, Friday 3 to 6

Millie   Monday 8 to 2, Thursday 12 to 6, Friday 9 to 5, Saturday 8 to 12

Debbie Tuesday 9 to 5, Wednesday 12 to 6, Thursday 8 to 12, Saturday 9 to 5

Arthur Monday 2 to 6, Wednesday 9 to 5, Friday 8 to 3, Saturday 12 to 6

Carl   Monday 2 to 6, Tuesday 12 to 6, Thursday 9 to 5, Saturday 10 to 6

Use the chart from Exercise 10 for Exercises 11–16.

11. Who is working on Saturday? on Monday?

12. How many hours is Debbie scheduled to work for the week?

13. Susan wants to take Wednesday morning off. Who can she get to work for her?

14. Carl earns $4.15 per hour. How much will he earn if he works all the hours on his schedule?

★ **15.** Arthur earns $5.89 per hour at the Writer's Block. He also earns $135 per week making deliveries. How much will he earn this week?

★ **16.** Everyone worked the hours which were scheduled. What is the total hours worked by all the employees?

Use the position code to find the product or quotient.

Here's how. $\triangleright \times \triangleleft = \dfrac{6}{7} \times \dfrac{1}{5} = \dfrac{6}{35}$

1. $\triangledown \times \triangle$ **2.** $\triangleright \div \triangle$ **3.** $\triangleleft \times \triangledown$ **4.** $\triangle \div \triangledown$

5. $\triangle \times \triangleright$ **6.** $\triangle \div \triangleright$ **7.** $\triangleleft \times \triangleright$ **8.** $\triangle \div \triangleleft$

Correct or incorrect? Write *C* or *I*.

9. $2 \div \dfrac{1}{9} = \dfrac{1}{18}$ **10.** $\dfrac{4}{5} \div 3 = \dfrac{4}{15}$ **11.** $8 \times \dfrac{1}{2} = 16$ **12.** $3\dfrac{1}{2} \times \dfrac{1}{3} = 1\dfrac{1}{6}$

13. $\dfrac{4}{7} \div \dfrac{16}{21} = \dfrac{3}{4}$ **14.** $\dfrac{2}{9} \div 2 = \dfrac{1}{9}$ **15.** $\dfrac{4}{9} \times \dfrac{3}{8} = 6$ **16.** $8\dfrac{1}{4} \times 1\dfrac{5}{6} = 30\dfrac{1}{8}$

17. Match the product or quotient with a letter to solve the riddle.

What do you call music to drive by?

N $4\dfrac{1}{2} \div 2\dfrac{5}{8}$ **R** $1\dfrac{1}{3} \times \dfrac{1}{2}$ **T** $\dfrac{4}{7} \div \dfrac{5}{8}$

A $\dfrac{5}{6} \times \dfrac{3}{10}$ **O** $1\dfrac{1}{2} \div 2$ **C** $6 \times \dfrac{4}{5}$

A   ▦   ▦   ▦   ▦   ▦   ▦   ▦

   $4\dfrac{4}{5}$ $\dfrac{1}{4}$ $\dfrac{2}{3}$ $\dfrac{32}{35}$ $\dfrac{3}{4}$ $\dfrac{3}{4}$ $1\dfrac{5}{7}$

Solve.

18. Dinner rolls cost $2.16 per dozen at The Bread Basket. Make a table to show the prices of from 1 to 10 dinner rolls.

19. The Flower Stall sells 5 tulip bulbs for $2.95. Make a chart to show the prices of from 1 to 10 bulbs.

Multiply. Write the product in lowest terms. (*pages 260–261*)

1. $5 \times \frac{3}{8}$ **2.** $\frac{5}{6} \times 9$ **3.** $4 \times \frac{3}{8}$ **4.** $\frac{2}{5} \times 7$ **5.** $\frac{1}{6} \times 18$

Multiply. Write the product in lowest terms. (*pages 262–265*)

6. $\frac{1}{12} \times \frac{3}{4}$ **7.** $\frac{3}{7} \times \frac{4}{9}$ **8.** $\frac{3}{10} \times \frac{4}{9}$ **9.** $\frac{5}{8} \times \frac{2}{7}$ **10.** $\frac{2}{3} \times \frac{5}{6}$

Multiply. Write the product in lowest terms. (*pages 266–267*)

11. $4\frac{3}{8} \times \frac{4}{5}$ **12.** $3\frac{1}{5} \times 3\frac{3}{4}$ **13.** $2\frac{2}{3} \times 4\frac{1}{2}$ **14.** $1\frac{7}{9} \times 3\frac{3}{8}$ **15.** $2\frac{1}{3} \times 6\frac{2}{3}$

Divide. (*pages 268–269*)

16. $4 \div \frac{1}{2}$ **17.** $6 \div \frac{1}{8}$ **18.** $9 \div \frac{1}{7}$ **19.** $12 \div \frac{1}{3}$ **20.** $7 \div \frac{1}{10}$

Divide. Write the quotient in lowest terms. (*pages 270–271*)

21. $\frac{1}{5} \div 2$ **22.** $\frac{2}{3} \div 6$ **23.** $\frac{6}{7} \div 2$ **24.** $\frac{5}{8} \div 5$ **25.** $\frac{3}{10} \div 9$

Divide. Write the quotient in lowest terms. (*pages 272–273*)

26. $\frac{1}{3} \div \frac{3}{4}$ **27.** $\frac{2}{3} \div \frac{3}{5}$ **28.** $\frac{6}{7} \div \frac{7}{8}$ **29.** $\frac{7}{10} \div \frac{2}{5}$ **30.** $\frac{5}{9} \div \frac{2}{3}$

Divide. Write the quotient in lowest terms. (*pages 274–275*)

31. $\frac{1}{5} \div 2\frac{3}{10}$ **32.** $6\frac{2}{7} \div \frac{3}{14}$ **33.** $7\frac{1}{3} \div \frac{11}{12}$ **34.** $8\frac{3}{4} \div 2\frac{3}{4}$ **35.** $8\frac{1}{2} \div 1\frac{3}{4}$

Solve. (*pages 276–277*)

36. The Clearview Window Washing Service charges $2.75 per window. Make a table to show the cost of washing from 1 to 10 windows.

37. At the Gopo Deli, potato salad costs $.59 for 500 g. Make a chart to show the cost of 250 g, 500 g, 750 g, and 1 kg.

Extra practice on page 397

Computer Programming

Computers can do amazing things, but not without instructions. These instructions are called **programs.** BASIC (Beginners All-purpose Symbolic Instruction Code) is one of the many different programming languages. It uses a combination of words and letters to tell the computer what to do.

Each line of a program is given a number. The numbers are usually multiples of 10 to let programmers add a new line without renumbering.

Here's an example.

Line Number	Instruction
10	Print 6741/7
20	Print 85 * 76
30	End
14	Print 79 - 7

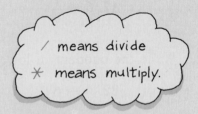

/ means divide
* means multiply.

This line should be between lines 10 and 20. If we make it any number between 10 and 20, the computer will do the calculations in the correct order.

In the program above, line 14 will be computed after line 10.

Once a program is in the computer, you can type RUN to have the computer complete the calculations. When this program is RUN the output is 963, 72, and 6460.

Write the output for the program.

1. 20   Print 678 − 49
    30   Print 1572 + 1861
    25   Print 70 * 9
    40   End

2. 40   Print 8595/5
    50   Print 67.9 − 39.61
    60   End
    55   Print 18.6 * 13.7
    42   Print 30 + 15

You can use the same program over and over if you use letters to stand for numbers. You can also have the computer print out exact words by using quotation marks.

Here's an example.

```
10    Print "Type in 2 numbers"

20    Input A, B

30    Let X = A * B

40    Print X

50    End
```

When you type RUN this is what you'll see.

```
RUN

TYPE IN 2 NUMBERS

?          A ? means it's your
           turn to type in numbers
           for A and B.
```

If you type in 68 and 35, your printout will look like this.

```
RUN

TYPE IN 2 NUMBERS

?   68    35

2380
```

Write the printout for the program using the given values.

3. 10 Print "Type in 2 numbers"
    20 Input A, B
    30 Let X = A − B
    40 Print X
    50 End
        A = 56,400 B = 3791

4. 10 Print "Type in 3 numbers"
    20 Input A, B, C
    30 Let X = (A + B) − C
    40 Print X
    50 End
        A = 3651 B = 286 C = 169

5. 10 Print "Type in 4 numbers"
    20 Input A, B, C, D
    30 Let X = (A * B) + (C/D)
    40 Print X
    50 End
        A = 75   B = 42
        C = 300   D = 50

6. 10 Print "Type in 4 numbers"
    20 Input A, B, C, D
    30 Print X
    25 Let X = (D − A) * (B/C)
    50 End
        A = 65   B = 2346
        C = 391   D = 782

Maintaining Skills

True or false? Write *T* or *F*.

1.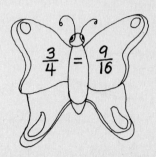
$\frac{3}{4} = \frac{9}{16}$

2.
$\frac{1}{3} = \frac{4}{12}$

3.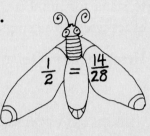
$\frac{1}{2} = \frac{14}{28}$

4.
$\frac{4}{5} = \frac{10}{12}$

5.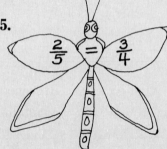
$\frac{2}{5} = \frac{3}{4}$

6.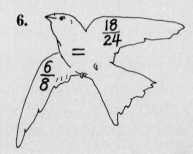
$\frac{6}{8} = \frac{18}{24}$

Correct or incorrect? Write *C* or *I*.

7. $\frac{7}{2} = 3\frac{1}{2}$

8. $\frac{12}{3} = 5$

9. $\frac{16}{6} = 2\frac{5}{6}$

10. $\frac{17}{9} = 1\frac{8}{9}$

11. $\frac{63}{8} = 7\frac{7}{8}$

12. $18 = \frac{108}{6}$

13. $\frac{39}{13} = 3\frac{1}{13}$

14. $5\frac{7}{8} = \frac{47}{8}$

Write as a terminating or repeating decimal.

15. $\frac{7}{9}$

16. $\frac{4}{100}$

17. $3\frac{1}{2}$

18. $\frac{79}{1000}$

19. $\frac{5}{8}$

20. $\frac{3}{11}$

Solve.

21. What part of the costume uses the least material? the most?

22. How much material is needed for the entire costume?

Shirt: $1\frac{1}{8}$ yd

Shoes: $\frac{7}{8}$ yd

Hat: $\frac{5}{6}$ yd

Pants: $1\frac{5}{12}$ yd

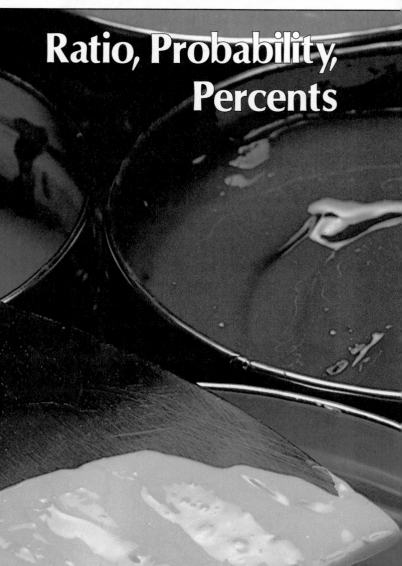

The primary colors can be mixed to make most of the other colors you see. Suppose a shade of purple requires 1 part red and 3 parts blue. If you have 5 L of red paint, how much blue will you need to make purple?

Ratio, Probability, Percents

Ratios

You can write a **ratio** to compare numbers or quantities.

The ratio of large clocks to small clocks is 2 to 4.

You can write ratios in several ways but you usually read them the same way.

$2:4$ ₒ°ᵒ 2 to 4 $\frac{2}{4}$ ₒ°ᵒ 2 to 4

When a ratio is written as a fraction, you can write the fraction in lowest terms.

$$\frac{2}{4} = \frac{1}{2}$$

Exercises

For each picture, write a ratio as a fraction in lowest terms.

1.

45 cm

73 cm

$\dfrac{\text{length of arm}}{\text{length of leg}}$ ⟹ ☐/☐

2.

$\dfrac{\text{trucks}}{\text{cars}}$ ⟹ ☐/☐

3.

ROME APPLES   Delicious

$\dfrac{\text{Rome apples}}{\text{Delicious apples}}$ ⟹ ☐/☐ = ☐/☐

4.

240 g   480 g

$\dfrac{\text{grams in small container}}{\text{grams in large container}}$ ⟹ ☐/☐ = ☐/☐

Write a ratio as a fraction in lowest terms to compare the numbers in the table.

Brandon School Talent Show

Acts	Singing	Dancing	Gymnastics	Magic	Musical Instruments	Yodeling
Number	32	15	21	6	41	1

5. ratio of gymnastics to dancing acts

6. ratio of yodeling to magic acts

7. ratio of gymnastics acts to all acts

8. ratio of magic to dancing acts

9. ratio of singing to yodeling acts

10. ratio of magic to singing acts

11. ratio of singing to musical instrument acts

12. ratio of musical instrument acts to all acts

Books in the Runkle School Library

Type	History	Science	Fiction	Biography	Sports	Hobbies
Number	448	375	876	337	593	167

13. ratio of history books to fiction

14. ratio of fiction to biography

15. ratio of science books to sports books

16. ratio of history books to science books

17. ratio of hobby books to biographies

18. ratio of sports books to hobby books

Time for A Change

Sometimes ratios compare measurements. When they do, you must be certain the measurements are written in the same units.

Example. $\dfrac{3\,cm}{1\,m} = \dfrac{3\,cm}{100\,cm} = \dfrac{3}{100}$

Rewrite the ratio so that both terms are expressed in the same unit. If possible, write the ratio in lowest terms.

19. $\dfrac{12\ minutes}{1\ hour}$

20. $\dfrac{3\ kg}{150\ g}$

21. $\dfrac{35\ mm}{50\ cm}$

22. $\dfrac{5\ days}{6\ weeks}$

23. $\dfrac{250\ mL}{1\ L}$

Rates

A **rate** is a ratio that compares different kinds of quantities or objects.

Todd can paint 9 signs in 3 hours. You can write this in two ways.

$$\frac{9 \text{ signs}}{3 \text{ hours}} \quad \text{or} \quad \frac{9}{3}.$$

To find the rate per hour, or **unit rate,** write an equivalent ratio with a denominator of 1.

$$\frac{9}{3} = \frac{3}{1}$$

Todd paints at the rate of 3 signs per hour.

Exercises

Complete.

1. $\frac{24}{8} = \frac{\blacksquare}{1}$ 　　　　 **2.** $\frac{10}{5} = \frac{\blacksquare}{1}$ 　　　　 **3.** $\frac{12}{3} = \frac{\blacksquare}{1}$ 　　　　 **4.** $\frac{20}{4} = \frac{\blacksquare}{1}$

5. $\frac{165}{5} = \frac{\blacksquare}{1}$ 　　　　 **6.** $\frac{216}{3} = \frac{\blacksquare}{1}$ 　　　　 **7.** $\frac{36}{9} = \frac{\blacksquare}{1}$ 　　　　 **8.** $\frac{132}{6} = \frac{\blacksquare}{1}$

Complete the table.

9.

Dollars earned	$48.50	?	?	?
Number of days	1	2	5	10

10.

Revolutions	$33\frac{1}{3}$	?	?	?	?
Minutes	1	2	7	10	25

Write the unit rate.

Example. 150 students for 3 teachers ⟹ 50 students per teacher

11. 10 eggs for 5 omelets 　　　 **12.** 850 km in 10 hours 　　　 **13.** $36 in 9 hours

14. 500 words in 25 lessons

15. 120 books on 5 shelves

16. $72 for 12 kg

17. 50 sandwiches for 25 people

18. $2275 for 7 months

19. 540 words in 9 minutes

20. $2.42 for 11 stamps

21. 1200 people in 50 rows

22. 2250 m in 15 minutes

23. 40 tokens for 5 rides

24. 600 flowers for 15 bouquets

25. 3 in. of rain in 6 days

26. 1400 mL of flour for 2 recipes

27. 800 nails in 20 boxes

28. 270 m of string in 9 balls

29. 25 records for $174.50

30. 478 books for 239 students

31. $1600 for 5 cameras

It Pays to Advertise

Newspaper advertising is expensive. Most business people think that the increase in sales pays for the advertising.

**Toledo Daily News
Retail Advertising Rates**

Rate per day		Number of lines	Ad size
Mon.–Sat.	Sun.		
$3.05	$3.72	per line	will vary
$1670	$2037	600	$\frac{1}{4}$ page
$2505	$3056	800	$\frac{1}{3}$ page
$3287	$4010	1200	$\frac{1}{2}$ page
$6475	$7900	2400	Full page

Use the table to answer the questions.

32. An art store wants to run a 555 line ad on Monday. Is it cheaper to buy a $\frac{1}{4}$ page ad or to pay by the line?

33. Waverly Cinema is running a $\frac{1}{2}$ page ad on Friday, Saturday, and Sunday. How much will this cost?

34. The weekly advertising budget for the Camera Shop is $8500. Can they afford to run a $\frac{1}{3}$ page ad on Sunday, Monday, and Saturday?

★ **35.** The Jog Shop is running a 68 line ad on Tuesday, Thursday, and Friday. They are running a $\frac{1}{2}$ page ad on Saturday. How much will this cost?

Proportions

Penny played Tagalong against her computer. Penny won 8 games out of 24. At this rate how many times can Penny expect to win if she plays 48 games?

To solve this problem you can write a **proportion.** A proportion is an equation that says two ratios or rates are equivalent.

$$\frac{8}{24} = \frac{n}{48} \quad \Rightarrow \quad \frac{8}{24} = \frac{8 \times 2}{24 \times 2} = \frac{16}{48} \quad \Rightarrow \quad n = 16$$

If Penny wins at the same rate, she can expect to win 16 times in 48 games.

Exercises

Complete the proportion.

1. $\frac{3}{10} = \frac{6}{n}$

2. $\frac{15}{2} = \frac{150}{x}$

3. $\frac{9}{2} = \frac{a}{20}$

4. $\frac{350}{7} = \frac{y}{1}$

5. $\frac{16}{8} = \frac{4}{a}$

6. $\frac{80}{24} = \frac{10}{y}$

7. $\frac{30}{45} = \frac{6}{a}$

8. $\frac{9}{12} = \frac{3}{n}$

9. $\frac{3}{6} = \frac{n}{36}$

10. $\frac{2}{19} = \frac{a}{95}$

11. $\frac{56}{64} = \frac{7}{x}$

12. $\frac{25}{3} = \frac{50}{y}$

13. $\frac{8}{5} = \frac{24}{a}$

14. $\frac{45}{20} = \frac{y}{4}$

15. $\frac{11}{15} = \frac{22}{x}$

16. $\frac{20}{30} = \frac{n}{210}$

17. $\frac{17}{3} = \frac{x}{9}$

18. $\frac{24}{14} = \frac{a}{7}$

19. $\frac{37}{2} = \frac{74}{y}$

20. $\frac{15}{3} = \frac{x}{1}$

21. $\frac{27}{33} = \frac{n}{11}$

22. $\frac{14}{6} = \frac{7}{a}$

23. $\frac{20}{16} = \frac{x}{8}$

24. $\frac{8}{3} = \frac{a}{21}$

25. $\frac{15}{8} = \frac{30}{n}$

26. $\frac{26}{5} = \frac{78}{a}$

27. $\frac{13}{4} = \frac{a}{16}$

28. $\frac{19}{6} = \frac{y}{30}$

29. $\frac{50}{60} = \frac{5}{x}$

30. $\frac{80}{120} = \frac{20}{a}$

31. $\frac{4}{380} = \frac{1}{y}$

32. $\frac{99}{33} = \frac{a}{11}$

33. $\frac{46}{20} = \frac{y}{10}$

34. $\frac{51}{17} = \frac{n}{1}$

35. $\frac{16}{80} = \frac{4}{n}$

36. $\frac{30}{35} = \frac{6}{y}$

37. $\frac{49}{63} = \frac{7}{x}$

38. $\frac{24}{64} = \frac{3}{n}$

39. $\frac{2}{7} = \frac{x}{35}$

40. $\frac{5}{17} = \frac{20}{a}$

Farmer's Market

Solve.

41. Mr. MacDonald needs 3 horses to pull each wagon. How many horses does he need to pull 6 wagons?

42. Mrs. Pierce earned $6.40 selling 8 loaves of bread. How much can she earn selling 24 loaves of bread?

43. Mr. Strauss bought 3 peaches for $.89. He also bought a dozen eggs for $1.06. How much did he spend?

★ **44.** Elizabeth has ivy, fern, palm and fig plants. The ratio of ivy plants to ferns is 3 to 5. The ratio of ferns to palms is 2 to 4. The ratio of ivy plants to figs is 2 to 5. There are 6 ivy plants. How many ferns does Elizabeth have? How many palms? How many figs?

Copy the figure. Write the numbers from 1 to 8 in the squares so that no two consecutive numbers touch on a side or corner.

Take a Break

Cross Multiplying

Cross multiplying is another way to solve a proportion.

Look at these examples. The symbol $\stackrel{?}{=}$ is used when you are checking to see if a proportion is true.

$$\frac{4}{5} \stackrel{?}{\times} \frac{8}{10}$$

$$4 \times 10 \stackrel{?}{=} 5 \times 8$$
$$40 = 40$$

The proportion is true.

$$\frac{8}{10} \stackrel{?}{\times} \frac{12}{18}$$

$$8 \times 18 \stackrel{?}{=} 10 \times 12$$
$$144 \stackrel{?}{=} 120$$

The proportion is not true.

Here's how to solve an equation to find the missing number in a proportion.

$$\frac{10}{6} = \frac{n}{36}$$

$$6 \times n = 10 \times 36$$
$$6 \times n = 360$$
$$n = 360 \div 6$$
$$n = 60$$

> $6 \times 60 = 360$
> so $n = 60$

Exercises

Complete. Is the proportion true? Write *Yes* or *No*.

1. $\frac{2}{6} \stackrel{?}{=} \frac{3}{9}$

$2 \times 9 = $ �

$6 \times 3 = $ ▩

2. $\frac{6}{8} \stackrel{?}{=} \frac{8}{12}$

$6 \times 12 = $ ▩

$8 \times 8 = $ ▩

3. $\frac{3}{12} \stackrel{?}{=} \frac{2}{8}$

$3 \times 8 = $ ▩

$12 \times 2 = $ ▩

4. $\frac{4}{2} \stackrel{?}{=} \frac{18}{9}$

$4 \times 9 = $ ▩

$2 \times 18 = $ ▩

5. $\frac{6}{4} \stackrel{?}{=} \frac{15}{10}$

$6 \times 10 = $ ▩

$4 \times 15 = $ ▩

6. $\frac{4}{9} \stackrel{?}{=} \frac{6}{27}$

$4 \times 27 = $ ▩

$9 \times 6 = $ ▩

7. $\frac{5}{6} \stackrel{?}{=} \frac{4}{7}$

$5 \times 7 = $ ▩

$4 \times 6 = $ ▩

8. $\frac{3}{8} \stackrel{?}{=} \frac{4}{12}$

$3 \times 12 = $ ▩

$4 \times 8 = $ ▩

9. $\frac{5}{15} \stackrel{?}{=} \frac{7}{21}$

$5 \times 21 = $ ▩

$7 \times 15 = $ ▩

Complete the proportions.

10. $\frac{6}{10} = \frac{n}{25}$

$10 \times n = 6 \times 25$

$10 \times n = 150$

$n = 150 \div 10$

$n = \blacksquare$

11. $\frac{6}{8} = \frac{21}{y}$

$6 \times y = 8 \times 21$

$6 \times y = 168$

$y = 168 \div 6$

$y = \blacksquare$

12. $\frac{8}{12} = \frac{r}{18}$

$12 \times r = 8 \times 18$

$12 \times r = 144$

$r = 144 \div 12$

$r = \blacksquare$

Cross multiply to complete the proportion.

13. $\frac{1}{4} = \frac{n}{28}$

14. $\frac{7}{8} = \frac{b}{32}$

15. $\frac{8}{6} = \frac{20}{a}$

16. $\frac{9}{w} = \frac{12}{4}$

17. $\frac{12}{8} = \frac{z}{18}$

18. $\frac{y}{50} = \frac{30}{75}$

19. $\frac{8}{a} = \frac{14}{7}$

20. $\frac{18}{15} = \frac{30}{e}$

21. $\frac{12}{b} = \frac{54}{45}$

22. $\frac{h}{27} = \frac{42}{54}$

23. $\frac{5}{10} = \frac{24}{m}$

24. $\frac{20}{16} = \frac{n}{44}$

25. $\frac{20}{c} = \frac{30}{21}$

26. $\frac{12}{7} = \frac{48}{d}$

27. $\frac{15}{33} = \frac{10}{f}$

28. $\frac{44}{77} = \frac{a}{56}$

Balancing Act

Solve. Use a proportion.

29. Randy's heart beats 145 times in 2 minutes. How many times does it beat in 30 minutes?

Hint: $\frac{145}{2} = \frac{n}{30}$

30. A pool is being filled at the rate of 200 L of water every 25 minutes. How long will it take to pump 10,000 L of water?

Hint: $\frac{200}{25} = \frac{10,000}{n}$

★ **31.** Suppose your watch gains 4 seconds every 8 hours. How many minutes will it gain in a week?

Probability

When you toss a coin, there are two possible **outcomes.** There is 1 chance in 2 of the outcome being a head. The **probability** of a head is 1 out of 2 or $\frac{1}{2}$. The probability of a tail is also $\frac{1}{2}$.

The spinner can stop on any of the 6 equal-size sections. To find the probability (P) of landing on a star ($\star$) you can use this formula.

$$P(\star) = \frac{\text{number of } \star \text{ outcomes}}{\text{total number of outcomes}}$$

$$P(\star) = \frac{3}{6} = \frac{1}{2}$$

The probability of an impossible event is 0. The probability of an event that must occur is 1.

Exercises

Complete.

	Activity	Possible Outcomes	Probability
1.	Tossing a number cube	1 2 3 4 5 6	$P(4) = \dfrac{\blacksquare}{6}$
2.	Choosing an envelope	2 3 4 5	2, 3, ■, ■	$P(3) = \dfrac{\blacksquare}{4}$
3.	Spinning a spinner	$\stackrel{\wedge}{\star}, \triangle, \triangle, \bigcirc, \blacksquare, \blacksquare$ ■, ■	$P(\stackrel{\wedge}{\star}) = \dfrac{\blacksquare}{8} = \dfrac{\blacksquare}{2}$ $P(\triangle) = \dfrac{\blacksquare}{\blacksquare} = \dfrac{\blacksquare}{4}$

There are 3 green, 7 red, and 2 yellow marbles in a jar. They are all the same size and shape. You choose a marble without looking. Write the probability of the outcome.

4. a green marble   **5.** a red marble   **6.** a yellow marble   **7.** a purple marble

Daisy invited 18 people to a party. The guests included 4 cousins, 2 aunts, 10 friends, and 2 uncles. Write the probability that the first guest arriving at the party is the following.

8. a cousin   **9.** a friend   **10.** an uncle   **11.** a nephew

A letter from the word ENGINEER is chosen without looking. Write the probability of the outcome.

12. the letter E   **13.** the letter N   **14.** a vowel   **15.** a consonant

Making Predictions

You can use probabilities to make predictions. The probability of the spinner stopping on a 3 is $\frac{1}{4}$. The probability of the spinner not stopping on a 3 is $1 - \frac{1}{4} = \frac{3}{4}$.

Since $\frac{1}{4}$ is less than $\frac{3}{4}$ it is more likely that the spinner will not stop on a 3.

Solve.

16. The Franklin School sold 348 raffle tickets to raise money for playground equipment. Mr. Marcos bought 5 tickets. Is it more likely that he will win the prize or not win the prize?

17. There are 67 books on a library shelf. Of the 67 books, 29 include pictures. If you choose a book at random are you more likely to choose one with pictures, or one without pictures?

★ **18.** The 1000th customer at Maxie's Market will get $5\frac{1}{2}$ times the amount of money he or she has. Bea has $10.75. How much could she win?

Probability

Room 18 had a drawing to assign jobs and parts for the class play. The 16 jobs and 16 parts for the play were written on slips of paper and put into two boxes. Without looking, everyone drew a slip from each box.

Jobs	number
make posters	2
make costumes	6
make sets	6
make tickets	2
Total Jobs	16

Parts	number
Bus driver	1
Passengers	10
Street Signs	3
Horses	2
Total Parts	16

Suppose you are the first person to choose. The probability of choosing *make posters* is $\frac{2}{16}$. The probability of choosing *bus driver* is $\frac{1}{16}$. The probability of choosing *make posters* and *bus driver* is $\frac{2}{16} \times \frac{1}{16} = \frac{2}{256} = \frac{1}{128}$.

In general, if none of the choices has been taken, you can use this formula to get the probability that two events will occur.

$$P(A \text{ and } B) = P(A) \times P(B)$$

$$P(\textit{make posters} \text{ and } \textit{bus driver}) = \frac{2}{16} \times \frac{1}{16} = \frac{2}{256} = \frac{1}{128}$$

Exercises

Suppose you pick a marble, without looking, from each container. The table shows the possible outcomes.

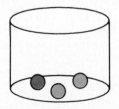 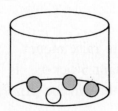

Outcome Table

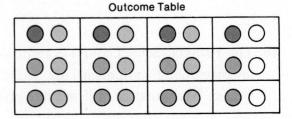

Write the probability.

1. a red and a green marble

2. 2 marbles

3. a blue and a white marble

4. a red and a white marble

5. a blue and a green marble

6. 2 red marbles

7. 2 green marbles

8. a blue and a red marble

294

The Bright family wrote their choices for pets and pet names on slips of paper. The 5 choices for each were put into two boxes. Suppose a slip is drawn, without looking, from each box.

Pets   Names

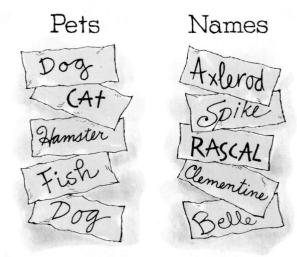

Write the probability that the pet will be the following.

9. hamster named Spike

10. fish named Axlerod

11. turtle named Rover

12. cat named Rascal

13. dog named Clementine

14. dog named Belle

15. gerbil named Caesar

16. fish named Spike

All or Nothing

Write 0 or 1 to show the probability.

17. Choosing a red sock from a drawer of 10 red socks.

18. Choosing a brown crayon from a box of 7 yellow crayons.

Checkpoint A

Write a ratio as a fraction to compare the figures. (*pages 284–285*)

1. ◯ to △   2. △ to ⬡

Write the unit rate. (*pages 286–287*)

3. $80 for 5 books

4. 75 km in 25 minutes

Complete the proportion. (*pages 288–289*)

5. $\frac{6}{24} = \frac{n}{48}$ 6. $\frac{3}{7} = \frac{12}{n}$

Cross multiply to complete the proportion. (*pages 290–291*)

7. $\frac{4}{n} = \frac{20}{25}$ 8. $\frac{n}{8} = \frac{6}{24}$

A box has 2 red, 2 blue, and 3 white marbles. What is the probability of choosing the following? (*pages 292–293*)

9. a red marble   10. a blue marble

Suppose you choose 1 marble from each jar. Write the probability. (*pages 294–295*)

11. 2 white marbles

12. 1 blue and 1 white marble

Meaning of Percent

The Watts Happening Light Bulb Company estimates that 94 out of every 100 bulbs they make will last for 1000 hours.

You can write the fraction $\frac{94}{100}$ as 94%, read *ninety-four percent.*

PERCENT MEANS PER 100. THE SYMBOL FOR PERCENT IS %.

These examples show how to write a percent as a fraction in lowest terms.

$$31\% = \frac{31}{100} \qquad 80\% = \frac{80}{100} = \frac{4}{5} \qquad 5\% = \frac{5}{100} = \frac{1}{20}$$

These examples show how to write a fraction as a percent.

- When the denominator is 100, just write the numerator with a percent symbol.

$$\frac{9}{100} = 9\% \qquad \frac{47}{100} = 47\%$$

- When the denominator is not 100, first write an equivalent fraction with a denominator of 100.

$$\frac{1}{5} = \frac{20}{100} = 20\%$$

Exercises

Complete to write the percent as a fraction in lowest terms.

1. $11\% = \frac{\blacksquare}{100}$

2. $40\% = \frac{\blacksquare}{100} = \frac{\blacksquare}{\blacksquare}$

3. $85\% = \frac{\blacksquare}{100} = \frac{\blacksquare}{\blacksquare}$

4. $29\% = \frac{\blacksquare}{100}$

5. $50\% = \frac{\blacksquare}{100} = \frac{\blacksquare}{\blacksquare}$

6. $12\% = \frac{\blacksquare}{100} = \frac{\blacksquare}{\blacksquare}$

7. $7\% = \frac{\blacksquare}{100}$

8. $90\% = \frac{\blacksquare}{100} = \frac{\blacksquare}{\blacksquare}$

9. $4\% = \frac{\blacksquare}{100} = \frac{\blacksquare}{\blacksquare}$

Complete to write the fraction as a percent.

10. $\frac{67}{100} = \blacksquare\%$

11. $\frac{7}{10} = \frac{\blacksquare}{100} = \blacksquare\%$

12. $\frac{1}{4} = \frac{\blacksquare}{100} = \blacksquare\%$

13. $\frac{73}{100} = \blacksquare\%$

14. $\frac{9}{10} = \frac{\blacksquare}{100} = \blacksquare\%$

15. $\frac{4}{5} = \frac{\blacksquare}{100} = \blacksquare\%$

Write as a percent.

16. $\frac{17}{100}$ **17.** $\frac{8}{10}$ **18.** $\frac{1}{2}$ **19.** $\frac{1}{4}$ **20.** $\frac{1}{25}$ **21.** $\frac{2}{5}$

22. $\frac{19}{20}$ **23.** $\frac{47}{100}$ **24.** $\frac{7}{25}$ **25.** $\frac{1}{20}$ **26.** $\frac{13}{20}$ **27.** $\frac{14}{25}$

28. $\frac{43}{50}$ **29.** $\frac{1}{50}$ **30.** $\frac{53}{100}$ **31.** $\frac{11}{20}$ **32.** $\frac{9}{25}$ **33.** $\frac{3}{5}$

Write as a fraction in lowest terms.

34. 40%   **35.** 57%   **36.** 75%   **37.** 6%   **38.** 1%   **39.** 15%

40. 2%   **41.** 65%   **42.** 67%   **43.** 39%   **44.** 84%   **45.** 60%

46. 85%   **47.** 43%   **48.** 10%   **49.** 72%   **50.** 99%   **51.** 20%

Public Opinion

Solve.

52. In a survey, $\frac{3}{5}$ of the people interviewed said they listened to the radio for at least 45 minutes per day. What percent is this?

53. At Research Inc., 15% of the employees work part-time. What fraction of the employees work part-time?

★ **54.** When Muriel makes telephone surveys, about $\frac{1}{4}$ of the people she calls aren't home. What percent of the people are home?

★ **55.** Jed asked his classmates what percent of their allowances they spent on food. The table shows their response. What percent said they spent 25% on food?

Number of people	8	4	6	2
Percent spent on food	15%	25%	35%	50%

A Percent of a Number

The town manager of Hot Springs earned $31,500 before receiving an 11% pay increase. What was the amount of the increase?

You can write a percent as a fraction and multiply.

$$11\% = \frac{11}{100} \quad \Rightarrow \quad \frac{11}{100} \times 31{,}500 = \$3465$$

The amount of the increase was $3465.

These examples also show how to find a percent of a number.

What is 40% of 30?

$$40\% = \frac{40}{100} = \frac{2}{5} \quad \Rightarrow \quad \frac{2}{5} \times 30 = 12$$

What is 85% of 60?

$$85\% = \frac{85}{100} = \frac{17}{20} \quad \Rightarrow \quad \frac{17}{20} \times 60 = 51$$

Exercises

Complete.

1. 50% of 20 = $\frac{1}{2} \times 20$ = ▨
   50% of 70 = ▨ × 70 = ▨

2. 25% of 60 = $\frac{1}{4} \times 60$ = ▨
   25% of 48 = ▨ × 48 = ▨

3. 10% of 90 = ▨ × 90 = ▨
   10% of 120 = ▨ × 120 = ▨

4. 75% of 64 = ▨ × 64 = ▨
   75% of 16 = ▨ × 16 = ▨

5. 60% of 35 = ▨ × 35 = ▨
   60% of 80 = ▨ × 80 = ▨

6. 70% of 90 = ▨ × 90 = ▨
   70% of 30 = ▨ × 30 = ▨

7. 15% of 10 = ▨ × 10 = ▨
   15% of 25 = ▨ × 25 = ▨

8. 88% of 50 = ▨ × 50 = ▨
   88% of 100 = ▨ × 100 = ▨

What is the number?

9. 90% of 50   **10.** 20% of 75   **11.** 30% of 60

12. 80% of 75   **13.** 50% of 42   **14.** 30% of 40

15. 25% of 56   **16.** 80% of 45   **17.** 20% of 25

18. 75% of 36   **19.** 10% of 70   **20.** 40% of 10

21. 70% of 50   **22.** 60% of 95   **23.** 25% of 200

24. 90% of 300   **25.** 40% of 250   **26.** 75% of 160

27. 80% of 410   **28.** 70% of 220   **29.** 10% of 190

30. 50% of 394   **31.** 20% of 350   **32.** 60% of 240

33. 36% of 400   **34.** 57% of 82   **35.** 91% of 550

Cityside

Complete the table.

	Employee	Salary	Percent Increase	Amount of Increase
36.	Gus Ziesel	$15,800	5%	?
37.	Ruth Amati	$18,450	7%	?
38.	Jack Glick	$14,750	13%	?

Solve.

39. There are 18,000 voters in Elmira. In the last election, 70% of them voted. How many voted?

40. Miller's Falls raised $9000 for a town pool. The town spent $\frac{1}{5}$ of the money for surveying. What percent is this?

Complete.

★ **41.** (85% of 40) + (50% of 50) = ▨

★ **42.** (20% of 100) − (25% of 36) = ▨

★ **43.** (18% of 100) × (30% of 90) = ▨

★ **44.** (65% of 300) ÷ (20% of 25) = ▨

Decimals and Percent

In a survey, 27 out of 100 people said they owned a home computer.

You can write the decimal, 0.27, as a percent

$$0.27 = \frac{27}{100} = 27\%$$

Sometimes you can't write a fraction with a denominator of 100. When this happens, you first divide to write the fraction as a decimal.

Fraction	Divide to write the fraction as a decimal.	Write the decimal as a percent.
$\frac{7}{8}$	$\begin{array}{r} 0.875 \\ 8\overline{)7.000} \end{array}$	$0.875 = 87.5\%$

Move the decimal point 2 places to the right.

Exercises

Complete to write the decimal as a percent.

1. $0.63 = \frac{\blacksquare}{100} = \blacksquare\%$ **2.** $0.05 = \frac{\blacksquare}{100} = \blacksquare\%$ **3.** $0.45 = \frac{\blacksquare}{100} = \blacksquare\%$

4. $0.04 = \frac{\blacksquare}{100} = \blacksquare\%$ **5.** $0.03 = \frac{\blacksquare}{100} = \blacksquare\%$ **6.** $0.07 = \frac{\blacksquare}{100} = \blacksquare\%$

7. $0.9 = \frac{\blacksquare}{100} = \blacksquare\%$ **8.** $0.11 = \frac{\blacksquare}{100} = \blacksquare\%$ **9.** $0.6 = \frac{\blacksquare}{100} = \blacksquare\%$

Complete to write the percent as a decimal.

10. $38\% = \frac{\blacksquare}{100} = 0.\blacksquare\blacksquare$ **11.** $2\% = \frac{\blacksquare}{100} = 0.\blacksquare\blacksquare$ **12.** $93\% = \frac{\blacksquare}{100} = 0.\blacksquare\blacksquare$

13. $8\% = \frac{\blacksquare}{100} = 0.\blacksquare\blacksquare$ **14.** $7\% = \frac{\blacksquare}{100} = 0.\blacksquare\blacksquare$ **15.** $1\% = \frac{\blacksquare}{100} = 0.\blacksquare\blacksquare$

16. $20\% = \frac{\blacksquare}{100} = 0.\blacksquare$ **17.** $70\% = \frac{\blacksquare}{100} = 0.\blacksquare$ **18.** $40\% = \frac{\blacksquare}{100} = 0.\blacksquare$

Write as a percent.

19. 0.23   **20.** 0.3   **21.** 0.15   **22.** 0.03   **23.** 0.48

24. 0.8   **25.** 0.82   **26.** 0.12   **27.** 0.1   **28.** 0.09

29. 0.07   **30.** 0.4   **31.** 0.02   **32.** 0.79   **33.** 0.11

Write as a percent. If the answer is a repeating decimal round to the nearest hundredth.

Example. $\frac{8}{11}$ ⇨ $11\overline{)8.0000}$ (0.7272) ⇨ 0.727272... ⇨ 73%

34. $\frac{5}{18}$ **35.** $\frac{3}{8}$ **36.** $\frac{9}{11}$ **37.** $\frac{4}{5}$ **38.** $\frac{5}{8}$

39. $\frac{1}{12}$ **40.** $\frac{5}{6}$ **41.** $\frac{3}{4}$ **42.** $\frac{2}{15}$ **43.** $\frac{8}{9}$

44. $\frac{1}{3}$ **45.** $\frac{4}{8}$ **46.** $\frac{8}{10}$ **47.** $\frac{16}{20}$ **48.** $\frac{1}{25}$

Connections

Write a fraction, a decimal, and a percent for the region.

49. A   **50.** B

51. G   **52.** M

53. B + C   **54.** A + B + C

★ **55.** E + K   ★ **56.** H + J

★ **57.** C + G   ★ **58.** A + B + F

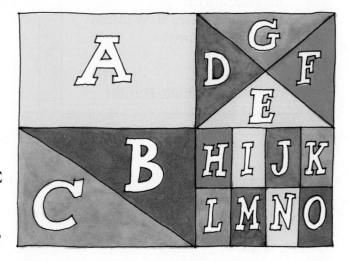

Calculator Corner

Suppose a car travels 6000 km per year. If the car travels an average of 4 km on a liter of gasoline, how much gas will it use in 5 years?

A Percent of a Number

You can write a percent as a decimal to find a percent of a number.

THE CITY TIMES

TODAY'S
MONEY
MANAGER

Dear Money Manager,

I read that I shouldn't spend more than 25% of my income for rent. I earn $2000 a month. How much rent can I afford?

Signed,
Apartment Hunter

Dear Apartment Hunter,

You can write the percent as a decimal and then multiply.

25% = 0.25
25% of 2000 = 0.25 × 2000
            = 500

I'd say you can afford to pay $500 a month.

Signed,
M.M.

Exercises

Complete.

1. 15% of 28 = ▦ × 28 = ▦

2. 46% of 57 = ▦ × 57 = ▦

3. 3% of 64 = ▦ × 64 = ▦

4. 8% of 92 = ▦ × 92 = ▦

5. 24% of 43 = ▦ × 43 = ▦

6. 52% of 86 = ▦ × 86 = ▦

7. 4% of 35 = ▦ × 35 = ▦

8. 7% of 23 = ▦ × 23 = ▦

9. 67% of 30 = ▦ × 30 = ▦

10. 33% of 96 = ▦ × 96 = ▦

11. 9% of 125 = ▦ × 125 = ▦

12. 5% of 75 = ▦ × 75 = ▦

What is the number?

13. 19% of 72

14. 81% of 48

15. 5% of 26

16. 2% of 87

17. 6% of 47

18. 32% of 54

19. 15% of 66

20. 11% of 94

21. 57% of 31

22. 4% of 26

23. 33% of 21

24. 95% of 53

25. 48% of 85

26. 18% of 76

27. 5% of 136

28. 24% of 49

29. 9% of 110

30. 73% of 58

31. 12% of 204

32. 61% of 125

33. 35% of 82

34. 86% of 39

35. 7% of 315

36. 28% of 64

Write < or > to compare the numbers.

37. 3% of 345 ▨ 5% of 325

38. 45% of 67 ▨ 50% of 58

39. 18% of 27 ▨ 62% of 48

40. 75% of 49 ▨ 80% of 62

Ask the Money Manager

Suppose you write a newspaper column that answers people's questions about money. How would you answer the letter?

41. Dear Money Manager,
I want to buy a new car that costs $9845. The sales tax is 3%. How much will the sales tax be?
Signed,
New Wheels

42. Dear Money Manager,
I want to buy a house that costs $78,500. The down payment is 20%. How much will the down payment be?
Signed,
House Hunter

★ **43.** Dear Money Manager,
I found a bookstore that gives a 15% discount on all books. How much can I save on a book that usually costs $15.98?
Signed,
Book Lover

★ **44.** Dear Money Manager,
Last month I saw a telescope that cost $387.50. Since then, the price has increased 7%. How much will it cost now?
Signed,
Star Gazer

One Number as a Percent of Another

Of the 20 families camping at Echo Lake Park, 7 were camping for the first time. What percent of the families were camping for the first time?

Follow these steps to write one number as a percent of another.

Write a fraction.	Write an equivalent fraction with a denominator of 100.	Write the fraction as a percent.
$\dfrac{7}{20}$	$\dfrac{7}{20} = \dfrac{n}{100} = \dfrac{35}{100}$	$\dfrac{35}{100} = 35\%$

7 is 35% of 20. The first-time campers were 35% of the total.

Exercises

Complete.

1. $\dfrac{3}{20} = \dfrac{n}{100}$ $\qquad$ $\dfrac{9}{20} = \dfrac{y}{100}$ $\qquad$ $\dfrac{13}{20} = \dfrac{a}{100}$

   3 is ▨% of 20. $\qquad$ 9 is ▨% of 20. $\qquad$ 13 is ▨% of 20.

2. $\dfrac{8}{50} = \dfrac{n}{100}$ $\qquad$ $\dfrac{12}{50} = \dfrac{a}{100}$ $\qquad$ $\dfrac{33}{50} = \dfrac{y}{100}$

   8 is ▨% of 50. $\qquad$ 12 is ▨% of 50. $\qquad$ 33 is ▨% of 50.

3. $\dfrac{18}{200} = \dfrac{a}{100}$ $\qquad$ $\dfrac{46}{200} = \dfrac{n}{100}$ $\qquad$ $\dfrac{74}{200} = \dfrac{y}{100}$

   18 is ▨% of 200. $\qquad$ 46 is ▨% of 200. $\qquad$ 74 is ▨% of 200.

Write the number as a percent of 25.

4. 4   **5.** 10   **6.** 12   **7.** 15

8. 21   **9.** 8   **10.** 6   **11.** 14

Write the number as a percent of 50.

12. 7   **13.** 16   **14.** 22   **15.** 30

16. 35   **17.** 25   **18.** 45   **19.** 5

Write the number as a percent of 200.

20. 8   **21.** 26   **22.** 34   **23.** 42

24. 50   **25.** 68   **26.** 82   **27.** 130

Write the number as a percent of 300.

28. 3   **29.** 15   **30.** 36   **31.** 54

32. 75   **33.** 102   **34.** 126   **35.** 180

Camping Trip

Solve.

36. On Monday 24 people signed up for a hike. When they found out how long the hike was, 6 dropped out. What percent dropped out?

37. The Rosens have $500 to spend on a camping trip. They expect to spend 25% of their money on food. How much will they spend on food?

38. Tanya sold her comic book collection for $35. She spent $11 on a new backpack. What percent did she spend on the backpack?

Checkpoint B

Write as a percent.
(*pages 296–297*)

1. $\frac{18}{100}$ **2.** $\frac{15}{20}$

Write as a fraction in lowest terms.

3. 38%   **4.** 55%

What is the percent of the number? (*pages 298–299*)

5. 60% of 50   **6.** 20% of 18

7. 75% of 200   **8.** 46% of 10

Write as a percent.
(*pages 300–301*)

9. 0.87   **10.** 0.09

Write as a decimal.

11. 18%   **12.** 6%

What is the percent of the number? (*pages 302–303*)

13. 22% of 50   **14.** 80% of 65

15. 4% of 36   **16.** 10% of 785

Write the number as a percent of 40. (*pages 304–305*)

17. 8   **18.** 20

19. 4   **20.** 12

Problem Solving · USING FORMULAS

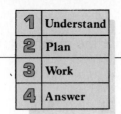

1	Understand
2	Plan
3	Work
4	Answer

Formulas are rules that you can use to solve problems.
Here's an example.

A passenger train between two towns travels at a rate of 95 km
per hour. It takes 3 hours to travel from one town to the other.
How far apart are the towns?

You can use the following formula to solve the problem.

distance (km) = rate (km/hour) × time (hours)

$$d = r \times t$$
$$d = 95 \times 3$$
$$= 285 \text{ km}$$

The towns are 285 km apart.

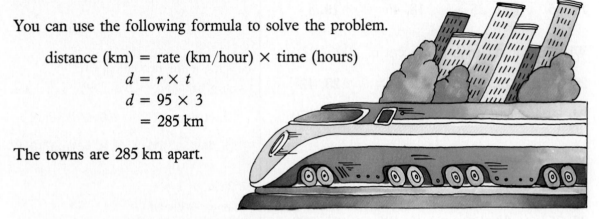

Use the distance formula to complete the table.

		r(km/hour)	t(hours)	$r \times t$
1.	jet at cruising speed	950	3	?
2.	6th grader on a bike	16	4.5	?
3.	satellite orbiting earth	27,400	2.8	?
4.	house fly	8	0.25	?
5.	gazelle	65.5	0.75	?

Solve.

6. A car is traveling at the rate of 80 km per hour. How far
will it travel in 10 minutes?

7. A small sailboat is crossing a lake that is 5 km wide. The
boat is traveling at the rate of 22 km per hour. How long
will it take to get across?

8. The three-toed sloth is one of the slowest moving land
animals. It travels at the rate of about 2.4 m per minute.
At this rate, how long will it take a sloth to travel 144 m?

You can use the following formula to estimate the average person's weight when you know the height.

weight (kg)   height (m)

$w = 97 \times (h - 1.02)$

Use the formula to complete the table.

	h	$h - 1.02$	$97 \times (h - 1.02)$
9.	1.21	?	?
10.	1.52	?	?
11.	1.16	?	?

Solve.

12. A basketball star is 2.4 m tall. Estimate his weight in kilograms.

13. A 4.5 m tall giraffe can weigh 1350 kg. Can you use the formula to find a giraffe's weight?

Use the formula to solve the problem.

14. Eddie took a taxi to the airport which is 12 km from his home. What was the fare?

(fare)   distance (km)

$f = \$1.75 + (\$1.50 \times d)$

15. A window washer was eating lunch outside of the 54th floor of a building. She dropped her apple and watched it fall to the ground 194 m below. How long did it take the apple to reach the ground?

distance (m)   time (seconds)

$d = 4.8 \times t^2$

★ **16.** Weather forecasters can predict how long a hurricane will last by measuring its diameter. How long would you expect a hurricane to last if it had a diameter of 38 km?

diameter (km)   time (hours)

$d^3 = 857 \times t^2$

307

Write a ratio as a fraction to compare the items in the table.

Jeremy's Lunchbox

item	sandwich	milk	carrot sticks	walnuts
number	2	1	18	10

1. sandwiches to carrot sticks

2. walnuts to milk

3. milk to sandwiches

4. carrot sticks to walnuts

Is the proportion true? Write *Yes* or *No*.

5. $\frac{5}{8} \overset{?}{=} \frac{7}{16}$

6. $\frac{3}{5} \overset{?}{=} \frac{12}{20}$

7. $\frac{3}{6} \overset{?}{=} \frac{4}{8}$

8. $\frac{12}{18} \overset{?}{=} \frac{4}{36}$

To determine a move on the transportation track, a player must spin each spinner. The player then moves that number of spaces of that color. Write the probability of the outcome.

9. Blue and 3

10. Red and 1

11. White and 2

Correct or incorrect? Write *C* or *I*.

12. $\frac{68}{100} = 68\%$

13. $\frac{4}{5} = 20\%$

14. $0.38 = 38\%$

15. $0.07 = 70\%$

16. 50% of 20 = 10

17. 70% of 100 = 7

18. 88% of 150 = 132

Solve.

19. A plane is flying at a speed of 1040 km per hour. How far will it fly in 5 hours?

Write a ratio as a fraction to compare the objects.
(*pages 284–285*)

□ △ ○ □ ○ ○ ◇ ⬡

1. □ to △   **2.** ○ to □   **3.** △ to ◇

Write the unit rate. (*pages 286–287*)

4. 100 books on 5 shelves   **5.** $3.60 for 9 envelopes   **6.** 20 km in 4 hours

Complete the proportions. (*pages 288–291*)

7. $\frac{7}{35} = \frac{n}{70}$ **8.** $\frac{n}{4} = \frac{1}{2}$ **9.** $\frac{13}{17} = \frac{39}{n}$ **10.** $\frac{8}{24} = \frac{n}{6}$

Suppose you choose a marble from each jar. Write the
probability of choosing the following. (*pages 292–295*)

11. 2 blue marbles

12. 1 blue and 1 white marble

Write as a percent. (*pages 296–297; 300–301*)

13. $\frac{72}{100}$ **14.** $\frac{3}{4}$ **15.** 0.57   **16.** 0.03

What is the percent of the number? (*pages 298–299; 302–303*)

17. 30% of 80   **18.** 65% of 200   **19.** 9% of 17   **20.** 18% of 175

Write the number as a percent of 80. (*pages 304–305*)

21. 8   **22.** 40   **23.** 10   **24.** 35

Solve. (*pages 306–307*)

25. Marion built a sandbox that measured 120 cm by 180 cm by
60 cm. How many cubic centimeters of sand are needed to
fill the box?

Patterns

Look at the problem below to see why mathematics is called the study of patterns.

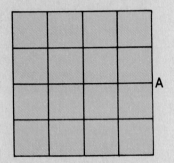

How many squares of all sizes can you find in figure A?

You could try counting all the squares. Since this would be boring and confusing, try looking for a pattern.

There is only 1 square in this diagram. It has a side with a length of 1 unit. You can write this as $1 \times 1 = 1^2$.

In this diagram, there are several squares.

1^2 1   square has a side 2 units long.

2^2 +4   squares have a side 1 unit long.

    5   or $1^2 + 2^2$ squares

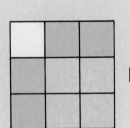

There are even more squares in this diagram.

1^2 1   square has a side 3 units long.

2^2 4   squares have a side 2 units long.

3^2 +9   squares have a side 1 unit long.

    14   or $1^2 + 2^2 + 3^2$ squares

Now you can tell how many squares are in figure A above.

$$1^2 + 2^2 + 3^2 + 4^2 = 1 + 4 + 9 + 16 = 30 \text{ squares}$$

Use the pattern above. How many squares are in a diagram of the given size?

1. 5 by 5   **2.** 6 by 6   **3.** 8 by 8   **4.** 10 by 10   **5.** 15 by 15

Complete the geometric patterns.

6. 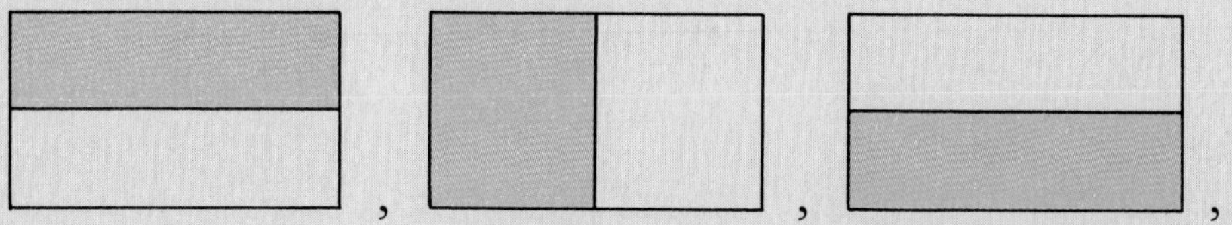 ■

7. 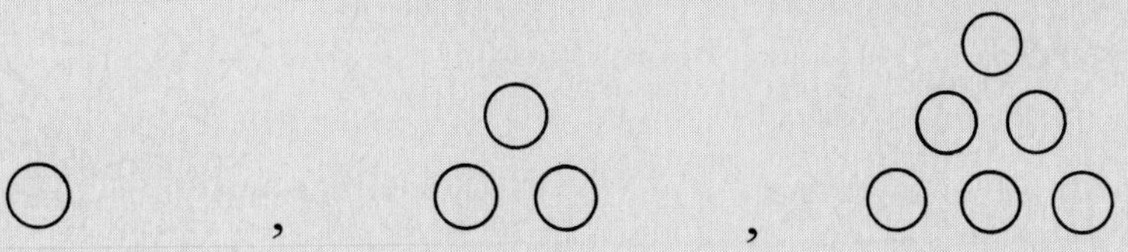 ■

8. 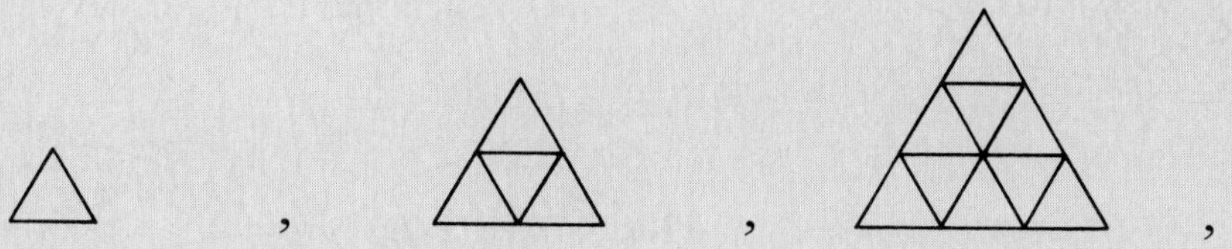 ■

9. 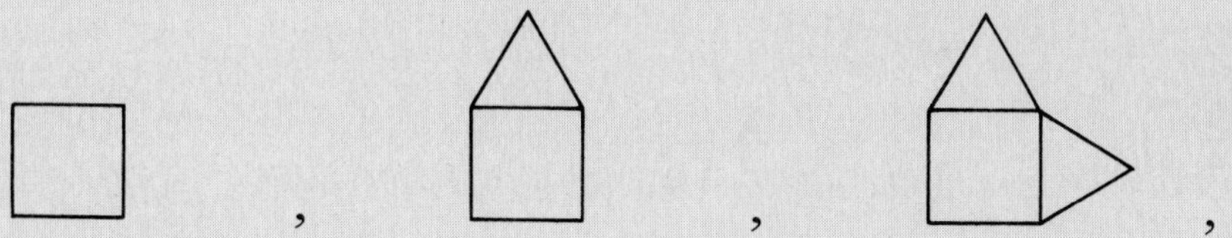 ■

Complete the number patterns.

10. 17, 25, 33, 41, ■, ■, ■

11. 56, 49, 42, 35, ■, ■, ■

12. 0.1, 0.01, 0.001, 0.0001, ■, ■, ■

13. $\frac{1}{2}, \frac{2}{3}, \frac{3}{4}, \frac{4}{5}, \frac{5}{6}$, ■, ■, ■

Solve.

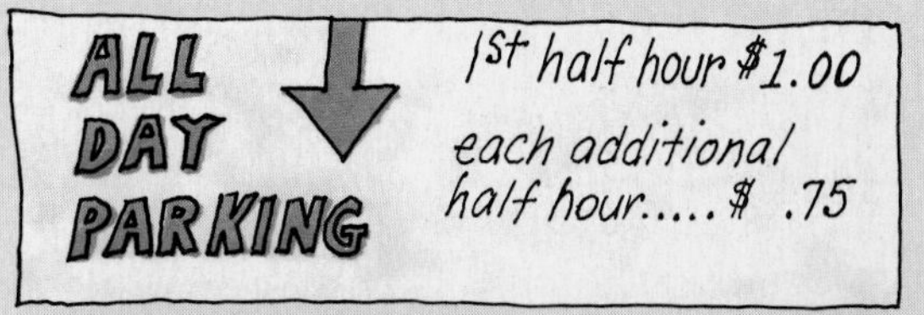

14. Make a table to show the cost of parking for from 1 to 5 hours. How much does it cost to park for 3 hours? for $4\frac{1}{2}$ hours?

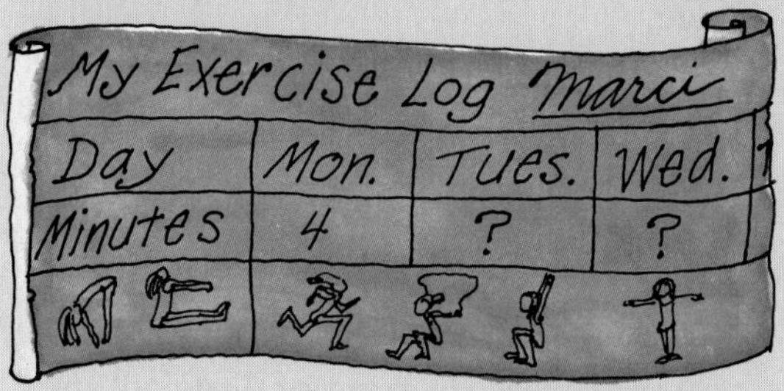

★ **15.** Marci started an exercise program. She exercised for 4 minutes the first day. For the next 7 days, she increased her time by $\frac{1}{2}$ the previous day's time. How many minutes will she exercise on the 8th day?

Maintaining Skills

Add, subtract, multiply, or divide.

1. $13 \div 2$

2. $103 - 19$

3. $29 + 93$

4. 60×13

5. $21 + 15 + 6$

6. 106×30

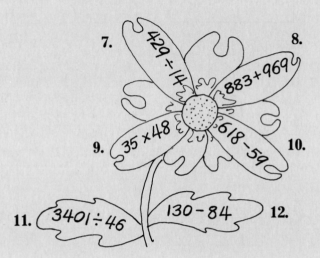

7. $429 \div 14$

8. $883 + 969$

9. 35×48

10. $618 - 59$

11. $3401 \div 46$

12. $130 - 84$

Match.

13. $\frac{2}{3} + 1\frac{3}{4}$ **A.** $7\frac{2}{3}$

14. $\frac{5}{6} \times \frac{7}{8}$ **B.** $1\frac{5}{6}$

15. $2\frac{5}{9} \div \frac{1}{3}$ **C.** $2\frac{5}{12}$

16. $3\frac{1}{4} - 1\frac{5}{12}$ **D.** $\frac{42}{65}$

17. $1\frac{2}{5} \div 2\frac{1}{6}$ **E.** $1\frac{7}{24}$

18. $4\frac{1}{8} - 2\frac{5}{6}$ **F.** $\frac{35}{48}$

Solve.

19. Of the flowers in the garden, $\frac{1}{3}$ are red. Of the red flowers, $\frac{3}{4}$ are roses. What fraction of the flowers in the garden are red roses?

20. The gardener used $\frac{5}{6}$ bag of lime to fertilize the grass. If there were $2\frac{1}{2}$ bags of lime to start, how much lime was left?

Geometry and Measurement

All aboard! Though this town looks real, it's only a model. It's built on the HO scale which means the models are $\frac{1}{87}$ as large as the real thing. If the model train is 0.24 m long, how long would the real train be?

12

Symmetry

If you can fold a figure so that both halves fit exactly on one another the figure is **symmetrical.** The fold is called a **line of symmetry.**

Some figures have more than one line of symmetry.

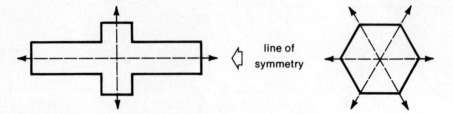

Some figures have no lines of symmetry.

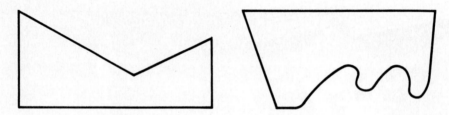

Exercises

Is the fold a line of symmetry? Write *Yes* or *No*.

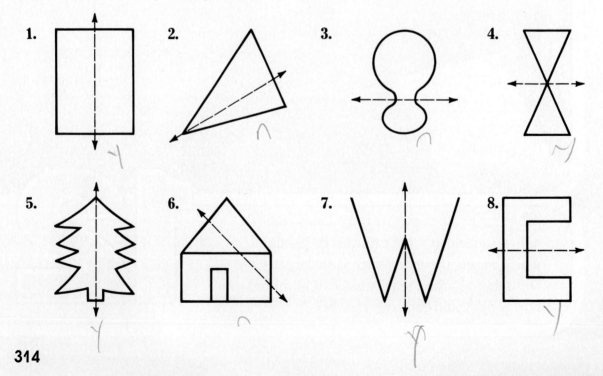

1.   2.   3.   4.

5.   6.   7.   8.

314

Copy the figure. Draw all the lines of symmetry.

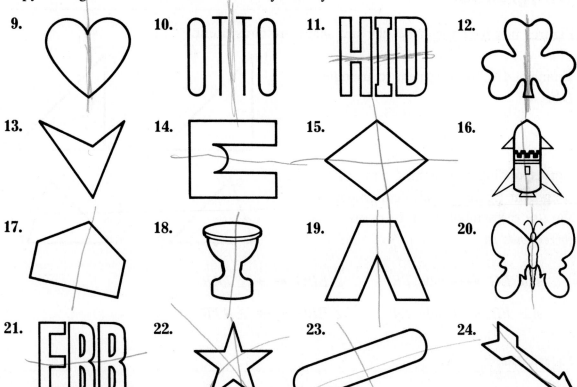

9.   10. OTTO   11. HID   12.

13.   14. E   15.   16.

17.   18.   19.   20.

21. EBB   22.   23.   24.

Mirror Image

Copy the figure. Complete the drawing so that the dashed line is a line of symmetry.

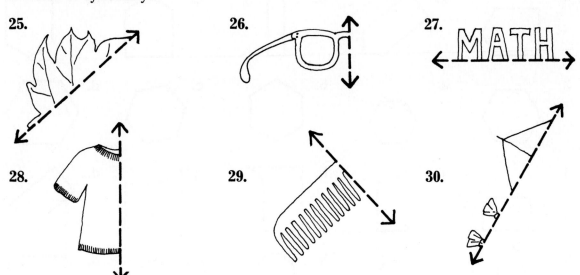

25.   26.   27. MATH

28.   29.   30.

Congruence

Figures that have the same size and shape are **congruent.**

Triangle *ABC* is congruent to triangle *DEF.*

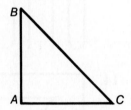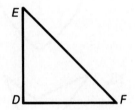

Corresponding or matching parts of congruent figures are also congruent. We use the symbol ⟷ to mean *corresponds to.*

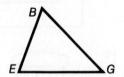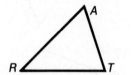

side *EG* ⟷ side *TR*   ∠*EBG* ⟷ ∠*TAR*

side *EB* ⟷ side *TA*   ∠*BEG* ⟷ ∠*ATR*

Exercises

Which figures are congruent to the first figure? Write *a, b, c,* or *d.*

1.   a.   b.   c.   d.

2.   a.   b.   c.   d.

3.   a.   b.   c.   d.

4.   a.   b.   c.   d.

5.   a.   b.   c.   d.

Complete to show which parts of triangle *RUT* correspond to parts of triangle *FOX*.

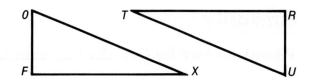

6. side *FO* ⟷ side ▨

7. side *OX* ⟷ side ▨

8. side *FX* ⟷ side ▨

9. ∠*FOX* ⟷ ∠▨

10. ∠*XFO* ⟷ ∠▨

11. ∠*OXF* ⟷ ∠▨

Complete to show which parts of figure *BARK* correspond to parts of figure *LIME*.

12. side *BA* ⟷ side ▨

13. side *KR* ⟷ side ▨

14. side *AR* ⟷ side ▨

15. ∠*RAB* ⟷ ∠▨

16. ∠*BKR* ⟷ ∠▨

17. ∠*ARK* ⟷ ∠▨

What's My Measure?

Angles that have the same measurement are congruent angles.
∠*ABC* is congruent to ∠*DEF*

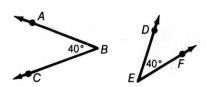

Are the angles congruent? Write *Yes* or *No*.

18.

19.

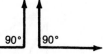

20.

Solve.

★ **21.** I am one of two acute angles in a right triangle. I am congruent to the other acute angle. How many degrees do I measure?

★ **22.** The two other angles of a triangle are congruent. I measure 80°. How many degrees does each congruent angle measure?

Arrange the 7 dots so that you can have 6 segments with 3 dots on each segment.

317

Similarity

Figures that have the same shape are **similar.**

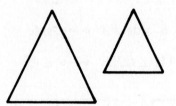

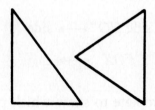

The triangles are similar.

The quadrilaterals are similar.

The triangles are not similar.

Exercises

Are the triangles similar? Write *Yes* or *No*.

1.
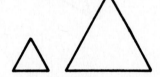

2.

3.
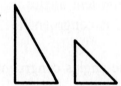

4.
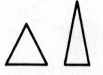

5.

6.

7.

8.
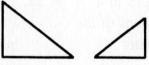

9.
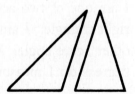

Are the figures similar? Write *Yes* or *No*.

10.
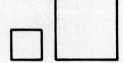

11.
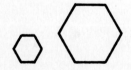

12.
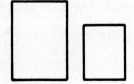

13.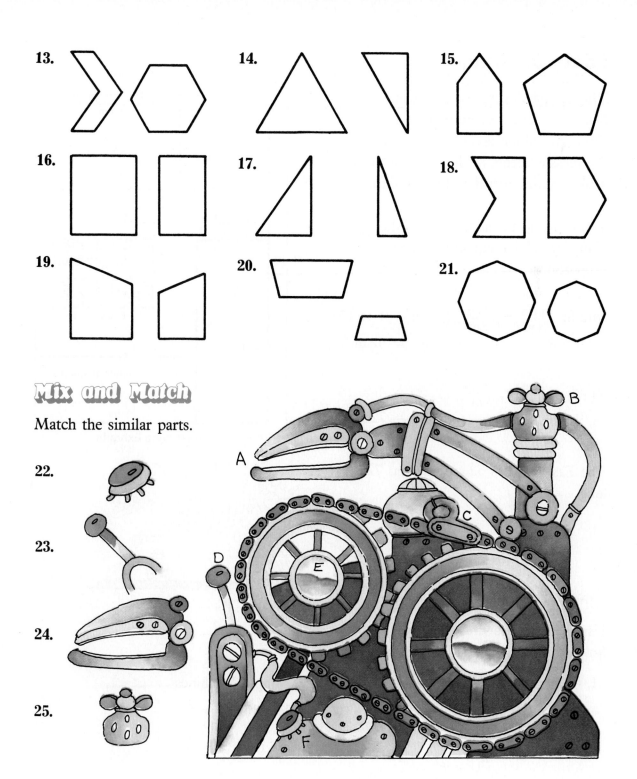

14.

15.

16.

17.

18.

19.

20.

21.

Mix and Match

Match the similar parts.

22.

23.

24.

25.

True or false? Write *T* or *F*.

★ **26.** All congruent figures are similar.

★ **27.** All similar figures are congruent.

Scale Drawing

The exhibit director of the Science Museum made a **scale drawing** to show the exhibit areas. The **scale** of the measurements in the drawing to the actual measurements is 1 cm to 4 m.

You can find the actual size of the East Wing by solving equations using proportions.

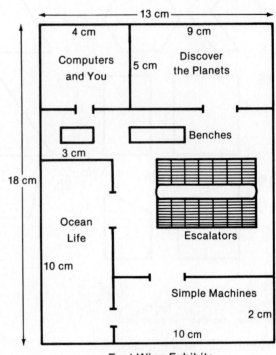

East Wing Exhibits

width: $\dfrac{1 \text{ cm}}{4 \text{ m}} \times \dfrac{13 \text{ cm}}{w \text{ m}}$ ⟹ $w = 4 \times 13$
$\qquad\qquad\qquad\qquad\qquad = 52 \text{ m}$

length: $\dfrac{1 \text{ cm}}{4 \text{ m}} \times \dfrac{18 \text{ cm}}{l \text{ m}}$ ⟹ $l = 4 \times 18$
$\qquad\qquad\qquad\qquad\qquad = 72 \text{ m}$

The East Wing is 52 m wide and 72 m long.

Exercises

Use the scale drawing above.
Solve to find the actual size of the exhibit area.

1. Computers and You

length: $\dfrac{1}{4} = \dfrac{5}{l}$

width: $\dfrac{1}{4} = \dfrac{4}{w}$

2. Simple Machines

length: $\dfrac{1}{4} = \dfrac{2}{l}$

width: $\dfrac{1}{4} = \dfrac{11}{w}$

3. Discover the Planets

length: $\dfrac{1}{4} = \dfrac{5}{l}$

width: $\dfrac{1}{4} = \dfrac{9}{w}$

4. Ocean Life

length: $\dfrac{1}{4} = \dfrac{10}{l}$

width: $\dfrac{1}{4} = \dfrac{3}{w}$

A building plan is drawn with a scale of 2 cm to 10 m. What length in the building does the length on the plan represent?

5. 1 cm   **6.** 4 cm   **7.** 5 cm

8. 10.5 cm   **9.** 25.5 cm   **10.** 13.8 cm

A plan for a summer camp is drawn with a scale of 3 cm to 1 km. What length in the camp does the length on the plan represent?

11. 6 cm   **12.** 12 cm   **13.** 4 cm

14. 12.3 cm   **15.** 15.6 cm   **16.** 7.3 cm

Museum Math

A dinosaur exhibit has a scale of 0.5 cm to 2 m. What was the actual size of the dinosaur?

17.

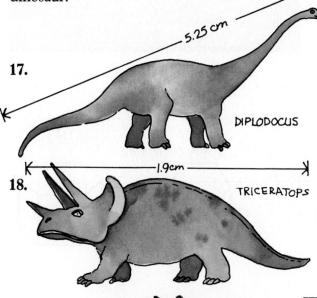

5.25 cm

DIPLODOCUS

18.

1.9cm

TRICERATOPS

19.

STEGOSAURUS

0.9 cm

Is the fold a line of symmetry? Write *Yes* or *No*. (*pages 314–315*)

1. 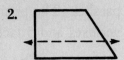   **2.**

Complete to show which parts of triangle *MAT* correspond to triangle *FUN*. (*pages 316–317*)

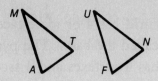

3. side *MA* ⟷ side ▓

4. side *MT* ⟷ side ▓

5. ∠ *TAM* ⟷ ∠ ▓

Are the figures similar? Write *Yes* or *No*. (*pages 318–319*)

6.

7.

A map is drawn to the scale of 2 cm to 25 km. What is the actual distance between towns that are the given distance apart on the map? (*pages 320–321*)

8. 10 cm   **9.** 25 cm

10. 6.8 cm   **11.** 15.7 cm

Prisms and Pyramids

A **prism** is a space figure with 5 or more sides or **faces.** Two of the faces, called **bases,** must be congruent and parallel. The prism below has 6 vertexes and 5 faces.

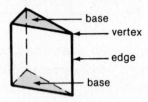

A **pyramid** has 4 or more faces. Only one is called the base. The pyramid below has 4 vertexes and 4 faces.

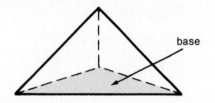

Exercises

Is the figure a prism or a pyramid?

1.

2.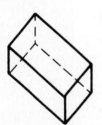

3.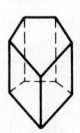

4.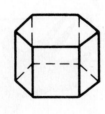

5.

6.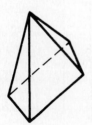

7.

8.

Use the figure to complete the table.

9. 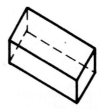 10.   11.  12.

13. 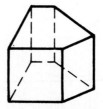 14.  15. 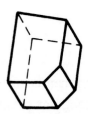 16.

	V = number of vertexes	F = number of faces	E = number of edges	V + F	(V + F) − E
9.	?	?	?	?	?
10.	?	?	?	?	?
11.	?	?	?	?	?
12.	?	?	?	?	?
13.	?	?	?	?	?
14.	?	?	?	?	?
15.	?	?	?	?	?
16.	?	?	?	?	?

Paper Folding

What figure do you form if you fold the pattern along the dotted lines?

17. 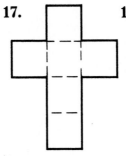 18. 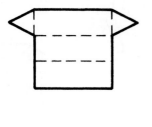 19.  20.

Volume of a Rectangular Prism

The **volume** of a figure is the amount of space it contains. We use cubic units to measure volume.

You can use the following formula to find the volume of a rectangular prism.

Volume = length × width × height
$$V = l \times w \times h$$

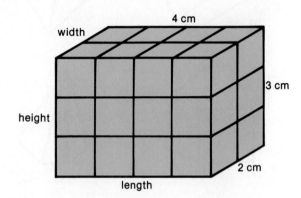

Here's how to use the formula to find the volume of the rectangular prism at the right.

$$V = 4 \times 2 \times 3$$
$$= 8 \times 3$$
$$= 24 \text{ cm}^3$$

24 cubic centimeters

The volume is 24 cm³.

Exercises

What is the volume if the edges have the given lengths?

1.

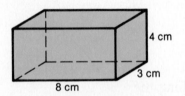

$V = \boxed{} \times \boxed{} \times \boxed{} = \boxed{} \text{ cm}^3$

2.

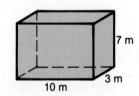

$V = \boxed{} \times \boxed{} \times \boxed{} = \boxed{} \text{ m}^3$

3.

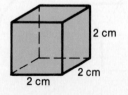

$V = \boxed{} \times \boxed{} \times \boxed{} = \boxed{} \text{ cm}^3$

4.

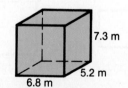

$V = \boxed{} \times \boxed{} \times \boxed{} = \boxed{} \text{ m}^3$

What is the volume if the edges have the given lengths?

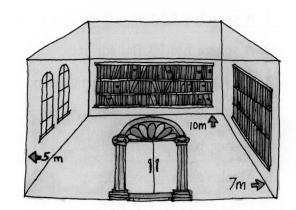

5. $AB = 18$ cm
$BC = 9$ cm
$CD = 7$ cm

6. $AB = 15$ cm
$BC = 8$ cm
$CD = 6$ cm

7. $AB = 9$ m
$BC = 5$ m
$CD = 4$ m

8. $AB = 2.0$ m
$BC = 1.1$ m
$CD = 0.9$ m

9. $AB = 11$ m
$BC = 6$ m
$CD = 4$ m

10. $AB = 21$ cm
$BC = 10$ cm
$CD = 8$ cm

11. $AB = 5$ m
$BC = 4$ m
$CD = 2$ m

12. $AB = 4.0$ cm
$BC = 18$ cm
$CD = 0.7$ cm

13. $AB = 0.42$ m
$BC = 0.32$ m
$CD = 0.09$ m

14. $AB = 5.2$ cm
$BC = 5.2$ cm
$CD = 7.3$ cm

15. $AB = 1.3$ m
$BC = 1.3$ m
$CD = 5.9$ m

16. $AB = 3.5$ cm
$BC = 1.5$ cm
$CD = 0.8$ cm

17. $AB = 16.2$ m
$BC = 12.6$ m
$CD = 10.0$ m

Taking Up Space

Use the figure at the right. Solve.

18. How many square meters of carpet will the library need?

19. How many cubic meters of space are there to be heated?

Complete.

★ **20.** If the length and width of a room are doubled, the number of cubic meters to be heated is ▓ times as great.

★ **21.** Double the length, width, and height of a room. The volume of space to heat is ▓ times as great.

Cylinders, Cones, and Spheres

Every point on a **sphere** is the same distance from the center. The distance from the center to any point on the sphere is called the radius.

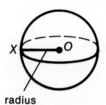

radius

A **cylinder** has two circular bases that are congruent and parallel.

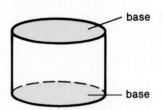

base

base

A **cone** has one circular base and one vertex.

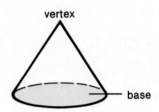

vertex

base

Exercises

Complete.

1. A cone has ▦ flat surface and ▦ curved surface.

2. A sphere has ▦ flat surfaces.

3. A cylinder has ▦ flat surfaces and ▦ curved surface.

4. A cylinder has ▦ vertexes.

5. A cone has ▦ vertex.

6. A sphere has ▦ vertexes.

Name the shape.

7.

8.

9.

10.

11.

12.

13.

14.

15.

Making Tracks

Suppose an ant travels the dotted path around the shape. What figure is made by the ant's tracks?

16.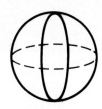

17.

18.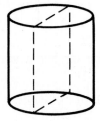

19.

20.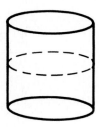

21.

Calculator Corner

The volume of a cube is 11,390,625 cm³. What is the length of each edge?

Volume of a Cylinder

What is the volume of the jar? You can use the formula for volume of a cylinder to find out.

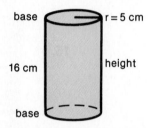

Volume (V) = Area of base (B) × height (h)

$$V = B \times h$$
$$\approx (3.14 \times 5^2) \times 16$$
$$\approx 78.5 \times 16$$
$$\approx 1256 \text{ cm}^3$$

The jar has a volume of about 1256 cm^3.

Exercises

Complete.

1. $B = 15 \text{ cm}^2$, $h = 10 \text{ cm}$

$V = \blacksquare \times \blacksquare = \blacksquare \text{ cm}^3$

2. $B = 20 \text{ cm}^2$, $h = 5 \text{ cm}$

$V = \blacksquare \times \blacksquare = \blacksquare \text{ cm}^3$

3. $B = 8 \text{ cm}^2$, $h = 16 \text{ cm}$

$V = \blacksquare \times \blacksquare = \blacksquare \text{ cm}^3$

4. $r = 10 \text{ cm}$, $h = 40 \text{ cm}$

$V \approx 3.14 \times \blacksquare^2 \times \blacksquare = \blacksquare \text{ cm}^3$

5. $r = 2 \text{ m}$, $h = 10 \text{ m}$

$V \approx 3.14 \times \blacksquare^2 \times \blacksquare = \blacksquare \text{ m}^3$

6. $r = 5 \text{ cm}$, $h = 11 \text{ cm}$

$V \approx 3.14 \times \blacksquare^2 \times \blacksquare = \blacksquare \text{ cm}^3$

Find the volume of a cylinder with the given area of base (B) and height (h).

7. $B = 20 \text{ cm}^2$

$h = 10 \text{ cm}$

8. $B = 30 \text{ cm}^2$

$h = 10 \text{ cm}$

9. $B = 20 \text{ cm}^2$

$h = 4 \text{ cm}$

10. $B = 22\,\text{cm}^2$
$h = 6\,\text{cm}$

11. $B = 9\,\text{m}^2$
$h = 3\,\text{m}$

12. $B = 15\,\text{cm}^2$
$h = 14\,\text{cm}$

13. $B = 21.6\,\text{cm}^2$
$h = 13.5\,\text{cm}$

14. $B = 46.4\,\text{cm}^2$
$h = 25.7\,\text{cm}$

15. $B = 0.6\,\text{m}^2$
$h = 0.9\,\text{m}$

16. $B = 15.8\,\text{cm}^2$
$h = 6.5\,\text{cm}$

17. $B = 0.9\,\text{cm}^2$
$h = 1.6\,\text{cm}$

18. $B = 22.5\,\text{cm}^2$
$h = 3.6\,\text{cm}$

Find the volume of a cylinder with the given radius (r) and height (h).

19. $r = 5\,\text{cm}$
$h = 20\,\text{cm}$

20. $r = 10\,\text{cm}$
$h = 8\,\text{cm}$

21. $r = 20\,\text{cm}$
$h = 15\,\text{cm}$

22. $r = 25\,\text{cm}$
$h = 9\,\text{cm}$

23. $r = 8\,\text{m}$
$h = 10\,\text{m}$

24. $r = 6\,\text{m}$
$h = 7\,\text{m}$

25. $r = 3\,\text{cm}$
$h = 12\,\text{cm}$

26. $r = 7\,\text{cm}$
$h = 8\,\text{cm}$

27. $r = 5\,\text{cm}$
$h = 10\,\text{cm}$

28. $r = 6\,\text{cm}$
$h = 0.5\,\text{cm}$

29. $r = 3\,\text{m}$
$h = 1.5\,\text{m}$

30. $r = 10\,\text{cm}$
$h = 2.6\,\text{cm}$

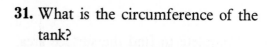

Waterways

Solve.

31. What is the circumference of the tank?

32. What is the area of one base of the tank?

33. What is the volume of water the tank will hold?

5m

10m

Surface Area

How much screening is needed to make a bird feeder that is 18 cm wide, 12 cm long, and 20 cm high?

The figure below shows how the bird feeder would look if it were unfolded and placed on a flat surface.

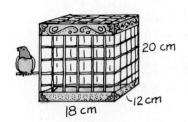

To find the **surface area** of a rectangular prism, add the areas of the faces.

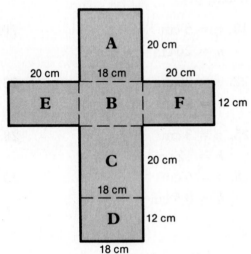

Face	$l \times w$	Area
A	$20 \times 18 =$	360 cm^2
B	$12 \times 18 =$	216 cm^2
C	$20 \times 18 =$	360 cm^2
D	$12 \times 18 =$	216 cm^2
E	$12 \times 20 =$	240 cm^2
F	$12 \times 20 =$	$+240 \text{ cm}^2$
Surface area ⟹		1632 cm^2

It takes 1632 cm^2 of screening for the bird feeder.

Exercises

1.

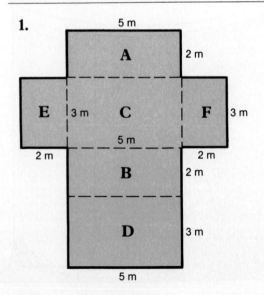

Complete to find the surface area.

Face	$l \times w$	Area
A	$2 \times 5 =$	▨ m^2
B	$2 \times 5 =$	▨ m^2
C	$3 \times 5 =$	▨ m^2
D	▨ $\times$ ▨ $=$	▨ m^2
E	▨ $\times$ ▨ $=$	▨ m^2
F	▨ $\times$ ▨ $=$	$+$ ▨ m^2
Surface area ⟹		▨ m^2

What is the surface area?

2.
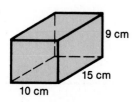
9 cm
15 cm
10 cm

3.
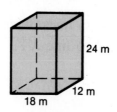
24 m
12 m
18 m

4.
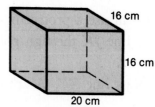
16 cm
16 cm
20 cm

5.
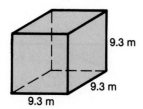
9.3 m
9.3 m
9.3 m

6.
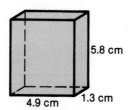
5.8 cm
4.9 cm
1.3 cm

7.
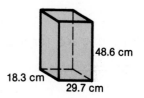
48.6 cm
18.3 cm
29.7 cm

Going Around in Circles

To find the surface area of a cylinder, add the areas of the
2 bases and the area of the curved surface.

Area of bases

Remember... a cylinder has 2 bases.

$A = 2 \times (\pi \times r^2)$
$\approx 2 \times (3.14 \times 36)$
≈ 226.08 cm^2

Area of curved surface

$A = \pi \times 2 \times r \times h$
$\approx 3.14 \times 2 \times 6 \times 10$
≈ 376.80 cm^2

Surface area ⇨
  226.08
+ 376.80
  602.88 cm^2

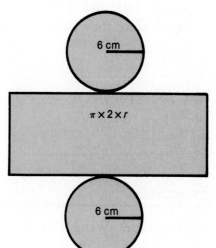

r = 6 cm
10 cm

6 cm
π × 2 × r
6 cm

What is the surface area of the cylinder?

8.
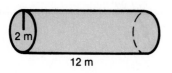
2 m
12 m

9.
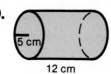
5 cm
12 cm

10.
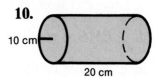
10 cm
20 cm

Drawing Parallel Lines

You can use a protractor to draw parallel lines. Here's how to draw line *JK* through point *R*, parallel to line *XY*.

- Draw line *XY*. Mark point *R*.

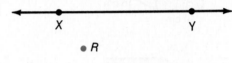

- Draw line *RS* through *R*, crossing line *XY*.

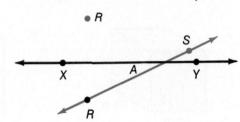

- Measure ∠*SAY*. In this figure it measures 25°.

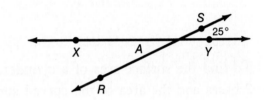

- Draw ∠*ARK* with a measure of 25°. Angles *SAY* and *ARK* are congruent angles since they have the same measure.

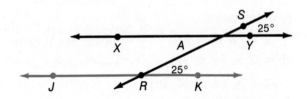

Line *JK* is parallel to line *XY*.

Exercises

True or false? Write *T* or *F*.

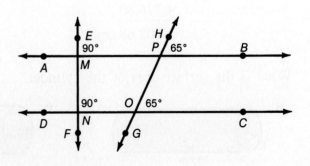

1. Line *AB* is parallel to line *DC*.

2. Line *EF* is perpendicular to line *HG*.

3. Line *DC* is perpendicular to line *AB*.

4. ∠*EMB* is congruent to ∠*MNO*.

5. ∠*GOC* is congruent to ∠*ONM*.

Use a protractor and centimeter ruler to draw the figure.

6. Draw line *DE* parallel to line *XY*.

7. Draw line *OR* parallel to line *PS*.

8. Draw a rectangle that is 4 cm wide and 5 cm long.

9. Draw a square that is 3 cm on each side.

10. Draw a rectangle that is 8 cm wide and 2 cm long.

11. Draw a square that is 6.7 cm long on each side.

12. Draw line *SR* perpendicular to line *JK*.

Around and About

You can use a compass to make designs. First draw a circle.

Next, using the same setting draw a curve that crosses the circle in two points.

Repeat this step 5 more times placing the point of the compass on the point where the curve crossed the circle.

Use a compass to make these designs.

13.

★ **14.**

Checkpoint B

How many vertexes, faces, and edges does the figure have? (*pages 322–323*)

1.   **2.**

What is the volume of the rectangular prism? (*pages 324–325*)

3.

What is the volume of the
4 cm
7 cm
8 cm

Name the shape. (*pages 326–327*)

4.   **5.**

What is the volume of the cylinder with the given radius (*r*) and height (*h*)? (*pages 328–329*)

6. $r = 6\,m$ **7.** $r = 4\,m$
   $h = 15\,m$ $h = 12\,m$

What is the surface area of the figure? (*pages 330–331*)

8.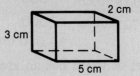
2 cm
3 cm
5 cm

Draw the figure. (*pages 332–333*)

9. Draw line *MJ* parallel to line *GL*.

10. Draw a square that is 6 cm long on each side.

Problem Solving · PROBLEM FORMULATION

1	Understand
2	Plan
3	Work
4	Answer

Oscar went to the lumber yard to buy materials to build a doghouse. He went home empty-handed because he hadn't planned what he was going to do.

The salesperson wrote down these questions for Oscar.

1. How much wood do you need?
2. How much paint do you need?
3. Do you need glue, or nails, or paint brushes?
4. How much do you want to spend?

Oscar went home and solved these problems to answer the questions.

Step 1: Oscar drew these plans. Then he found the surface area.

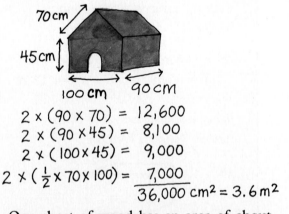

$2 \times (90 \times 70) = 12,600$
$2 \times (90 \times 45) = 8,100$
$2 \times (100 \times 45) = 9,000$
$2 \times (\frac{1}{2} \times 70 \times 100) = 7,000$
$36,000 \text{ cm}^2 = 3.6 \text{ m}^2$

One sheet of wood has an area of about 3 m^2. Oscar decided he needed two sheets.

Step 2: Oscar found that a 1 L can of paint would cover 9 m^2. He decided that one can was enough.

Step 3: Oscar had glue, nails, and brushes so he didn't need to buy them.

Step 4: Oscar had $40 to spend. The plywood cost $36. He had $4 left for paint. He chose a can that cost $3.50 rather than one that cost $5.50.

After gathering the information he needed, Oscar went back to the lumber yard. He bought 2 sheets of wood and 1 can of paint. He had what he needed and he knew how much it would cost.

Write the letters of the questions you'd need to answer to complete the activity. Then write one other question you'd need to answer.

1. Plan a meal.
   a. How much do a dozen roses cost?
   b. How many people are coming?
   c. What color sweater will you wear?
   d. At what time should you start dinner?

2. Paint your bedroom.
   a. How large is the room?
   b. How much paint do you need?
   c. Do you need more than one coat of paint?
   d. At what time of day will you paint?

3. Start a savings account.
   a. What is the minimum deposit?
   b. How much interest does the bank pay?
   c. When is the bank open?
   d. What kind of computers does the bank use?

4. Decide how much money you need for a vacation.
   a. How long will you be gone?
   b. How many people will be going?
   c. What time will you be leaving?
   d. How many pairs of socks should you take?

Write four questions you'd have to answer to complete the activity.

5. You are in charge of posters, tickets, and programs for the school Glee Club concert. You know that you will need 10 posters, 200 tickets, and 200 programs. You can spend $25.

6. You agree to plan a birthday party for your 5 year old cousin. You know that there will be 10 guests. You must buy paper goods, favors, and refreshments.

★ 7. Your parents have agreed to let you start a vegetable garden.

★ 8. You want to start a collection. You don't know whether to choose stamps or coins.

Is the fold a line of symmetry? Write *Yes* or *No*.

1.   **2.** 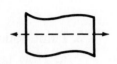   **3.**   **4.**

True or false? Write *T* or *F*.

5. Congruent figures have the same shape and size.

6. Similar triangles must be the same size.

7. All right angles are congruent angles.

8. A pyramid has three faces and two bases.

9. A cone has one circular base and one vertex.

Use a centimeter ruler and the scale on the map to find the actual distance between the cities.

10. Savannah and Riceboro

11. Baxley and Vidalia

12. Jesup and Surrency

Scale:
2.5 cm = 32 km

Use the figure at the right.

13. What is the surface area?

14. What is the volume?

4 cm
8 cm
10 cm

Write the letters of the questions you'd have to answer to complete the activity.

15. Planning a garage sale.
    a. Where can you have the sale?   **b.** How much should you charge?

    c. How much do apples cost?   **d.** Should you make posters?

Is the fold a line of symmetry? Write *Yes* or *No*. (*pages 314–315*)

1.   **2.** 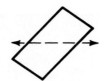 **3.**   **4.**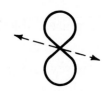

Look at the figures on the right. (*pages 316–319*)

5. Are triangles *ABC* and
   DEF similar?

A building plan has a scale of 1 cm to 4 m. What length does
the length on the plan represent? (*pages 320–321*)

6. 2 cm   **7.** 5 cm   **8.** 10 cm   **9.** 8 cm   **10.** 6 cm

Complete. (*pages 322–323; 326–327*)

11. A cylinder has ▨ flat surfaces and ▨ vertexes.

What is the volume of the rectangular prism or cylinder?
(*pages 324–325; 328–329*)

12. $l = 14$ m, $w = 9$ m, $h = 8$ m   **13.** $r = 6$ cm, $h = 18$ cm

What is the surface area of the figure
at the right? (*pages 330–331*)

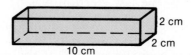

Draw the figure. (*pages 332–333*)

14. Draw line *XY* parallel to line *RS*   **15.** Draw a rectangle that is 12 cm
                                                          wide and 15 cm long.

Write the letters of the questions you'd have to answer to
complete the activity. (*pages 334–335*)

16. You want to buy carpeting.
   a. How many rooms do you have?   **b.** How much do floor tiles cost?

   c. Do you want wall-to-wall carpeting?   **d.** How much does paint cost?

Making Predictions

Porpoise Publications developed a new magazine called Persnickety. They took a survey and projected that 13% of the population would buy the new magazine. How many copies should be shipped to a chain of stores that serves 250,000 people?

If the survey sample is correct, 13% of the 250,000 people are likely to buy the magazine.

$$13\% = 0.13$$

$$0.13 \times 250,000 = 32,500$$

About 32,500 copies of Persnickety should be shipped.

Sometimes it's more convenient to use ratios to make predictions.

In a certain city, the ratio of eligible voters to the number who actually voted in the last election was 5:3. If there were 80,000 eligible voters, how many voted in the last election?

If the sample is representative, $\frac{3}{5}$ of the people voted.

$$\frac{3}{5} \times 80,000 = 48,000$$

You would expect that 48,000 people voted.

Solve.

1. In a survey of pet food buyers, 46% chose Spunky Mix as their pets' favorite brand. Chunky Chow was the choice of 54%. If 151,556 people were surveyed, how many chose Chunky Chow?

2. The ratio of jazz records to the number of country records sold in one town is 3:5. Zounds Sounds buys a total of 256,000 of the two kinds of records each year. How many of these should be country?

4. In a survey, a car dealer asked 500 customers whether they liked small cars or large cars better. The dealer found that 225 liked large cars better. What ratio of small cars to large cars should the dealer use when placing the next car order? In an order of 750 cars, how many should be small cars?

6. Alpha Research took a survey to find how many people liked Whirlwind Window Wash better than other brands. Of the 300 people surveyed, 48 preferred Whirlwind. What percent projection should the company make about the preference for Whirlwind? If a store has 88 customers in one week who are buying window cleaner, how many can be expected to buy Whirlwind?

7. To estimate the number of deer in a wildlife preserve a scientist captured 75 deer. She then marked and released them. A week later she captured 25 deer and found that 3 of them were marked. How many deer should she estimate are in the forest?

3. A supermarket analyst found that 16% of the fruit brought in spoiled before it was sold. The Market Basket bought 3500 kg of peaches. How much of this can they expect to sell before it spoils?

5. On an assembly line, 400 television sets were checked for defects. Of those checked, 32 had defects. What percent were not defective? If a store orders 150 sets, how many of the sets can they expect to be free of defects?

Maintaining Skills

Measure the angle. Write *A*, *O*, or *R* to show whether it is acute, obtuse, or right.

Match the proportions.

9. $\frac{4}{8}$ **A.** $\frac{1}{3}$

10. $\frac{5}{15}$ **B.** $\frac{3}{6}$

11. $\frac{4}{20}$ **C.** $\frac{12}{54}$

12. $\frac{14}{21}$ **D.** $\frac{5}{25}$

13. $\frac{2}{9}$ **E.** $\frac{6}{9}$

Choose the correct answer. Write *a*, *b*, or *c*.

14. 35% of 20   **a.** 0.7   **15.** 86% of 42   **a.** 3.612
                  b. 70   **b.** 36.12
                  c. 7   **c.** 361.2

16. 75% of 50   **a.** 375   **17.** 6% of 320   **a.** 1.92
                  b. 37.5   **b.** 19.2
                  c. 3.75   **c.** 192

Solve.

18. Angela bought a kite that cost $18.50. The sales tax was 5%. What was the total cost of her purchase?

19. Terry spent 3 hours doing homework. He spent 25% of the time on math. How much time did he spend on math?

Statistics and Integers

Have you ever heard the saying "It's only the tip of the iceberg"? Though it looks enormous, only $\frac{1}{9}$ of the floating ice mass is above sea level. How much is hidden from view?

Range and Mode

The owner of a coin shop kept track of the number of customers he had each day. During the first two weeks in April, the numbers varied from 36 to 102.

The difference between the greatest and least numbers is called the **range.**

$$102 - 36 = 66$$

	Mint Condition Coin Shop Customer Count			
	Week			
Day	**Apr. 3**	**Apr. 10**	**Apr. 17**	**Apr. 24**
Mon.	36	42		
Tues.	39	49		
Wed.	63	91		
Thurs.	86	91		
Fri.	91	102		

The **mode** is 91 because that number appears most often. If no number appears more than once, there is no mode. If there are two or more numbers that appear the same number of times and more often than any of the other numbers, then there is more than one mode.

Exercises

Complete.

1. numbers: 13, 15, 16, 16, 19
range: $19 - 13 = $ ▨
mode: ▨

2. numbers: 87, 91, 94, 94, 94
range: $94 - 87 = $ ▨
mode: ▨

3. numbers: 59, 63, 57, 65, 58, 64
range: $65 - $ ▨ $ = $ ▨
mode: ▨

4. numbers: 125, 136, 136, 172, 134
range: ▨ $ - 125 = $ ▨
mode: ▨

Write the range and mode.

5. 17, 12, 18, 21, 23, 29, 18

6. 41, 56, 28, 35, 44, 41

7. 76, 74, 61, 92, 74, 78, 85

8. 271, 258, 316, 294, 271

9. 9, 7, 6, 8, 6, 11

10. 36, 29, 42, 34, 38, 36, 40

11. 150, 162, 158, 156, 160, 156

12. 1.8, 2.3, 1.5, 1.7, 2.0, 1.7

The table shows the monthly savings for six families for five months.

Monthly Savings					
Family	Jan.	Feb.	Mar.	April	May
Johnsons	$100	$200	$ 75	$150	$175
Riveras	$212	$280	$125	$300	$420
Takases	$400	$200	0	$275	$200
Corcorans	$375	$300	$175	$265	$350
Roeschs	0	$180	$175	$225	$250

13. For January, what is the range? the mode?

14. For February, what is the range? the mode?

15. For the Corcorans, what is the range? the mode?

16. For January, February, and March combined what is the range?

17. For April, what is the range? the mode?

18. For the Johnsons, Riveras, and Takases combined what is the range?

19. For the Riveras, what is the range? the mode?

20. For the five months what is the range? the savings?

Solve.

21. The price of coins depends on their condition. A dealer has five 1930 Buffalo nickels. They cost $.65, $.95, $1.75, $6.00 and $45.00. What is the range of these prices? the mode?

★ **22.** Molly spent $68.50 on coins, $3.79 on a coin collector's book, and $8.50 on a coin album. The sales tax is 8%. How much change should she receive from $100?

Write three 2-digit numbers that give the same number whether upside-down or right-side up. Now write eight 4-digit numbers that are the same both ways.

Mean and Median

The table shows the prices of several 10-speed bikes. One way to describe the prices is to say that they are all between $109 and $249.

Another way to describe the prices is to give their **average,** or **mean.** The example shows how to find the average price of the bikes.

10-Speed Bicycles	
Brand	**Price**
Scruffy	$109
Pedal-Up	$249
Roller	$169
Run Around	$175
Grand Sport	$220

Add the prices.

$109
249
169
175
+ 220
———
$922

Divide the sum by the number of addends.

$$5\overline{)\$922.00} \quad \$184.40$$

The average price for the five bikes is $184.40.

The middle number in an ordered set of data is called the **median.** When you find the median, you know that 50% of the numbers in the set are less than that number, and 50% are greater.

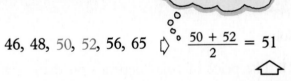

When there are two middle numbers, find their mean.

$109, $169, $175, $220, $249

⬆
median

46, 48, 50, 52, 56, 65 $\quad \dfrac{50 + 52}{2} = 51$

⬆
median

Exercises

Complete.

1. numbers: 5, 6, 7, 8, 9
mean: ▨ ÷ 5 = ▨
median: ▨

2. numbers: 39, 41, 44, 46
mean: ▨ ÷ 4 = ▨
median: ▨ ÷ 2 = ▨

3. numbers: 125, 133, 134
mean: ▨ ÷ 3 = ▨
median: ▨

4. numbers: 68, 56, 52, 40
mean: ▨ ÷ 4 = ▨
median: ▨ ÷ 2 = ▨

5. numbers: 75, 80, 90, 95
mean: ▨ ÷ 4 = ▨
median: ▨ ÷ 2 = ▨

6. numbers: 136, 142, 140
mean: ▨ ÷ 3 = ▨
median: ▨

Write the mean and the median. Round the mean to the nearest
whole number.

7. 21, 19, 17, 11, 24, 16

8. 18, 27, 31, 14, 27

9. 78, 45, 39, 62, 70

10. 39, 47, 51, 49, 42, 50

11. 28, 56, 44, 32, 52, 27

12. 126, 134, 205, 163, 215

13. 130, 128, 180, 149

14. 2, 8, 6, 1, 12, 16

Write the mean and the median. Round the mean to the same
decimal place as the list of numbers.

15. 1.5, 2.8, 1.9, 2.5

16. 0.39, 0.21, 0.26, 0.24

17. 8.62, 7.99, 8.43, 7.86, 8.04

18. 3.5, 3.7, 4.2, 4.6, 3.8, 4.5

19. 2.45, 3.04, 2.69, 2.48

20. 9.21, 9.88, 8.69, 9.08, 8.89

Taking Stock

Wonderland Books • Inventory Control Book Sales Week of Jan. 6						
Type	**Mon.**	**Tues.**	**Wed.**	**Thurs.**	**Fri.**	**Sat.**
Travel	8	3	15	6	4	7
Health	12	50	35	48	22	61
Mystery	16	23	28	15	26	37
History	6	3	0	10	12	8

Write the number. Round the mean to the nearest whole number.

21. What was the mean number of
travel books sold?

22. What was the mean number of
mystery books sold?

23. What was the median number of
health books sold?

24. What was the median number of
history books sold?

25. What was the total number of books
sold on Wednesday?

★ **26.** Write a fraction and a decimal to
show what part of Saturday's sales
were history books.

Double Bar Graphs

Video City offered a $5.00 discount on any video game purchased with a coupon in February. The manager made a **double bar graph** to compare sales with the coupon and without the coupon.

In the first week 80 games were sold with a coupon and 75 games were sold without a coupon.

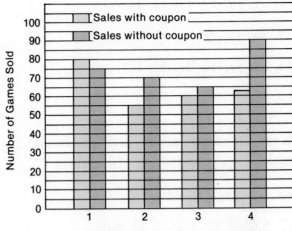

SALES OF VIDEO GAMES

Exercises

Use the graph above to answer the question.

1. How many games were sold with a coupon in the third week?

2. In which week were the most games sold without a coupon?

3. What were the total sales of video games for each week?

4. In which weeks were the total sales greater than 130 games?

5. What was the range of sales without the coupon?

6. What was the range of sales with the coupon?

7. How many fewer games were sold with a coupon than without a coupon?

8. What was the mean number of games sold each week without a coupon?

9. What was the mean number of games sold each week with a coupon?

10. What was the total number of games sold for the month?

Use the graph to answer the question.

During the first semester how many attended the workshop?

11. dramatics   **12.** science

13. computer   **14.** cooking

What was the total number attending workshops?

15. first semester

16. second semester

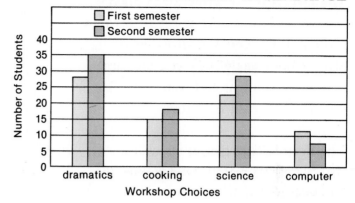

AFTER SCHOOL WORKSHOP ATTENDANCE

What was the difference in workshop attendance between first and second semester in the following?

17. dramatics   **18.** cooking   **19.** science   **20.** computer

21. What was the mean number taking cooking for the two semesters?

22. Which workshops had more than 15 people attending second semester?

Graph and Compare

Draw a bar graph to compare the data in the table.

23.

Mayfair Movie Attendance							
Time	Sun.	Mon.	Tues.	Wed.	Thur.	Fri.	Sat.
Afternoon	335	127	142	111	231	488	561
Evening	1086	792	641	374	398	1288	1575

★ **24.**

Wanda's Weekly Test Scores						
	Week					
Subject	1	2	3	4	5	6
Math	90	72	93	84	81	93
Spelling	94	86	73	86	90	95
Science	90	84	86	92	87	81

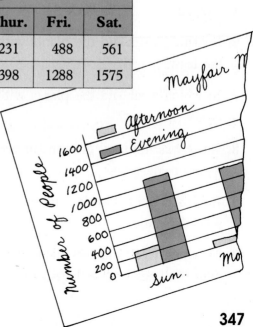

Line Graphs

The makers of Allegrow Plant Food tried an experiment. For six weeks they measured the growth of two sets of plants. Both sets were given the same amount of sunlight and water, but one set was also given Allegrow.

The **double line graph** shows the changes in the plant's heights over the six week period.

By the third week, the plants with Allegrow had grown about 2.4 cm. Those without Allegrow had grown about 1.5 cm.

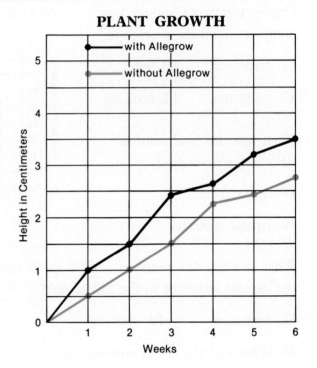

PLANT GROWTH

Exercises

Use the graph above to answer the question.
What was the difference in growth between the sets of plants for the week?

1. week 2   **2.** week 3   **3.** week 4   **4.** week 5   **5.** week 6

6. In which week did the plants with Allegrow grow the most? the least?

7. In which week did the plants without Allegrow grow the most? the least?

8. What was the total growth for the plants with Allegrow? without Allegrow?

9. In which week was the amount of growth the same for both sets of plants?

10. In which week did the plants without Allegrow grow more than the ones with Allegrow?

Use the graph to answer the questions.

FOOD-ON-THE-MOVE DELIVERIES

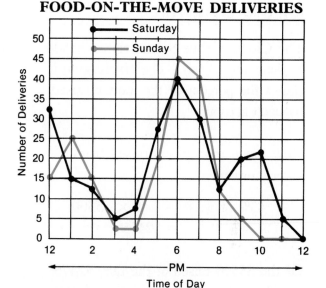

11. Were more deliveries made at 12 noon on Saturday or Sunday?

12. At which time were the greatest number of deliveries made on Saturday? on Sunday?

13. What was the total number of deliveries made on Saturday? on Sunday?

14. What was the mean number of deliveries made in an hour on Saturday? on Sunday?

15. Between which two times was the change in the number of deliveries the greatest on Saturday? on Sunday?

16. About how many more deliveries were made at 6 o'clock on Sunday than at 6 o'clock on Saturday?

17. Food-on-the-Move is considering closing at 10 P.M. About how many deliveries would they lose on Saturday? on Sunday?

AGE	HEIGHT (cm)
9	130
10	135
11	141
12	146
13	152
14	158
15	165
16	170
17	170

Away We Grow

Milton kept a record of his height on nine birthdays. Draw a line graph to show Milton's growth.

18. What was the range of Milton's height for the nine years?

19. Between which two birthdays did Milton grow the most?

20. Between which two birthdays did Milton grow the least?

★ 21. What is the mean amount Milton grew each year?

349

Circle Graphs

The Clover Grove School raised $5500 at their annual fair. The **circle graph** shows the percent of the money raised by each activity.

How much money was raised from entertainment?

$$45\% \text{ of } 5500 = 0.45 \times \$5500$$
$$= \$2475$$

Of the $5500 raised at the fair, $2475 was from entertainment.

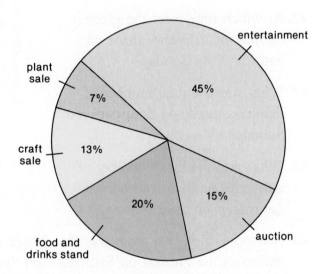

CLOVER GROVE FUND RAISING

entertainment
45%
plant sale
7%
craft sale
13%
20%
15%
auction
food and drinks stand

Exercises

Use the graph above to answer the question.

1. What is the sum of the percents on the graph?

2. Which activity raised the most money? the least?

3. What percent of the money was raised from the craft sale?

4. Was more money raised by the auction or the craft sale?

5. How much money was raised by the plant sale?

6. How much money was raised by the auction? by the craft sale?

7. How much more money was raised by the craft sale than the plant sale?

8. How much less money was raised by the auction than the entertainment?

9. How much was raised from food and drinks?

10. Which activities raised more than $800?

The graph shows what percent of the town's $100,000 community development budget was spent on each item.

COMMUNITY BUDGET

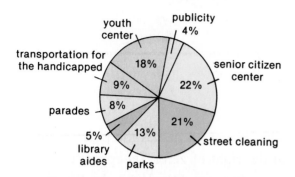

11. What percent was spent on the senior and youth centers?

12. What percent was spent on parks and transportation for the handicapped?

13. How much more was spent on parks than on publicity?

14. How much more was spent on parades than on library aides?

15. How much was spent on publicity, parades, and street cleaning combined?

Your Turn

The Orlando family had $400 to spend on camping gear.

16. Copy and complete the graph to show how much was spent on each item.

tents: 50%
sleeping bags: 25%
back packs: 15%
cooking gear: 10%

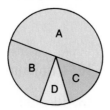

Write the range and mode.
(*pages 342–343*)

1. 9, 5, 7, 9, 6, 3, 4, 8

Write the mean and median.
(*pages 344–345*)

2. 10, 7, 6, 13, 4

Use the graph. (*pages 346–347*)

JUANITA'S EARNINGS

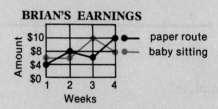

3. How much more did Juanita save than she spent in June?

Use the graph. (*pages 348–349*)

BRIAN'S EARNINGS

4. How much did Brian earn in the 4 weeks?

The circle graph shows what percent of $600 a swim club spent on each item. (*pages 350–351*)

5. How much for warm-up suits?

6. How much for stop watches?

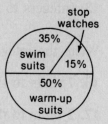

Integers

Whole numbers and their opposites are called **integers.** Look at the number line. Points to the right of zero are called positive integers. Points to the left of zero are called negative integers.

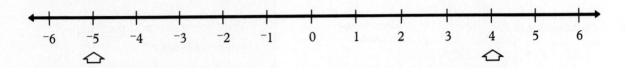

The integer ⁻5 read *negative 5* names the point 5 units to the left of zero. Its opposite is ⁺5, read *positive five*.

The integer ⁺4 names the point 4 units to the right of zero. Its opposite is ⁻4. You can write ⁺4 without the ⁺ sign, as just 4.

Exercises

Write the missing numbers.

1.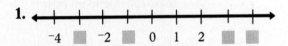

2.

3.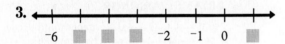

4.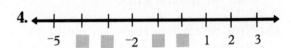

Complete.

5. ⁻15 is ▦ units to the ▦ of zero.

6. 11 is ▦ units to the ▦ of zero.

7. 7 is ▦ units to the ▦ of zero.

8. ⁻8 is ▦ units to the ▦ of zero.

9. The opposite of 9 is ▦.

10. The opposite of ⁻5 is ▦.

11. We read 8 as ▦.

12. We read ⁻1 as ▦.

13. Integers to the right of zero are ▦.

14. Integers to the left of zero are ▦.

Write the integer.

15. 7 units to the right of 0

16. 4 units to the left of zero

17. 2 units to the left of 0

18. 18 units to the right of zero

19. 6 units to the right of 1

20. 2 units to the left of ⁻1

21. 3 units to the left of ⁻5

22. 5 units to the right of 2

Write the integer between the two integers.

23. 5, 7   **24.** ⁻8, ⁻10   **25.** ⁻1, 1   **26.** 12, 14

27. ⁻16, ⁻14   **28.** ⁻4, ⁻6   **29.** 2, 4   **30.** ⁻6, ⁻8

Write the opposite of each integer.

31. ⁻10   **32.** 11   **33.** 2   **34.** ⁻18   **35.** ⁻4   **36.** 17

37. 6   **38.** ⁻7   **39.** ⁻15   **40.** 14   **41.** 5   **42.** ⁻1

Ups and Downs

Write the integer for the phrase. Then write its opposite.

Example. Climb down 4 stairs, ⁻4 ▷ Climb up 4 stairs, 4

43. lost $10

44. gain 3 kg

45. 14 km north

46. move forward 11 m

47. sell 2 books

48. 7 hours ago

49. increase 9 g

50. 5°C above zero

Write an integer to name the number in the sentence. Then give its opposite.

51. The elevator went up 2 floors.

52. It was 20 seconds before lift off.

53. Florence withdrew $15 from her savings account.

Write an integer to show the final number.

★ **54.** Al received $10 for his birthday. He spent $3.00 on a new fish, and $2.00 on art supplies.

★ **55.** Vicki went from the 3rd floor to the 2nd floor and then up 4 floors.

Comparing Integers

On Tuesday the temperature was 3°C. On Wednesday it was
⁻5°C. On which day was it warmer?

You can compare integers by comparing their positions on a
number line. The greater of two integers is always the one
farther to the right.

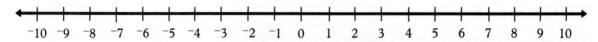

3 is to the right of ⁻5.
$$3 > {}^-5$$
so $3°C > {}^-5°C$

It was warmer on Tuesday.

Here are more examples.

⁻7 is to the left of ⁻4.
$${}^-7 < {}^-4$$

⁻5 is to the right of ⁻8.
$${}^-5 > {}^-8$$

Exercises

Write *right* or *left* to complete. Then write < or >.

1. ⁻4 is to the ▨ of 9

2. 3 is to the ▨ of ⁻7

3. ⁻8 is to the ▨ of ⁻1

4. 5 is to the ▨ of ⁻5

5. ⁻10 is to the ▨ of ⁻12

6. 2 is to the ▨ of 7

7. 5 is to the ▨ of 0

8. ⁻6 is to the ▨ of ⁻8

Write < or > to compare the integers.

9. ⁻9 ▨ 2

10. ⁻3 ▨ ⁻8

11. 3 ▨ ⁻5

12. 4 ▨ ⁻4

13. ⁻10 ▨ 10

14. 7 ▨ ⁻3

15. ⁻4 ▨ ⁻5

16. ⁻7 ▨ ⁻3

17. ⁻12 ▓ 5   **18.** 34 ▓ ⁻18   **19.** ⁻15 ▓ ⁻9   **20.** 15 ▓ ⁻10

21. 7 ▓ 0   **22.** ⁻13 ▓ 15   **23.** ⁻19 ▓ 0   **24.** ⁻12 ▓ 5

25. 25 ▓ ⁻6   **26.** 45 ▓ 37   **27.** ⁻34 ▓ 13   **28.** 100 ▓ ⁻100

Write in order from least to greatest.

29. ⁻5, 3, ⁻7, 4

30. ⁻3, ⁻8, 7, 0

31. ⁻8, ⁻10, ⁻4, 1, ⁻3

32. 10, ⁻6, 4, ⁻7, ⁻4

33. ⁻12, 5, 10, ⁻9, 2

34. 2, ⁻5, ⁻2, 0, ⁻11

Complete by writing *greater* or *less*.

35. Any positive integer is ▓ than any negative integer.

36. Any positive integer is ▓ than 0.

37. Any negative integer is ▓ than 0.

Write On

38. Write the integers that are greater than ⁻4 and less than 2.

39. Write the integers that are less than ⁻2 and greater than ⁻10.

40. On Wednesday the temperature was ⁻5° and on Thursday it was ⁻10°. On which day was the temperature lower?

★ **41.** Amy's cabin is 50 m above sea level. Tom's cabin is 45 m below sea level. Whose cabin is higher?

Look for the pattern. Write the missing numbers.

1	4	9	16	?	?	?

3	5	7	?	?	?

2	2	?	?	?

0	?	?	?

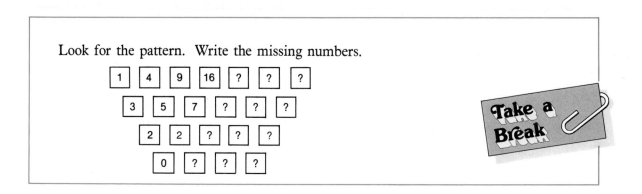

Take a Break

Adding Integers

Helen drove her car 6 km east on the highway. She missed the correct exit. She turned around and drove 2 km west.

The number line shows what happens when you add integers.

To add 6 and ⁻2 move from 0 to 6, then move 2 units to the left.

$$6 + {}^-2 = 4$$

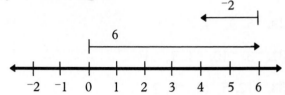

To add ⁻8 and 5 move from 0 to ⁻8, then move 5 units to the right.

$${}^-8 + 5 = {}^-3$$

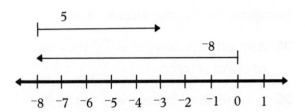

Exercises

Complete.

1.

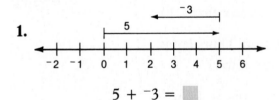

$$5 + {}^-3 = \blacksquare$$

2.

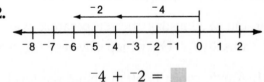

$${}^-4 + {}^-2 = \blacksquare$$

3.

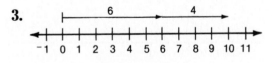

$$6 + 4 = \blacksquare$$

4.

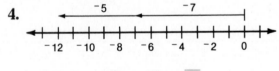
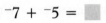

$${}^-7 + {}^-5 = \blacksquare$$

5.

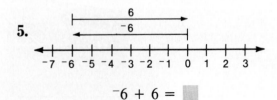

$${}^-6 + 6 = \blacksquare$$

6.

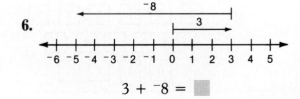

$$3 + {}^-8 = \blacksquare$$

Add.

7. $4 + 5$	**8.** $^-1 + {}^-8$	**9.** $13 + {}^-9$	**10.** $^-11 + 5$
11. $^-3 + 12$	**12.** $6 + {}^-11$	**13.** $^-14 + 9$	**14.** $15 + {}^-8$
15. $2 + {}^-5$	**16.** $^-5 + {}^-7$	**17.** $^-16 + 8$	**18.** $8 + {}^-2$
19. $^-7 + {}^-4$	**20.** $10 + {}^-4$	**21.** $18 + {}^-9$	**22.** $0 + {}^-7$
23. $^-17 + 8$	**24.** $9 + {}^-3$	**25.** $0 + 9$	**26.** $12 + {}^-5$
27. $6 + {}^-8$	**28.** $^-3 + {}^-10$	**29.** $^-15 + 6$	**30.** $^-27 + 9$

Moving Along

Solve.

31. In a board game, Phyllis earned $100 on one turn. On her next turn she lost $200. What was the total gain or loss after the two turns?

32. Clive wrote a check for $30.00. The next day he deposited $25 in his account. What was the gain or loss after the two transactions were made?

★ **33.** A bus driver drove 300 km east. He then drove 800 km west. How far was he from his starting point?

★ **34.** The circumference of a round lake is 800.7 m. If Hal swims across at its widest point, how far will he swim?

Calculator Corner

One centimeter of rain is equivalent to 12 cm of snow. A record for rainfall is 184.05 cm in 24 hours. How much snow would this have been?

Subtracting Integers

The number line shows that $5 - 2 = 5 + {}^-2 = 3$.

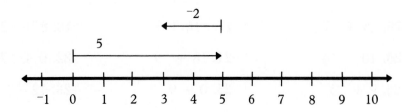

Subtracting an integer is the same as adding its opposite. Here are more examples.

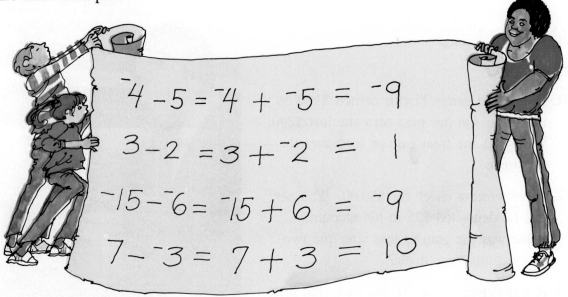

$${}^-4 - 5 = {}^-4 + {}^-5 = {}^-9$$
$$3 - 2 = 3 + {}^-2 = 1$$
$${}^-15 - {}^-6 = {}^-15 + 6 = {}^-9$$
$$7 - {}^-3 = 7 + 3 = 10$$

Exercises

Complete.

1. $8 - 2 = 8 + \boxed{} = \boxed{}$

2. $1 - 2 = 1 + \boxed{} = \boxed{}$

3. ${}^-6 - {}^-4 = {}^-6 + \boxed{} = \boxed{}$

4. $2 - {}^-4 = 2 + \boxed{} = \boxed{}$

5. $10 - {}^-3 = 10 + \boxed{} = \boxed{}$

6. ${}^-10 - {}^-3 = {}^-10 + \boxed{} = \boxed{}$

7. $8 - 7 = 8 + \boxed{} = \boxed{}$

8. ${}^-8 - 7 = {}^-8 + \boxed{} = \boxed{}$

9. ${}^-5 - {}^-5 = {}^-5 + \boxed{} = \boxed{}$

10. $8 - {}^-8 = 8 + \boxed{} = \boxed{}$

11. $0 - {}^-9 = 0 + \boxed{} = \boxed{}$

12. $0 - 9 = 0 + \boxed{} = \boxed{}$

Subtract.

13. $9 - 7$ **14.** $3 - {}^-6$ **15.** ${}^-16 - {}^-7$ **16.** ${}^-10 - {}^-5$

17. $13 - 9$ **18.** ${}^-8 - 4$ **19.** $11 - 5$ **20.** ${}^-2 - 8$

21. ${}^-12 - 6$ **22.** $1 - {}^-3$ **23.** $7 - {}^-8$ **24.** ${}^-17 - 8$

25. ${}^-6 - 2$ **26.** $0 - {}^-5$ **27.** $14 - 5$ **28.** $18 - 10$

29. $8 - {}^-3$ **30.** $5 - {}^-1$ **31.** ${}^-15 - 6$ **32.** ${}^-9 - 7$

33. ${}^-4 - 0$ **34.** $16 - 9$ **35.** $10 - {}^-2$ **36.** $12 - 8$

Opposites Attract

Solve.

37. The temperature is ${}^-5°C$. It becomes $7°$ colder. What is the new temperature?

38. The temperature was $8°C$ on Tuesday and ${}^-4°C$ on Wednesday. What was the change in temperature from Tuesday to Wednesday?

Follow the path from start to finish.

★ **39.**

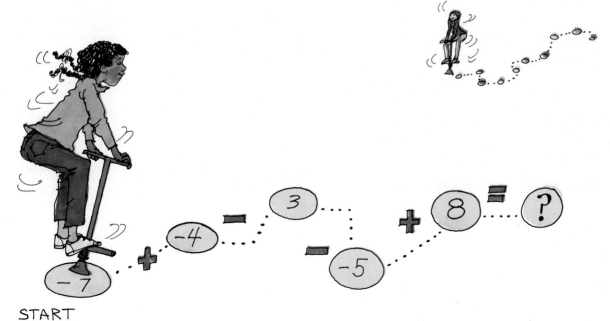

START

Graphing Number Pairs

You can use **ordered pairs** of integers to locate points on a grid.

To locate a point on a grid, start at 0. The first integer tells you to move right or left. The second tells you to move up or down.

The point (2, 5) is 2 units to the right and 5 units up.

The point (⁻3, ⁻4) is 3 units to the left and 4 units down.

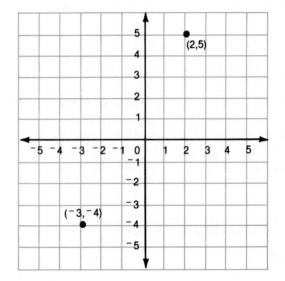

Exercises

Write the ordered pair for the directions.

1. to the right 5, then down 7

2. to the left 3, then down 8

3. to the left 8, then up 5

4. to the right 4, then up 2

5. to the right 0, then down 1

6. to the left 6, then up 6

Write the letter that names the ordered pair.

7. (⁻5, 3)   **8.** (8, 0)

9. (4, 1)   **10.** (⁻1, 7)

11. (⁻8, ⁻4)   **12.** (6, ⁻2)

13. (⁻3, ⁻3)   **14.** (5, 3)

15. (⁻7, 1)   **16.** (2, ⁻2)

17. (2, 6)   **18.** (⁻4, 1)

19. (⁻6, ⁻5)   **20.** (3, ⁻4)

21. (⁻4, ⁻8)   **22.** (8, ⁻6)

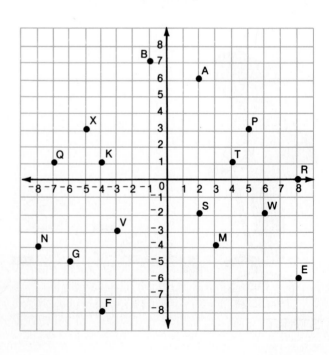

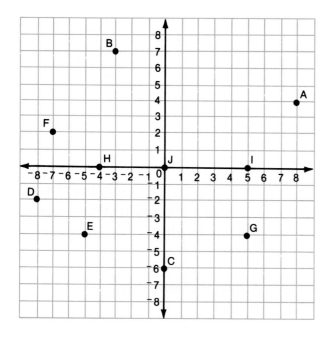

Write the ordered pair for the letter.

23. *A*   **24.** *B*

25. *C*   **26.** *D*

27. *E*   **28.** *F*

29. *G*   **30.** *H*

31. *I*   **32.** *J*

True Grid

33. Locate each point on a grid. Join the points in order. What do you see?

A	$(^-1, ^-7)$	*I*	$(1, 9)$
B	$(^-1, ^-6)$	*J*	$(0, 10)$
C	$(1, ^-6)$	*K*	$(^-1, 9)$
D	$(1, ^-7)$	*L*	$(^-1, 6)$
E	$(3, ^-7)$	*M*	$(^-2, 5)$
F	$(2, ^-5)$	*N*	$(^-2, ^-5)$
G	$(2, 5)$	*O*	$(^-3, ^-7)$
H	$(1, 6)$	*P*	$(^-1, ^-7)$

Write the integer. (*pages 352–353*)

1. 3 points to the right of zero

2. 6 points to the left of zero

3. 14 points to the left of zero

4. 2 points to the right of zero

Write $<$ or $>$ to compare the integers. (*pages 354–355*)

5. $^-4$ ▨ $^-5$ **6.** 3 ▨ $^-2$

7. 9 ▨ 12 **8.** $^-6$ ▨ 1

Add. (*pages 356–357*)

9. $2 + ^-1$ **10.** $^-5 + 3$

11. $^-4 + ^-6$ **12.** $7 + 5$

Subtract. (*pages 358–359*)

13. $3 - 2$ **14.** $7 - ^-4$

15. $^-2 - ^-5$ **16.** $^-8 - 2$

Write the ordered pair for the letter. (*pages 360–361*)

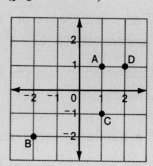

17. *D*   **18.** *C*

19. *A*   **20.** *B*

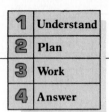

1	Understand
2	Plan
3	Work
4	Answer

Problem Solving · INTERPRETING A CHART

On a cold, windy day it often feels colder than it is. This is due to the effect of the wind chill factor.

WIND CHILL CHART

Temperature (°C)

Temp	6	10	20	30	40	50	60
20	20	18	16	14	13	13	12
16	16	14	11	9	7	7	6
12	12	9	5	3	1	0	0
8	8	5	0	−3	−5	−6	−7
4	4	0	−5	−8	−11	−12	−13
0	0	−4	−10	−14	−17	−18	−19
−4	−4	−8	−15	−20	−23	−25	−26
−8	−8	−13	−21	−25	−29	−31	−32
−12	−12	−17	−26	−31	−35	−37	−39
−16	−16	−22	−31	−37	−41	−43	−45
−20	−20	−26	−36	−43	−47	−49	−51
−24	−24	−31	−42	−48	−53	−56	−58
−28	−28	−35	−47	−54	−59	−62	−64
−32	−32	−40	−52	−60	−65	−68	−70
−36	−36	−44	−57	−65	−71	−74	−77
−40	−40	−49	−63	−71	−77	−80	−83

Wind Speed (kilometers per hour)

Suppose the thermometer reading is −8°C and the wind speed is 10 km per hour. You can find how cold it feels by looking at the Wind Chill Chart.

- Find the wind speed of 10 km per hour
- Then find −8°C

With the wind chill factor, it feels like −13°C.

Use the chart above. How cold will it feel on a day with the given temperature and wind speed?

1. Wind speed: 20 km per hour
   Temperature: −8°C

2. Wind speed: 10 km per hour
   Temperature: −24°C

3. Wind speed: 50 km per hour
   Temperature: −36°C

4. Wind speed: 30 km per hour
   Temperature: 20°C

What is the thermometer reading?

5. Wind speed: 30 km per hour
   Wind chill factor: −31°C

6. Wind speed: 60 km per hour
   Wind chill factor: −19°C

7. Wind speed: 40 km per hour
   Wind chill factor: −47°C

8. Wind speed: 6 km per hour
   Wind chill factor: 0°C

Solve.

9. The captain of a fishing boat decided that his crew couldn't go out if the wind chill was ⁻35°C or below. The temperature is ⁻8°C. The wind speed is 30 km per hour. Will the crew go out?

10. In Juneau, Alaska the lowest temperature on a certain day was ⁻4°C. The highest temperature was 8° warmer. The wind speed was 30 km per hour. How cold did it feel at the highest temperature?

11. Suppose the temperature was ⁻4°C. The wind speed changed from 10 km per hour to 20 km per hour. What was the change in how cold it felt?

12. On one day the temperature, with the wind chill, changed from ⁻35°C to ⁻47°C. The wind speed was 40 km per hour. What was the actual change in temperature?

13. On Tuesday, the wind chill factor was ⁻8°C. The wind speed increased 4 km per hour, but the wind chill factor was still ⁻8°C. What was the thermometer reading?

★ 14. You're planning an ice skating party. You decide to go bowling if the wind chill drops below 0°C. The temperature is 10°C. The wind speed is 25 km per hour. Will you go skating or bowling?

Unit Review

1. Write the letter that names the ordered pair to solve the riddle.

What did the highway say to the street?

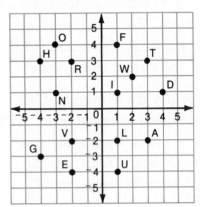

(1, 1) | ($^-$4, 3) (3, $^-$2) ($^-$2, $^-$2) ($^-$2, $^-$4)

(3, 3) ($^-$4, 3) (3, $^-$2) (3, 3)

(3, 3) (1, 1) ($^-$2, 3) ($^-$2, $^-$4) (4, 1)

($^-$2, 3) (1, $^-$4) ($^-$3, 1) (4, 1) ($^-$3, 4) (2, 2) ($^-$3, 1)

(1, 4) ($^-$2, $^-$4) ($^-$2, $^-$4) (1, $^-$2) (1, 1) ($^-$3, 1) ($^-$4, $^-$3)

Is the statement true or false? Write *T* or *F*.

2. $^-7 > 3$ **3.** $^-4 < 4$ **4.** $^-5 + 3 = ^-8$ **5.** $^-4 - ^-4 = ^-1$

Use the graph to answer the question.

6. How many people attended the 7:00 show on Monday?

7. How much gas was sold on day 3?

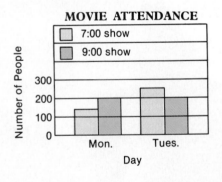

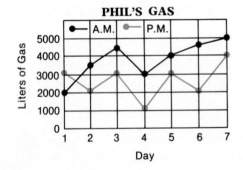

Write the mean, mode, median and range.

8. 3, 7, 5, 2, 4, 7, 1   **9.** 2, 5, 4, 3, 5, 6

Solve.

10. The smallest sharks weigh about 0.028 kg. Would a bucket containing 15 of these sharks weigh 1 kg?

Write the range and mean. (*pages 342–345*)

1. 2, 9, 7, 8, 3, 7, 5

2. 6, 12, 19, 4, 8, 6, 10

Use the graph to answer the question. (*pages 346–349*)

3. How many more children than adults visited in week 1?

4. How many houses did Herb clean in the 4 weeks?

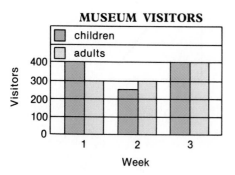

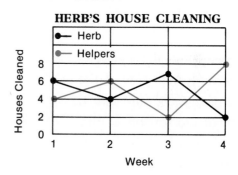

The circle graph shows the percent of 500 items sold at a fruit stand. (*pages 350–351*)

5. How many apples were sold?

6. How many oranges were sold?

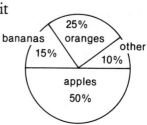

Write < or > to compare the integers. (*pages 352–355*)

7. ⁻3 ▨ 3

8. ⁻5 ▨ ⁻7

9. 8 ▨ ⁻12

10. ⁻17 ▨ ⁻21

Add or subtract. (*pages 356–359*)

11. 6 + ⁻3

12. ⁻7 – 4

13. ⁻9 + ⁻8

14. ⁻3 – ⁻5

Write the ordered pair for the letter. (*pages 360–361*)

15. A

16. B

17. C

18. D

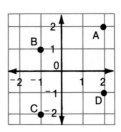

Solve. (*pages 362–363*)

19. Cheryl usually works $2\frac{1}{2}$ hours a day for 5 days each week. How many hours does she work in a week?

Enrichment

The Pythagorean Theorem

A Greek mathematician named Pythagoras proved a very interesting relationship among the sides of right triangles.

In a right triangle, the longest side is called the **hypotenuse.** The other sides are called **legs.**

If you count the squares drawn on each side of the triangle, you'll find that the sum of the squares of the legs is equal to the square of the hypotenuse.

In this triangle $a^2 + b^2 = c^2$.
$$3^2 + 4^2 = 5^2$$
$$9 + 16 = 25$$

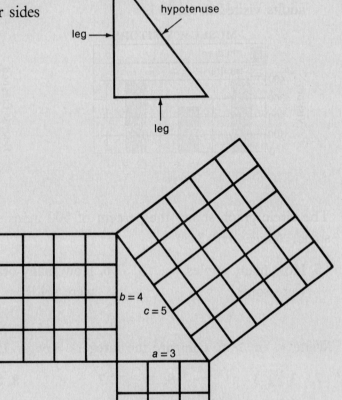

What is the length of the hypotenuse in the right triangle?

1.

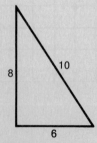

2.

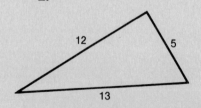

3.

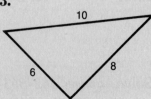

Write an equation you can use to find the missing number.
Then solve the equation.

Example.
$$a^2 + b^2 = c^2$$
$$(12)^2 + b^2 = (37)^2$$
$$144 + b^2 = 1369$$
$$b^2 = 1225$$
$$b = 35$$

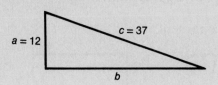

4.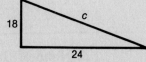

5.

6.

7.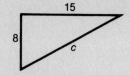

8.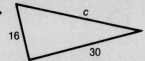

9.

Is the triangle a right triangle? Write *Yes* or *No.*

10.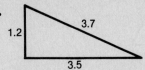

11.

12.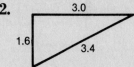

The table shows the square roots of some numbers.
Use the table to write *n* to the nearest whole number.

13.

14.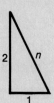

15.

16.

n^2	n
5	2.236
10	3.162
11	3.317
13	3.606
25	5
40	6.325
42	6.481
44	6.633
50	7.071
65	8.062

Choose the best answer. Write *a*, *b*, *c*, or *d*.

Choose the pair of figures described.

1. They are congruent.

a.   **b.** 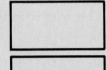   **c.** 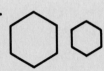   **d.** None of these

2. They are similar.

a.   **b.**   **c.** 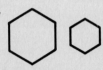   **d.** None of these

3. Which figure does not have a line of symmetry?

a.   **b.**    **c.**   **d.** None of these

A building plan is drawn to the scale 1 cm to 8 m. What length does the following length on the plan represent?

4. 5 cm
  a. 40 m
  b. 86 m
  c. 2 m
  d. None of these

5. 12 cm
  a. 40 m
  b. 96 m
  c. 48 m
  d. None of these

6. 16 cm
  a. 2 m
  b. 108 m
  c. 128 m
  d. None of these

Complete. Write *a*, *b*, *c*, or *d* for ▓.

7. The prism has ▓ vertices.

  a. 8
  b. 6
  c. 4
  d. None of these

8. The prism has ▓ faces.

  a. 5
  b. 4
  c. 6
  d. None of these

What is the volume of the rectangular prism or cylinder?

9. base = 6 cm
width = 4 cm
height = 12 cm

   a. 120 cm³
   b. 144 cm³
   c. 288 cm³
   d. None of these

10. radius = 22 cm
height = 5 cm

   a. 110 cm³
   b. 1519.76 cm³
   c. 7488 cm³
   d. None of these

11. radius = 4 m
height = 8 m

   a. 50.24 m³
   b. 100.48 m³
   c. 401.92 m³
   d. None of these

12. base = 10 m
width = 5 m
height = 20 m

   a. 500 m³
   b. 100 m³
   c. 1000 m³
   d. None of these

Complete. Write *a*, *b*, *c*, or *d* for ▦.

13. A sphere has ▦ vertexes.

   a. 0
   b. 1
   c. many
   d. None of these

14. A cylinder has ▦ bases.

   a. 1
   b. 2
   c. 0
   d. None of these

What is the surface area of the rectangular prism?

15.

   a. 52 m²
   b. 24 m²
   c. 70 m²
   d. None of these

16.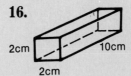

   a. 8 cm²
   b. 40 cm²
   c. 88 cm²
   d. None of these

Solve.

17. A soccer team played 20 games. They won 8 and lost 12. What percent of the games did they win?

   a. 25%
   b. 40%
   c. 30%
   d. None of these

Applying Your Skills

Discounts Save You Money

THRIFTY TRAVEL AGENCY
SPEND 4 NIGHTS AT A BEACHFRONT HOTEL!
FULL PRICE $325
Now offering a 20% discount

The Thrifty Travel Agency often gives a **discount,** or certain percent off the cost of a trip, to attract customers.

This is how to find the cost of the trip in the ad with a 20% discount.

Write the percent as a decimal.

$$20\% = 0.20$$

Multiply the full cost by the decimal.

$$\begin{array}{r} \$325 \\ \times\,.20 \\ \hline \$65.00 \end{array}$$

Subtract the amount of the discount from the full cost.

$$\begin{array}{r} \$325.00 \\ -\,65.00 \\ \hline \$260.00 \end{array}$$

These are other discounts that Thrifty has listed. Find the amount of the discount.

1. 10% discount on a $45 bus trip to Houston

2. 20% discount on a $277 one way flight to Miami

3. 5% discount on a $75 round trip train train fare

4. 15% discount on a $400 weekend summer cruise

5. 30% discount on an $80-a-day hotel room

6. 25% discount on a $30 dinner in San Francisco

7. 20% discount on a $30-a-day car rental

8. 10% discount on a $350 camping and hiking trip

Day-by-Day Discount put discount tags on some items to sell them quickly. How much would a customer pay for each item?

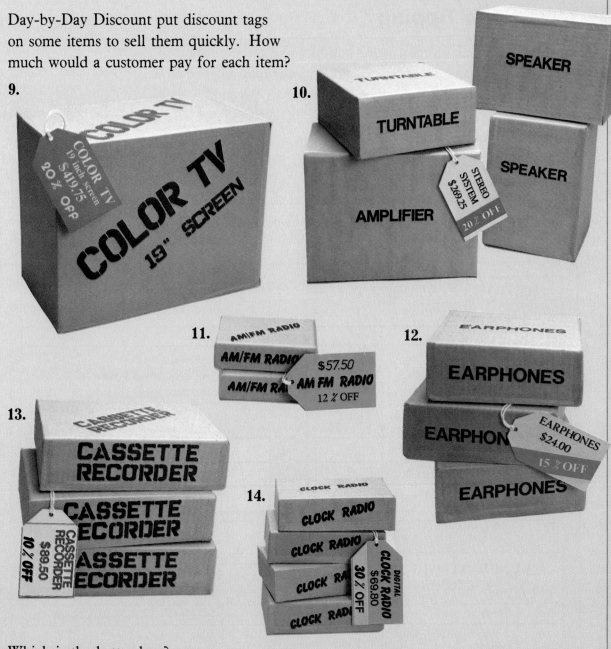

9.

COLOR TV
19 inch screen
$419.75
20% OFF

COLOR TV
19" SCREEN

10.

TURNTABLE

SPEAKER

AMPLIFIER

SPEAKER

STEREO SYSTEM
$269.25
20% OFF

11.

AM/FM RADIO
AM/FM RADIO
AM/FM RA

$57.50
AM FM RADIO
12% OFF

12.

EARPHONES
EARPHONES
EARPHON
EARPHONES

EARPHONES
$24.00
15% OFF

13.

CASSETTE RECORDER
CASSETTE RECORDER
ASSETTE ECORDER

CASSETTE RECORDER
$89.50
10% OFF

14.

CLOCK RADIO
CLOCK RADIO
CLOCK RAD
CLOCK RAD
CLOCK RADI

DIGITAL CLOCK RADIO
$69.80
30% OFF

Which is the better buy?

15. A $60 jacket at a 20% discount or the same jacket reduced by $15?

16. A $15 dinner reduced by $3 or the same dinner at a 25% discount?

17. A $4.50 ticket to a ball game reduced by a dollar or the same ticket reduced by 20%?

18. A $120 35mm camera at a 20% discount or the same camera reduced by $30?

Applying Your Skills

Taxes and Tipping

There is a sales tax on most items you buy and often on food in restaurants. Suppose there is a 5% tax on your food total of $4 at a restaurant. How much tax do you pay?

Write the percent as 0.05 and multiply the food total by the decimal.

$$\begin{array}{r} \$4 \\ \times 0.05 \\ \hline \$.20 \end{array}$$

You pay $.20 tax.

Complete these order forms from different states. Round the tax to the nearest cent.

MIDTOWN RESTAURANT ORDER

No.	Item		Cost
1	vegetable soup, bowl		$ 1.50
1	cheese sandwich		$ 1.95
1	cole slaw		$ .50
1	sliced fresh fruit		$ .60
1	milk		$ .55
1.		Food total	?
2.		Tax 6%	?
3.		Total	?

FARLEY'S ORDER

No.	Item		Cost
3	shrimp		$ 23.25
3	lettuce and tomato		$ 4.50
3	baked potatoes		$ 2.10
3	strawberries		$ 2.40
4.		Total food	?
5.		Tax 6%	?
6.		Total	?

LUNCH-AT-THE-MALL ORDER

No.	Item		Cost
4	chicken noodle soup, bowls		$6.00
4	chef's salad bowls		$15.80
4	yogurt salad dressing		$ 2.40
2	whole wheat crackers		$ .60
4	fruit in season		$ 3.00
7.		Total food	?
8.		Tax 7%	?
9.		Total	?

APPLE TREE INN ORDER

No.	Item		Cost
2	tuna salad plates		$ 11.00
1	fruit salad plate		$ 4.50
2	whole wheat rolls		$ .40
1	crackers and cheese		$ 1.35
2	fruit cups		$ 1.50
3	milk		$ 1.65
10.		Food total	?
11.		Tax 8%	?
12.		Total	?

The usual tip for people who give service is 15% of a bill. A restaurant tip is based on the total food cost before the tax is added.

What is the usual tip on these food totals?

13. $18   **14.** $21   **15.** $64   **16.** $84   **17.** $36   **18.** $42

Solve.

19. Seven people stopped for lunch at a restaurant. The cost of the food was $84. The restaurant added a 15% tip and a 6% tax to their bill. How much was the total bill?

20. Five people dined out. They paid $75, including tax and tip. Their taxi fare home was $6.20 and they paid a 15% tip rounded to the nearest ten cents. How much did their evening out cost altogether?

21. Six friends stopped at a hotel to have breakfast. The total food cost was $36. They then had to add a $2.16 tax and a $5.40 tip. The friends agreed to share the total bill evenly. How much did the hotel breakfast cost each of the six friends?

22. Each of two groups ate meals costing $50. One group added 20% for both tax and tip to their bill. The second group added 5% for the tax and then 15% on the total including the tax. Did the first or the second group pay more? How much more?

Applying Your Skills

The Cost of Electricity

A **watt** is a unit of power needed to make something run. A **kilowatt** equals 1000 watts.

Suppose a radio takes 70 watts per hour to run. Suppose it is used 1200 hours per year. The cost of electricity is $.095 per kilowatt hour. To find how much the radio costs to run per year, follow these steps.

Multiply to find the total watts used per year.

Divide to find the number of kilowatt hours.

Now multiply to find the total cost. Round to the nearest cent.

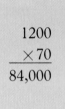

```
                        84
  1200        1000)84,000              $.095
  ×70         -80 00                   ×84
  84,000        4 000                  380
              -4 000                   7600
                   0                   $7.980  ▷ $7.98
```

The radio costs about $7.98 to run each year.

Complete the chart.

ESTIMATED USE OF SOME APPLIANCES					
Appliance	Watts Per Hour	Hours Per Year	Kilowatt Hours Per Year	Rate in cents	Cost Per Year
1. Automatic Washer	515	200	?	$.107	?
2. Dryer	4840	200	?	$.107	?
3. Color TV	200	2200	?	$.107	?
4. Clock	2	8760	?	$.107	?
5. Room Air Conditioner	1500	1000	?	$.107	?
6. Hair Dryer	750	50	?	$.107	?

ESTIMATED YEARLY COSTS OF RUNNING APPLIANCES

Appliance	Cost
dishwasher	$61.20
refrigerator with freezer	$51.15
garbage disposal	$ .69
stove with oven	$27.02
refrigerator with frostless freezer	$42.07
toaster	$ .90
stove with self-cleaning oven	$27.71

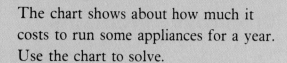

The chart shows about how much it costs to run some appliances for a year. Use the chart to solve.

7. How much can be saved per year with a regular oven rather than a self-cleaning oven?

8. Suppose your garbage disposal broke six months after you bought it. About how much did it cost to run before it broke?

9. What is the cost of running a dishwasher, a refrigerator with a freezer, a stove with a regular oven, and a toaster per year?

10. What is the difference in cost between running a refrigerator that is frostless and one that is not?

On an electric bill, you are told the total number of kilowatt hours you used and the total amount you owe. Many people don't realize that in most states the total owed includes an extra fuel charge. The fuel charge is for the same number of kilowatt hours used, but at a different rate.

How much is each bill without the added cost for fuel?

	Fuel Cost per Kilowatt Hour	Kilowatt Hours Used	Total Fuel Cost	Total Bill	Bill Without Fuel Cost
11.	$.047	208	?	$22.27	?
12.	$.046	284	?	$28.56	?
13.	$.042	317	?	$20.21	?
14.	$.051	296	?	$31.48	?

Enrichment

Probability Problems

The first three books returned to the library, one day, are on the librarian's desk. The books are either fiction or non-fiction. The chances of either are equally likely. What is the probability that only 2 of the books are non-fiction?

You may draw a tree diagram to show all the possibilities.

The diagram shows that there are 8 possibilities.
$$4 \times 2 = 8$$

Of the 8 possibilities, three show that two of the books are non-fiction.

(F, N, N) (N, F, N) (N, N, F)

The probability that 2 of the books are non-fiction is 3 out of 8.

$$P(2 \text{ non-fiction books}) = \frac{3}{8}$$

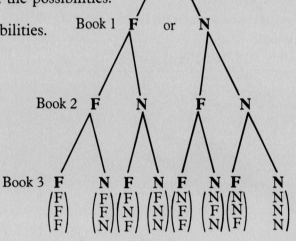

Copy and complete the diagram.
Then list the possibilities to solve.

1. Four students will each win a watch. Each watch is either electronic or wind-up. The chances of either are equally likely. What is the probability that 3 students will win electronic watches?

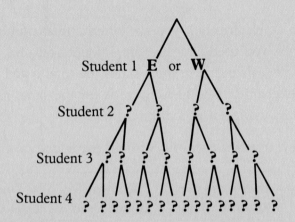

Make a diagram of the possibilities.
Then list the possibilities to solve.

2. Three people are waiting for either an up or a down elevator. The chances of either are equally likely. What is the probability that 2 people are waiting for a down elevator?

Table of Measures

TIME

60 seconds (s) = 1 minute (min)
60 minutes = 1 hour (h)
24 hours = 1 day (d)
7 days = 1 week

365 days ⎫
52 weeks ⎬ = 1 year (y)
12 months ⎭
10 years = 1 decade
100 years = 1 century

Metric

LENGTH

10 millimeters (mm) = 1 centimeter (cm)
10 centimeters = 1 decimeter (dm)
10 decimeters ⎫
100 centimeters ⎭ = 1 meter
10 meters = 1 dekameter (dam)
10 dekameters = 1 hectameter (hm)
10 hectameters ⎫
1000 meters ⎭ = 1 kilometer (km)

AREA

100 square millimeters = 1 square centimeter
(mm^2)   (cm^2)
10,000 square centimeters = 1 square meter (m^2)
10,000 square meters = 1 hectare (ha)

VOLUME

1000 cubic millimeters = 1 cubic centimeter
(mm^3)   (cm^3)
1,000,000 cubic centimeters = 1 cubic meter (m^3)

MASS

1000 milligrams (mg) = 1 gram (g)
1000 grams = 1 kilogram (kg)

CAPACITY

1000 milliliters (mL) = 1 liter (L)

United States Customary

LENGTH

12 inches (in.) = 1 foot (ft)
3 feet ⎫
36 inches ⎭ = 1 yard (yd)
5280 feet ⎫
1760 yards ⎭ = 1 mile (mi)

AREA

144 square inches (m^2) = 1 square foot (ft^2)
9 square feet = 1 square yard (yd^2)
4840 square yards = 1 acre (A)

VOLUME

1728 cubic inches = 1 cubic foot (ft^3)
27 cubic feet = 1 cubic yd (yd^3)

WEIGHT

16 ounces (oz) = 1 pound (lb)
2000 pounds = 1 ton (t)

CAPACITY

8 fluid ounces (fl oz) = 1 cup (c)
2 cups = 1 pint (pt)
2 pints = 1 quart (qt)
4 quarts = 1 gallon (gal)

UNIT 1 Extra Practice

For use after Checkpoint A

Pages 8–9

Complete.

1. $9 + \blacksquare = 7 + 9$ **2.** $2 + (5 + 3) = (2 + 5) + \blacksquare$ **3.** $6 + 4 = \blacksquare$

$10 - 4 = \blacksquare$

Pages 10–11

Solve the equation.

4. $2 + a = 7$ **5.** $3 + n = 9$ **6.** $n - 3 = 5$ **7.** $x + 6 = 11$

8. $n - 9 = 4$ **9.** $y - 3 = 4$ **10.** $9 + x = 17$ **11.** $a - 5 = 2$

Pages 12–13

Write the standard form.

12. three million, thirty-eight **13.** 19 billion, 29 million, 147 thousand, 9

Pages 14–15

Write $<$ or $>$ to compare the numbers.

14. 793 $\blacksquare$ 794 **15.** 3704 $\blacksquare$ 3740 **16.** 62,951 $\blacksquare$ 7,938

17. 89,456 $\blacksquare$ 98,517 **18.** 3,874,603 $\blacksquare$ 3,875,842

For use after Checkpoint B

Pages 16–17

1. 61	**2.** 347	**3.** 856	**4.** 911	**5.** $3.98
+83	+ 29	8	39	.37
		+265	+547	+ 1.38

Pages 18–19

6. 92	**7.** 74	**8.** 733	**9.** 832	**10.** 454
− 7	−28	−416	− 85	− 98

Pages 20–21

11. 90	**12.** 3002	**13.** 5060	**14.** 7007	**15.** 2000
−46	− 135	− 389	− 1934	− 1461

Pages 22–23

16. 37,632	**17.** 13,092	**18.** $7253.16	**19.** 308,031
+68,969	− 5,738	+9478.08	− 198,992

Pages 24–25

Write the standard numeral.

20. CXLVI **21.** MMXLIII **22.** CCDMMXXXIV

Write the Roman numeral.

23. 46 **24.** 369 **25.** 1938 **26.** 4716

Extra Practice   UNIT 1

Pages 8–11

$7 + a = 10$
$7 + 3 = 10$
so $a = 3$

Complete.

1. $7 + 5 = \blacksquare + 7$

2. $(3 + 6) + 5 = 3 + (\blacksquare + 5)$

Solve the equation.

3. $2 + b = 6$

4. $x - 6 = 3$

5. $6 + m = 13$

Pages 12–15

28,431 $\blacksquare$ 28,143

28,431 $>$ 28,143

Write the standard form.

1. 6 million, 28 thousand, 432

2. 62 million, 216

3. 9 billion, 400 thousand, 16

4. 2 million, 48 thousand

Write $<$ or $>$ to compare the numbers.

5. 439,863 $\blacksquare$ 438,863

6. 623,591 $\blacksquare$ 72,391

7. 6,004,398 $\blacksquare$ 5,937,398

8. 9,361,594 $\blacksquare$ 9,361,693

Pages 16–23

$$\begin{array}{r} 5\,7,9\,0\,4 \\ +\,3\,8,1\,3\,7 \\ \hline 9\,6,0\,4\,1 \end{array}$$

$$\begin{array}{r} 4\,0\,0\,9 \\ -\,2\,8\,7\,6 \\ \hline 1\,1\,3\,3 \end{array}$$

1.
$$\begin{array}{r} 752 \\ +\ 89 \\ \hline \end{array}$$

2.
$$\begin{array}{r} 847 \\ -\,329 \\ \hline \end{array}$$

3.
$$\begin{array}{r} 5098 \\ +\,921 \\ \hline \end{array}$$

4.
$$\begin{array}{r} 2767 \\ -\,893 \\ \hline \end{array}$$

5.
$$\begin{array}{r} 3467 \\ +5693 \\ \hline \end{array}$$

6.
$$\begin{array}{r} 4006 \\ -\,248 \\ \hline \end{array}$$

7.
$$\begin{array}{r} 8000 \\ -1536 \\ \hline \end{array}$$

8.
$$\begin{array}{r} 34,861 \\ +27,495 \\ \hline \end{array}$$

9.
$$\begin{array}{r} 85,500 \\ -67,479 \\ \hline \end{array}$$

10.
$$\begin{array}{r} 125,678 \\ +246,108 \\ \hline \end{array}$$

11.
$$\begin{array}{r} \$634.91 \\ +789.45 \\ \hline \end{array}$$

12.
$$\begin{array}{r} \$900.60 \\ -\ 68.79 \\ \hline \end{array}$$

Pages 24–25

L   XX   IV
$\triangledown$ $\triangledown$ $\triangledown$
$50 + 20 + 4 = 74$

Write the standard numeral.

1. LIX

2. CXVI

3. XLIV

4. MCM

5. IX

6. XXXI

7. MCMIV

8. DCXX

Pages 26–27

1. Understand
2. Plan
3. Work
4. Answer

1. Harry bought a rubber bone for $1.27, a food dish for $3.98, and a large sack of puppy food for $7.49. How much did he spend?

UNIT 2 Extra Practice

For use after Checkpoint A

Pages 34–35

Round to the nearest hundred.

1. 632 **2.** 879 **3.** 387 **4.** 352 **5.** 965

Pages 36–37

Round to the nearest thousand.

6. 8265 **7.** 4530 **8.** 2607 **9.** 49,780 **10.** 62,598

Pages 38–39

Estimate the sum or difference.

11. 685	**12.** 964	**13.** 4282	**14.** 13,894
+ 41	− 337	− 2739	+ 6,236

Pages 40–41

Estimate the sum or difference.

15. $.94	**16.** $3.49	**17.** $48.32	**18.** $4.09
+.61	− 2.26	− 6.81	8.32
			+ .92

For use after Checkpoint B

Pages 42–43

Measure the segment to the nearest centimeter.

1. ——————— **2.** ——————— **3.** ———————

Pages 44–45

Choose the more likely measurement.
Write *a* or *b*.

4. the length of a camera **a.** 14 mm **b.** 14 cm

5. the length of a basketball court **a.** 26 m **b.** 26 cm

Pages 46–47

Choose the more likely measurement.
Write *a* or *b*.

6. the mass of a pair of sneakers **a.** 1 g **b.** 1 kg

7. the amount of juice in a can **a.** 3 mL **b.** 3 L

Pages 48–49

8. 1 ft 5 in.	**9.** 2 yd 1 ft	**10.** 2 ft 7 in.
+ 8 in.	− 1 yd 2 ft	+ 2 ft 9 in.

Pages 50–51

11. 2 qt 1 pt	**12.** 3 gal 1 qt	**13.** 7 lb 7 oz
+ 1 qt 1 pt	− 1 gal 2 qt	+ 6 lb 12 oz

Extra Practice UNIT 2

Pages 34–41

$$\begin{array}{r} 8573 \ \lozenge \ 8600 \\ + \ 326 \ \lozenge \ + \ 300 \\ \hline 8900 \end{array}$$

Round to the nearest hundred. Estimate the sum or difference.

1. 397 + 130	**2.** 483 + 152	**3.** 764 − 247	**4.** 968 − 620
5. 3598 − 1743	**6.** 8374 + 7428	**7.** 49,813 + 6,749	**8.** 75,298 + 16,853

Round to the nearest dollar. Estimate the sum or difference.

9. $ 4.15 + 12.87	**10.** $6.79 + 2.23	**11.** $52.39 − 25.82	**12.** $42.99 + 37.19

Pages 42–43

Measure to the nearest centimeter.

1. _____ **2.** _____ **3.** _____

4. _____ **5.** _____ **6.** _____

Pages 44–47

The height of a door might be 200 cm.

Choose the more likely measurement. Write *a* or *b*.

1. the length of a pen	**a.** 15 m	**b.** 15 cm
2. the mass of an ice cube	**a.** 50 kg	**b.** 50 g
3. the amount of soup in a can	**a.** 40 L	**b.** 400 mL
4. the height of a basketball hoop	**a.** 3 m	**b.** 3 km

Pages 48–51

$$\begin{array}{r} 1 \ ft \ \ 8 \ in. \\ + \qquad 9 \ in. \\ \hline 1 \ ft \ 17 \ in. \\ \lozenge \\ 2 \ ft \ 5 \ in. \end{array}$$

1. 7 yd 2 ft + 2 yd 2 ft	**2.** 3 qt − 1 qt 1 pt	**3.** 4 lb 12 oz + 6 lb 8 oz
4. 3 ft 7 in. − 1 ft 11 in.	**5.** 7 lb 8 oz − 2 lb 12 oz	**6.** 4 qt 1 pt + 3 qt 1 pt

Pages 52–53

1. Understand
2. Plan
3. Work
4. Answer

1. Jacques bowled 3 games. His scores were 112, 132, and 128. The league record was 171. What was his total score for the 3 games?

UNIT 3 Extra Practice

For use after Checkpoint A

Pages 60–61

Complete.

1. $5 \times 4 = \blacksquare \times 5$ **2.** $3 \times (8 \times 6) = (3 \times \blacksquare) \times 6$ **3.** $6 \times 1 = \blacksquare$

Pages 62–63

4. $\begin{array}{r} 86 \\ \times 7 \\ \hline \end{array}$ **5.** $\begin{array}{r} 68 \\ \times 4 \\ \hline \end{array}$ **6.** $\begin{array}{r} 529 \\ \times 6 \\ \hline \end{array}$ **7.** $\begin{array}{r} 831 \\ \times 5 \\ \hline \end{array}$

8. $\begin{array}{r} 3147 \\ \times 3 \\ \hline \end{array}$ **9.** $\begin{array}{r} 5768 \\ \times 9 \\ \hline \end{array}$ **10.** $\begin{array}{r} 29{,}876 \\ \times 8 \\ \hline \end{array}$ **11.** $\begin{array}{r} 43{,}762 \\ \times 9 \\ \hline \end{array}$

Pages 64–65

12. $\begin{array}{r} 358 \\ \times 10 \\ \hline \end{array}$ **13.** $\begin{array}{r} 679 \\ \times 100 \\ \hline \end{array}$ **14.** $\begin{array}{r} 362 \\ \times 800 \\ \hline \end{array}$ **15.** $\begin{array}{r} 74 \\ \times 600 \\ \hline \end{array}$

Pages 66–67

Write the LCM of the numbers.

16. 8 and 3   **17.** 7 and 21   **18.** 6 and 9   **19.** 18 and 24

20. 5 and 15   **21.** 8 and 20   **22.** 3 and 5   **23.** 9 and 10

For use after Checkpoint B

Pages 68–69

1. $\begin{array}{r} 48 \\ \times 93 \\ \hline \end{array}$ **2.** $\begin{array}{r} 91 \\ \times 43 \\ \hline \end{array}$ **3.** $\begin{array}{r} 945 \\ \times 78 \\ \hline \end{array}$ **4.** $\begin{array}{r} 127 \\ \times 86 \\ \hline \end{array}$

5. $\begin{array}{r} 236 \\ \times 17 \\ \hline \end{array}$ **6.** $\begin{array}{r} 4278 \\ \times 87 \\ \hline \end{array}$ **7.** $\begin{array}{r} 3654 \\ \times 28 \\ \hline \end{array}$ **8.** $\begin{array}{r} 6429 \\ \times 59 \\ \hline \end{array}$

Pages 70–71

9. $\begin{array}{r} 999 \\ \times 888 \\ \hline \end{array}$ **10.** $\begin{array}{r} 264 \\ \times 196 \\ \hline \end{array}$ **11.** $\begin{array}{r} 7839 \\ \times 75 \\ \hline \end{array}$ **12.** $\begin{array}{r} 2738 \\ \times 614 \\ \hline \end{array}$

13. $\begin{array}{r} 4193 \\ \times 263 \\ \hline \end{array}$ **14.** $\begin{array}{r} 75{,}243 \\ \times 102 \\ \hline \end{array}$ **15.** $\begin{array}{r} 76{,}729 \\ \times 815 \\ \hline \end{array}$ **16.** $\begin{array}{r} 39{,}017 \\ \times 482 \\ \hline \end{array}$

Pages 72–73

Estimate the product.

17. $\begin{array}{r} 94 \text{ cm} \\ \times 6 \\ \hline \end{array}$ **18.** $\begin{array}{r} 78 \text{ mL} \\ \times 37 \\ \hline \end{array}$ **19.** $\begin{array}{r} \$7.99 \\ \times 36 \\ \hline \end{array}$ **20.** $\begin{array}{r} \$8.31 \\ \times 437 \\ \hline \end{array}$

Pages 74–75

Write the product.

21. 4^3 **22.** 5^2 **23.** 2^4 **24.** 12^1 **25.** 3^3

26. 5^3 **27.** 15^2 **28.** 2^6 **29.** 7^3 **30.** 4^4

Extra Practice   UNIT 3

Pages 60–71

$$929$$
$$\times 687$$
$$\overline{6\,503}$$
$$74\,320$$
$$\underline{557\,400}$$
$$\overline{638{,}223}$$

1. 436
$\times 8$

2. 56
$\times 7$

3. 64
$\times 37$

4. 328
$\times 27$

5. 735
$\times 10$

6. 469
$\times 100$

7. 3984
$\times 38$

8. 6781
$\times 59$

9. 246
$\times 813$

10. 7048
$\times 297$

11. 8453
$\times 827$

12. 3829
$\times 761$

13. 4109
$\times 349$

14. 11,391
$\times 658$

15. 27,037
$\times 506$

16. 86,319
$\times 772$

Multiples of 3 and 4
less than 15.

3: 3, 6, 9, 12
4: 4, 8, 12

12 is the LCM.

Write the LCM of the numbers.

13. 2 and 3   **14.** 4 and 9   **15.** 3 and 10

16. 6 and 8   **17.** 4 and 11   **18.** 6 and 14

19. 6 and 9   **20.** 8 and 14   **21.** 12 and 18

22. 10 and 30   **23.** 3 and 13   **24.** 25 and 4

Pages 72–73

94 cm ⇨ 90 cm
$\times 16$ ⇨ $\times 20$
1800 cm

Estimate the product.

1. 645 kg
$\times 9$

2. $9.26
$\times 38$

3. 378 mL
$\times 24$

4. $7.35
$\times 68$

5. 372 g
$\times 42$

6. $89.50
$\times 6$

7. 351 cm
$\times 16$

8. $69.85
$\times 52$

Pages 74–75

$4^3 = 4 \times 4 \times 4$

$= 64$

Write the product.

1. 3^4 **2.** 12^1 **3.** 2^5 **4.** 5^2 **5.** 7^3

6. 2^3 **7.** 4^1 **8.** 9^2 **9.** 6^3 **10.** 12^2

Pages 76–77

1. Understand
2. Plan
3. Work
4. Answer

Use a picture to help solve the problem.

1. Bob has 3 pairs of pants and 3 shirts. How many different outfits does he have using 1 pair of pants and 1 shirt?

UNIT 4 Extra Practice

For use after Checkpoint A

Pages 84–85

Solve.

1. $42 \div 7 = n$ 2. $a \div 7 = 9$ 3. $y \times 8 = 48$

Pages 86–87

4. $2\overline{)457}$ 5. $7\overline{)856}$ 6. $9\overline{)8199}$ 7. $4\overline{)24,217}$

Pages 88–89

8. $5\overline{)1050}$ 9. $9\overline{)5473}$ 10. $6\overline{)6140}$ 11. $8\overline{)8087}$

Pages 90–91

Write the GCF of the numbers.

12. 8 and 18 13. 7 and 11 14. 36 and 64 15. 56 and 98

Pages 92–93

Is the first number divisible by the second? Write *Yes* or *No*.

16. 180; 5 17. 317; 2 18. 585; 10 19. 355; 5

For use after Checkpoint B

Pages 94–95

1. $40\overline{)509}$ 2. $90\overline{)956}$ 3. $60\overline{)1852}$ 4. $20\overline{)1937}$

5. $50\overline{)726}$ 6. $80\overline{)947}$ 7. $30\overline{)229}$ 8. $70\overline{)808}$

Pages 96–97

9. $24\overline{)216}$ 10. $43\overline{)340}$ 11. $67\overline{)389}$ 12. $71\overline{)654}$

13. $15\overline{)119}$ 14. $33\overline{)261}$ 15. $56\overline{)325}$ 16. $97\overline{)544}$

Pages 98–99

17. $26\overline{)843}$ 18. $19\overline{)940}$ 19. $32\overline{)3186}$ 20. $86\overline{)4698}$

21. $65\overline{)913}$ 22. $38\overline{)549}$ 23. $72\overline{)891}$ 24. $47\overline{)868}$

Pages 100–101

25. $32\overline{)8427}$ 26. $19\overline{)3980}$ 27. $32\overline{)5232}$ 28. $54\overline{)11,125}$

29. $14\overline{)26,154}$ 30. $71\overline{)90,161}$ 31. $54\overline{)61,073}$ 32. $38\overline{)81,901}$

Pages 102–103

33. $327\overline{)90,325}$ 34. $651\overline{)26,980}$ 35. $408\overline{)79,007}$ 36. $126\overline{)3089}$

37. $125\overline{)11,628}$ 38. $461\overline{)50,816}$ 39. $717\overline{)814,961}$ 40. $359\overline{)66,781}$

Pages 104–105

Estimate the quotient.

41. $67\overline{)41,983}$ 42. $32\overline{)10,163}$ 43. $631\overline{)478,554}$ 44. $751\overline{)34,900}$

45. $51\overline{)249,601}$ 46. $18\overline{)610,311}$ 47. $394\overline{)122,315}$ 48. $618\overline{)54,016}$

Extra Practice   UNIT 4

Pages 84–85

$x \div 9 = 3$
$27 \div 9 = 3$
$x = 27$

Solve.

1. $9 \times 6 = y$

2. $72 \div 9 = n$

3. $x \times 6 = 54$

4. $n \div 7 = 5$

5. $4 \times y = 28$

6. $48 \div n = 8$

Pages 86–93

$$9 \overline{)\,731} \quad \begin{array}{r} 81 \ \text{R2} \\ \end{array}$$
-72
11
-9
2

1. $4\overline{)78}$

2. $6\overline{)525}$

3. $8\overline{)674}$

4. $4\overline{)783}$

5. $5\overline{)601}$

6. $6\overline{)5120}$

Write the GCF.

7. 6 and 21

8. 8 and 24

9. 10 and 35

10. 12 and 28

11. 13 and 39

12. 18 and 30

Pages 94–103

$$38\overline{)\,2798} \quad \begin{array}{r} 73 \ \text{R24} \\ \end{array}$$
-266
138
-114
24

1. $36\overline{)257}$

2. $72\overline{)589}$

3. $59\overline{)423}$

4. $45\overline{)3821}$

5. $27\overline{)9653}$

6. $63\overline{)5289}$

7. $32\overline{)7548}$

8. $46\overline{)28,957}$

9. $74\overline{)581,236}$

10. $68\overline{)7591}$

11. $52\overline{)33,815}$

12. $83\overline{)115,715}$

13. $31\overline{)11,784}$

14. $48\overline{)29,063}$

15. $76\overline{)497,008}$

16. $615\overline{)88,614}$

17. $308\overline{)2759}$

18. $217\overline{)51,123}$

19. $285\overline{)33,988}$

20. $827\overline{)43,815}$

21. $687\overline{)469,752}$

Pages 104–105

$$29\overline{)917} \ \diamond \ 30\overline{)900} \quad \begin{array}{r} 30 \\ \end{array}$$

Estimate the quotient.

1. $27\overline{)891}$

2. $43\overline{)283}$

3. $36\overline{)476}$

4. $557\overline{)4192}$

5. $253\overline{)11,683}$

6. $807\overline{)326,851}$

Pages 106–107

1. Understand
2. Plan
3. Work
4. Answer

1. In a touch football game, the Hurricanes beat the Tornadoes by 21 points. The Hurricanes scored 35 points. What was the Tornadoes' score?

2. A group of 183 students went to camp by school buses. Each bus could seat 36 students. How many buses were needed?

Pages 122–123

Write the decimal.

1. 5 and 2 tenths   **2.** 4 tenths

Pages 124–125

3. 118 and 9 hundredths   **4.** 8 and 21 hundredths

5. 3251 ten-thousandths   **6.** 51 hundred-thousandths

Pages 126–127

Write < or > for ▓.

7. 0.495 ▓ 0.5   **8.** 0.58 ▓ 0.57   **9.** 7.18 ▓ 6.18

Pages 128–129

10. 3.92	**11.** 4.900	**12.** 28.45	**13.** 3.51
+4.84	+8.613	17.37	4.515
		42.7	5.6
		+47.03	+6.894

For use after Checkpoint B

Pages 130–131

1. 4.2	**2.** 8.73	**3.** 25.057	**4.** 39.07
−1.6	−4.5	−11.259	−2.382

Pages 132–133

Write the new balance.

	DATE	CHECK NUMBER	CHECKS OR DEPOSITS	AMOUNT OF CHECK		AMOUNT OF DEPOSIT		BALANCE	
								790	05
5.	5/17		Deposit			235	50	?	
6.	5/25	403	Stuffy's Insulation Co.	300	75			?	
7.	5/29	404	Nick's Shoe Repair	10	85			?	
8.	6/8	405	Dr. Markowitz	32	50			?	

Pages 134–135

Round to the nearest thousandth.

9. 0.5921   **10.** 2.5185   **11.** 3.6098   **12.** 5.21645

13. 1.7852   **14.** 16.7019   **15.** 83.0191   **16.** 35.6152

Pages 136–137

Round to the nearest tenth. Estimate.

17. 0.83	**18.** 0.71	**19.** 0.96	**20.** 12.48
+0.971	−0.42	+1.23	−3.573

Pages 122–127

6 and 24 thousandths
⇨
6.024

Write the decimal.

1. 7 tenths

2. 7 and 31 hundredths

3. 428 thousandths

4. 9 and 8 thousandths

5. 53 ten-thousandths

6. 18 and 9 hundredths

0.709 ▨ 0.78
0.709 < 0.780

Write < or > for ▨.

7. 8.205 ▨ 8.206

8. 0.9 ▨ 0.86

Pages 128–133

$$\begin{array}{r} 62.576 \\ -18.139 \\ \hline 44.437 \end{array}$$

1. $\begin{array}{r} 3.4 \\ +5.8 \\ \hline \end{array}$

2. $\begin{array}{r} 8.03 \\ -5.12 \\ \hline \end{array}$

3. $\begin{array}{r} 92.458 \\ +0.931 \\ \hline \end{array}$

4. $\begin{array}{r} 873.5 \\ +390.7 \\ \hline \end{array}$

5. $\begin{array}{r} 5.6 \\ -3.8 \\ \hline \end{array}$

6. $\begin{array}{r} 74.2 \\ -41.59 \\ \hline \end{array}$

7. $\begin{array}{r} 0.924 \\ -0.376 \\ \hline \end{array}$

8. $\begin{array}{r} 78.01 \\ -44.253 \\ \hline \end{array}$

9. $\begin{array}{r} \$59.62 \\ +28.34 \\ \hline \end{array}$

10. $\begin{array}{r} 81.27 \\ +28.3 \\ \hline \end{array}$

11. $\begin{array}{r} \$4.75 \\ -2.49 \\ \hline \end{array}$

12. $\begin{array}{r} \$51.95 \\ -34.89 \\ \hline \end{array}$

Pages 134–137

Round 5.68 to the
nearest tenth.
Round up to 5.7.
5.68 ⇨ 5.7

Round to the nearest tenth.

1. 7.85

2. 14.43

3. 15.98

4. 5.24

Round to the nearest hundredth.

5. 0.988

6. 1.184

7. 2.042

8. 6.897

Estimate.

$$\begin{array}{r} 8.25 \; ⇨ \quad 8.3 \\ +6.31 \; ⇨ \; +6.3 \\ \hline 14.6 \end{array}$$

Round to the nearest tenth. Estimate.

9. $\begin{array}{r} 0.74 \\ +0.92 \\ \hline \end{array}$

10. $\begin{array}{r} 0.08 \\ +0.14 \\ \hline \end{array}$

11. $\begin{array}{r} 5.295 \\ -3.57 \\ \hline \end{array}$

12. $\begin{array}{r} 6.14 \\ -2.15 \\ \hline \end{array}$

Pages 138–139

1. Understand
2. Plan
3. Work
4. Answer

1. When a book is opened, the product of the page numbers is
4160. What are the page numbers?

UNIT 6 Extra Practice

For use after Checkpoint A

Pages 146–147

| 1. 0.7 ×6 | 2. 3.87 ×45 | 3. 0.027 ×329 | 4. 0.36 ×2714 |

Pages 148–149

| 5. 0.9 ×0.7 | 6. 4.9 ×0.6 | 7. 2.86 ×3.1 | 8. 68.7 ×0.47 |

Pages 150–151

| 9. 0.0836 ×0.42 | 10. 0.1647 ×0.09 | 11. 1.847 ×0.015 | 12. 0.08 ×0.009 |

| 13. 0.01 ×0.07 | 14. 0.071 ×0.009 | 15. 1.015 ×0.004 | 16. 0.041 ×0.002 |

Pages 152–153

Estimate the product.

| 17. 486 ×0.8 | 18. 0.413 ×78 | 19. 9.21 ×6.3 | 20. 84.2 ×0.06 |

For use after Checkpoint B

Pages 154–155

1. $8\overline{)18.88}$ 2. $9\overline{)614.7}$ 3. $31\overline{)20.398}$

4. $5\overline{)42.5}$ 5. $47\overline{)11.797}$ 6. $81\overline{)1.944}$

Pages 156–157

7. 2.48×10 8. $483.5 \div 100$ 9. 5.97×1000

Pages 158–159

10. $0.9\overline{)5.157}$ 11. $3.2\overline{)3.816}$ 12. $4.3\overline{)11.567}$

13. $6.7\overline{)142.71}$ 14. $1.1\overline{)60.17}$ 15. $3.8\overline{)6.004}$

Pages 160–161

16. $0.06\overline{)72.54}$ 17. $0.24\overline{)3.948}$ 18. $1.35\overline{)0.999}$

Pages 162–163

Divide. Round the quotient to the nearest hundredth.

19. $6\overline{)72.19}$ 20. $2.4\overline{)11.233}$ 21. $0.35\overline{)0.925}$

Pages 164–165

Estimate the quotient.

22. $4.8\overline{)34.97}$ 23. $7.32\overline{)419.8}$ 24. $9.94\overline{)5921.8}$

Pages 166–167

Write the missing number.

25. 5.68 m = ▓ cm   26. 2.9 km = ▓ m   27. 4980 cm = ▓ m

Extra Practice UNIT 6

Pages 146–151

$$\begin{array}{r} 6.48 \\ \times 3.2 \\ \hline 1296 \\ 19440 \\ \hline 20.736 \end{array}$$

1. 0.7
   ×6

2. 4.08
   ×9

3. 0.48
   ×0.3

4. 1.249
   ×1.8

5. 9.56
   ×4.3

6. 0.82
   ×0.64

7. 72.9
   ×1.7

8. 0.206
   ×25

Pages 152–153

$$\begin{array}{r} 2.8 \\ \times 8.1 \end{array} \begin{array}{c} \Diamond \\ \Diamond \end{array} \begin{array}{r} 3 \\ \times 8 \\ \hline 24 \end{array}$$

Estimate the product.

1. 468
   ×9.3

2. 56.2
   ×0.8

3. 0.09
   ×7.1

4. 80.36
   ×2.4

Pages 154–161

$38.7 \div 9 = 4.3$

$45.2 \div 10 = 4.52$
$45.2 \times 100 = 4520$

$$0.59\overline{)9.44} \ \Diamond \ 59\overline{)944}$$ (quotient 16)

1. $150.5 \div 7$

2. $406.4 \div 16$

3. $657.6 \div 48$

4. $751.2 \div 6$

5. $18.29 \div 59$

6. $35.7 \div 3$

7. $6.78 \div 10$

8. 493.8×100

9. 583.4×100

10. $14.61 \div 100$

11. 38.5×1000

12. $501.7 \div 1000$

13. $0.8\overline{)5.6}$

14. $5.8\overline{)37.12}$

15. $0.27\overline{)9.855}$

16. $0.06\overline{)23.94}$

17. $0.45\overline{)8.739}$

18. $3.4\overline{)0.799}$

Pages 162–167

$$5.8\overline{)42.1} \ \Diamond \ 6\overline{)42}$$ (quotient 7)

Divide. Round the quotient to the nearest hundredth.

1. $0.8\overline{)29.17}$

2. $1.6\overline{)33}$

3. $2.8\overline{)0.891}$

Estimate the quotient.

4. $6.6\overline{)35.42}$

5. $18.9\overline{)98.9}$

6. $12.4\overline{)278.9}$

Complete.

7. 580 cm = ▨ m

8. 49 m = ▨ km

9. 2.84 km = ▨ m

Pages 168–169

1. Understand
2. Plan
3. Work
4. Answer

1. Lori Wilson bought 62 L of unleaded gasoline for 36.5¢ per liter. How much will she receive in change if she gives the cashier $30.00?

UNIT 7 Extra Practice

For use after Checkpoint A

Pages 176–177

Use the figure on the right.

1. Name 5 segments

2. Name 5 angles

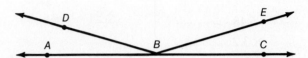

Pages 178–179

Is the angle acute, obtuse, or right? Write *A*, *O*, or *R*.

3. 31°   4. 90°   5. 134°   6. 89°

Pages 180–181

List the pair of lines described.

7. Parallel lines

8. Perpendicular lines

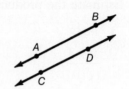
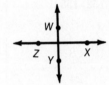

Pages 182–183

Choose the correct answer. Write *a* or *b*.

9.

a. rectangle
b. triangle

10.

a. rhombus
b. polygon

Pages 184–185

How big is the third angle of the triangle?

11. 30°, 40°   12. 68°, 45°   13. 101°, 37°

For use after Checkpoint B

Pages 186–187

What is the perimeter of the figure with sides of the given lengths?

1. 6 cm, 8 cm, 3 cm, 2 cm, 9 cm   2. 56 mm, 39 mm, 48 mm

Pages 188–189

What is the circumference of the circle with the given diameter?

3. 4m   4. 18 cm   5. 50 mm   6. 200 km

Pages 190–191

What is the area of the rectangle with the given length (*l*) and width (*w*)?

7. $w = 9\,\text{cm}$ 8. $w = 25\,\text{m}$ 9. $w = 97\,\text{km}$ 10. $w = 1000\,\text{cm}$
$l = 5\,\text{cm}$ $l = 13\,\text{m}$ $l = 35\,\text{km}$ $l = 53\,\text{cm}$

Pages 192–193

What is the area of the circle with the given radius?

11. 3 km   12. 12 m   13. 7 mm   14. 24 cm

Pages 176–181

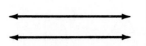

Parallel lines

Perpendicular lines

Do the lines look parallel or perpendicular?

1. *ZQ* and *XS*   **2.** *PY* and *YR*

3. *RY* and *SX*   **4.** *PY* and *XS*

Write *A*, *O*, or *R* to show whether the angle is acute, obtuse or right.

5. $\angle PYR$ **6.** $\angle QRY$

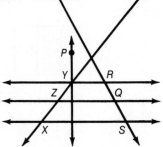

Pages 182–185

rectangle

Choose the correct answer. Write *a* or *b*.

1.

a. rhombus
b. polygon

2.

a. triangle
b. trapezoid

3.

a. parallelogram
b. square

Pages 186–189

Perimeter is the distance around a figure.

$C \approx 3.14 \times d$

What is the perimeter of a figure with sides of the given length?

1. 8 km, 19 km, 21 km   **2.** 15 m, 22 m, 17 m, 27 m

3. 2.5 m, 3.7 m, 5.9 m   **4.** 2.48 cm, 3.72 cm, 4.91 cm

What is the circumference of the circle with the given diameter?

5. 7 cm   **6.** 11 m   **7.** 20 km   **8.** 51 mm

Pages 190–193

$A = l \times w$
$A = (b \times h) \div 2$
$A \approx 3.14 \times r^2$

What is the area of the figure?

1. a rectangle with length of 28 cm and width of 17 cm

2. a right triangle with base 16 m and height of 7 m

Pages 194–195

1. Understand
2. Plan
3. Work
4. Answer

Write a number phrase to complete the sentence.

1. Tony's shirts cost $12.50 each.
   Let s = number of shirts bought.
   Then, ▓ = cost of the shirts.

UNIT 8 Extra Practice

For use after Checkpoint A

Pages 202–203

Write the fraction for the shaded part.

1.  2. 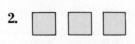 3.   4.

Pages 204–205

Complete.

5. $\frac{1}{8} = \frac{\blacksquare}{24}$ 6. $\frac{5}{9} = \frac{\blacksquare}{36}$ 7. $\frac{3}{4} = \frac{\blacksquare}{20}$ 8. $\frac{4}{7} = \frac{\blacksquare}{21}$

Pages 206–207

Write in lowest terms.

9. $\frac{4}{6}$ 10. $\frac{10}{20}$ 11. $\frac{21}{49}$ 12. $\frac{10}{15}$

13. $\frac{5}{30}$ 14. $\frac{12}{45}$ 15. $\frac{16}{36}$ 16. $\frac{3}{39}$

Pages 208–209

Write $<$ or $>$ for $\blacksquare$.

17. $\frac{3}{5} \blacksquare \frac{7}{15}$ 18. $\frac{7}{8} \blacksquare \frac{5}{6}$ 19. $\frac{4}{7} \blacksquare \frac{1}{2}$ 20. $\frac{5}{12} \blacksquare \frac{13}{36}$

For use after Checkpoint B

Pages 210–211

Write as a fraction.

1. $3\frac{3}{4}$ 2. $4\frac{5}{7}$ 3. $1\frac{5}{12}$ 4. $2\frac{4}{5}$

Pages 212–213

Write as a mixed number or whole number.

5. $\frac{13}{6}$ 6. $\frac{31}{8}$ 7. $\frac{56}{4}$ 8. $\frac{42}{5}$

Pages 214–215

Write as a decimal.

9. $\frac{9}{10}$ 10. $\frac{654}{1000}$ 11. $\frac{51}{100}$ 12. $\frac{7}{100}$

Pages 216–217

13. $\frac{4}{5}$ 14. $3\frac{7}{20}$ 15. $\frac{11}{40}$ 16. $1\frac{12}{25}$

Pages 218–219

Write as a repeating decimal. Show your answer using a bar.

17. $\frac{2}{11}$ 18. $\frac{7}{12}$ 19. $\frac{9}{22}$ 20. $\frac{2}{3}$

21. $\frac{7}{9}$ 22. $\frac{15}{18}$ 23. $\frac{11}{15}$ 24. $\frac{13}{22}$

Pages 202–209

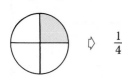

$\frac{3}{4} = \frac{3 \times 5}{4 \times 5} = \frac{15}{20}$

$\frac{16}{40} = \frac{16 \div 8}{40 \div 8} = \frac{2}{5}$

$\frac{1}{2} < \frac{5}{8}$

Write the fraction for the shaded part.

1.   **2.**   **3.**

Complete.

4. $\frac{1}{2} = \frac{\blacksquare}{16}$ **5.** $\frac{2}{3} = \frac{\blacksquare}{9}$ **6.** $\frac{5}{6} = \frac{\blacksquare}{18}$

Write in lowest terms.

7. $\frac{4}{8}$ **8.** $\frac{9}{12}$ **9.** $\frac{12}{16}$ **10.** $\frac{8}{10}$

11. $\frac{8}{24}$ **12.** $\frac{14}{21}$ **13.** $\frac{28}{32}$ **14.** $\frac{18}{45}$

Write $<$ or $>$ for $\blacksquare$.

15. $\frac{2}{3} \blacksquare \frac{5}{6}$ **16.** $\frac{3}{5} \blacksquare \frac{1}{2}$ **17.** $\frac{5}{16} \blacksquare \frac{1}{4}$

Pages 210–215

$3\frac{2}{5} = \frac{17}{5}$

$\frac{8}{3} = 2\frac{2}{3}$

Write as a fraction.

1. $1\frac{2}{3}$ **2.** $2\frac{3}{4}$ **3.** $4\frac{3}{5}$ **4.** $3\frac{5}{6}$

Write as a mixed number or whole number.

5. $\frac{10}{2}$ **6.** $\frac{13}{4}$ **7.** $\frac{23}{7}$ **8.** $\frac{50}{9}$

Pages 216–219

$\frac{5}{8} \Rightarrow 8)\overline{5.000}^{\,0.625}$

$\frac{1}{3} \Rightarrow 3)\overline{1.00}^{\,0.33...} \Rightarrow 0.\overline{3}$

Write as a terminating or repeating decimal.

1. $\frac{3}{4}$ **2.** $\frac{27}{100}$ **3.** $\frac{7}{16}$ **4.** $\frac{3}{5}$

5. $\frac{5}{6}$ **6.** $\frac{4}{7}$ **7.** $\frac{17}{20}$ **8.** $\frac{4}{9}$

Pages 220–221

1. Understand
2. Plan
3. Work
4. Answer

1. The Road Runner's Running Club bought 24 pairs of running shorts for $198.00. How much does 1 pair of shorts cost?

UNIT 9 Extra Practice

For use after Checkpoint A

Pages 236–237

Measure to the nearest $\frac{1}{16}$ in.

1. _____

2. _____

3. _____

4. _____

Pages 238–239

Add or subtract. Write the answer in lowest terms.

5. $\frac{3}{11} + \frac{5}{11}$

6. $\frac{5}{9} - \frac{2}{9}$

7. $\frac{15}{16} - \frac{5}{16}$

8. $\frac{5}{18} + \frac{3}{18}$

Pages 240–241

Add. Write the sum in lowest terms.

9. $\begin{array}{r} \frac{1}{4} \\ + \frac{7}{8} \\ \hline \end{array}$

10. $\begin{array}{r} \frac{5}{16} \\ + \frac{1}{8} \\ \hline \end{array}$

11. $\begin{array}{r} \frac{11}{21} \\ + \frac{4}{7} \\ \hline \end{array}$

12. $\begin{array}{r} \frac{7}{10} \\ + \frac{1}{2} \\ \hline \end{array}$

Pages 242–243

13. $\begin{array}{r} 1\frac{1}{8} \\ + 2\frac{3}{4} \\ \hline \end{array}$

14. $\begin{array}{r} 2\frac{4}{5} \\ + 1\frac{1}{3} \\ \hline \end{array}$

15. $\begin{array}{r} 3\frac{5}{6} \\ + 2\frac{1}{4} \\ \hline \end{array}$

16. $\begin{array}{r} 1\frac{1}{2} \\ + 6\frac{5}{7} \\ \hline \end{array}$

For use after Checkpoint B

Pages 244–245

Subtract. Write the difference in lowest terms.

1. $\begin{array}{r} \frac{11}{12} \\ - \frac{5}{6} \\ \hline \end{array}$

2. $\begin{array}{r} \frac{2}{3} \\ - \frac{1}{8} \\ \hline \end{array}$

3. $\begin{array}{r} \frac{9}{10} \\ - \frac{3}{8} \\ \hline \end{array}$

4. $\begin{array}{r} \frac{5}{6} \\ - \frac{7}{9} \\ \hline \end{array}$

Pages 246–247

5. $\begin{array}{r} 4\frac{5}{6} \\ - 2\frac{1}{6} \\ \hline \end{array}$

6. $\begin{array}{r} 5\frac{9}{10} \\ - 1\frac{3}{5} \\ \hline \end{array}$

7. $\begin{array}{r} 8\frac{7}{9} \\ - 8\frac{1}{4} \\ \hline \end{array}$

8. $\begin{array}{r} 5\frac{5}{6} \\ - 2\frac{3}{8} \\ \hline \end{array}$

Pages 248–249

9. $\begin{array}{r} 7 \\ - 3\frac{3}{8} \\ \hline \end{array}$

10. $\begin{array}{r} 10\frac{1}{4} \\ - 3\frac{3}{4} \\ \hline \end{array}$

11. $\begin{array}{r} 6\frac{1}{5} \\ - 4\frac{4}{5} \\ \hline \end{array}$

12. $\begin{array}{r} 8\frac{3}{10} \\ - 2\frac{7}{10} \\ \hline \end{array}$

Pages 250–251

13. $\begin{array}{r} 5\frac{3}{8} \\ - 1\frac{5}{6} \\ \hline \end{array}$

14. $\begin{array}{r} 7\frac{5}{9} \\ - 2\frac{2}{3} \\ \hline \end{array}$

15. $\begin{array}{r} 7\frac{2}{7} \\ - 3\frac{2}{3} \\ \hline \end{array}$

16. $\begin{array}{r} 6\frac{5}{12} \\ - 4\frac{3}{4} \\ \hline \end{array}$

Pages 236–237

Measure to the nearest $\frac{1}{16}$ in.

1. _____ 2. _____

3. _____ 4. _____

Pages 238–243

$$5\frac{3}{4} = 5\frac{9}{12}$$

$$+2\frac{2}{3} = +2\frac{8}{12}$$

$$\overline{\phantom{+2\frac{2}{3}} \quad 7\frac{17}{12}}$$

$$= 7 + 1\frac{5}{12}$$

$$= 8\frac{5}{12}$$

Add. Write the sum in lowest terms.

1. $\frac{1}{8}$ $+\frac{5}{8}$

2. $\frac{2}{3}$ $+\frac{5}{9}$

3. $\frac{7}{10}$ $+\frac{1}{2}$

4. $\frac{3}{4}$ $+\frac{1}{6}$

5. $\frac{5}{6}$ $+\frac{1}{8}$

6. $\frac{5}{6}$ $+\frac{4}{9}$

7. $3\frac{1}{4}$ $+2\frac{1}{3}$

8. $5\frac{5}{12}$ $+2\frac{7}{8}$

Pages 244–251

$$6\frac{2}{5} = 6\frac{6}{15}$$

$$-3\frac{2}{3} = -3\frac{10}{15}$$

$$= 5\frac{21}{15}$$

$$= -3\frac{10}{15}$$

$$2\frac{11}{15}$$

Subtract. Write the difference in lowest terms.

1. $\frac{7}{9}$ $-\frac{4}{9}$

2. $\frac{7}{9}$ $-\frac{1}{3}$

3. $\frac{4}{7}$ $-\frac{1}{2}$

4. $\frac{7}{8}$ $-\frac{1}{4}$

5. $4\frac{8}{9}$ $-2\frac{5}{9}$

6. $7\frac{11}{12}$ $-3\frac{7}{8}$

7. $9\frac{2}{3}$ $-5\frac{1}{4}$

8. $8\frac{3}{4}$ $-6\frac{2}{9}$

9. $5\frac{1}{6}$ $-2\frac{5}{6}$

10. 9 $-7\frac{3}{10}$

11. $4\frac{1}{3}$ $-2\frac{3}{5}$

12. $3\frac{3}{8}$ $-1\frac{2}{3}$

Pages 252–253

1. Understand
2. Plan
3. Work
4. Answer

Write a simpler problem. Use it to solve the original problem.

1. Carlton bought $13\frac{7}{10}$ gal of gas that cost $1.419 per gallon. How much did he spend?

2. In a bread slicing contest, the winner sliced a $360\frac{1}{4}$ in. loaf into 1441 slices. How thick was each slice?

Pages 260–261

Multiply. Write the product in lowest terms.

1. $4 \times \frac{5}{8}$ **2.** $\frac{3}{7} \times 8$ **3.** $5 \times \frac{3}{7}$ **4.** $\frac{5}{6} \times 11$

5. $6 \times \frac{1}{2}$ **6.** $28 \times \frac{4}{7}$ **7.** $\frac{3}{5} \times 60$ **8.** $\frac{3}{8} \times 17$

Pages 262–263

9. $\frac{1}{3} \times \frac{4}{7}$ **10.** $\frac{5}{8} \times \frac{3}{4}$ **11.** $\frac{7}{10} \times \frac{3}{5}$ **12.** $\frac{2}{3} \times \frac{4}{5}$

13. $\frac{2}{3} \times \frac{5}{8}$ **14.** $\frac{7}{8} \times \frac{2}{5}$ **15.** $\frac{3}{4} \times \frac{1}{8}$ **16.** $\frac{6}{7} \times \frac{3}{14}$

Pages 264–265

17. $\frac{2}{3} \times \frac{7}{10}$ **18.** $\frac{8}{21} \times \frac{3}{10}$ **19.** $\frac{3}{8} \times \frac{4}{15}$ **20.** $\frac{5}{6} \times \frac{12}{20}$

21. $\frac{1}{5} \times \frac{15}{18}$ **22.** $\frac{9}{10} \times \frac{5}{6}$ **23.** $\frac{7}{8} \times \frac{24}{35}$ **24.** $\frac{14}{25} \times \frac{10}{21}$

Pages 266–267

25. $4 \times 1\frac{1}{4}$ **26.** $1\frac{3}{4} \times 2\frac{2}{5}$ **27.** $1\frac{3}{10} \times 1\frac{2}{3}$ **28.** $2\frac{2}{7} \times 1\frac{2}{5}$

29. $3\frac{1}{3} \times 4\frac{1}{4}$ **30.** $5\frac{1}{6} \times 1\frac{5}{7}$ **31.** $2\frac{5}{8} \times 1\frac{2}{3}$ **32.** $1\frac{7}{12} \times 2\frac{2}{5}$

Pages 268–269

Divide. Write the quotient in lowest terms.

1. $7 \div \frac{3}{5}$ **2.** $18 \div \frac{7}{10}$ **3.** $14 \div \frac{5}{8}$ **4.** $21 \div \frac{3}{7}$

5. $8 \div \frac{1}{5}$ **6.** $13 \div \frac{2}{10}$ **7.** $50 \div \frac{3}{4}$ **8.** $62 \div \frac{2}{3}$

Pages 270–271

9. $\frac{2}{3} \div 8$ **10.** $\frac{2}{9} \div 2$ **11.** $\frac{5}{6} \div 3$ **12.** $\frac{3}{4} \div 5$

13. $\frac{1}{8} \div 5$ **14.** $\frac{2}{5} \div 7$ **15.** $\frac{4}{9} \div 9$ **16.** $\frac{7}{8} \div 4$

Pages 272–273

17. $\frac{2}{3} \div \frac{3}{4}$ **18.** $\frac{6}{7} \div \frac{7}{8}$ **19.** $\frac{4}{5} \div \frac{1}{10}$ **20.** $\frac{3}{5} \div \frac{8}{15}$

21. $\frac{1}{2} \div \frac{3}{8}$ **22.** $\frac{2}{5} \div \frac{4}{9}$ **23.** $\frac{11}{12} \div \frac{22}{24}$ **24.** $\frac{15}{42} \div \frac{12}{21}$

Pages 274–275

25. $2\frac{1}{7} \div \frac{3}{7}$ **26.** $\frac{3}{21} \div 1\frac{1}{2}$ **27.** $1\frac{1}{3} \div 2$ **28.** $6\frac{3}{4} \div 2\frac{1}{8}$

29. $8\frac{2}{3} \div 5\frac{1}{4}$ **30.** $4\frac{7}{8} \div 3\frac{2}{3}$ **31.** $14\frac{3}{8} \div 5\frac{2}{3}$ **32.** $9\frac{2}{3} \div 18\frac{3}{4}$

Extra Practice UNIT 10

Pages 260–267

$2\frac{2}{3} \times 3\frac{3}{5}$

$2\frac{2}{3} = \frac{8}{3}$

$3\frac{3}{5} = \frac{18}{5}$

$\frac{8}{\cancel{3}} \times \frac{\overset{6}{\cancel{18}}}{5} = \frac{48}{5} = 9\frac{3}{5}$

Multiply. Write the product in lowest terms.

1. $\frac{2}{3} \times 5$ **2.** $\frac{7}{8} \times 9$ **3.** $6 \times \frac{4}{5}$ **4.** $18 \times \frac{3}{8}$

5. $\frac{5}{13} \times \frac{2}{5}$ **6.** $\frac{2}{3} \times \frac{7}{20}$ **7.** $\frac{17}{18} \times \frac{21}{34}$ **8.** $\frac{8}{9} \times \frac{5}{12}$

9. $1\frac{5}{6} \times 2$ **10.** $3\frac{3}{4} \times 4\frac{1}{4}$ **11.** $2\frac{2}{7} \times 1\frac{2}{5}$ **12.** $3\frac{5}{8} \times 2\frac{1}{4}$

13. $2\frac{5}{8} \times 1\frac{2}{3}$ **14.** $5\frac{1}{2} \times 4\frac{5}{8}$ **15.** $4\frac{3}{8} \times 2\frac{2}{5}$ **16.** $3\frac{7}{12} \times 2\frac{5}{6}$

17. $4\frac{1}{2} \times 2\frac{5}{8}$ **18.** $7\frac{1}{3} \times 6\frac{7}{8}$ **19.** $3\frac{3}{4} \times 2\frac{9}{10}$ **20.** $6\frac{7}{8} \times 1\frac{1}{2}$

21. $5\frac{1}{3} \times 6\frac{2}{7}$ **22.** $4\frac{2}{5} \times 2\frac{1}{2}$ **23.** $10\frac{2}{3} \times 7\frac{4}{5}$ **24.** $11\frac{1}{6} \times 5\frac{1}{7}$

Pages 268–275

$2\frac{3}{4} \div 3\frac{2}{3}$

$2\frac{3}{4} = \frac{11}{4}$

$3\frac{2}{3} = \frac{11}{3}$

$\frac{11}{4} \div \frac{11}{3} = \frac{\cancel{11}}{4} \times \frac{3}{\cancel{11}}$

$= \frac{3}{4}$

Divide. Write the quotient in lowest terms.

1. $8 \div \frac{4}{5}$ **2.** $14 \div \frac{6}{11}$ **3.** $\frac{5}{6} \div 5$ **4.** $\frac{5}{7} \div 3$

5. $\frac{5}{9} \div \frac{2}{3}$ **6.** $\frac{8}{9} \div \frac{4}{9}$ **7.** $\frac{4}{7} \div \frac{3}{5}$ **8.** $\frac{3}{8} \div \frac{9}{10}$

9. $2 \div 3\frac{2}{3}$ **10.** $2\frac{3}{4} \div 1\frac{5}{8}$ **11.** $3\frac{2}{5} \div 1\frac{1}{2}$ **12.** $2\frac{1}{6} \div 4\frac{5}{8}$

13. $3\frac{1}{6} \div 1\frac{2}{3}$ **14.** $2\frac{1}{4} \div 1\frac{2}{5}$ **15.** $3\frac{3}{8} \div 3\frac{1}{2}$ **16.** $2\frac{2}{3} \div 3\frac{4}{9}$

17. $1 \div \frac{3}{8}$ **18.** $7\frac{1}{2} \div 5\frac{2}{3}$ **19.** $6\frac{1}{8} \div 4\frac{3}{8}$ **20.** $7\frac{9}{10} \div 5\frac{3}{7}$

21. $6\frac{1}{2} \div 4\frac{1}{3}$ **22.** $1\frac{1}{3} \div 6\frac{4}{5}$ **23.** $5\frac{1}{7} \div 4\frac{6}{9}$ **24.** $2\frac{2}{3} \div 5\frac{1}{8}$

25. $7\frac{1}{3} \div 4\frac{4}{5}$ **26.** $3\frac{3}{4} \div 4\frac{1}{2}$ **27.** $10\frac{2}{3} \div 5\frac{1}{2}$ **28.** $1\frac{1}{9} \div 2\frac{4}{5}$

Pages 276–277

1. Understand
2. Plan
3. Work
4. Answer

1. The Muddville Market sells 6 oranges for $1.38. Make a chart to show the price of from 1 to 10 oranges. How much do 15 oranges cost?

UNIT 11 Extra Practice

Pages 286–287

Write the unit rate.

1. 750 words in 25 lessons

2. 1800 people in 75 rows

Pages 288–289

3. $\frac{1}{7} = \frac{n}{21}$

4. $\frac{4}{5} = \frac{16}{a}$

5. $\frac{5}{6} = \frac{x}{18}$

6. $\frac{7}{19} = \frac{56}{n}$

Pages 290–291

Solve by cross multiplication.

7. $\frac{15}{40} = \frac{3}{a}$

8. $\frac{x}{15} = \frac{18}{30}$

9. $\frac{28}{60} = \frac{n}{15}$

10. $\frac{17}{3} = \frac{51}{n}$

Pages 292–293

A letter is chosen, without looking, from the word PARALLELOGRAM. Write the probability of the outcome.

11. the letter A

12. the letter L

13. a vowel.

Pages 294–295

Suppose you pick a marble, without looking, from each container. Write the probability of the outcome.

14. 2 green marbles

15. 1 white and 1 green

16. 1 green and 1 red

17. 1 red and 1 white

Pages 296–297

Write as a percent.

1. $\frac{79}{100}$

2. $\frac{9}{10}$

3. $\frac{3}{20}$

4. $\frac{4}{5}$

5. $\frac{9}{20}$

6. $\frac{13}{25}$

Pages 298–299

What is the number?

7. 20% of 10

8. 35% of 62

9. 80% of 94

10. 95% of 241

Pages 300–301

Write as a percent.

11. 0.83

12. 0.67

13. 0.05

14. 0.94

15. 0.01

Pages 302–303

What is the number?

16. 17% of 35

17. 87% of 94

18. 9% of 65

19. 45% of 159

Pages 304–305

Write the number as a percent of 200.

20. 18

21. 120

22. 170

23. 46

24. 180

Extra Practice   UNIT 11

Pages 284–291

$$\frac{\$125.00}{25 \text{ persons}} = \frac{\$5.00}{1 \text{ person}}$$

Rate: $5 per person

$$\frac{7}{9} = \frac{b}{36}$$

$9 \times b = 7 \times 36$

$b = 28$

Write the unit rate.

1. 351 m in 9 hours

2. 560 revolutions in 8 seconds

3. $37.40 for 187 stamps

4. 3760 m in 20 minutes.

Solve.

5. $\frac{3}{8} = \frac{6}{n}$

6. $\frac{2}{x} = \frac{8}{36}$

7. $\frac{a}{5} = \frac{27}{15}$

8. $\frac{5}{n} = \frac{30}{18}$

9. $\frac{3}{16} = \frac{x}{48}$

10. $\frac{12}{a} = \frac{3}{10}$

11. $\frac{4}{5} = \frac{16}{n}$

12. $\frac{x}{9} = \frac{6}{18}$

Pages 292–295

Tossing two coins

The probability of getting HT is $\frac{1}{4}$.

A box containing letter tiles has 2 A's, 4 B's, 6 T's, and 12 M's. What is the probability of picking the following at random?

1. an A

2. a B

3. a T

4. an M

Pages 296–303

20% of 150

20% = 0.20

0.20 × 150 = 30

What is the number?

1. 20% of 50

2. 10% of 40

3. 90% of 80

4. 19% of 43

5. 27% of 35

6. 33% of 51

Pages 304–305

What % of 240 is 12?

$n \times 240 = 12$

$n = 12 \div 240$

$n = 5\%$

Write the number as a percent of 200.

1. 10

2. 28

3. 38

4. 140

5. 180

6. 40

7. 72

8. 56

9. 125

10. 130

Pages 306–307

1. Understand
2. Plan
3. Work
4. Answer

1. Make a chart to show the cost of a taxi ride for from 1 to 10 miles. How much does it cost to ride a taxi for $7\frac{1}{2}$ miles?

TAXI FOR RENT
$.85 plus $.75
for each $\frac{1}{2}$ mile

UNIT 12 Extra Practice

Right For use after Checkpoint A

Pages 314–315

Copy the figure. Draw the line of symmetry.

1. **2.** 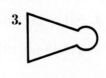 **3.** **4.**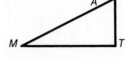

Pages 316–317

Complete to show which parts of triangle *MAT* correspond to parts of triangle *BOX*.

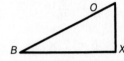

5. side *MA* ⟷ side ▓ **6.** ∠ *TAM* ⟷ ∠ ▓ **7.** ∠ *XBO* ⟷ ∠ ▓

Pages 318–319

Are the shapes similar? Write *Yes* or *No*.

8. 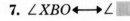 **9.** 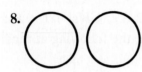 **10.**

Pages 320–321

A building plan is drawn to the scale 1 cm to 5 m. What length in the building does the length on the plan stand for?

11. 2 cm **12.** 6 cm **13.** 10 cm **14.** 50 cm

For use after Checkpoint B

Pages 322–325

What is the volume of a rectangular prism if the lengths of 3 edges are the following?

1. 12 cm, 8 cm, 5 cm **2.** 64 mm, 20 mm, 35 mm

Pages 326–329

Find the volume of a cylinder with the given area of base (*B*) and height (*h*).

3. $B = 20 \text{ cm}^2$ $h = 5 \text{ cm}$ **4.** $B = 5.8 \text{ m}^2$ $h = 0.9 \text{ m}$

Pages 330–331

Find the surface area.

5.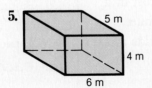

6.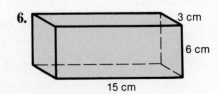

Pages 314–321

Congruent triangles

Scale: 1 cm to 3 m

$$\frac{1\,cm}{3\,m} = \frac{6\,cm}{n\,m}$$

$$n = 18\,m$$

Are the figures similar, congruent, or both?

1.  **2.**  **3.**

A building plan is drawn to the scale 1 cm to 3 m. What length in the building does the length on the plan stand for?

4. 4 cm   **5.** 3 cm   **6.** 7 cm   **7.** 5.5 cm

Pages 322–331

rectangular prism:
$V = l \times h \times w$

cylinder:
$V = B \times h$

What is the volume?

1. 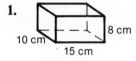   **2.**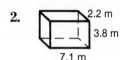

What is the volume of the cylinder with the given area of base (*B*) and height (*h*)?

3. $B = 155\,m^2$ **4.** $B = 13\,mm^2$ **5.** $B = 79\,cm^2$ **6.** $B = 28\,cm^2$
   $h = 10\,m$ $h = 17\,mm$ $h = 2.7\,cm$ $h = 5\,cm$

Surface area equals the sum of the areas of the faces.

What is the surface area?

7. 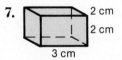   **8.**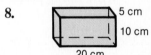

Pages 332–333

Line *AB* is parallel to line *MN*.

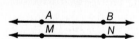

Use a protractor and centimeter ruler to draw the figure.

1. Draw line DE parallel to line JK.

2. Draw line UV parallel to line CD.

3. Draw a square with sides that are 4 cm each.

Pages 334–335

1. Understand
2. Plan
3. Work
4. Answer

Write the letter of the question you would need to answer to complete the activity.

1. You are planning a day at the zoo.
   a. What is the admission charge?
   b. Can you feed the animals?

UNIT 13 Extra Practice

For use after Checkpoint A

Pages 342–345

Write the range, mode, mean, and median.

1. 42, 45, 36, 29, 58, 42

2. 8.0, 8.5, 8.0, 8.8, 7.3

Pages 346–347

Use the bar graph on the right.

3. How many more cars refueled in the A.M. than in the P.M.?

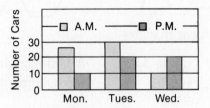

Pages 348–349

Use the line graph on the right.

4. What was the total amount collected in January?

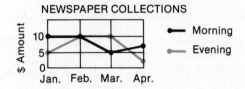

Pages 350–351

A group of 60 students planted trees. The circle graph shows what percent of the students performed each task.

5. How many students dug holes?

6. How many watered trees?

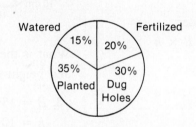

For use after Checkpoint B

Pages 352–353

Write the opposite of the integer.

1. $^-11$ 2. 18   3. 22   4. $^-3$

Pages 354–355

Write < or > to compare the integers.

5. $^-9$ ▢ $^-3$ 6. 5 ▢ $^-6$ 7. 0 ▢ $^-10$

Pages 356–357

8. $^-5 + ^-9$ 9. $4 + ^-8$ 10. $^-3 + 11$

Pages 358–359

11. $5 - ^-2$ 12. $^-8 - 9$ 13. $^-7 - ^-3$

Pages 360–361

Write the ordered pair for the letter

14. A   15. B   16. C   17. D

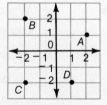

Extra Practice UNIT 13

Pages 342–345

9, 14, 15, 17, 15
Sum is 70; mean
is 70 ÷ 5 = 14

What are the range, mode, mean, and median?

1. 5, 7, 3, 12, 7, 14

2. 9, 13, 7, 15, 10, 13, 17

3. 33, 16, 24, 48, 17, 24

4. 98, 103, 72, 107, 86, 98

Pages 346–351

Tina collected
$13.00 on Tuesday.

The double line graph shows how
much Tina and Eric collected each
day for the Community Fund
Drive.

1. On which days did Tina collect
the same amount?

2. How much did Eric collect on
Wednesday?

3. What was the total that Tina
and Eric collected in the four
days?

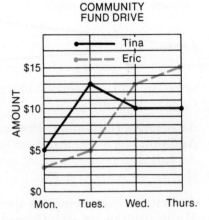

COMMUNITY FUND DRIVE

Pages 352–359

5 + ⁻11 = ⁻6
5 − ⁻11 = 5 + 11
= 16

Add or subtract.

1. ⁻8 + ⁻9

2. 4 − 12

3. 3 − ⁻10

4. ⁻4 + 17

5. ⁻2 − 8

6. 11 + ⁻15

Pages 360–361

Across
▷
(1, ⁻2)
◁
Down

Write the letter for the number pair.

1. (1, ⁻1)

2. (⁻2, ⁻1)

3. (1, 1)

4. (⁻2, 1)

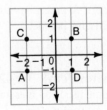

Pages 362–363

1. Understand
2. Plan
3. Work
4. Answer

Use the chart to answer the question.

1. What is the distance
between St. Louis and
Tampa?

Distance Between Cities (km)			
	Detroit	Tampa	St. Louis
Detroit	0	1922	821
Tampa	1922	0	1648
St. Louis	821	1648	0

Glossary

acute angle (p. 178) An angle with a measure of less than 90 degrees.

addend (p. 8) A number that is added. In 5 + 6 = 11, the addends are 5 and 6.

angle (p. 176) Two rays with a common endpoint. Example. $\angle ABC$:

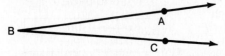

area (p. 190) The amount of surface inside a figure.

Associative (Grouping) Property of Addition (p. 8) Changing the grouping of the addends does not change the sum. Example. (4 + 7) + 6 = 4 + (7 + 6)

Associative (Grouping) Property of Multiplication (p. 60) Changing the grouping of the factors does not change the product. Example. $(3 \times 5) \times 2 = 3 \times (5 \times 2)$

average (mean) (p. 344) The quotient found by dividing the sum of a set of addends by the number of addends.

base (p. 80) Our number system is called a base 10 system because we group in powers of 10 when we write numbers.
(p. 322) A prism has two bases that are congruent and parallel.

centimeter (cm) (p. 42) A standard metric unit used for measuring lengths. 1 cm = 10 millimeters.

circle graph (p. 350) A graph used to show fractions or percents of a whole.

circumference (C) (p. 188) The distance around a circle. $C = 2 \times \pi \times r$

common factor (p. 90) A number which is a factor of two or more numbers. Example. 1, 2, 3, and 6 are common factors of 12 and 18.

common multiple (p. 66) A number which is a multiple of two or more numbers. Example. 20 is a common multiple of 4 and 5.

Commutative (Order) Property of Addition (p. 8) Changing the order of the addends does not change the sum. Example. 5 + 9 = 9 + 5

Commutative (Order) Property of Multiplication (p. 60) Changing the order of the factors does not change the product. Example. $3 \times 7 = 7 \times 3$

composite number (p. 91) A number that has more than two factors.

cone (p. 326) A shape in space with a flat, circular base and one vertex.

congruent (p. 316) Having the same size and shape.

corresponding parts (p. 316) Matching parts of congruent figures.

cylinder (p. 326) A shape in space with two parallel, congruent, circular bases.

decimal (p. 122) A number which uses a decimal point to show tenths or hundredths, such as 1.2 or 2.38.

decimal point (p. 122) A decimal point is used to separate whole numbers from tenths.

degree (p. 178) A small unit angle used to measure angles.

denominator (p. 202) 3 is the denominator in the fraction $\frac{2}{3}$.

diameter (p. 188) A segment through the center of a circle that connects two points on the circle.

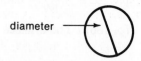

diameter

Distributive Property (p. 62) One of the factors can be rewritten to make the multiplication easier. Example.
$68 \times 3 = (60 + 8) \times 3 = (60 \times 3) + (8 \times 3)$

dividend (p. 86) 16 is the dividend in $16 \div 4$ and in $8\overline{)16}$.

divisor (p. 86) 4 is the divisor in $8 \div 4$ and in $4\overline{)36}$.

double bar graph (p. 346) A bar graph that compares two sets of data.

double line graph (p. 348) A line graph that compares two sets of data.

equation (p. 10) A sentence using numbers. It always has an = sign.

equilateral triangle (p. 184) A triangle with three equal sides and three equal angles.

equivalent fractions (p. 204) The diagram shows that $\frac{1}{3}$ and $\frac{2}{6}$ are equivalent fractions.

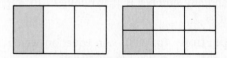

exponent (p. 74) In 5^3, 3 is the exponent. It shows that 5 is used as a factor 3 times. Example. $5^3 = 5 \times 5 \times 5$

factors (p. 60) Numbers that are multiplied. Example. In $3 \times 2 = 6$, the factors are 3 and 2.

formula (p. 21) A rule used to write an equation. Example. $A = l \times w$ is a formula.

fraction (p. 202) A number such as $\frac{1}{2}$ or $\frac{6}{10}$.

gram (g) (p. 46) A standard metric unit used for measuring mass. 1000 g = 1 kg.

greatest common factor (GCF) (p. 90) The greatest number which is a factor of two or more numbers. 4 is the GCF of 12 and 16.

hexagon (p. 183) A 6-sided polygon.

hypotenuse (p. 366) The longest side in a right triangle.

integers (p. 352) Whole numbers and their opposites.
Example: 1, 2, 3, . . . and $-1, -2, -3, . . .$

isosceles triangle (p. 184) A triangle that has two equal sides and two equal angles.

least common denominator (LCD) (p. 208) The least common multiple of the denominators of two or more fractions.
Example. 15 is the LCD of $\frac{1}{3}$ and $\frac{2}{5}$.

least common multiple (LCM) (p. 66) The smallest multiple shared by two or more numbers. 30 is the LCM of 6 and 10.

line (p. 176) A line has no endpoints. It goes on and on in two directions.

line of symmetry (p. 314) A fold line of a figure that makes the two parts match exactly.

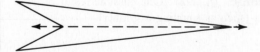

liter (L) (p. 46) A standard metric unit used for measuring volumes. 1000 mL = 1 L.

lowest terms (p. 206) When there is no common factor other than 1 that will divide the numerator and denominator of a fraction, then it is in lowest terms.

mean (or average) (p. 344) The quotient found by dividing the sum of a set of addends by the number of addends.

median (p. 344) The number that comes in the middle of a group of numbers when they are arranged in order. Example. 35, 32, 30, 15, 14. The median is 30.

meter (m) (p. 44) A standard metric unit used for measuring length. 1 m = 100 cm.

mixed numbers (p. 210) A whole number plus a fraction. Example. $2\frac{1}{3}$.

mode (p. 342) The number or numbers in a set of data that appear most often. Example. 24, 16, 24, 24, 21, 46. The mode is 24.

multiple (p. 66) The product of two numbers is a multiple of each number. 15 is a multiple of 3 and of 5.

numerator (p. 202) 2 is the numerator in the fraction $\frac{2}{3}$.

obtuse angle (p. 178) An angle with a measure greater than 90°, but less than 180°.

octagon (p. 183) An 8-sided polygon.

Opposites Property of Addition and Subtraction (p. 8) Addition and subtraction are opposites. One undoes the other. Example: 3 + 5 = 8   8 − 5 = 3

ordered pair (p. 360) A pair of numbers such as (3, ⁻2) in which the order shows the location of a point on a grid.

outcome (p. 292) One possible result of an action (such as spinning a spinner).

parallel lines (p. 180) Lines that never intersect. Example. *AB* is parallel to *CD*.

parallelogram (p. 182) A quadrilateral with opposite sides parallel.

pentagon (p. 183) A 5-sided polygon.

percent (p. 296) Hundredths written with a % sign. Example. $83\% = \frac{83}{100} = 0.83$

perimeter (p. 186) The distance around a figure.

perpendicular lines (p. 180) Two lines that intersect to form right angles. Example. *AB* is perpendicular to *CD*.

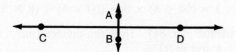

Pi (p. 188) A Greek letter which we use to stand for the number 3.14.

polygon (p. 182) A figure formed by joining three or more segments.

prime number (p. 91) A number that has exactly two factors, 1 and itself. Example. 7 is a prime number. 10 is not a prime number.

prism (p. 322) A shape in space with two bases that are parallel, congruent polygons.

probability (p. 292) The probability of an outcome is the ratio of the number of favorable outcomes to the total number of possible outcomes.

Property of One (p. 60) The product of one and any number is that number. Example. 7 × 1 = 7.

proportion (p. 288) An equation which states that two ratios are equivalent. Example. $\frac{3}{4} = \frac{n}{12}$; $n = 9$.

pyramid (p. 322) A shape in space with a base that is a polygon. All other faces are triangles and meet at one point.

quadrilateral (p. 182) A four-sided polygon.

quotient (p. 86) The answer in division.

radius (p. 188) A segment from any point on a circle to its center.

range (p. 342) The difference between the greatest and least numbers in a set of data. Example. 15, 27, 6, 32. The range is 26.

ratio (p. 284) A comparison of two numbers. It can be written in many ways, 2:9, 2 to 9, $\frac{2}{9}$.

ray (p. 176) Part of a line with a point on one end. To name a ray we state the endpoint first.

ray CB

reciprocal (p. 268) One number is the reciprocal of another if their product is 1. The reciprocal of 2 is $\frac{1}{2}$.

rectangle (p. 182) A parallelogram with four right angles.

repeating decimal (p. 218) A decimal in which the division never ends, and gives a quotient in which one or more of the digits repeats.

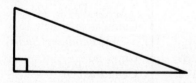
Example. $\frac{1}{3}$ ◇ $3\overline{)1.000}$ ··· ◇ $0.\overline{3}$

rhombus (p. 182) A parallelogram with four equal sides.

right angle (p. 178) An angle with a measure of 90°.

right triangle (p. 184) A triangle with one 90° angle.

scale (p. 320) The ratio of the size of a figure on a drawing to the actual size of the figure.

segment (p. 176) A part of a line. It has two endpoints.

sides (p. 182) The segments that form a polygon.

similar figures (p. 318) Figures that have the same shape.

simplify (p. 206) To divide the numerator and denominator of a fraction by the same nonzero number. $\frac{4}{12} = \frac{4 \div 4}{12 \div 4} = \frac{1}{3}$

sphere (p. 326) A shape in space, the points of which are the same distance from a point called the center.

square (p. 182) A rhombus with four right angles.

square root (p. 75) The square root of 9 is 3 because $3^2 = 9$.

standard form (p. 12) The usual, short form of a number. The standard form for 5 hundreds, 7 tens, 3 ones is 573.

surface area (p. 330) The sum of the areas of all the surfaces of a figure.

symmetrical (p. 314) A figure is symmetrical if it can be folded so that both halves fit exactly on one another.

terminating decimal (p. 218) A decimal in which the division ends because the final remainder is zero.

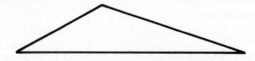
Example. $\frac{1}{5}$ ◇ $5\overline{)1.00}$ ◇ 0.20

trapezoid (p. 182) A quadrilateral with exactly one pair of opposite sides parallel.

triangle (p. 184) A three-sided polygon.

vertex (p. 176, 322, 326) The point at which two rays meet to form an angle. The point at which two sides of a polygon or three or more edges of a shape in space meet.

volume (p. 324) The number of cubic units contained in a figure.

Zero Property of Addition (p. 8) The sum of zero and any number is that number. Example. $3 + 0 = 3$

Zero Property of Multiplication (p. 60) The product of zero and any number is zero. Example. $12 \times 0 = 0$

Index

Credits

Cover design and art direction by Kirchoff/Wohlberg, Inc.
Photograph by Larry Voigt.

Production of *Applying Your Skills* sections by Ligature Publishing Services, Inc.
Photography by James L. Ballard and Associates, Inc.

Answers for Unit Opener Questions

UNIT 2: Probably not   UNIT 3: 34 spirals   UNIT 4: 20 minutes   UNIT 5: 999.9 m
UNIT 6: blue   UNIT 9: About 108 floors   UNIT 10: About 3200 people   UNIT 11: 15 L
UNIT 12: About 21 m   UNIT 13: $8/9$ of the iceberg